D1479970

Illustrated C# 2005

■ ■ ■

Daniel Solis

Apress®

Illustrated C# 2005

Copyright © 2006 by Daniel Solis

All rights reserved. No part of this work may be reproduced or transmitted in any form or by any means, electronic or mechanical, including photocopying, recording, or by any information storage or retrieval system, without the prior written permission of the copyright owner and the publisher.

ISBN-13 (pbk): 978-1-59059-723-1

ISBN-10 (pbk): 1-59059-723-0

Printed and bound in the United States of America 9 8 7 6 5 4 3 2 1

Trademarked names may appear in this book. Rather than use a trademark symbol with every occurrence of a trademarked name, we use the names only in an editorial fashion and to the benefit of the trademark owner, with no intention of infringement of the trademark.

Lead Editor: Matthew Moodie
Technical Reviewer: Christophe Nasarre
Editorial Board: Steve Anglin, Ewan Buckingham, Gary Cornell, Jason Gilmore, Jonathan Gennick, Jonathan Hassell, James Huddleston, Chris Mills, Matthew Moodie, Dominic Shakeshaft, Jim Sumser, Matt Wade
Project Manager | Production Director: Grace Wong
Copy Edit Manager: Nicole Flores
Copy Editors: Damon Larson, Sharon Wilkey
Assistant Production Director: Kari Brooks-Copony
Production Editor: Katie Stence
Compositor: Pat Christenson
Proofreader: Lori Bring
Indexer: Michael Brinkman
Cover Designer: Kurt Krames
Manufacturing Director: Tom Debolski

Distributed to the book trade worldwide by Springer-Verlag New York, Inc., 233 Spring Street, 6th Floor, New York, NY 10013. Phone 1-800-SPRINGER, fax 201-348-4505, e-mail orders-ny@springer-sbm.com, or visit http://www.springeronline.com.

For information on translations, please contact Apress directly at 2560 Ninth Street, Suite 219, Berkeley, CA 94710. Phone 510-549-5930, fax 510-549-5939, e-mail info@apress.com, or visit http://www.apress.com.

The information in this book is distributed on an "as is" basis, without warranty. Although every precaution has been taken in the preparation of this work, neither the author(s) nor Apress shall have any liability to any person or entity with respect to any loss or damage caused or alleged to be caused directly or indirectly by the information contained in this work.

The source code for this book is available to readers at http://www.apress.com in the Source Code/ Download section. You will need to answer questions pertaining to this book in order to successfully download the code.

*I would like to dedicate this book to
my parents, Sal and Amy;
and to Sian and Sue.*

Contents at a Glance

About the Author xxi
About the Technical Reviewer xxiii
Acknowledgments. xxv
Introduction xxvii

■CHAPTER 1   C# and the .NET Framework 1
■CHAPTER 2   Overview of C# Programming 15
■CHAPTER 3   Types, Storage, and Variables 29
■CHAPTER 4   Classes: The Basics. 43
■CHAPTER 5   Methods. 61
■CHAPTER 6   More About Classes 95
■CHAPTER 7   Classes and Inheritance 139
■CHAPTER 8   Expressions and Operators 171
■CHAPTER 9   Statements. 209
■CHAPTER 10   Namespaces and Assemblies. 239
■CHAPTER 11   Exceptions 265
■CHAPTER 12   Structs 285
■CHAPTER 13   Enumerations. 295
■CHAPTER 14   Arrays. 307
■CHAPTER 15   Delegates 333
■CHAPTER 16   Events 353
■CHAPTER 17   Interfaces 371
■CHAPTER 18   Conversions 397
■CHAPTER 19   Generics 427
■CHAPTER 20   Enumerators and Iterators. 455
■CHAPTER 21   Attributes 481

CHAPTER 22 Preprocessor Directives 503

CHAPTER 23 Other Topics 515

INDEX 543

Contents

About the Author xxi

About the Technical Reviewer. xxiii

Acknowledgments. xxv

Introduction xxvii

▓CHAPTER 1   **C# and the .NET Framework** 1

Before .NET 2
   Windows Programming in the Late 1990s 2
   Goals for the Next-Generation Platform 2
Enter Microsoft .NET 3
   Components of the .NET Framework. 3
   An Improved Programming Environment 4
Compiling to the Common Intermediate Language (CIL). 7
Compiling to Native Code and Execution 8
   Overview of Compilation and Execution 9
The Common Language Runtime (CLR) 10
The Common Language Infrastructure (CLI) 11
   Important Parts of the CLI 12
Review of the Acronyms 13

▓CHAPTER 2   **Overview of C# Programming** 15

A Simple C# Program. 16
   More About SimpleProgram 17
Identifiers and Keywords 18
   Naming Conventions. 19
   Keywords 19
Main: The Starting Point of a Program 20
Whitespace 20
Statements. 21
   Simple Statements 21
   Blocks 21

Text Output from a Program 22
    Write 22
    WriteLine. 23
    The Format String 23
    Substituting Values 24
    Multiple Markers and Values. 25
Comments: Annotating the Code 26
    More About Comments 27
    Documentation Comments 27
    Summary of Comment Types 28

■CHAPTER 3 **Types, Storage, and Variables** 29

A C# Program Is a Set of Type Declarations 30
A Type Is a Template 31
Instantiating a Type 31
Data Members and Function Members. 32
    Types of Members 32
Predefined Types 33
    More About the Predefined Types 34
User-Defined Types 35
The Stack and the Heap 36
    The Stack 36
    The Heap. 37
Value Types and Reference Types. 38
    Storing Members of a Reference Type Object 38
    Categorizing the C# Types. 39
Variables. 40
    Variable Declarations 40
    Multiple-Variable Declarations 42
    Using the Value of a Variable. 42

■CHAPTER 4 **Classes: The Basics** 43

Overview of Classes. 44
    A Class Is an Active Data Structure 44
Programs and Classes: A Quick Example. 45
Declaring a Class 46

Class Members 47

    Fields 47

    Methods 49

Creating Variables and Instances of a Class 50

Allocating Memory for the Data 50

    Combining the Steps 51

Instance Members 52

Access Modifiers 53

    Private and Public Access 53

Accessing Members from Inside the Class 56

Accessing Members from Outside the Class 57

Putting It All Together 58

CHAPTER 5   **Methods** 61

The Structure of a Method 62

    Code Execution in the Method Body 63

Local Variables 64

    Local Variables Inside Nested Blocks 65

    Flow-of-Control 66

Method Invocations 67

Return Values 68

    The Return Statement and Void Methods 70

Parameters 72

    Formal Parameters 72

    Actual Parameters 73

Value Parameters 75

Reference Parameters 78

Output Parameters 81

Parameter Arrays 84

    Method Invocation 85

    Expanded Form 85

    Arrays As Actual Parameters 88

Summary of Parameter Types 88

Stack Frames 89

Recursion 91

Method Overloading 93

■CHAPTER 6   **More About Classes** 95

Class Members... 96
    Order of Member Modifiers.................................. 96
Instance Class Members.. 98
Static Fields... 99
Accessing Static Members from Outside the Class 100
    Example of a Static Field............................... 100
    Lifetimes of Static Members............................. 101
Static Function Members 102
Other Static Class Member Types 103
Constants.. 104
    Constants Are Like Statics.............................. 105
    Local Constants... 106
Properties... 107
    Property Declarations and Accessors 108
    A Property Example...................................... 109
    Using a Property 110
    Properties and Associated Fields 111
    Performing Other Calculations 113
    Read-Only and Write-Only Properties 114
    A Computed, Read-Only Property Example 115
    Example of Properties and Databases..................... 116
    Static Properties 117
Instance Constructors 118
    Constructors with Parameters 119
    Default Constructors.................................... 120
Static Constructors.. 121
    Example of a Static Constructor......................... 122
Accessibility of Constructors................................ 122
Finalizers 123
    Calling the Finalizer 124
Comparison of Constructors and Finalizers 124
The readonly Modifier 125
The this Keyword 126

Indexers 127
    What Is an Indexer? 128
    Indexers and Properties 128
    Declaring an Indexer. 129
    The set Accessor. 130
    The get Accessor. 131
    More About Indexers. 131
    Declaring the Indexer for the Employee Example 132
    An Additional Example of an Indexer 133
    Indexer Overloading 134
Access Modifiers on Accessors 135
Partial Classes. 136

■CHAPTER 7   **Classes and Inheritance**. 139

Class Inheritance 140
Accessing the Inherited Members 141
    All Classes are Derived From Class object 142
Hiding Members of a Base Class 143
Base Access 145
Using References to a Base Class 146
    Virtual and Override Methods 148
    Overriding a Method Marked override. 150
Constructor Execution 153
    Constructor Initializers 154
    Class Access Modifiers 156
Inheritance Between Assemblies. 157
Member Access Modifiers. 159
    Regions Accessing a Member. 160
    Public Member Accessibility 161
    Private Member Accessibility 161
    Protected Member Accessibility 162
    Internal Member Accessibility. 162
    Protected Internal Member Accessibility. 163
    Summary of Member Access Modifiers 164
Abstract Members 165
Abstract Classes 166
    Example of an Abstract Class and an Abstract Method 167
Sealed Classes 168
External Methods 168

■CHAPTER 8   **Expressions and Operators** 171

Expressions 172
Literals 173
    Integer Literals. 174
    Real Literals 176
    Character Literals 177
    String Literals. 178
Order of Evaluation. 180
    Precedence 180
    Associativity 181
    Parenthesized Expressions 181
Simple Arithmetic Operators. 182
The Remainder Operator 183
Relational and Equality Comparison Operators 184
    Comparison and Equality Operations. 185
Increment and Decrement Operators 186
Conditional Logical Operators. 188
Logical Operators 190
Shift Operators 192
Assignment Operators 194
    Compound Assignment 195
The Conditional Operator. 196
Unary Arithmetic Operators. 198
User-Defined Type Conversions. 199
    Explicit Conversion and the Cast Operator 201
Operator Overloading. 202
    Restrictions on Operator Overloading 203
    Example of Operator Overloading. 203
The typeof Operator 205

■CHAPTER 9   **Statements**. 209

What Are Statements?. 210
Expression Statements 211
Flow-of-Control Statements 212
The if Statement 213
The if...else Statement. 214

The switch Statement 215

    A Switch Example 217

    More on the switch Statement 218

    Switch Labels. 219

The while Loop 220

The do Loop. 221

The for Loop 223

    Scope of Variables in a for Statement 225

    Multiple Expressions in the Initializer and Iterator. 226

Jump Statements 227

The break Statement 227

The continue Statement 228

Labeled Statements 229

    Labels 229

The Scope of Labeled Statements. 230

The goto Statement 231

    The goto Statement Inside a switch Statement. 231

The using Statement 232

    Packaging Use of the Resource 233

    Example of the using Statement. 234

    Multiple Resources and Nesting. 235

    Another Form of the using Statement 236

Other Statements 237

CHAPTER 10 **Namespaces and Assemblies**. 239

Referencing Other Assemblies. 240

    The mscorlib Library. 243

Namespaces 245

    Namespace Names. 247

    More About Namespaces. 248

    Namespaces Spread Across Files 249

    Nesting Namespaces 250

The using Directives. 251

    The using Namespace Directive. 251

    The using Alias Directive 252

The Structure of an Assembly 253

The Identity of an Assembly 255

Strongly Named Assemblies.. 257

    Creating a Strongly Named Assembly....................... 258

Private Deployment of an Assembly 259

Shared Assemblies and the GAC 260

    Installing Assemblies into the GAC.......................... 260

    Side-by-Side Execution in the GAC 261

Configuration Files 262

Delayed Signing 263

■CHAPTER 11   **Exceptions** 265

What Are Exceptions? 266

The try Statement.. 267

    Handling the Exception................................... 268

The Exception Classes... 269

The catch Clause 270

Examples Using Specific catch Clauses 271

The catch Clauses Section 272

The finally Block 273

Finding a Handler for an Exception 274

Searching Further... 275

    General Algorithm 276

    Example of Searching Down the Call Stack 277

Throwing Exceptions 280

Throwing Without an Exception Object............................. 282

■CHAPTER 12   **Structs**.. 285

What Are Structs?... 286

Structs Are Value Types... 287

Assigning to a Struct 288

Constructors and Finalizers 289

    Instance Constructors.................................... 289

    Static Constructors 291

    Summary of Constructors and Finalizers 291

Field Initializers 292

Inheritance.. 292

Boxing and Unboxing... 292

Structs As Return Values and Parameters 293

Additional Information About Structs............................... 293

■CHAPTER 13   **Enumerations** 295

Enumerations 296
Underlying Types and Values 297
Setting the Underlying Type 298
Setting Explicit Values for the Members 298
Implicit Member Numbering 299
Bit Flags 300
The Flags Attribute 301
Example Using Bit Flags................................... 303
More About Enums... 304

■CHAPTER 14   **Arrays** 307

Arrays 308
Definitions... 308
Important Details.. 308
Types of Arrays.. 309
An Array As an Object 310
One-Dimensional and Rectangular Arrays 311
Declaring a One-Dimensional Array or a Rectangular Array 311
Instantiating a One-Dimensional or Rectangular Array 312
Accessing Array Elements..................................... 313
Initializing an Array.. 314
Automatic Initialization.................................. 314
Explicit Initialization of One-Dimensional Arrays 314
Explicit Initialization of Rectangular Arrays.................. 315
Syntax Points for Initializing Rectangular Arrays.............. 315
Shortcut Syntax.. 316
Putting It All Together.................................... 316
Jagged Arrays 317
Declaring a Jagged Array 318
Shortcut Instantiation 318
Instantiating a Jagged Array 319
Sub-Arrays in Jagged Arrays 320
Comparing Rectangular and Jagged Arrays...................... 321
The foreach Statement 322
The Iteration Variable Is Read-Only 323
The foreach Statement with Multidimensional Arrays 324
Array Covariance.. 326

Useful Inherited Array Members 327
    The Clone Method 329
Comparing Array Types 331

■CHAPTER 15   **Delegates** 333

What Is a Delegate? 334
Declaring the Delegate Type 335
Creating the Delegate Object 336
Assigning Delegates 338
Combining Delegates 339
Adding Methods to Delegates 340
Deleting Methods from a Delegate 341
Invoking a Delegate 342
Delegate Example 343
Invoking Delegates with Return Values 344
Invoking Delegates with Reference Parameters 345
Anonymous Methods 346
    Using Anonymous Methods 347
    Syntax of Anonymous Methods 348
    Scope of Variables and Parameters 351

■CHAPTER 16   **Events** 353

Events Are Like Delegates 354
    An Event Has a Private Delegate 355
Overview of Source Code Components 356
Declaring an Event 357
    An Event Is a Member 358
    The Delegate Type and EventHandler 358
Raising an Event 359
Subscribing to an Event 360
    Removing Event Handlers 362
    Adding Anonymous Method Event Handlers 363
Standard Event Usage 364
    Using the EventArgs Class 364
    Passing Data by Extending EventArgs 364
    Using the Custom Delegate 365
The MyTimerClass Code 367
Event Accessors 369

■CHAPTER 17   **Interfaces** 371

What Is an Interface? 372
    Example Using the IComparable Interface 373
Declaring an Interface 376
Implementing an Interface 378
    Example with a Simple Interface 379
An Interface Is a Reference Type 380
Implementing Multiple Interfaces 382
Implementing Interfaces with Duplicate Members 383
References to Multiple Interfaces 384
An Inherited Member As an Implementation 386
Explicit Interface Member Implementations 388
    Accessing Explicit Interface Member Implementations 391
Interfaces Can Inherit Interfaces 392
Using the as Operator with Interfaces 393
    Example of Different Classes Implementing an Interface 394

■CHAPTER 18   **Conversions** 397

What Are Conversions? 398
Implicit Conversions 399
Explicit Conversions and Casting 400
    Casting 400
Types of Conversions 402
Numeric Conversions 402
    Implicit Numeric Conversions 403
    Overflow Checking Context 404
    Explicit Numeric Conversions 406
Reference Conversions 410
    Implicit Reference Conversions 411
    Explicit Reference Conversions 413
    Valid Explicit Reference Conversions 414
Boxing Conversions 416
    Boxing Creates a Copy 417
Unboxing Conversions 418
    The Unboxing Conversions 419

User-Defined Conversions.. 420
    Constraints on User-Defined Conversions 420
    Example of a User-Defined Conversion...................... 421
    Evaluating User-Defined Conversions 423
    Example of a Multi-Step User-Defined Conversion............ 423
The is Operator 425
The as Operator 426

■CHAPTER 19   Generics.. 427

What Are Generics?... 428
    A Stack Example 428
Generics in C#... 430
    Continuing with the Example 431
Generic Classes 432
Declaring a Generic Class...................................... 433
Creating a Constructed Type 433
Creating Variables and Instances............................... 435
    The Stack Example Using Generics 437
    Comparing the Generic and Non-Generic Stack 439
Constraints on Type Parameters 440
    Where Clauses... 441
    Constraint Types and Order.............................. 442
Generic Structs 443
Generic Interfaces... 444
    An Example Using Generic Interfaces 445
    Generic Interface Implementations Must Be Unique........... 446
Generic Delegates 447
Generic Methods.. 449
    Declaring a Generic Method 449
    Invoking a Generic Method 450
    Example of a Generic Method............................ 452

■CHAPTER 20   Enumerators and Iterators 455

Enumerators and Enumerable Types 456
    Using the foreach Statement............................. 456
    Types of Enumerators 457

Using the IEnumerator Interface. 458
    Declaring an IEnumerator Enumerator 461
The IEnumerable Interface 463
    Example Using IEnumerable and IEnumerator. 464
The Non-Interface Enumerator. 466
The Generic Enumeration Interfaces. 468
The IEnumerator<T> Interface. 469
The IEnumerable<T> Interface 472
Iterators 474
    Iterator Blocks 475
    More about Iterators 476
Producing Enumerables and Enumerators. 477
Using an Iterator to Produce an Enumerable 478
Using an Iterator to Produce an Enumerator 479

■CHAPTER 21   **Attributes** 481

What Is an Attribute? 482
    A Quick Preview 483
    The Stages of an Attribute. 484
Applying an Attribute 485
    Multiple Attributes. 486
    Other Targets. 486
    Global Attributes 487
    Predefined Attributes 488
Using Custom Attributes 489
    Declaring a Custom Attribute 489
    Using Attribute Constructors 490
    Specifying the Constructor 490
    Using the Constructor. 491
    Positional and Named Parameters in Constructors. 492
    Restricting the Usage of an Attribute. 494
    Using Suggested Practices for Custom Attributes. 496
Accessing an Attribute. 496
    Using the IsDefined Method 497
    Using the GetCustomAttributes Method 498
Using Reserved Attributes. 499
    The Obsolete Attribute 499
    The Conditional Attribute 499

■CHAPTER 22   **Preprocessor Directives**. 503

What Are Preprocessor Directives?. 504
General Rules 504
The #define and #undef Directives 506
Conditional Compilation. 507
          The Conditional Compilation Constructs 508
Diagnostic Directives 511
Line Number Directives 512
Region Directives 513
The #pragma warning Directive. 514

■CHAPTER 23   **Other Topics** 515

Miscellaneous Topics. 516
Strings 516
          Using Class StringBuilder. 517
          Formatting Numeric Strings 518
Parsing Strings to Data Values 523
Nullable Types. 524
          Creating a Nullable Type 524
          Using Nullable User-Defined Types 529
Method Main 531
Documentation Comments 533
          Inserting Documentation Comments 534
Nested Types. 537
          Example of a Nested Class 538
          Visibility and Nested Types 539

■INDEX 543

About the Author

 **DAN SOLIS** holds a Bachelor of Arts in biology and English, and initially worked in research on the structure of metal crystals, until he found that he enjoyed programming much more than working in a lab. He also holds a Master of Science degree in computer science from the University of California at Santa Barbara, where he concentrated on programming languages and compiler design.

Dan has been programming professionally for more than 20 years, with more than half that time working as a consultant and contract programmer, including several projects for Microsoft Consulting Services. His consulting projects have ranged from programs for mutual fund analysis and supply chain management to systems for missile tracking. He has also taught courses on various programming languages, Windows programming, UNIX internals, and a number of other topics, in both the United States and Europe.

Dan's first programming language was C, but he soon became intrigued by the journal articles about a new language called "C with Classes." Eventually that language was renamed C++ and released to the world. He began using C++ as soon as he could get access to a compiler, and eventually started teaching training seminars on the language as well.

With the advent of C# and .NET, he has moved on to enjoying the myriad advantages of the new language and platform, and has been working with them enthusiastically ever since.

About the Technical Reviewer

 **CHRISTOPHE NASARRE** is a development architect for Business Objects, a company that develops desktop and web-based business intelligence solutions. In his spare time, Christophe writes articles for *MSDN* magazine, MSDN/Vista, and ASPToday; and has been reviewing books on Win32, COM, MFC, .NET, and WPF since 1996.

Acknowledgments

I want to thank Sian for supporting and encouraging me on a daily basis, and I also want to thank my parents and family for their continued love and support.

I also want to express my sincere gratitude to the people at Apress who have worked with me to bring this book to fruition. I really appreciate that they understood and appreciated what I was trying to do, and worked with me to achieve it. Thanks to all of you.

Introduction

The purpose of this book is to teach you the fundamentals and mechanics of the C# programming language. Most books teach programming primarily using text. That's great for novels, but many of the important concepts of programming languages can best be understood through a combination of words, figures, and tables.

Many of us think visually, and figures and tables can help clarify and crystallize our understanding of a concept. In several years of teaching programming languages, I have found that the pictures I drew on the whiteboards were the things that most quickly helped the students understand the concepts I was trying to convey.

Illustrations alone, however, are not sufficient to explain a programming language and platform. The goal of this book is to find the best combination of words and illustrations to give you a thorough understanding of the language, and to allow the book to serve as a reference resource as well.

This book is written for anyone who wants an introduction to the C# programming language—from the novice to the seasoned programmer. For those just getting started in programming, I have included the basics. For seasoned programmers, the content is laid out succinctly, and in a form that will allow you to go directly to the information required without having to wade through oceans of words. For both sets of programmers, the content itself is presented graphically, in a form that should make the language easy to learn. Enjoy!

■■■

CHAPTER 1

C# and the .NET Framework

Before .NET

Enter Microsoft .NET

Compiling to the Common Intermediate Language (CIL)

Compiling to Native Code and Execution

The Common Language Runtime (CLR)

The Common Language Infrastructure (CLI)

Review of the Acronyms

Before .NET

The C# programming language was designed for developing programs for Microsoft's .NET Framework. This chapter will take a brief look at where .NET came from, and its basic architecture. Just to make sure you're starting on the right foot, let me take this opportunity to remind you of what is hopefully the obvious: C# sharp is pronounced *see sharp*.[1]

Windows Programming in the Late 1990s

In the late 1990s, Windows programming using the Microsoft platform had fractured into a number of branches. Most programmers were using Visual Basic (VB), C, or C++. Some C and C++ programmers were using the raw Win32 API, but most C++ programmers were using MFC (Microsoft Foundation Classes). Others had moved to COM (the Component Object Model).

All these technologies had their own problems. The raw Win32 API was not object-oriented, and using it required a lot more work than MFC. MFC was object-oriented, but it was inconsistent and getting old. COM, although conceptually simple, was complex in its actual coding, and required lots of ugly, inelegant plumbing.

Another shortcoming of all these programming technologies was that they were aimed primarily at developing code for the desktop rather than the Internet. At the time, programming for the Web was an afterthought and seemed very different from coding for the desktop.

Goals for the Next-Generation Platform

What we really needed was a new start—an integrated, object-oriented development framework that would bring consistency and elegance back to programming. To meet this need, Microsoft set out to develop a code execution environment and a code development environment that met the goals illustrated in Figure 1-1.

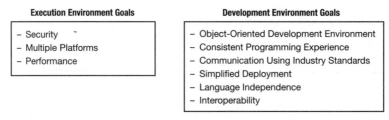

Figure 1-1. *Goals for the next-generation platform*

---

1. I was once interviewing for a contract C# programming position when the human resources interviewer asked me how much experience I'd had programming in "see pound" (instead of "see sharp")! It took me a second to realize what he was talking about.

Enter Microsoft .NET

In 2002, Microsoft released the .NET Framework, which promised to address the old problems and meet the goals for the next-generation system. The .NET Framework is a much more consistent and object-oriented environment than either the MFC or COM programming technologies. Some of its features include the following:

- *Multiple platforms*: The system runs on a broad range of computers, from servers and desktop machines to PDAs and cell phones.

- *Industry standards*: The system uses industry standard communication protocols, such as XML, HTTP, SOAP, and WSDL.

- *Security*: The system can provide a much safer execution environment, even in the presence of code obtained from suspect sources.

Components of the .NET Framework

The .NET Framework is made up of three components, as shown in Figure 1-2. The execution environment is called the *Common Language Runtime (CLR)*. The CLR manages program execution at run time, including the following:

- Memory management

- Code safety verification

- Code execution

- Garbage collection

The programming tools include everything required for coding and debugging, including the following:

- The Visual Studio integrated development environment

- .NET-compliant compilers (e.g., C#, VB, JScript, and managed C++)

- Debuggers

- Server-side improvements, such as ASP.NET

The *Base Class Library (BCL)* is a large class library used by the .NET Framework and available for you to use in your programs as well.

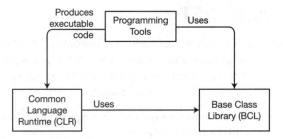

Figure 1-2. *Components of the .NET Framework*

An Improved Programming Environment

The .NET Framework offers programmers considerable improvements over previous Windows programming environments. A brief overview of its features and their benefits is given in the following sections.

Object-Oriented Development Environment

The CLR, the BCL, and C# have all been designed to be thoroughly object-oriented and act as a well-integrated environment.

The system provides a consistent, object-oriented model of programming for both local programs and distributed systems. It also provides a software development interface for both application programming and web development, consistent across a broad range of targets, from servers to cell phones.

Automatic Garbage Collection

The CLR has a tool called the *Garbage Collector (GC)*, which automatically manages memory.

- The GC automatically deletes objects from memory that your program will no longer access.

- The GC relieves the programmer of tasks that he or she has traditionally had to perform, such as deallocating memory and hunting for memory leaks. Hunting for memory leaks can be difficult and time-consuming, so this is no small feature.

Interoperability

The .NET Framework was designed for interoperability between different .NET languages, the operating system, and COM.

- .NET language interoperability allows software modules written using different .NET languages to interact.
    - A program written in one .NET language can use and even inherit from a class written in another .NET language, as long as certain rules are followed.
    - Because of its ability to easily integrate modules produced in different programming languages, the .NET Framework is sometimes described as *language agnostic*.

- The *platform invoke (P/Invoke)* features allow code written for .NET—called managed code—to call and use code not written for .NET, such as the Win32 system calls.

- The .NET Framework allows interoperability with COM, in that .NET software components can call COM components, and COM components can call .NET components.

No COM Required

The .NET Framework frees the programmer from the COM legacy. As a C# programmer, you do not need to use COM, and therefore do not need any of the following:

- *The* IUnknown *interface*: In COM, all objects must implement interface IUnknown. In contrast, all .NET objects derive from a single class called object. Interface programming is still an important part of .NET, but it is no longer the central theme.

- *Type libraries*: In .NET, information about a program's types is kept together with the code in the program file, not in a separate type library the way it is in COM.

- *Reference counting*: The programmer no longer has to keep track of references to objects. In .NET, the GC keeps track of references and deletes objects when appropriate.

- HRESULT: The HRESULT data type used in COM to return runtime error codes is not used in .NET. Instead, all runtime errors produce *exceptions*.

- *The registry*: This system-wide database that holds information about the operating system and application configurations is not used when deploying .NET applications. This simplifies installation and removal of programs.

Simplified Deployment

Deploying programs written for the .NET Framework can be considerably easier than it was previously, for the following reasons:

- .NET programs do not need to be registered with the registry. In the simplest case, a program just needs to be copied to the target machine.

- *Side-by-side execution* allows different versions of a DLL to exist on the same machine. This means that every executable can have access to the version of the DLL for which it was built.

Type Safety

The CLR checks and ensures the type safety of parameters and other data objects—even between components written in different programming languages.

The Base Class Library

The .NET Framework supplies an extensive base class library, called, not surprisingly, the *Base Class Library (BCL)*. It is also called the *Framework Class Library*. You can use this extensive set of available code when writing your own programs. Some of the categories of base classes provided are as follows:

- *General base classes*: Provide you with an extremely powerful set of tools for a wide range of programming tasks, such as string manipulation, security, and encryption

- *Windows Forms classes*: For building Windows GUI applications

- *ASP.NET classes*: For building web-based applications

- *ADO.NET classes*: For database manipulation

Compiling to the Common Intermediate Language (CIL)

The compiler for a .NET language takes a source code file and produces an output file called an *assembly*. In non-.NET terms, an assembly is either an executable or a DLL. The process is illustrated in Figure 1-3.

- The code in the assembly is not native machine code, but an intermediate language called the *Common Intermediate Language* (*CIL*).

- Among other things, the assembly contains the following:
  - The program's CIL
  - Metadata about the types used in the program
  - Metadata about references to other assemblies

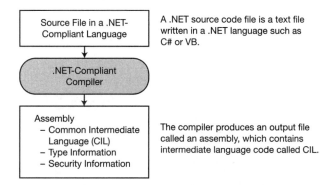

Figure 1-3. *The compilation process*

The acronym for the intermediate language has changed over time. Other terms for the CIL that you might encounter are IL (Intermediate Language), and MSIL (Microsoft Intermediate Language), which was used during initial development and early documentation.

Compiling to Native Code and Execution

The program is not compiled to native machine code until it is called to run. At run time, the CLR performs the following steps (as shown in Figure 1-4):

- It checks the assembly's security characteristics.

- It allocates space in memory.

- It sends the assembly's executable code to the *Just-In-Time (JIT) compiler*, which compiles portions of it to native code.

The executable code in the assembly is compiled by the JIT compiler as it is needed, and cached in case it is called again later in the program. That way, the code only has to be compiled to native code once. Code that is not called is not compiled to native code.

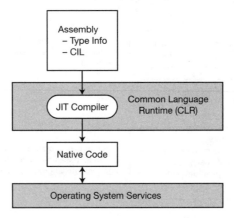

Figure 1-4. *Compilation to native code occurs at run time*

Once the CIL is compiled to native code, the CLR manages it as it runs, performing such tasks as releasing orphaned memory, checking array bounds, checking parameter types, and managing exceptions. For this reason

- Code written for the .NET Framework is called *managed code*, and needs the CLR.

- Code that does not require the CLR is called *unmanaged code*.

Microsoft also supplies a tool called the *Native Image Generator*, or *Ngen*, which takes an assembly and produces native code for the processor.

Overview of Compilation and Execution

The same compilation and execution process is followed regardless of the language of the original source files. Figure 1-5 illustrates the entire compilation and runtime processes for three programs written in different languages.

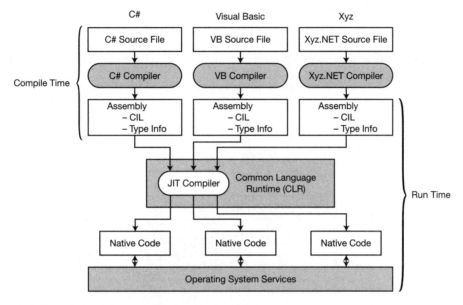

Figure 1-5. *Overview of the compile-time and runtime processes*

The Common Language Runtime (CLR)

The core component of the .NET Framework is the CLR, which sits on top of the operating system and manages program execution, as shown in Figure 1-6. The CLR also provides the following:

- Automatic garbage collection

- Security and authentication

- Extensive programming functionality through access to the BCL—including functionality such as web services and data services

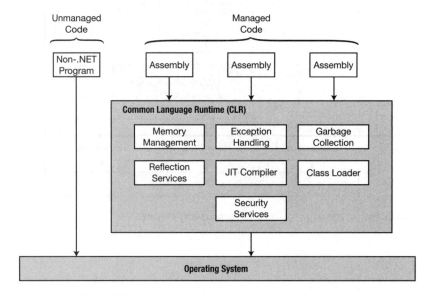

Figure 1-6. *Overview of the CLR*

The Common Language Infrastructure (CLI)

Every programming language has a set of intrinsic types representing such objects as integers, floating point numbers, characters, and so on. Historically, the characteristics of these types have varied from one programming language to another, and from platform to platform. For example, the number of bits constituting an integer has varied widely depending on the language and platform.

This non-uniformity, however, will not work if we want programs to play well with programs and libraries written in other languages. In order for there to be order and cooperation, there must be a set of standards.

The *Common Language Infrastructure (CLI)* is a set of standards that ties all the components of the .NET Framework into a cohesive, consistent system. It lays out the *concepts* and *architecture* of the system, and specifies the rules and conventions to which all the software must adhere. The components of the CLI are illustrated in Figure 1-7.

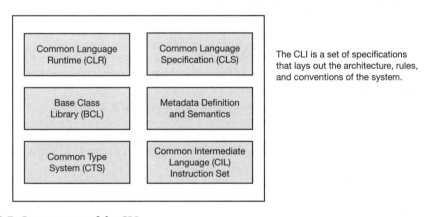

The CLI is a set of specifications that lays out the architecture, rules, and conventions of the system.

Figure 1-7. *Components of the CLI*

Both the CLI and C# have been approved as open international standard specifications by Ecma International. (The name "Ecma" used to be an acronym for the European Computer Manufacturers Association, but it's now just a word in itself.) Ecma members include Microsoft, IBM, Hewlett Packard, Adobe, and many other corporations associated with computers and consumer electronics.

Important Parts of the CLI

Although most programmers don't need to know the details of the CLI specifications, you should at least be familiar with the two specifications discussed in the following sections.

Common Type System (CTS)

The *Common Type System* (*CTS*) defines the characteristics of the types that must be used in managed code. Some important aspects of the CTS are the following:

- The CTS defines a rich set of intrinsic types, with fixed, specific characteristics for each type.

- The types provided by a .NET-compliant programming language generally map to some specific subset of this defined set of intrinsic types.

- One of the most important characteristics of the CTS is that *all* types are derived from a common base class—called object.

Common Language Specification (CLS)

The *Common Language Specification* (*CLS*) specifies the rules, properties, and behaviors of a .NET-compliant programming language.

The topics include data types, class construction, and parameter passing.

Review of the Acronyms

This chapter has covered a lot of .NET acronyms, so Figure 1-8 is included to help you keep them straight.

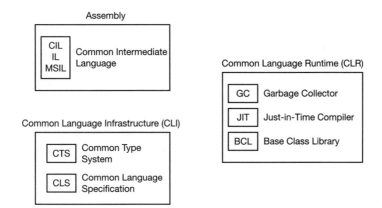

Figure 1-8. *The .NET acronyms*

CHAPTER 2

■ ■ ■

Overview of C# Programming

A Simple C# Program
Identifiers and Keywords
Main: The Starting Point of a Program
Whitespace
Statements
Text Output from a Program
Comments: Annotating the Code

A Simple C# Program

This chapter will lay the groundwork for studying C#. Since code samples will be used extensively throughout the text, you first need to see what a C# program looks like and what its various parts mean.

I will start by demonstrating a simple program and explaining its components one by one. This will introduce you to a range of topics, from the structure of a C# program to the method of producing program output to the screen.

With these source code preliminaries under your belt, you can then use code samples freely throughout the rest of the text. So, unlike the following chapters, where one or two topics will be covered in detail, this chapter will touch on many topics with a minimum of explanation.

Let's start by looking at a simple C# program. The complete program source is shown in the top shaded area in Figure 2-1. As shown, the code is contained in a text file called SimpleProgram.cs. As you read through it, don't worry about understanding all the details. Table 2-1 gives a line-by-line description of the code.

- When the code is compiled and executed, it displays the string "Hi there!" in a window on the screen.

- One line contains two contiguous slash characters. These characters—and everything following them on the line—are ignored by the compiler. This is called a *single-line comment*.

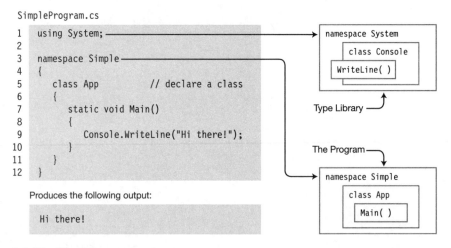

Figure 2-1. *The SimpleProgram programn*

Table 2-1. *The SimpleProgram Program, Line by Line*

Line Number	Description
Line 1	Tells the compiler that this program uses types from the System namespace.
Line 3	Declares a new namespace, called Simple.
	• The new namespace starts at the open curly brace on line 4 and extends through the matching curly brace on line 12.
	• Any types declared within this section are members of the namespace.
Line 5	Declares a new class type, called App.
	• Any members declared between the matching curly braces on lines 6 and 11 are members that make up this class.
Line 7	Declares a method called Main as a member of class App.
	• In this program, Main is the only member of the App class.
	• Main is a special function used by the compiler as the starting point of the program.
Line 9	Contains only a single, simple statement; this line constitutes the body of Main.
	• Simple statements are terminated by a semicolon.
	• This statement uses a class called Console, in namespace System, to print out the message to a window on the screen.
	• Without the using statement in line 1, the compiler wouldn't have known where to look for class Console.

More About SimpleProgram

A C# program consists of one or more type declarations. Much of this book is spent explaining the different types that you can create and use in your programs. The types in a program can be declared in any order. In the SimpleProgram example, only the class type is declared.

A *namespace* is a set of type declarations associated with a name. SimpleProgram creates a new namespace called Simple, and uses a predefined namespace called System.

To compile the program, you can use Visual Studio or the command-line compiler. To use the command-line compiler, use the following command:

```
csc SimpleProgram.cs
```

In this command, csc is the name of the command-line compiler and SimpleProgram.cs is the name of the source file.

Identifiers and Keywords

Identifiers are character strings used to name things such as variables, methods, parameters, and a host of other programming constructs that will be covered later.

You can create self-documenting identifiers by concatenating meaningful words into a single descriptive name, using uppercase and lowercase letters (e.g., CardDeck, PlayersHand, FirstName, SocSecurityNum). Certain characters are allowed or disallowed at certain positions in an identifier. These rules are illustrated in Figure 2-2.

- The alphabetic and underscore characters (a through z, A through Z, and _) are allowed at any position.

- Digits are not allowed in the first position, but are allowed everywhere else.

- The @ character is allowed in the first position of an identifier, but not anywhere else. The use of the @ character, although allowed, is discouraged for general use.

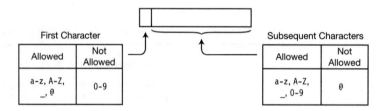

Figure 2-2. *Characters allowed in identifiers*

Identifiers are case sensitive. For instance, the variable names myVar and MyVar are different identifiers. It is generally a bad idea, however, to have identifiers that differ only in the case of some of the letters.

As an example, in the following code snippet, the variable declarations are all valid and declare different integer variables. But using such similar names will make coding more error-prone and debugging more difficult. Those debugging your code at some later time will not be pleased.

```
// Valid syntactically, but don't do this!
int totalCycleCount;
int TotalCycleCount;
int TotalcycleCount;
```

Naming Conventions

The *C# Language Specification* suggests that certain casing conventions be used in creating identifiers. The suggested guidelines for casing are described and summarized in Table 2-2.

For most identifiers, the Pascal casing style should be used. In this style, each of the words combined to make an identifier is capitalized—for example, `FirstName` and `LastName`.

Table 2-2. *Recommended Identifier Naming Styles*

Style Name	Description	Recommended Use	Examples
Pascal casing	Each word in the identifier is capitalized.	Use for most identifiers.	CardDeck, DealersHand
Camel casing	Each word in the identifier, *except the first*, is capitalized.	Use for parameters and local variables.	totalCycleCount, randomSeedParam
Uppercase	The identifier is composed of all uppercase letters.	Use only for abbreviations.	IO, DMA, XML

Keywords

Keywords are the character string tokens used to define the C# language. A complete list of the C# keywords is given in Table 2-3.

Some important things to know about keywords are the following:

- Keywords cannot be used as variable names or any other form of identifier, unless prefaced with the @ character.

- All C# keywords consist entirely of lowercase letters. .NET type names, however, use Pascal casing.

Table 2-3. *The C# Keywords*

abstract	const	extern	int	out	short	typeof
as	continue	false	interface	override	sizeof	uint
base	decimal	finally	internal	params	stackalloc	ulong
bool	default	fixed	is	private	static	unchecked
break	delegate	float	lock	protected	string	unsafe
byte	do	for	long	public	struct	ushort
case	double	foreach	namespace	readonly	switch	using
catch	else	goto	new	ref	this	virtual
char	enum	if	null	return	throw	void
checked	event	implicit	object	sbyte	true	volatile
class	explicit	in	operator	sealed	try	while

Main: The Starting Point of a Program

Every C# program must have one class with a method (function) called Main. In the SimpleProgram program shown previously, it was declared in a class called App.

- The starting point of execution of every C# program is at the first instruction in Main.

- The name Main *must be capitalized*.

- The simplest form of Main is the following:

```
static void Main( )
{
   Statements
}
```

Whitespace

Whitespace in a program refers to characters that do not have a visible output character. Whitespace in source code is ignored by the compiler, but is used by the programmer to make the code clearer and easier to read. Some of the whitespace characters include the following:

- Space

- Tab

- New line

- Carriage return

For example, the following code fragments are treated exactly the same by the compiler in spite of their differences in appearance:

```
// Nicely formatted
Main()
{
   Console.WriteLine("Hi, there!");
}

// Just concatenated
Main(){Console.WriteLine("Hi, there!");}
```

Statements

The statements in C# are very similar to those of C and C++. This section will introduce the general form of statements; the specific statement forms will be covered in Chapter 9.

Simple Statements

A *statement* is a source code instruction describing a type or telling the program to perform an action.

- A *simple statement* is terminated by a semicolon.

For example, the following code is a sequence of two simple statements. The first statement defines a variable named var1 and initializes its value to 5. The second statement prints the value of variable var1 to the screen.

```
int var1 = 5;
System.Console.WriteLine("The value of var1 is {0}", var1);
```

Blocks

A *block* is a sequence of zero or more statements enclosed by a matching set of curly braces; it acts as a single syntactic statement.

You can create a block from the set of two statements in the preceding example by enclosing the statements in matching curly braces, as shown in the following code:

```
{
    int var1 = 5;
    System.Console.WriteLine("The value of var1 is {0}", var1);
}
```

Some important things to know about blocks are the following:

- You can use a block whenever the syntax requires a statement but the action you need requires more than one simple statement.

- Certain program constructs *require* blocks. In these constructs, you cannot substitute a simple statement for the block.

- Although a simple statement is terminated by a semicolon, a block is *not* followed by a semicolon. (Actually, the compiler will *allow* it—but it's not good style.)

```
{
                    ↓ Terminating semicolon                        Terminating semicolon
                                                                              ↓
    int var2 = 5;
    System.Console.WriteLine("The value of var1 is {0}", var1);
}
    ↑  No terminating semicolon
```

Text Output from a Program

A *console window* is a simple command prompt window that allows a program to display text and receive input from the keyboard. The BCL supplies a class called Console (in the System namespace), which contains methods for inputting and outputting data to a console window.

Write

Write is a member of the Console class. It sends a text string to the program's console window. In its simplest form, Write sends a literal string of text to the window. The string must be enclosed in quotation marks.

The following line of code shows an example of using the Write member:

```
Console.Write("This is trivial text.");
                        ↑
                   Output string
```

This code produces the following output in the console window:

```
This is trivial text.
```

As another example, the following code sends three literal strings to the program's console window:

```
System.Console.Write ("This is text1.");
System.Console.Write ("This is text2.");
System.Console.Write ("This is text3.");
```

This code produces the output that follows. Notice that Write does not append a newline character after the string, so the output of the three statements runs together on a single line.

```
This is text1.This is text2.This is text3.
       ↑              ↑              ↑
     First         Second         Third
    statement     statement      statement
```

WriteLine

WriteLine is another member of Console; it performs the same functions as Write, but appends a newline character to the end of each output string.

For example, if you use the preceding code, but use WriteLine instead of Write, the output is on separate lines:

```
System.Console.WriteLine("This is text 1.");
System.Console.WriteLine("This is text 2.");
System.Console.WriteLine("This is text 3.");
```

This code produces the following output in the console window:

```
This is text 1.
This is text 2.
This is text 3.
```

The Format String

The general form of the Write and WriteLine statements takes more than a single parameter.

- If there is more than a single parameter, the parameters are separated by commas.

- The first parameter must always be a string, and is called the *format string*.

- The parameters following the format string are called *substitution values*. The substitution values are numbered, starting at 0.

The syntax is as follows:

```
Console.WriteLine( FormatString, SubVal0, SubVal1, SubVal2, ... );
```

For example, the following statement has two substitution values, numbered 0 and 1. Their values are 3 and 6, respectively.

```
Console.WriteLine("Two sample integers are {0} and {1}.", 3, 6);
```
                    Format string   Substitution values

Substituting Values

Substitution values are used to display the values of program data and variables. To use them, do the following:

- Place these values or variables as substitution values, after the format string.

- Include *substitution markers* in the format string.

A substitution marker marks the position in the format string where a value should be substituted in the output string. It consists of an integer enclosed in a set of matching curly braces. The integer is the numeric position of the substitution value to be used.

There are two things to note in the following example:

- The format string of this WriteLine statement includes two substitution markers and two integer substitution values.

- When the statement is executed, the substitution markers are replaced by the substitution values in the output string.

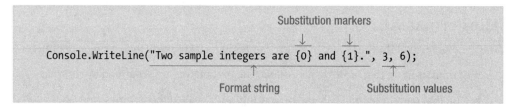

This code displays the following on the screen:

```
Two sample integers are 3 and 6.
```

Multiple Markers and Values

In C#, you can use any number of markers and any number of values.

- The values can be used in any order.

- The values can be substituted any number of times in the format string.

For example, the following statement uses three markers and only two values. Notice that value 1 is used before value 0, and that value 1 is used twice.

```
Console.WriteLine("Three integers are {1}, {0} and {1}.", 3, 6);
```

This code displays the following on the screen:

```
Three integers are 6, 3 and 6.
```

A marker must not attempt to reference a value at a position beyond the length of the list of values. If it does, however, it will not produce a compile error, but a runtime error (called an exception).

For example, in the following statement there are two substitution values, with positions 0 and 1. The second marker, however, references position 2—which does not exist. This will produce a runtime error.

```
                               Position 0   Position 1
                                   ↓     ↓
Console.WriteLine("Two integers are {0} and {2}.", 3, 6);     // Error!
                                         ↑
                          There is no position 2 value.
```

Comments: Annotating the Code

You have already seen single-line comments, so here I'll discuss the second type of inline comments—*delimited comments*—and mention a third type called documentation comments.

- Delimited comments have a start marker and an end marker.

- Text between the matching markers is ignored by the compiler.

- Delimited comments can span any number of lines.

For example, the following code shows a delimited comment spanning multiple lines.

```
↓Beginning of comment spanning multiple lines
/*
    This text is ignored by the compiler.
    Unlike single-line comments, delimited comments
    like this one can span several lines.
*/
↑ End of comment
```

A delimited comment can also span just part of a line. For example, the following statement shows text commented out of the middle of a line. The result is the declaration of a single variable, var2.

```
Beginning of comment
       ↓
int /*var 1,*/ var2;
                ↑
        End of comment
```

■**Note** Single-line and delimited comments behave in C# just as they do in C and C++.

More About Comments

There are several other important things you need to know about comments:

- Nested comments are not allowed. Only one comment can be in effect at a time.

- The comment that starts first is in effect until the end of its scope. The scope for particularly comment types is as follows:

  - For single-line comments, the end of the current line
  - For delimited comments, the first *end delimiter* encountered

The following attempts at comments are incorrect:

```
↓ Opens the comment
/* This is an attempt at a nested comment.
    /* ←Ignored because it is inside a comment
        Inner comment
    */ ←Closes the comment because it is the first end delimiter encountered
*/ ←Syntax error because it has no opening delimiter

↓ Opens the comment          ↓ Ignored because it is inside a comment
// Single-line comment    /* Nested comment?
                        */ ←Incorrect because it has no opening delimiter
```

Documentation Comments

C# also provides a third type of comment: the *documentation comment*. Documentation comments contain XML text that can be used to produce program documentation. Comments of this type look like single-line comments, except that they have three contiguous slashes rather than two. I will cover documentation comments in Chapter 23.

The following code shows the form of documentation comments:

```
/// <summary>
/// This class does...
/// </summary>
class Program
{
    ...
```

Summary of Comment Types

Inline comments are sections of text that are ignored by the compiler but are included in the code to document it. Programmers insert comments into their code to explain and document it. Table 2-4 gives a summary of the comment types.

Table 2-4. *Comment Types*

Type	Start	End	Description
Single-line	//		The text from the beginning marker to the end of the current line is ignored by the compiler.
Delimited	/*	*/	The text between the start and end markers is ignored by the compiler.
Documentation	///		Comments of this type contain XML text that is meant to be extracted by a tool to produce program documentation.

■ ■ ■

CHAPTER 3

Types, Storage, and Variables

A C# Program is a Set of Type Declarations

A Type is a Template

Instantiating a Type

Data Members and Function Members

Predefined Types

User-Defined Types

The Stack and the Heap

Value Types and Reference Types

Variables

A C# Program Is a Set of Type Declarations

If you were to broadly characterize the source code of C and C++ programs, you might say that a C program is a set of functions and data types, and that a C++ program is a set of functions and classes. A C# program, however, is a set of type declarations.

- The source code of a C# program or DLL is a set of one or more type declarations.
  - For an executable, one of the types declared must be a class that includes a method called Main.
  - For a DLL, none of the classes can declare a method called Main.

- A *namespace* is a way of grouping a related set of type declarations and giving the group a name. Since your program is a related set of type declarations, you will generally declare your program inside a namespace you create.

For example, the following code shows a program that consists of three type declarations. The three types are declared inside a new namespace called MyProgram.

```
namespace MyProgram                       // Create a new namespace.
{
    DeclarationOfTypeA                     // Declare a type.

    DeclarationOfTypeB                     // Declare a type.

    class C                               // Declare a type.
    {
        static void Main()
        {
            ...
        }
    }
}
```

Class libraries are sets of type declarations that are categorized into namespaces. Namespaces will be covered in more detail in Chapter 10.

A Type Is a Template

Since a C# program is just a set of type declarations, learning C# consists of learning how to create and use types. So the first thing you need to do is to look at what a type is.

You can start by thinking of a type as a *template* for creating a data structure. It is not the data structure itself, but it specifies the characteristics of objects constructed from the template.

A type has the following:

- A name

- A data structure to contain its components

- Behaviors and constraints

For example, Figure 3-1 illustrates the components of two types: short and int.

 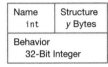

Figure 3-1. *A type is a template.*

Instantiating a Type

Creating an actual object from the type's template is called *instantiating* the type.

- The object created by instantiating a type is called either an *object* of the type or an *instance* of the type. The terms are interchangeable.

- Every data item in a C# program is an instance of some type—either a type provided by the language, provided by the BCL, or defined by the programmer.

Figure 3-2 illustrates the instantiation of objects of two predefined types.

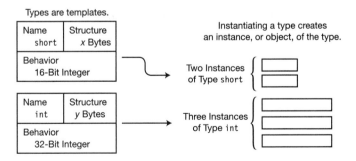

Figure 3-2. *Instantiating a type creates an instance.*

Data Members and Function Members

Some types, such as short, int, and long, are called *simple types*, and can only store a single data item.

Other types can store multiple data items. An *array*, for example, is a type that can store multiple items of the same type. The individual items are called elements, and they are referenced by a number, called an *index*. Arrays will be looked at in detail in Chapter 14.

Types of Members

Other types, however, can contain data items of many different types. The individual elements in these types are called *members*, and, unlike arrays, in which each member is referred to by a number, these members have distinct names.

There are two types of members: data members and function members.

- *Data members* store data that is relevant to the object of the class or to the class itself.

- *Function members* execute code. Function members define how the type can act.

For example, Figure 3-3 shows some of the data members and function members of type XYZ. It contains two data members and two function members.

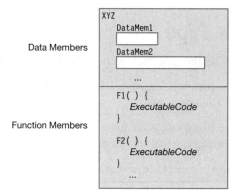

Figure 3-3. *Types specify data members and function members.*

Predefined Types

C# provides 15 predefined types, which are shown in Figure 3-4 and listed in Tables 3-1 and 3-2. They include 13 simple types and 2 non-simple types.

The names of all the predefined types consist of *all lowercase* characters. The predefined simple types include the following:

- 11 numeric types, including
  - Various lengths of signed and unsigned integer types.
  - Floating point types—float and double.
  - A high-precision decimal type called decimal. Unlike float and double, type decimal can represent decimal fractional numbers exactly. It is often used for monetary calculations.
- A Unicode character type, called char.
- A Boolean type, called bool. Type bool represents Boolean values and must be one of two values—either true or false.

Note Unlike C and C++, numeric values do not have a Boolean interpretation in C#.

The two non-simple types are the following:

- Type string, which is a sequence of Unicode characters.
- Type object, which is the type on which all other types are based.

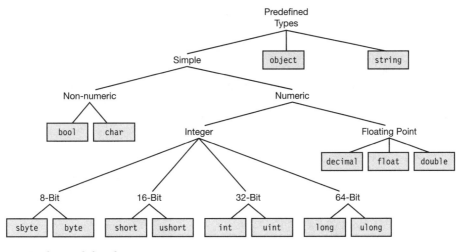

Figure 3-4. *The predefined types*

More About the Predefined Types

All the predefined types are mapped directly to underlying .NET types. The C# type names are just aliases for the .NET types, so using the .NET names works fine syntactically, although this is discouraged. Within a C# program, using the C# names is preferred to using the .NET names.

The predefined simple types represent a single item of data. They are listed in Table 3-1, along with the ranges of values they can represent and the underlying .NET types to which they map.

Table 3-1. *The Predefined Simple Types*

Name	Meaning	Range	.NET Framework Type
sbyte	8-bit unsigned integer	-128–127	System.SByte
byte	8-bit unsigned integer	0–255	System.Byte
short	16-bit unsigned integer	-32,768–32,767	System.Int16
ushort	16-bit unsigned integer	0–65,535	System.UInt16
int	32-bit signed integer	-2,147,483,648–2,147,483,647	System.Int32
uint	32-bit unsigned integer	0–4,294,967,295	System.UInt32
long	64-bit signed integer	$-9{,}223{,}372{,}036{,}854{,}775{,}808$ to $9{,}223{,}372{,}036{,}854{,}775{,}807$	System.Int64
ulong	64-bit unsigned integer	0–18,446,744,073,709,551,615	System.UInt64
float	Single-precision float	1.5×10^{-45}–3.4×10^{38}	System.Single
double	Double-precision float	5×10^{-324}–1.7×10^{308}	System.Double
bool	Boolean	true, false	System.Boolean
char	Unicode character	U+0000–U+ffff	System.Char
decimal	Decimal value with 28-significant-digit precision	$\pm 1.0 \times 10^{28}$–$\pm 7.9 \times 10^{28}$	System.Decimal

The non-simple predefined types are somewhat more complex. Values of type string contain zero or more Unicode characters. The object type is the base class for all other types in the system, including the predefined, simple types. These are shown in Table 3-2.

Table 3-2. *The Predefined Non-Simple Types*

Name	Meaning	.NET Framework Type
object	The base class from which all other types are derived.	System.Object
string	A sequence of Unicode characters.	System.String

User-Defined Types

Besides the 15 predefined types provide by C#, you can also create your own types, called *user-defined types*.

There are six *kinds of types* you can create, as follows:

- class types
- struct types
- array types
- num types
- delegate types
- interface types

Types are created using a *type declaration*, which includes the following information:

- The kind of type you are creating

- The name of the new type

- A declaration (name and specification) of each of the type's members—except for array and delegate types, which do not have named members

Once you have declared a type, you can create and use objects of the type just as if they were predefined types. But whereas using predefined types is a one-step process in which you simply instantiate the objects, using user-defined types is a two-step process. You first declare the type and then instantiate objects of the type. This is illustrated in Figure 3-5.

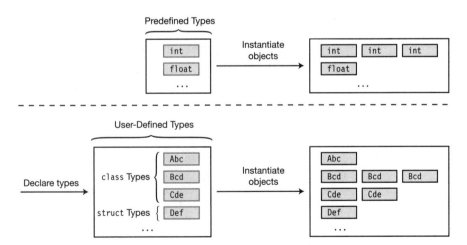

Figure 3-5. *The predefined types require instantiation only. The user-defined types require two steps: declaration and instantiation.*

The Stack and the Heap

While a program is running, its data must be stored in memory. How much memory is required for an item, and where and how it is stored, depends on its type.

A running program uses two regions of memory to store data: the *stack* and the *heap*.

The Stack

The system takes care of all stack manipulation. You, as the programmer, don't need to do anything with it explicitly. But understanding its basic functions will give you a better understanding of what your program is doing when it is running, and allow you to better understand the C# documentation and literature.

The stack is an array of memory that acts as a last-in, first-out (LIFO) data structure. It stores several types of data:

- The values of certain types of variables

- The program's current execution environment

- Parameters passed to methods

Facts About Stacks

The following are additional facts you should know about stacks:

- Data can only be added to and deleted from the top of the stack.

- Placing a data item at the top of the stack is called *pushing* the item onto the stack.

- Deleting an item from the top of the stack is called *popping* the item from the stack.

Figure 3-6 illustrates the functions and terminology of the stack.

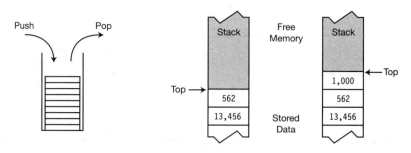

Data items are *pushed* onto the top of the stack and *popped* from the top of the stack.

Pushing an integer (e.g., 1,000) onto the stack moves the top of the stack up.

Figure 3-6. *Pushing and popping on the system stack*

The Heap

The *heap* is an area where chunks of memory can be allocated to store certain kinds of data. Unlike the stack, memory can be allocated and deallocated from the heap in any order. Figure 3-7 shows a program that has allocated four items from the heap.

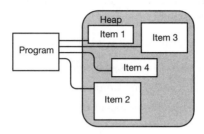

Figure 3-7. *The memory heap*

Although your program can allocate memory from the heap, it cannot deallocate it. Instead, the CLR's Garbage Collector (GC) automatically cleans up orphaned heap objects when it determines that your code will no longer access them. This frees you from what in other programming languages can be an error-prone task. Figure 3-8 illustrates the garbage collection process.

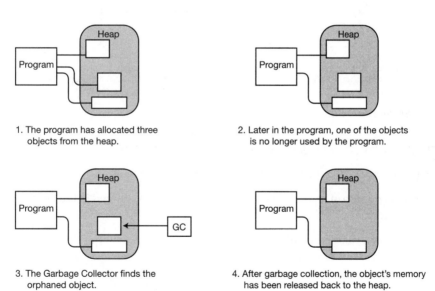

1. The program has allocated three objects from the heap.

2. Later in the program, one of the objects is no longer used by the program.

3. The Garbage Collector finds the orphaned object.

4. After garbage collection, the object's memory has been released back to the heap.

Figure 3-8. *Automatic garbage collection in the heap*

Value Types and Reference Types

The *type* of a data item defines how much memory is required to store it, the data members that comprise it, and the functions that it is able to execute. The type also determines where an object is stored in memory—the stack or the heap.

Types are divided into two categories: value types and reference types. Objects of these types are stored differently in memory.

- *Value types* require only a single segment of memory—which stores the actual data.

- *Reference types* require two segments of memory:
    - The first contains the actual data—and is located in the heap.
    - The second is a reference that points to where in the heap the data is stored.

Data that is not a member of another type is stored as shown in Figure 3-9. For value types, data is stored on the stack. For reference types, the actual data is stored in the heap and the reference is stored on the stack.

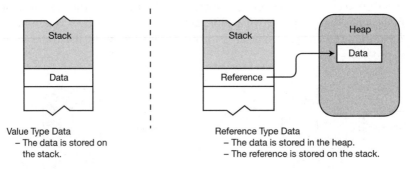

Figure 3-9. *Storing data that is not part of another type*

Storing Members of a Reference Type Object

These types, however, are not always stored as shown in Figure 3-9.

- The data portion of an object of a reference type is *always* stored in the heap, as shown in the figure.

- The data of a value type object or the reference of a reference type object can be stored in either the stack or the heap, depending on the circumstances.

Suppose, for example, that you have an instance of a reference type, called MyType, that has two members—a value type member and a reference type member. How is it stored? Is the value type member stored on the stack and the reference type split between the stack and the heap as shown in Figure 3-9? The answer is no.

Remember that for a reference type, the data of an instance is *always* stored in the heap. Since both members are part of the object's data, they are both stored in the heap, regardless of whether they are value or reference types. Figure 3-10 illustrates the case of type MyType.

- Even though member A is a value type, it is stored in the heap because it is part of the data of the instance of MyType.

- Member B is a reference type, and therefore its data portion will always be stored in the heap, as shown by the small box marked "Data." What's different is that its reference is also stored in the heap, inside the data portion of the enclosing MyType object.

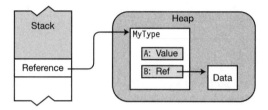

Figure 3-10. *Storage of data as part of a reference type*

■**Note** For any object of a reference type, all its data members are stored in the heap, regardless of whether they are of value type or reference type.

Categorizing the C# Types

Table 3-3 shows all the types available in C# and what kinds of types they are—value types or reference types. I will cover each type in this text.

Table 3-3. *Value Types and Reference Types in C#*

	Value Types			Reference Types
Predefined Types	sbyte short int long bool	byte ushort uint ulong	float double char decimal	object string
User-Defined Types	struct enum			class interface delegate array

Variables

A general-purpose programming language must allow a program to store and retrieve data.

- A *variable* is a name that represents data stored in memory during program execution.

- C# provides four categories of variables, each of which will be discussed in detail. The four types are as follows:
  - Local variables
  - Fields
  - Parameters
  - Array elements

Variable Declarations

A variable must be declared before it can be used. The variable declaration defines the variable, and accomplishes two things:

- It gives the variable a name.

- It allows the compiler to allocate memory for it.

A simple variable declaration requires at least a type and a name. The following declaration defines a variable named var2, of type int:

```
Type
  ↓
int var2;
      ↑
    Name
```

For example, Figure 3-11 represents the declaration of four variables and their places on the stack.

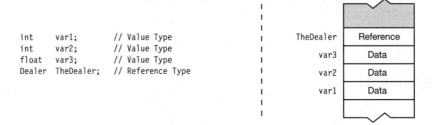

Figure 3-11. *Value type and reference type variable declarations*

Variable Initializers

Besides declaring a variable's name and type, a declaration can also initialize its memory to a specific value.

A *variable initializer* consists of an equals sign followed by the initializing value, as shown here:

```
        Initializer
            ↓
int var2 = 17;
```

Local variables without initializers have an undefined value, and cannot be used until they have been assigned a value. Attempting to use an undefined variable causes the compiler to produce an error message.

Figure 3-12 shows a number of local variable declarations on the left, and the resulting stack configuration on the right. Some of the variables have initializers and others do not.

```
int     var1;                // Value Type
int     var2 = 17;           // Value Type
float   var3 = 26.843F;      // Value Type
Dealer  Dealer1;             // Reference Type
Dealer  Dealer2 = null;      // Reference Type
```

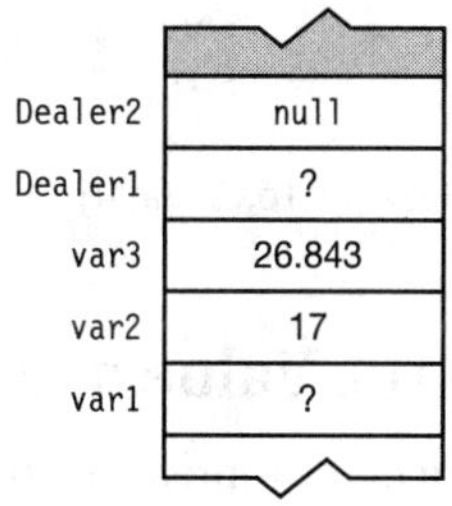

Dealer2	null
Dealer1	?
var3	26.843
var2	17
var1	?

Figure 3-12. *Variable initializers*

Automatic Initialization

Some kinds of variables are automatically set to default values if they are declared without an initializer, and others are not. Variables that are not automatically initialized to default values contain undefined values until the program assigns them a value. Table 3-4 shows which types of variables are automatically initialized and which are not.

Table 3-4. *Types of Variables*

Variable Type	Stored In	Auto-Initialized	Use
Local variables	Stack or stack and heap	No	Used for local computation inside a function member
Class fields	Heap	Yes	Members of a class
Struct fields	Stack or heap	Yes	Members of a struct
Parameters	Stack	No	Used for passing values into and out of a method
Array elements	Heap	Yes	Members of an array

Multiple-Variable Declarations

You can declare multiple variables in a single declaration statement. The rules for multiple-variable declarations are as follows:

- To declare multiple variables in a single statement, separate the variable names with commas. Initializers can be included with the variable names.

- The variables in a multiple-variable declaration must all be of the same type.

For example, the following code shows two valid declaration statements with multiple variables. Notice that the initialized variables can be mixed with uninitialized variables as long as they are separated by commas. The last declaration statement is invalid because it attempts to declare different types of variables in a single statement.

```
// Variable declarations--some with initializers, some without
int    var3 = 7, var4, var5 = 3;
double var6, var7 = 6.52;


Type    Different type
  ↓         ↓
int var8, float var9;        // Wrong! Can't mix types (int & float)
```

Using the Value of a Variable

A variable name represents the value stored by the variable. You can use the value by using the variable name.

For example, the value of var2 is retrieved from memory and placed at the position of the variable name, like so:

```
Console.WriteLine("{0}", var2);
```

CHAPTER 4

■■■

Classes: The Basics

Overview of Classes
Programs and Classes: A Quick Example
Declaring a Class
Class Members
Creating Variables and Instances of a Class
Allocating Memory for the Data
Instance Members
Access Modifiers
Accessing Members from Inside the Class
Accessing Members from Outside the Class
Putting It All Together

Overview of Classes

In the previous chapter, you saw that C# provides six user-defined types. The most important of these, and the one I will cover first, is the *class*. Since the topic of classes in C# is a large one, its discussion will be spread over the next several chapters.

A Class Is an Active Data Structure

Before the days of object-oriented analysis and design, programmers thought of a program as just a sequence of instructions. The focus at that time was on structuring and optimizing those instructions. With the advent of the object-oriented paradigm, the focus changed from optimizing instructions to organizing a program's data and functions into encapsulated sets of logically related data items and functions, called classes.

A class is a data structure that can store data and execute code. It contains the following:

- *Data members*, which store data associated with the class or an instance of the class. Data members generally model the attributes of the real-world object the class represents.

- *Function members*, which execute code. Function members generally model the functions and actions of the real-world object that the class represents.

A C# class can have any number of data and function members. The members can be any combination of nine possible member types. These member types are shown in Table 4-1. The ones I will cover in this chapter—*fields* and *methods*—are checked in the table.

Table 4-1. *Types of Class Members*

Data Members Store Data	Function Members Execute Code	
✓ Fields	✓ Methods	❑ Operators
❑ Constants	❑ Properties	❑ Indexers
	❑ Constructors	❑ Events
	❑ Finalizers	

■**Note** Classes are encapsulated sets of logically related data items and functions that generally represent objects in the real world or a conceptual world.

Programs and Classes: A Quick Example

A running C# program is a group of interacting type objects, most of which are instances of classes. For example, suppose you have a program simulating a poker game. When it is running, it has an instance of a class called Dealer, whose job it is to run the game, and several instances of a class called Player, which represent the players of the game.

The Dealer object stores such information as the current state of the card deck and the number of players. Its actions include shuffling the deck and dealing the cards.

The Player class is very different. It stores such information as the player's name and the amount of money left to bet, and performs such actions as analyzing the player's current hand and placing bets. The running program is illustrated in Figure 4-1.

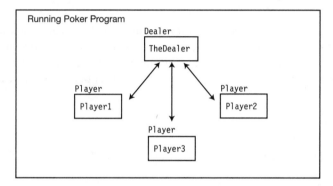

Figure 4-1. *The objects in a running program*

A real program would undoubtedly contain dozens of other classes besides Dealer and Player. These would include classes such as Card and Deck. Each class models some *thing* that is a component of the poker game.

■Note A running program is a set of objects interacting with each other.

Declaring a Class

Although types int, double, and char are defined by C#, as you can probably guess, classes Dealer and Player are not defined by the language. If you want to use them in a program, you will have to define them yourself. You do this by writing a *class declaration*.

A *class declaration* defines the characteristics and members of a new class. It does not create an instance of the class, but creates the template from which class instances will be created. The class declaration provides the following:

- The class name

- The members of the class

- The characteristics of the class

The following is an example of the minimum syntax for a class declaration. The curly braces contain the member declarations that make up the *class body*. Class members can be declared in any order inside the class body. This means that it is perfectly fine for the declaration of a member to refer to another member that is not yet defined until further down in the class declaration.

```
Keyword    Class name
   ↓           ↓
class MyExcellentClass
{
    MemberDeclarations
}
```

For example, the following code shows the outlines of three class declarations:

```
class Dealer                                // Class declaration
{
    ...
}

class Player                                // Class declaration
{
    ...
}
```

Note Since a class declaration "defines" a new class, you will often see a class declaration referred to as a "class definition" both in the literature and in common usage among programmers.

Class Members

Fields and methods are the most important of the class member types. Fields are data members and methods are function members.

Fields

A *field* is a variable that belongs to a class.

- It can be of any type, either predefined or user-defined.

- Like all variables, fields store data, and have the following characteristics:
  - They can be written to.
  - They can be read from.

The minimum syntax for declaring a field is the following:

```
Type
 ↓
Type Identifier;
         ↑
      Field name
```

For example, the following class contains the declaration of field `MyField`, which can store an `int` value:

```
class MyClass
{   Type
      ↓
    int MyField;
         ↑
}       Field name
```

Note Unlike C and C++, there are *no global variables* (i.e., variables or fields) declared outside of a type. All fields belong to a type, and must be declared within the type declaration.

Explicit and Implicit Field Initialization

Since a field is a kind of variable, the syntax for a *field initializer* is the same as that of the variable initializer in the previous chapter.

- A *field initializer* is part of the field declaration, and consists of an equals sign followed by an expression that evaluates to a value.

- The initialization value must be determinable at compile time.

```
class MyClass
{
    int F1 = 17;
}              ↑
           Field initializer
```

- If no initializer is used, the value of a field is set by the compiler to a default value, determined by the type of the field. The default values for the simple types are given in Table 4-1. The default for reference types is null.

For example, the following code declares four fields. The first two fields are initialized implicitly. The second two fields are initialized explicitly with initializers.

```
class MyClass
{
    int    F1;                  // Initialized to 0    - value type
    string F2;                  // Initialized to null - reference type

    int    F3 = 25;             // Initialized to 25
    string F4 = "abcd";         // Initialized to "abcd"
}
```

Declarations with Multiple Fields

As with variables, you can declare multiple fields *of the same type* in the same statement by separating the names with commas. Different types cannot be mixed in a single declaration. For example, you can combine the four preceding declarations into two statements, with the exact same semantic result:

```
int    F1, F3 = 25;
string F2, F4 = "abcd";
```

Methods

A *method* is a named block of executable code that can be executed from many different parts of the program, and even from other programs. (There are also anonymous methods, which aren't named—but I'll cover these in Chapter 15.)

When a method is *called*, or *invoked*, it executes its code, and then returns to the code that called it. Some methods return a value to the position from which they were called. Methods correspond to *member functions* in C++.

The minimum syntax for declaring a method includes the following components:

- *Return type*: This states the type of value the method returns. If a method does not return a value, the return type is specified as void.

- *Name*: This is the name of the method.

- *Parameter list*: This consists of at least an empty set of matching parentheses. If there are parameters (which will be covered in the next chapter), they are listed between the parentheses.

- *Method body*: This consists of a matching set of curly braces, containing the executable code.

For example, the following code declares a class with a simple method called PrintNums. From the declaration, you can tell the following about PrintNums:

- It returns no value; hence, the return type is specified as void.

- It has an empty parameter list.

- It contains two lines of code in its method body.

```
class SimpleClass
{
  Return type      Parameter list
     ↓                  ↓
    void PrintNums (  )
    {
        Console.WriteLine("1");
        Console.WriteLine("2");
    }
}
```

■Note Unlike C and C++, there are *no global functions* (i.e., methods or functions) declared outside of a type declaration.

Creating Variables and Instances of a Class

The class declaration is just the blueprint from which instances of the class are created. Once a class is declared, you can create instances of the class.

- Classes are reference types, which, as you will remember from the last chapter, means that they require memory for both the actual data and the reference to the data.

- The reference to the data is stored in a variable of the class type. So, to create an instance of the class, you need to start by declaring a variable of the class type. If the variable is not initialized, its value is undefined.

Figure 4-2 illustrates defining the variable to hold the reference. At the top of the code on the left is a declaration for class `Dealer`. Below that is a declaration for class `App`, which contains method `Main`. `Main` declares variable `TheDealer` of type `Dealer`. Since the variable is uninitialized, its value is undefined, as shown on the right in the figure.

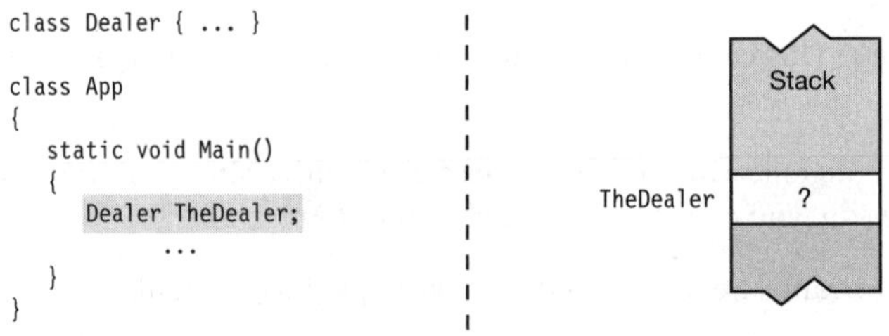

```
class Dealer { ... }

class App
{
    static void Main()
    {
        Dealer TheDealer;
            ...
    }
}
```

Figure 4-2. *Allocating memory for the reference of a class variable*

Allocating Memory for the Data

Declaring the variable of the class type allocates the memory to hold the reference, but not the memory to hold the actual data of the class object. To allocate memory for the actual data, you use the `new` operator.

- The `new` operator allocates and initializes memory for an instance of any specified type. It allocates the memory from either the stack or the heap, depending on the type.

- Use the `new` operator to form an *object-creation expression*, which consists of the following:
  - The keyword `new`.
  - The name of the type of the instance for which memory is to be allocated.
  - Matching parentheses, which might or might not include parameters. I'll discuss more about the possible parameters later.

```
Keyword   Parentheses are required.
  ↓           ↓
new TypeName ()
       ↑
     Type
```

- If the memory allocated is for a reference type, the object-creation expression returns a reference to the allocated and initialized instance of the type in the heap.

This is exactly what you need to allocate and initialize the memory to hold the class instance data. Use the new operator to create an object-creation expression, and assign the value returned by it to the class variable. Here's an example:

```
Dealer TheDealer;          // Declare variable for the reference.
TheDealer = new Dealer();  // Allocate memory for the class object.
              ‾‾‾‾‾‾‾‾‾‾
         Object-creation expression
```

The code on the left in Figure 4-3 shows the new operator used to allocate memory and create an instance of class Dealer, which is then assigned to the class variable. The memory structure is illustrated on the right side of the figure.

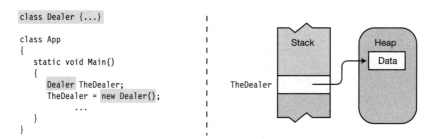

Figure 4-3. *Allocating memory for the data of a class variable*

Combining the Steps

The two steps can be combined by *initializing* the variable with the object-creation expression.

```
Declare variable
        ↓
Dealer TheDealer = new Dealer();        // Declare and initialize.
                   ‾‾‾‾‾‾‾‾‾‾‾‾
              ↑
        Initialize with an object-creation expression.
```

Instance Members

A class declaration acts as a blueprint from which you can create as many instances of the class as you like.

- *Instance members*: Each instance of a class is a separate entity that has its own set of the class members, distinct from the other instances of the same class. These are called *instance members* since they are associated with an instance of the class.

- *Static members*: Instance members are the default, but you can also declare members that are associated with the class, rather than the instance. These are called *static members*, and they will be looked at in Chapter 6.

For example, the following code shows the poker program with three instances of class Player. Each instance has a different value for the Name field. The code is illustrated in Figure 4-4.

```
class Dealer { ... }                           // Declare class
class Player {                                  // Declare class
   string Name;                                 // Field
      ...
}

class Program {
   static void Main()
   {
      Dealer TheDealer = new Dealer();
      Player Player1 = new Player();
      Player Player2 = new Player();
      Player Player3 = new Player();
      ...
   }
}
```

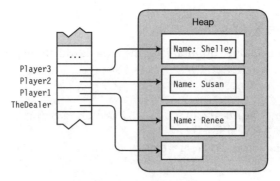

Figure 4-4. *Instance members are distinct between class objects.*

Access Modifiers

From within a class, any function member can access any other member of the class simply by using that member's name.

The *access modifier* is an optional part of a member declaration that specifies what other parts of the program have access to the member. The access modifier is placed before the simple declaration forms shown previously. The following is the syntax for fields and methods:

```
Fields
   AccessModifier Type Identifier;

Methods
   AccessModifier ReturnType MethodName ()
   {
      ...
   }
```

The five categories of member access are the following. I will describe the first two in this chapter, and the others in Chapter 7.

- `private`

- `public`

- `protected`

- `internal`

- `protected internal`

Private and Public Access

Private members are only accessible from within the class in which they are declared—other classes cannot see or access them.

- Private access is the default access level—so if a member is declared without an access modifier, it is a private member.

- You can also use the `private` access modifier to explicitly declare a member private.

- There is no semantic difference between declaring a private member implicitly as opposed to explicitly. They act exactly the same.

For example, the following two declarations both specify `private int` members:

```
        int MyInt1;          // Implicitly declared private
private int MyInt2;          // Explicitly declared private
   ↑
Access modifier
```

Public members are accessible to all other objects in the program. Use the `public` access modifier to specify public access.

```
Access modifier
    ↓
public int MyInt;
```

Depicting Public and Private Access

The figures in this text represent classes as labeled boxes, as shown in Figure 4-5.

- The class members are represented as smaller labeled boxes inside the class boxes.

- Private members are represented enclosed entirely within their class box.

- Public members are represented sticking partially outside their class box.

```
class Program
{
            int Member1;
    private int Member2;
    public  int Member3;
}
```

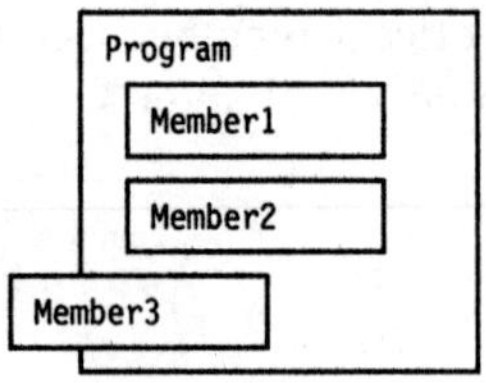

Figure 4-5. *Representing classes and members*

Example of Member Access

Class C1 declares both public and private fields and methods. Figure 4-6 illustrates the visibility of the members of class C1.

```
class C1
{
   int         F1;                    // Implicit private field
   private int F2;                    // Explicit private field
   public  int F3;                    // Public field

   void DoCalc()                      // Implicit private method
   {
      ...
   }

   public int GetVal()                // Public method
   {
      ...
   }
}
```

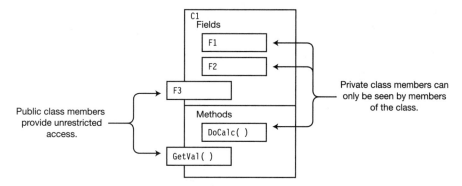

Figure 4-6. *Private and public class members*

Accessing Members from Inside the Class

As mentioned before, members of a class can access the other class members by just using their names.

For example, the following class declaration shows the methods of the class accessing the fields and other methods. Even though the fields and two of the methods are declared `private`, all the members of a class can be accessed by any method (or any function member) of the class. The code is illustrated in Figure 4-7.

```
class DaysTemp
{
   // Fields
   private int High = 75;
   private int Low  = 45;

   // Methods
   private int GetHigh()
   {
      return High;                       // Access private field
   }

   private int GetLow()
   {
      return Low;                        // Access private field
   }

   public float Average ()
   {
      return (GetHigh() + GetLow()) / 2;  // Access private methods
   }                        ↑            ↑
}                    Accessing the private methods
```

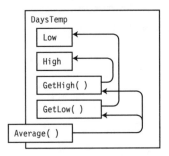

Figure 4-7. *Members within a class can freely access each other.*

Accessing Members from Outside the Class

To access a public instance member from outside the class, you must include the variable name and the member name, separated by a period (dot). This is called *dot-syntax notation*; it will be discussed in more detail later.

For example, the second line of the following code shows an example of accessing a method from outside the class:

```
DaysTemp MyDt = new DaysTemp();      // Create an object of the class.
float FValue = MyDt.Average();       // Access it from outside.
                 ↑       ↑
        Variable name  Member name
```

As an example, the following code declares two classes: DaysTemp and Program.

- The two fields in DaysTemp are declared public, so they can be accessed from outside the class.

- Method Main is a member of class Program. It creates a variable and object of class DaysTemp, and assigns values to the fields of the object. It then reads the values of the fields and prints them out.

```
class DaysTemp                              // Declare class DaysTemp
{
   public int High = 75;
   public int Low  = 45;
}

class Program                               // Declare class Program.
{
   static void Main()
   {
              Variable name
                   ↓
      DaysTemp Temp = new DaysTemp();        // Create the object.
   Variable name and field
           ↓
      Temp.High = 85;                        // Assign to the fields.
      Temp.Low  = 60;         Variable name and field
                                   ↓
      Console.WriteLine("High:  {0}", Temp.High );   // Read from fields.
      Console.WriteLine("Low:   {0}", Temp.Low  );
   }
}
```

This code produces the following output:

```
High:  85
Low:   60
```

Putting It All Together

The following code creates two instances and stores their references in variables named T1 and T2. Figure 4-8 illustrates T1 and T2 in memory. The code demonstrates the following three actions discussed so far in the use of a class:

- Declaring a class

- Creating instances of the class

- Accessing the class members (i.e., writing to a field and reading from a field)

```
class DaysTemp                              // Declare the class.
{
    public int High, Low;                   // Declare the instance fields.
    public int Avg()                        // Declare the instance method.
    {
        return (High + Low) / 2;
    }
}

class Class1
{
    static void Main()
    {
        DaysTemp T1 = new DaysTemp();
        // Create 2 instances of DaysTemp.
        DaysTemp T2 = new DaysTemp();

        // Write to the fields of each instance.
        T1.High = 76;  T1.Low  = 57;
        T2.High = 75;  T2.Low  = 53;

        // Read from the fields of each instance and call a method of
        // each instance.
        Console.WriteLine("T1: {0}, {1}, {2}", T1.High, T1.Low, T1.Avg ());
        Console.WriteLine("T2: {0}, {1}, {2}", T2.High, T2.Low, T2.Avg ());
                                                      ↑        ↑        ↑
    }                                              Field    Field   Method
}
```

This code produces the following output:

```
T1: 76, 57, 66
T2: 75, 53, 64
```

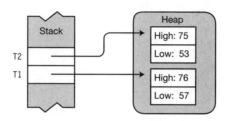

Figure 4-8. *Memory layout of instances T1 and T2*

CHAPTER 5

Methods

The Structure of a Method
Local Variables
Method Invocations
Return Values
Parameters
Value Parameters
Reference Parameters
Output Parameters
Parameter Arrays
Summary of Parameter Types
Stack Frames
Recursion
Method Overloading

The Structure of a Method

Essentially, a *method* is a block of code with a name. You can execute the code by using the method's name. You can pass data into a method and receive data as output.

As you saw in the previous chapter, a method is a function member of a class. Methods have two major sections, as shown in Figure 5-1—the method header and the method body:

- The *method header* specifies the method's characteristics, including the following:
  - Whether the method returns data
  - The name of the method
  - What types of input can be passed to the method

- The *method body* contains the sequence of executable code statements. Execution starts at the first statement in the method body and continues sequentially through the method.

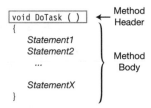

Figure 5-1. *The structure of a method*

The following example shows the form of the method header. I will cover each part in the following pages.

```
int MyMethod ( int intpar1, string strpar1 )
 ↑        ↑         ↑
Return  Method            Parameter
type    name              list
```

Methods can also be function members of another user-defined type called a struct, which is covered in Chapter 12. Most of what this chapter covers about class methods will also be true for struct methods.

For example, the following code shows a simple method called MyMethod, that, in turn, calls the WriteLine method several times:

```
void MyMethod()
{
    Console.WriteLine("First");
    Console.WriteLine("Last");
}
```

Code Execution in the Method Body

The method body is a *block*, which (as you will recall from Chapter 2) is a sequence of statements between curly braces. A block generally contains the following:

- Local variables

- Flow-of-control constructs

- Method invocations

- Blocks nested within it

Figure 5-2 shows an example of a method body and some of its components.

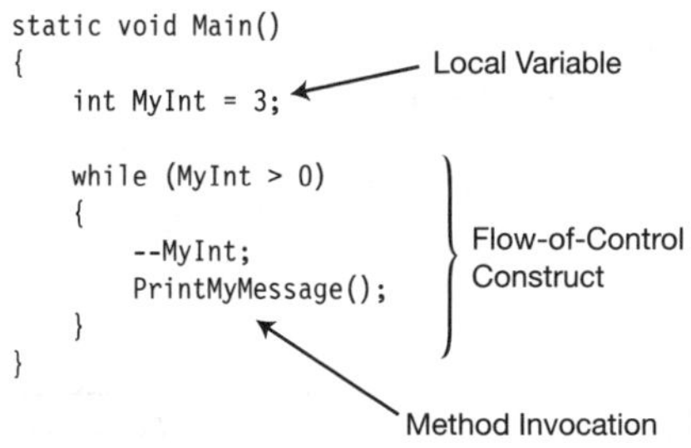

Figure 5-2. *Method body example*

Local Variables

Like fields, local variables store data. While fields usually store data about the state of the object, local variables are usually created to store data for local, or transitory, computations. Table 5-1 compares and contrasts local variables and instance fields.

The following line of code shows the syntax of local variable declarations. The optional initializer consists of the equals sign followed by a value to be used to initialize the variable.

```
         Variable name
             ↓
Type Identifier = Value;
                  ‾‾‾‾‾↑
              Optional initializer
```

- The existence of a local variable is limited to the block in which it is created.
  - It comes into existence at the point at which it is declared.
  - It goes out of existence when the block completes execution.
- You can declare local variables at any position in the method body.

The following example shows the declaration and use of three local variables of type int.

```
static void Main( )
{
   int FirstInt  = 15;
   int SecondInt = 13;

   int Total = FirstInt + SecondInt;
   ...
}
```

Table 5-1. *Instance Fields vs. Local Variables*

	Instance Field	Local Variable
Lifetime	Starts when the instance is created. Ends when the instance is no longer accessible.	Starts at the point in the block where it is declared. Ends when the block completes execution.
Implicit Initialization	Initialized to a default value for the type.	No implicit initialization. The value remains undefined until it is assigned to.
Storage Area	All the fields of a class are stored in the heap, regardless of whether they are value types or reference types.	Value type: stored on the stack. Reference type: reference stored on the stack, and data stored in the heap.

Local Variables Inside Nested Blocks

Method bodies can have other blocks nested inside them.

- There can be any number of blocks, and they can be sequential or nested further. Blocks can be nested to any level.

- Local variables can be declared inside nested blocks, and like all local variables, their lifetime is limited to the block in which they are declared.

Figure 5-3 illustrates the lifetimes of two local variables, showing the code and the state of the stack.

- Variable var1 is declared in the body of the method, before the nested block.

- Variable var2 is declared inside the nested block. It exists from the time it is declared, until the end of the block in which it was declared.

- When control passes out of the nested block, its local variables are popped from the stack.

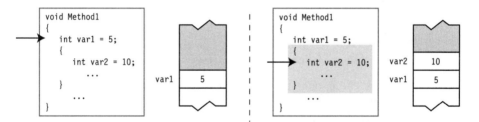

1. Variable var1 is declared before the nested block, and space is allocated for it on the stack.

2. Variable var2 is declared within the nested block, and space is allocated for it on the stack.

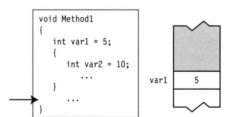

3. When execution passes out of the nested block, var2 is popped from the stack.

Figure 5-3. *The lifetime of a local variable*

Flow-of-Control

Methods contain most of the code for the actions that make up a program. The remainder is in other function members, such as properties and operators—but the bulk is in methods.

The term *flow-of-control* refers to the flow of execution through your program. By default, program execution moves sequentially from one statement to the next. The control statements allow you to modify the order of execution.

In this section, I will just mention some of the available control statements you can use in your code. Chapter 9 covers them in detail.

- *Selection statements:* These statements allow you to select which statement, or block of statements, to execute.
  - if: Conditional execution of a statement.
  - if...else: Conditional execution of one statement or another.
  - switch: Conditional execution of one statement from a set.

- *Iteration statements:* These statements allow you to loop, or iterate, on a block of statements.
  - for: Loop—testing at the top.
  - while: Loop—testing at the top.
  - do: Loop—testing at the bottom.
  - foreach: Execute once for each member of a set.

- *Jump statements:* These statements allow you to jump from one place in the block or method to another.
  - break: Exit the current loop.
  - continue: Go to the bottom of the current loop.
  - goto: Go to a named statement.
  - return: Return execution to the calling method.

For example, the following method shows several of the flow-of-control statements. Don't worry about the details.

```
void SomeMethod()
{
   int IntVal = 3;
   Equality comparison operator
               ↓
   if( IntVal == 3 )                          // if statement
      Console.WriteLine("Value is 3.");

   for( int i=0; i<5; i++ )                    // for statement
      Console.WriteLine("Value of i: {0}", i);
}
```

Method Invocations

You can call other methods from inside a method body.

- The phrases *call a method* and *invoke a method* are synonymous.

- You call a method by using its name, along with the parameter list, which I will discuss shortly.

For example, the following class declares a method called `PrintDateAndTime`, which is called from inside method `Main`.

```csharp
class MyClass
{
    void PrintDateAndTime( )                    // Declare the method.
    {
        DateTime dt = DateTime.Now;             // Get the current date and time.
        Console.WriteLine("{0}", dt);           // Write it out.
    }

    static void Main()                          // Declare the method.
    {
        MyClass mc = new MyClass();
        mc.PrintDateAndTime( );                 // Invoke the method.
    }        ↑                ↑
}        Method name   Empty parameter list
```

Figure 5-4 illustrates the sequence of actions when a method is called:

1. Execution of the current method suspends at that point of the invocation.

2. Control transfers to the beginning of the invoked method.

3. The invoked method executes until it completes.

4. Control returns to the calling method.

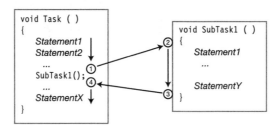

Figure 5-4. *Flow-of-control when calling a method*

Return Values

A method can return a value to the calling code. The returned value is inserted into the calling code at the position in the expression where the invocation occurred.

- To return a value, the method must declare a *return type* before the method name.

- If a method does not return a value, it must declare a return type of void.

The following code shows two method declarations. The first returns a value of type int. The second does not return a value.

```
Return type
  ↓
int GetHour()      { ... }
void DisplayHour() { ... }
  ↑
No value is returned.
```

A method that declares a return type must return a value from the method by using the following form of the return statement, which includes an expression after the keyword return. Every path through the method must end with a return statement of this form.

```
return Expression;                            // Return a value.
         ↑
Evaluates to a value of the return type
```

For example, the following code shows a method called GetHour, which returns a value of type int.

```
Return type
  ↓
int GetHour( )
{
    DateTime dt = DateTime.Now;            // Get the current date and time.
    int hour = dt.Hour;                    // Get the hour.

    return hour;                           // Return an int.
}        ↑
    Return statement
```

You can also return objects of user-defined types. For example, the following code returns an object of type MyClass.

```
Return type -- MyClass
     ↓
MyClass method3( )
{
    MyClass mc = new MyClass();
    ...
    return mc;                          // Return a MyClass object.
}          ↑
```

As another example, in the following code, method GetHour is called in the WriteLine statement in Main, and returns an int value to that position in the WriteLine statement.

```
class MyClass
{              ↓ Return type
    public int GetHour()
    {
        DateTime dt = DateTime.Now;       // Get the current date and time.
        int hour = dt.Hour;               // Get the hour.

        return hour;                      // Return an int.
    }          ↑
}            Return value


class Program
{
    static void Main()
    {                               Method invocation
        MyClass mc = new MyClass();          ↓
        Console.WriteLine("Hour: {0}", mc.GetHour());
    }                             ↑         ↑
}                      Instance name  Method name
```

The Return Statement and Void Methods

In the previous section, you saw that methods that return a value must contain return statements. Void methods do not require return statements. When the flow-of-control reaches the closing curly brace of the method body, control returns to the calling code. No value is inserted back into the calling code.

Often, however, you can simplify your program logic by exiting the method early, when certain conditions apply.

- You can exit from a method at any time by using the following form of the return statement, with no parameters:

```
return;
```

- This form of the return statement can be used only with methods declared void.

For example, the following code shows the declaration of a void method called SomeMethod, which has three possible places it might return to the calling code. The first two places are in branches called if statements, which are covered in Chapter 9. The last place is the end of the method body.

```
Void return type
   ↓
void SomeMethod()
{
   ...
   if( SomeCondition )                   // If ...
      return;                            // return to the calling code.

   ...

   if( OtherCondition )                  // If ...
      return;                            // return to the calling code.

   ...
}                                        // Return to the calling code.
```

The following code shows an example of a void method with a return statement. The method writes out a message only if the time is after noon. The process, illustrated in Figure 5-5, is as follows:

- First the method gets the current date and time. (Don't worry about understanding the details of this right now.)

- If the hour is less than 12 (that is, before noon), the return statement is executed, and control immediately returns to the calling method.

- If the hour is 12 or greater, the return statement is skipped, and the WriteLine statement is executed.

```
class MyClass {
    ↓ Void return type
    void TimeUpdate() {
        DateTime dt = DateTime.Now;         // Get the current date and time.
        if (dt.Hour < 12)                   // If the hour is less than 12,
            return;                         // then return.
            ↑
        Return to calling method.
        Console.WriteLine("It's afternoon!");   // Otherwise, print message.
    }

    static void Main() {
        MyClass mc = new MyClass();         // Create an instance of the class.
        mc.TimeUpdate();                    // Invoke the method.
    }
}
```

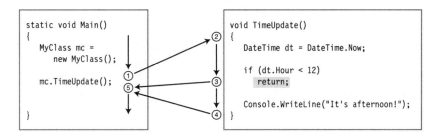

Figure 5-5. *Using a return statement with a void return type*

Parameters

So far, you have seen that methods are named units of code that can be called from many places in a program, and can return a single value to the calling code. Returning a single value is certainly valuable, but what if you need to return multiple values? Also, it would be useful to be able to pass data into a method when it starts execution. *Parameters* are special variables that allow you to do both these things.

Formal Parameters

Formal parameters are local variables that are declared in the method's parameter list, rather than in the body of the method.

The following method header shows the syntax of parameter declarations. It declares two formal parameters—one of type int, and the other of type float.

```
public void PrintSum( int x, float y )
{ ... }
                       Formal parameter declarations
```

- Because formal parameters are variables, they have a data type and a name, and can be written to and read from.

- Unlike a method's other local variables, the parameters are defined outside the method body and initialized before the method starts, except in one case, which I will cover shortly.

- The parameter list can have any number of formal parameter declarations, and the declarations must be separated by commas.

The formal parameters are used throughout the method body, for the most part, just like other local variables. For example, the following declaration of method PrintSum uses two formal parameters, x and y, and a local variable, Sum, all of type int.

```
public void PrintSum( int x, int y )
{
    int Sum = x + y;
    Console.WriteLine("Newsflash:  {0} + {1} is {2}", x, y, Sum);
}
```

Actual Parameters

When your code calls a method, the values of the formal parameters must be initialized before the code in the method begins execution.

- The expressions or variables used to initialize the formal parameters are called the *actual parameters*.

- The actual parameters are placed in the parameter list of the method invocation.

For example, the following code shows the invocation of method PrintSum that has two actual parameters of data type int.

```
PrintSum( 5, SomeInt );
         ↑    ↑
    Expression  Variable of type int
```

When the method is called, the value of each actual parameter is used to initialize the corresponding formal parameter. The method body is then executed. Figure 5-6 illustrates the relationship between the actual parameters and the formal parameters.

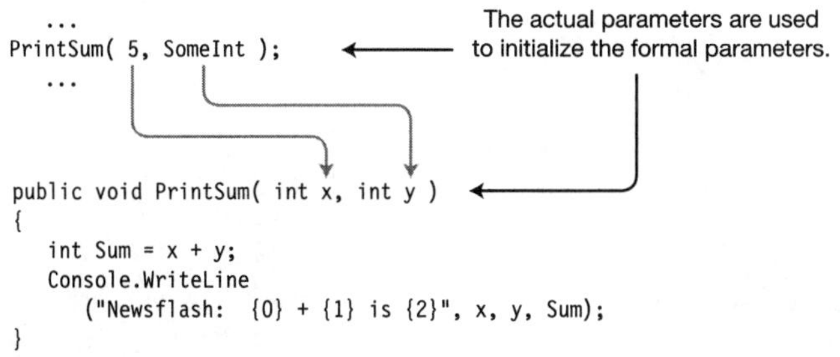

```
    ...
PrintSum( 5, SomeInt );  ◄────── The actual parameters are used
    ...                           to initialize the formal parameters.


public void PrintSum( int x, int y )  ◄──
{
    int Sum = x + y;
    Console.WriteLine
        ("Newsflash:  {0} + {1} is {2}", x, y, Sum);
}
```

Figure 5-6. *Actual parameters initialize the corresponding formal parameters.*

When you call a method, the following must be true:

- The number of actual parameters must be the same as the number of formal parameters (with one exception, which I will discuss later).

- Each actual parameter must match the type of the corresponding formal parameter.

An Example of Methods with Input Parameters

In the following code, class MyClass declares two methods—one that takes two integers and returns their sum, and another that takes two floats and returns their average.

```
class MyClass      Formal parameters
{                        ↓
   public int Sum(int x, int y)                      // Declare the method.
   {
      return x + y;                                  // Return the sum.
   }                      Formal parameters
                               ↓
   public float Avg(float Input1, float Input2)      // Declare the method.
   {
      return (Input1 + Input2) / 2.0F;               // Return the average.
   }
}


class Class1
{
   static void Main()
   {
      MyClass MyT = new MyClass();
      int SomeInt = 6;

      Console.WriteLine
         ("Newsflash:  Sum: {0} and {1} is {2}",
               5, SomeInt, MyT.Sum( 5, SomeInt ));      // Invoke the method.
                                        ↑
      Console.WriteLine              Actual parameters
         ("Newsflash:  Avg: {0} and {1} is {2}",
               5, SomeInt, MyT.Avg( 5, SomeInt ));      // Invoke the method.
   }                                    ↑
}                              Actual parameters
```

This code produces the following output:

```
Newsflash:  Sum: 5 and 6 is 11
Newsflash:  Avg: 5 and 6 is 5.5
```

Value Parameters

There are several kinds of parameters, which pass data to and from the method in slightly different ways. The kind you have been looking at so far is the default type and is called a *value parameter*.

When you use value parameters, data is passed to the method by copying the value of the actual parameter to the formal parameter. When a method is called, the system does the following:

- Allocates space on the stack for the formal parameter

- Copies the actual parameter to the formal parameter

An actual parameter for a value parameter does not have to be a variable. It can be any expression evaluating to the matching data type. For example, the following code shows two method calls. In the first, the actual parameter is a variable of type `float`. In the second, it is an expression that evaluates to `float`.

```
float func1( float Val )                         // Declare the method.
{ ... }           ↑
          Float data type


{
   float j = 2.6F;
   float k = 5.1F;     float variable
                          ↓
   float fValue1 = func1( k );                    // Method call
   float fValue2 = func1( (k + j) / 3 );          // Method call
   ...
                ↑
      Expression that evaluates to a float
```

Variables must be assigned to, before being used as actual parameters (except in the case of output parameters, which I will cover shortly). For reference types, the variable can be assigned either a reference or `null`.

Chapter 3 covered *value types*, which, as you will remember, are types that contain their own data. Don't be confused that I am now talking about *value parameters*. They are entirely different. Remember that *value parameters* are parameters where the value of the actual parameter is copied to the formal parameter.

For example, the following code shows a method called MyMethod, which takes two parameters—a variable of type MyClass and an int.

- The method adds 5 to both the field of the class and the int.

- You might also notice that MyMethod uses the modifier static, which you haven't seen before. You can ignore it for now. I will talk about static methods in Chapter 6.

```
class MyClass
{ public int Val = 20; }                          // Initialize the field to 20.

class Program                    Formal parameters
{                                      ↓
    static void MyMethod( MyClass f1, int f2 )
    {
        f1.Val = f1.Val + 5;                       // Add 5 to field of f1 param.
        f2     = f2 + 5;                           // Add 5 to second param.
    }

    static void Main( )
    {
        MyClass A1 = new MyClass();
        int     A2 = 10;

        MyMethod( A1, A2 );                        // Call the method.
    }              ↑
}            Actual parameters
```

Figure 5-7 illustrates the following about the values of the actual and formal parameters at various stages in the execution of the method:

- Before the method call, variables A1 and A2, which will be used as the actual parameters, are already on the stack.

- By the beginning of the method, the system has allocated space on the stack for the formal parameters, and copied the values from the actual parameters.
  - Since A1 is a reference type, the *reference* is copied, resulting in both the actual and formal parameters referring to the same object in the heap.
  - Since A2 is a value type, the *value* is copied, producing an independent data item.

- At the end of the method, both f2 and the field of object f1 have been incremented by 5.

- After method execution, the formal parameters are popped off the stack.
  - The value of A2, the value type, is *unaffected* by the activity in the method.
  - The value of A1, the reference type, however, *has been changed* by the activity in the method.

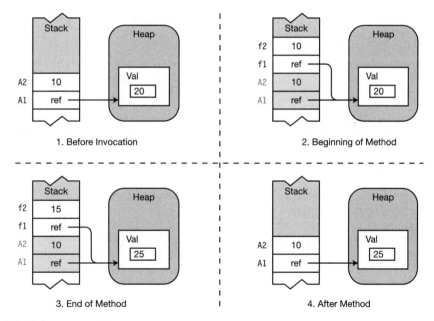

Figure 5-7. *Value parameters*

Reference Parameters

The second type of parameter is called a *reference parameter*.

- When using a reference parameter, you must use the `ref` modifier in both the declaration and the invocation of the method.

- The actual parameter *must* be a variable, which must be assigned to before being used as the actual parameter. If it is a reference type variable, it can be assigned a reference or the value `null`.

For example, the following code illustrates the syntax of the declaration and invocation.

```
              Include the ref modifier.
                      ↓
void MyMethod( ref int val )          // Method declaration
{ ... }

int y = 1;                            // Variable for the actual parameter
MyMethod ( ref y );                   // Method call
         ↑
    Include the ref modifier.

MyMethod ( ref 3+5 );                 // Error!
               ⊤
          Must use a variable.
```

Remember that value parameters allocate memory on the stack for the formal parameters. In contrast, reference parameters have the following characteristics:

- They do not allocate new memory on the stack for the formal parameters.

- A formal parameter name acts as an alias for the actual parameter variable, referring to the same memory location.

Since the formal parameter name and the actual parameter name reference the same memory location, clearly any changes made to the formal parameter during method execution will be visible after the method is completed, through the actual parameter variable.

For example, the following code shows method MyMethod, again, but this time the parameters are reference parameters rather than value parameters.

```
class MyClass
{ public int Val = 20; }                        // Initialize field to 20.

class Program          ref modifier      ref modifier
{                           ↓                 ↓
    static void MyMethod(ref MyClass f1, ref int f2)
    {
        f1.Val = f1.Val + 5;                    // Add 5 to field of f1 param.
        f2 = f2 + 5;                            // Add 5 to second param.
    }

    static void Main()
    {
        MyClass A1 = new MyClass();
        int A2 = 10;

        MyMethod(ref A1, ref A2);               // Call the method.
    }            ↑          ↑
}                    ref modifiers
```

Figure 5-8 illustrates the following about the values of the actual and formal parameters at various stages in the execution of the method:

- Before the method call, variables A1 and A2, which will be used as the actual parameters, are already on the stack.

- By the beginning of the method, the names of the formal parameters have been set as aliases for the actual parameters. Variables A1 and f1 refer to the same memory location, and A2 and f2 refer to the same memory location.

- At the end of the method, both f2 and the field of the object of f1 have been incremented by 5.

- After method execution, the names of the formal parameters are out of scope, but the values of both A1, the reference type, and A2, the value type, have been changed by the activity in the method.

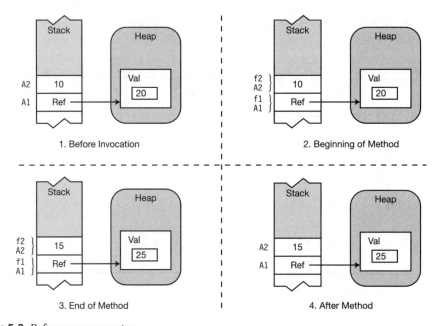

Figure 5-8. *Reference parameter*

Output Parameters

Output parameters are used to pass data from inside the method back out to the calling code. They are very similar to reference parameters. Like reference parameters, output parameters have the following requirements:

- You must use a modifier in both the method declaration and the invocation. With output parameters, the modifier is out, rather than ref.

- The actual parameter *must* be a variable—it cannot be another type of expression.

For example, the following code declares a method called MyMethod, which takes a single output parameter.

```
                  out modifier
                      ↓
void MyMethod( out int val )         // Method declaration
{ ... }

...
int y = 1;                           // Variable for the actual parameter
MyMethod ( out y );                  // Method call
             ↑
         out modifier
```

Like reference parameters, the formal parameters act as aliases for the actual parameters. Both the formal parameter and the actual parameter are names for the same memory location. Clearly, any changes made to a formal parameter in the method will be visible through the actual parameter variable after the method.

Unlike reference parameters, output parameters require the following:

- Before the method call, you do not have to initialize or assign values to the actual parameter variables. The initial values of the actual parameters are irrelevant.

- Inside the method, an output parameter must be assigned to, before it can be read from.

- Every output parameter *must be assigned to*, before the method exits.

Since the code inside the method must write to an output variable before it can read from it, it is impossible to send data *into* a method by using output parameters. As a matter of fact, if there is any execution path through the method that attempts to read the value of an output parameter before the method has assigned it a value, the compiler produces an error message.

```
                  ↓        ↓
public void Add2( out int InRef )
{
    int var1 = InRef + 2;     // Error! Cannot read from an output variable
}                ↑            // before it has been assigned to by the method.
```

For example, the following code again shows method MyMethod, but this time using output parameters.

```
class MyClass
{ public int Val = 20; }                    // Initialize field to 20.

class Program         out modifier       out modifier
{                          ↓                  ↓
    static void MyMethod(out MyClass f1, out int f2)
    {
        f1 = new MyClass();             // Create an object of the class.
        f1.Val = 25;                    // Assign to the class field.
        f2     = 15;                    // Assign to the int param.
    }

    static void Main()
    {
        MyClass A1 = null;
        int A2;

        MyMethod(out A1, out A2);       // Call the method.
    }             ↑       ↑
}                 out modifiers
```

Figure 5-9 illustrates the following about the values of the actual and formal parameters at various stages in the execution of the method:

- Before the method call, variables A1 and A2, which will be used as the actual parameters, are already on the stack.

- At the beginning of the method, the names of the formal parameters are set as aliases for the actual parameters. Variables A1 and f1 refer to the same memory location, and A2 and f2 refer to the same memory location. The *names* A1 and A2 are out of scope and cannot be accessed from inside the method.

- Inside the method, the code creates an object of type MyClass and assigns it to f1. It then assigns a value to f1's field and also assigns a value to f2. The assignment to f1 and f2 are both required, since they are output parameters.

- After method execution, the names of the formal parameters are out of scope, but the values of both A1, the reference type, and A2, the value type, have been changed by the activity in the method.

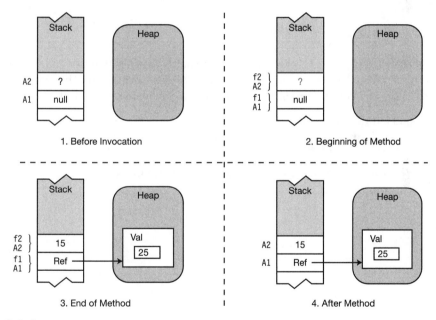

Figure 5-9. *Output parameters*

Parameter Arrays

In the parameter types I've covered so far, there must be exactly one actual parameter for each formal parameter. *Parameter arrays* are different in that they allow *zero or more* actual parameters for a particular formal parameter.

There can be only one parameter array in a parameter list. If there is one, it must be the last parameter in the list. To declare a parameter array, do the following:

- Use the params modifier before the data type.

- Place a set of empty square brackets after the data type.

The following method header shows the syntax for the declaration of a parameter array of type int. In this example, formal parameter InputList can represent zero or more actual int parameters.

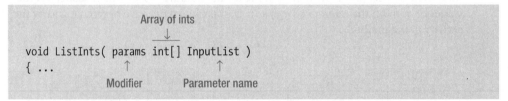

The empty set of square brackets after the type name specifies that the parameter will be an *array* of ints. You don't need to worry about the details of arrays here. They are covered in detail in Chapter 14. For our purposes here, though, all you need to know is that an array is

- An ordered set of data items of the same type

- Accessed by using a numerical index

- A reference type, and therefore stores all its data items in the heap

Method Invocation

You can supply the actual parameters in two ways. The forms you can use are the following:

- A comma-separated list of elements of the data type

```
ListInts( 10, 20, 30 );                          // Three ints
```

- A one-dimensional array of elements of the data type

```
int[] IntArray = {1, 2, 3};
ListInts( IntArray );                            // An array variable
```

Notice in these examples that you do not use the params modifier in the invocation. The use of the modifier in parameter arrays does not fit the pattern of the other parameter types.

- The other parameter types are consistent, in that they either use a modifier or do not use a modifier.
    - Value parameters take *no* modifier in *either* the declaration or the invocation.
    - Reference and output parameters require the modifier in *both* places.

- Parameter arrays, however,
    - Require the modifier in the declaration
    - Do not accept it in the invocation

Expanded Form

You will start by examining the form where you use separate actual parameters in the invocation. This is sometimes called the *expanded form*.

For example, the declaration of method ListInts in the following code matches all the method invocations below it, even though they have different numbers of actual parameters.

```
void ListInts( params int[] InputList ) { ... }      // Method declaration

...
ListInts( );                                  // 0 actual parameters
ListInts( 1, 2, 3 );                          // 3 actual parameters
ListInts( 4, 5, 6,  7 );                      // 4 actual parameters
ListInts( 8, 9, 10, 11, 12 );                 // 5 actual parameters
```

When you use an invocation with separate actual parameters for a parameter array, the compiler does the following:

- Takes the list of actual parameters and uses them to create and initialize an array in the heap.

- Stores the reference to the array in the formal parameter on the stack.

- If there are no actual parameters at the position corresponding to the formal parameter array, the compiler creates an array with 0 elements and uses that.

For example, the following code declares a method called ListInts, which takes a parameter array. Main declares three ints and passes them to the array.

```
class MyClass                      Parameter array
{                              _____↓_____
   public void ListInts( params int[] inVals )
   {
      if (inVals != null)
         for (int i = 0; i < inVals.Length; i++)    // Process the array.
         {
            inVals[i] = inVals[i] * 10;
            Console.WriteLine("{0}  ", inVals[i]); // Display new value.
         }
   }
}

class Program
{
   static void Main()
   {
      int first = 5, second = 6, third = 7;        // Declare three ints.

      MyClass mc = new MyClass();
      mc.ListInts( first, second, third );         // Call the method.
                 _____↑_____
                   Actual parameters
      Console.WriteLine("{0}, {1}, {2}", first, second, third);
   }
}
```

This code produces the following output:

```
50
60
70
5, 6, 7
```

Figure 5-10 illustrates the following about the values of the actual and formal parameters at various stages in the execution of the method:

- Before the method call, the three actual parameters are already on the stack.

- By the beginning of the method, the three actual parameters have been used to initialize an array in the heap, and the reference to the array has been assigned to formal parameter InputList.

- Inside the method, the code first checks to make sure that the array reference is not null, and then processes the array by multiplying each element in the array by 10, and storing it back.

- After method execution, the formal parameter, InputList, is out of scope.

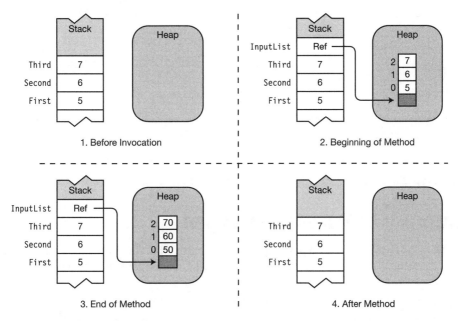

Figure 5-10. *Parameter arrays*

An important thing to remember about parameter arrays is that when the array is created in the heap, the values of the actual parameters are *copied* to the array. In this way, they are like value parameters:

- If the array parameter is a value type, the *values* are copied, and the actual parameters *cannot be affected* inside the method.

- If the array parameter is a reference type, the *references* are copied, and the objects referenced by the actual parameters *can be affected* inside the method.

Arrays As Actual Parameters

You can also create and populate an array before the method call, and pass the single array variable as the actual parameter. In this case, the compiler uses *your* array, rather than creating one.

For example, the following code uses method ListInts, declared in the previous example. In this code, Main creates an array and uses the array variable as the actual parameter, rather than using separate integers.

```
static void Main()
{
   int[] MyArr = new int[] { 5, 6, 7 };  // Create and initialize array.

   MyClass mc = new MyClass();
   mc.ListInts(MyArr);                    // Call method.

   foreach (int x in MyArr)
      Console.WriteLine("{0}", x);        // Print out each element.
}
```

This code produces the following output:

```
50
60
70
```

Summary of Parameter Types

Since there are four parameter types, it is sometimes difficult to remember their various characteristics. Table 5-2 summarizes them, making it easier to compare and contrast them.

Table 5-2. *Summary of Parameter Type Syntactic Usage*

Parameter Type	Modifier	Used at Declaration?	Used at Invocation?	Implementation
Value	None			The system copies the actual parameter to the formal parameter.
Reference	ref	Yes	Yes	The formal parameter aliases the actual parameter.
Output	out	Yes	Yes	The formal parameter aliases the actual parameter.
Array	params	Yes	No	This allows passing a variable number of actual parameters to a method.

Stack Frames

So far, you know that local variables and parameters are kept on the stack. Let's look at that organization a little further.

When a method is called, memory is allocated at the top of the stack, to hold a number of data items associated with the method. This chunk of memory is called the *stack frame* for the method.

- The stack frame contains memory to hold the following:
  - The return address—that is, where to resume execution when the method exits
  - Those parameters that allocate memory, that is, the value parameters of the method, and the parameter array if there is one
  - Various other administrative data items relevant to the method call
- When a method is called, its entire stack frame is pushed onto the stack.
- When the method exits, its entire stack frame is popped from the stack. Popping a stack frame is sometimes called *unwinding* the stack.

For example, the following code declares three methods. Main calls MethodA, which calls MethodB, creating three stack frames. As the methods exit, the stack unwinds.

```
class Program
{
   static void MethodA( int par1, int par2)
   {
      Console.WriteLine("Enter MethodA: {0}, {1}", par1, par2);
      MethodB(11, 18);                              // Call MethodB.
      Console.WriteLine("Exit  MethodA");
   }

   static void MethodB(int par1, int par2)
   {
      Console.WriteLine("Enter MethodB: {0}, {1}", par1, par2);
      Console.WriteLine("Exit  MethodB");
   }

   static void Main( )
   {
      Console.WriteLine("Enter Main");
      MethodA( 15, 30);                             // Call MethodA.
      Console.WriteLine("Exit  Main");
   }
}
```

This code produces the following output:

```
Enter Main
Enter MethodA: 15, 30
Enter MethodB: 11, 18
Exit  MethodB
Exit  MethodA
Exit  Main
```

Figure 5-11 shows how the stack frames of each method are placed on the stack when the method is called, and how the stack is unwound as the methods complete.

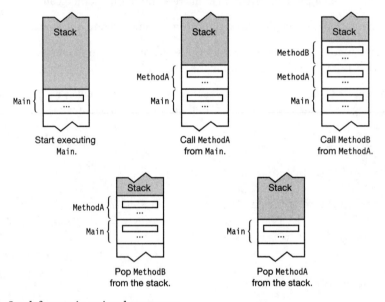

Figure 5-11. *Stack frames in a simple program*

Recursion

Besides calling other methods, a method can also call itself. This is called *recursion.*

Recursion can produce some very elegant code, such as the following method for comput-ing the factorial of a number. Notice that inside the method, the method calls itself, with an actual parameter of 1 less than its input parameter.

```
int Factorial(int InValue)
{
   if (InValue <= 1)
      return InValue;
   else
      return InValue * Factorial(InValue - 1);      // Call Factorial again.
                              ↑
                         Calls itself
}
```

The mechanics of a method calling itself are exactly the same as if it had called another, different method. A new stack frame is pushed onto the stack for each call to the method.

For example, in the following code, method Count calls itself with one less than its input parameter and then prints out its input parameter. As the recursion gets deeper, the stack gets larger.

```
class Program
{
   public void Count(int InVal)
   {
      if (InVal == 0)
         return;
      Count(InVal - 1);                // Invoke this method again.
        ↑
      Calls itself
      Console.WriteLine("{0} ", InVal);
   }

   static void Main()
   {
      Program pr = new Program();
      pr.Count(3);
   }
}
```

This code produces the following output:

1
2
3

Figure 5-12 illustrates the code. Notice that with an input value of 3, there are four different, independent stack frames for method Count. Each has its own value for input parameter InVal.

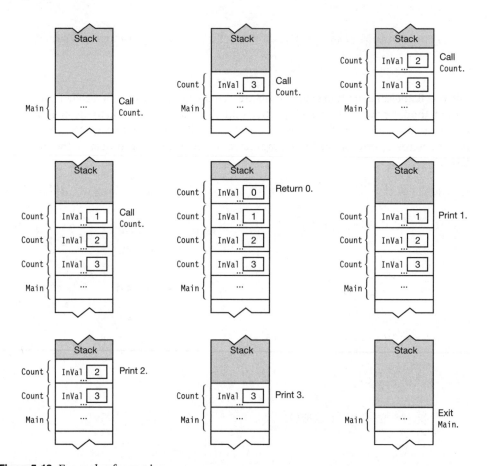

Figure 5-12. *Example of recursion*

Method Overloading

A class can have more than one method with the same name. This is called *method overloading*. Each method with the same name must have a different *signature* than the others.

- The signature of a method consists of the following information from the method header of the method declaration:
  - The name of the method
  - The number of parameters
  - The data types and order of the parameters
  - The parameter modifiers

- The return type is *not* part of the signature—although it is a common mistake to believe that it is.

- The *names* of the formal parameters are also not part of the signature.

```
Not part of signature
↓
long AddValues( int a, out int b) { ... }
     ─────────────────────────────
                  ↑
              Signature
```

For example, the following four methods are overloads of the method name AddValues.

```
class A
{
   long AddValues( int   a, int   b)          { return a + b; }
   long AddValues( int   a, int   b, int c)   { return a + b + c; }
   long AddValues( float a, float b)          { return a + b; }
   long AddValues( long  a, long  b)          { return a + b; }
}
```

The following code shows an illegal attempt at overloading the method name AddValues. The two methods differ on the return types and the names of the formal parameters. But they still have the same signature, because they have the same method name, and the number, types, and order of their parameters are the same. The compiler would produce an error message for this code.

```
class B           Signature
{        ─────────────────────────────
                         ↓
   long AddValues( long  a, long  b) { return a+b; }
   int  AddValues( long  c, long  d) { return a+b; }
}        ─────────────────────────────
                  ↑
              Signature
```

CHAPTER 6

■■■

More About Classes

Class Members
Instance Class Members
Static Fields
Static Function Members
Other Static Class Member Types
Constants
Properties
Instance Constructors
Static Constructors
Accessibility of Constructors
Finalizers
Comparison of Constructors and Finalizers
The readonly Modifier
The this Keyword
Indexers
Access Modifiers on Accessors
Partial Classes

Class Members

The previous two chapters covered two of the nine types of class members: fields and methods. In this chapter, I will introduce more class member types, and discuss the lifetimes of class members.

Table 6-1 shows a list of the class member types. Those that have already been introduced are marked with diamonds. Those that will be covered in this chapter are marked with a check. Those that will be covered later in the text are marked with empty check boxes.

Table 6-1. *Types of Class Members*

Data Members (Store Data)	Function Members (Execute Code)	
✦ Fields	✦ Methods	✓ Operators
✓ Constants	✓ Properties	✓ Indexers
	✓ Constructors	❑ Events
	✓ Finalizers	

Order of Member Modifiers

Previously, you saw that the declarations of fields and methods can include modifiers such as `public` and `private`. In this chapter, I will discuss a number of additional modifiers. Since many of these modifiers can be used together, the question that arises is: what order do they need to be in?

Class member declaration statements consist of the following: the core declaration, an optional set of *modifiers*, and an optional set of *attributes*. The syntax used to describe this structure is the following:

```
[ attributes ]   [ modifiers ]   CoreDeclaration
```

- The modifiers, if any, must be placed before the core declaration.

- The attributes, if any, must be placed before the modifiers and core declaration.

- The square brackets indicate that the set of components inside them is optional.

When a declaration has multiple modifiers, they can be placed in any order, before the core declaration. So far, I've only discussed two modifiers: public and private. When there are multiple attributes, they can be placed in any order, before the modifiers. I'll discuss attributes in Chapter 21.

For example, public and static are both modifiers that can be used together to modify certain declarations. Since they're both modifiers, they can be placed in either order. The following two lines are equivalent:

```
public static int MaxVal;

static public int MaxVal;
```

Figure 6-1 shows the order of the components as applied to the member types shown so far: fields and methods. Notice that the type of the field and the return type of the method are not modifiers—they are part of the core declaration.

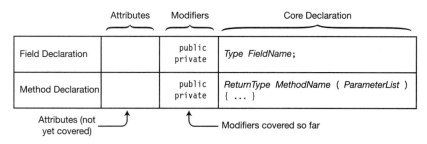

Figure 6-1. *Attributes, modifiers, and core declarations*

Instance Class Members

Class members can be associated with an instance or with the class. By default, members are associated with an instance. You can think of each instance of a class as having its own copy of each class member. These members are called *instance members*.

Changes to the value of one instance field do not affect the values of the members in any other instance. So far, the fields and methods you've looked at have all been instance fields and instance methods.

For example, the following code declares a class D with a single integer field Mem1. Main creates two instances of the class. Each instance has its own copy of field Mem1. Changing the value of one instance's copy of the field does not affect the values of the other instances' copies. Figure 6-2 shows the two instances of class D.

```
class D
{
    public int Mem1;
}

class Program
{
    static void Main()
    {
        D d1 = new D();
        D d2 = new D();
        d1.Mem1 = 10; d2.Mem1 = 28;

        Console.WriteLine("d1 = {0}, d2 = {1}", d1.Mem1, d2.Mem1);
    }
}
```

This code produces the following output:

```
d1 = 10, d2 = 28
```

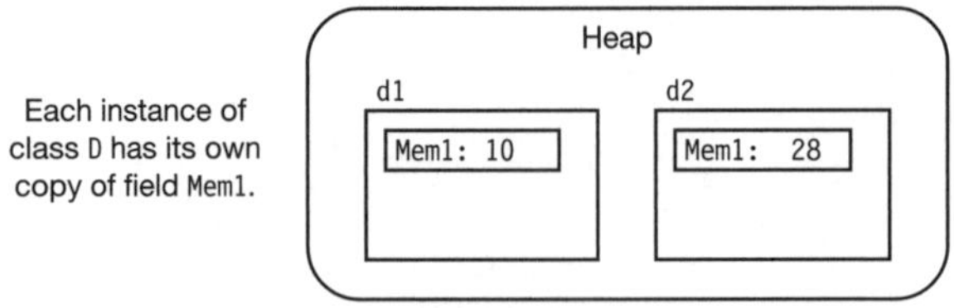

Each instance of
class D has its own
copy of field Mem1.

Figure 6-2. *Two instances with instance data members*

Static Fields

Besides instance fields, classes can also have *static fields*.

- A static field is *shared* by all the instances of the class.
  - With a static field, all the instances access the same memory location.
  - If the value of the memory location is changed by one instance, the change is visible to all the instances.

- The `static` modifier is used to declare a field static, as follows:

```
class D
{
    int Mem1;                // Instance field
    static int Mem2;         // Static field
      ↑
    Keyword
}
```

For example, the code in Figure 6-3 declares class D with static field Mem2 and instance field Mem1. Main defines two instances of class D.

- Because Mem2 is static, both instances of class D share a single Mem2 field.

- If Mem2 is changed in one instance, it is changed in the other as well.

- Member Mem1 is not declared `static`, so each instance has its own copy.

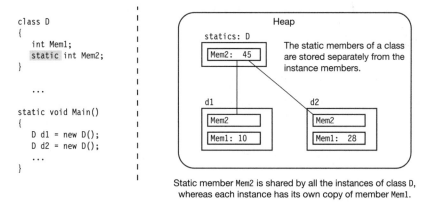

Figure 6-3. *Static and non-static data members*

Accessing Static Members from Outside the Class

In the previous chapter, you saw that dot-syntax notation is used to access instance members from outside the class. Dot-syntax notation consists of listing the instance name, followed by a dot, followed by the member name.

Static members, like instance members, are also accessed from outside the class using dot-syntax notation. But instead of using the *instance name*, you must use the *class name*, as follows:

```
Class name
↓
D.Mem2 = 5;                          // Accessing the static class member
  ↑
Member name
```

Example of a Static Field

The following code expands the preceding class D by adding two methods:

- One method sets the values of the two data members.

- The other method displays the values of the two data members.

```
class D {
    int       Mem1;
    static int Mem2;

    public void SetVars(int v1, int v2) // Set the values
    {   Mem1 = v1; Mem2 = v2; }
                    ↑  Access as if it were an instance field

    public void Display( string str )
    {   Console.WriteLine("{0}: Mem1= {1}, Mem2= {2}", str, Mem1, Mem2); }
}                                                                   ↑
                                        Access as if it were an instance field
class Program {
    static void Main()
    {
        D d1 = new D(), d2 = new D();   // Create two instances.

        d1.SetVars(2, 4);               // Set d1's values.
        d1.Display("d1");

        d2.SetVars(15, 17);             // Set d2's values.
        d2.Display("d2");

        d1.Display("d1");               // Display d1 again and notice that the
    }                                   // value of static member Mem2 has changed!
}
```

The preceding code produces the following output:

```
d1: Mem1= 2, Mem2= 4
d2: Mem1= 15, Mem2= 17
d1: Mem1= 2, Mem2= 17
```

Lifetimes of Static Members

Instance members come into existence when the instance is created, and go out of existence when the instance is destroyed. Static members, however, exist and are accessible even if there are *no instances* of the class.

Figure 6-4 illustrates a class D, with a static field, Mem2. Although Main does not define any instances of the class, it assigns the value 5 to the static field and prints it out.

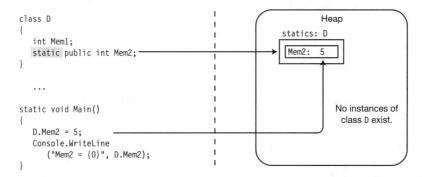

Figure 6-4. *Static field with no class instances*

The code in Figure 6-4 produces the following output:

```
Mem2 = 5
```

Note Static members exist even if there are no instances of the class.

Static Function Members

Besides static fields, there are also static function members.

- Static function members, like static fields, are independent of any class instance. Even if there are no instances of a class, you can call a static method.

- Static function members cannot access instance members. They can, however, access other static members.

For example, the following class contains a static field and a static method. Notice that the body of the static method accesses the static field.

```
class X
{
    static public int A;                        // Static field
    static public void PrintValA()              // Static method
    {
        Console.WriteLine("Value of A: {0}", A);
    }                                    ↑
}                                 Accessing the static field
```

The following code uses class X, defined in the preceding code. Figure 6-5 illustrates the code.

```
class Program
{
    static void Main()
    {
        X.A = 10;              // Use dot-syntax notation
        X.PrintValA();         // Use dot-syntax notation
    } ↑
} Class name
```

This code produces the following output:

```
Value of A: 10
```

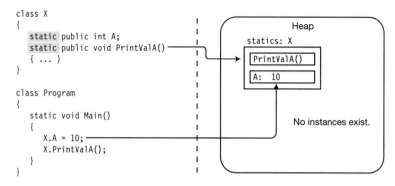

Figure 6-5. *Static methods of a class can be called even if there are no instances of the class.*

Other Static Class Member Types

The types of class members that can be declared static are shown checked in Table 6-2. The other member types cannot be declared static.

Table 6-2. *Class Member Types That Can Be Declared Static*

Data Members (Store Data)	Function Members (Execute Code)	
✓ Fields	✓ Methods	✓ Operators
Constants	✓ Properties	Indexers
	✓ Constructors	✓ Events
	Finalizers	

Constants

Of the nine class member types, two of them are *data* member types. The first, which has already been discussed, is fields. The second is *constants*. You can think of a *constant* as a type of "variable" for which the value cannot be changed.

- A constant *must be initialized* at its declaration.

- A constant *cannot be changed* after its declaration.

- There are two kinds of constants:
    - Member constants, which are like fields—except constant
    - Local constants, which are like local variables—except constant

The core declaration for a constant is shown following. Note that the syntax is the same as that of a field or variable declaration, except for the following:

- The addition of the keyword const in front

- The mandatory initializer

Note The keyword const is not a modifier, but part of the core declaration. It must be placed immediately before the type.

```
Keyword
  ↓
const Type Identifier = Value;
                         ↑
                  Initializer required
```

Note Unlike C and C++, in C# there are no global constants. Every constant must be declared within a type.

Constant members, like fields, are declared in the class declaration, as follows:

```
class MyClass
{
    const int IntVal = 100;      // Defines a constant named IntVal, of type int
          ↑             ↑        // and initializes its value to 100
}         Type      Initializer

const double PI = 3.1416;        // Error: cannot be declared outside a type
                                 // declaration
```

The value used to initialize a constant must be computable at compile time.

```
class MyClass
{
   const int IntVal1 = 100;
   const int IntVal2 = 2 * IntVal1;     // Fine. The value of IntVal1 was
}                                       // set in the previous line
```

You cannot assign to a constant after its declaration.

```
class MyClass
{
   const int IntVal;                    // Error: initialization is required.
   IntVal = 100;                        // Error: assignment is not allowed.
}
```

Constants Are Like Statics

Constants members act like static values. They are "visible" to every instance of the class, and they are available even if there are no instances of the class.

For example, the following code declares class X with constant field PI. Main does not create any instances of X, and yet it can use field PI and print its value.

```
class X
{
   public const double PI = 3.1416;
}

class Program
{
   static void Main()
   {
      Console.WriteLine("pi = {0}", X.PI);    // Use static field PI
   }
}
```

This code produces the following output:

```
pi = 3.1416
```

Unlike actual statics, however, constants do not have their own storage locations, and are substituted in by the compiler at compile time, in a manner similar to #define values in C and C++. This is shown in Figure 6-6, which illustrates the preceding code. Hence, although a constant member acts like a static, you cannot declare a constant as static.

```
static const double PI = 3.14;
  ↑
Error: can't declare a constant as static
```

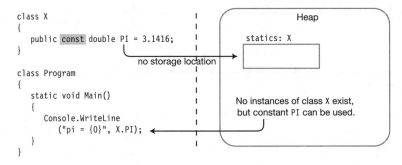

Figure 6-6. *Constant fields act like static fields, but do not have a storage location in memory.*

Local Constants

A local constant, like a local variable, is declared in a method body or code block, and goes out of scope at the end of the block in which it is declared. For example, in the following code, local constant PI goes out of scope at the end of Main.

```
static void Main()
{
   const double PI = 3.1416;                    // Local constant

   for (int radius = 1; radius <= 5; radius++)
   {
      double area = radius * radius * PI;       // Read from local constant
      Console.WriteLine
         ("Radius: {0}, Area: {1}", radius, area);
   }
}
```

Properties

A property is a member that represents an item of data in a class instance or class.

Using a property appears very much like writing to, or reading from, a field. The syntax is the same. For example, the following code shows the use of a class called MyClass that has both a public field and a public property. From their usage, you cannot tell them apart.

```
MyClass mc = new MyClass();

mc.MyField    = 5;                       // Assigning to a field
mc.MyProperty = 10;                      // Assigning to a property

WriteLine("{0} {1}", mc.MyField, mc.MyProperty); // Read field and property
```

A property, like a field, has the following characteristics:

- It is a named class member.

- It has a type.

- It can be assigned to and read from.

Unlike a field, however, a property is a *function member*.

- It does not allocate memory for data storage!

- It executes code.

A *property* is a named set of two matching methods called *accessors*.

- The set accessor is used for assigning a value to the property.

- The get accessor is used for retrieving a value from the property.

Figure 6-7 shows representations of a property. The code on the left shows the syntax of declaring a property named MyValue, of type int. The figure on the right shows how I will graphically represent properties in this text. The accessors are shown sticking out the back, because, as you shall soon see, they are not directly callable.

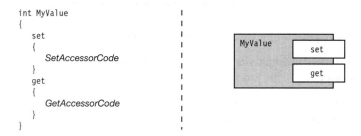

Figure 6-7. *An example property of type int, named MyValue*

Property Declarations and Accessors

Property accessors have predefined names and semantics. They are the set accessor and the get accessor. You can think of the set accessor as a method with a single parameter that "sets" the value of the property. The get accessor has no parameters and returns a value from the property.

- The set accessor always has the following:
  - A single, implicit value parameter named value, of the same type as the property
  - A return type of void

- The get accessor always has the following:
  - No parameters
  - A return type of the same type as the property

The structure of a property declaration is shown in Figure 6-8. Notice in the figure that neither accessor declaration has *explicit* parameter or return type declarations. They don't need them, because they are *implicit* in the type of the property.

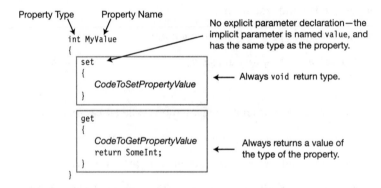

Figure 6-8. *The syntax and structure of a property declaration*

The implicit parameter value, in the set accessor, is a normal value parameter. Like other value parameters, you can use it to send data into a method body—or in this case, the accessor block. Once inside the block, you can use value like a normal variable, including assigning values to it.

Other important points about accessors are the following:

- All paths through the implementation of a get accessor *must* include a return statement that returns a value of the property type.

- The set and get accessors can be declared in either order, and no methods other than the accessors are allowed on a property.

A Property Example

The following code shows an example of the declaration of a class called C1 that contains a property named MyValue.

- Notice that the property itself does not have any storage. Instead, the accessors determine what should be done with data sent in, and what data should be sent out. In this case, the property uses a field called TheRealValue for storage.

- The set accessor takes its input parameter, value, and assigns that value to field TheRealValue.

- The get accessor just returns the value of field TheRealValue.

Figure 6-9 illustrates the code.

```
class C1
{
    private int TheRealValue;              // Field: memory allocated

    public int MyValue                     // Property: no memory allocated
    {
        set
        {
            TheRealValue = value;
        }

        get
        {
            return TheRealValue;
        }
    }
}
```

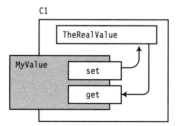

Figure 6-9. *Property accessors often use fields for storage*

Using a Property

You write to and read from a property in the same way you access a field. The accessors are called implicitly.

- To write to a property, use the property's name on the left side of an assignment statement.

- To read from a property, use the property's name in an expression.

For example, the following code contains an outline of the declaration of a property named MyValue. You write to and read from the property using just the property name, as if it were a field name.

```
int MyValue              // Property declaration
{
   set{ ... }
   get{ ... }
}
...
```
Property name
↓
```
MyValue = 5;             // Assignment: the set method is implicitly called
z = MyValue;             // Expression: the get method is implicitly called
```
↑
Property name

The appropriate accessor is called implicitly depending on whether you are writing to or reading from the property. You cannot explicitly call the accessors. Attempting to do so produces a compile error.

```
y = MyValue.get();       // Wrong! Can't explicitly call get accessor.
MyValue.set(5);          // Wrong! Can't explicitly call set accessor.
```

Properties and Associated Fields

A property is often associated with a field. A common practice is to encapsulate a field in a class by declaring it private, and declaring a public property to give controlled access to the field from outside the class.

For example, the following code uses the public property MyValue to give controlled access to private field TheRealValue.

```
class C1
{
    private int TheRealValue = 10;   // Field: memory allocated
    public  int MyValue              // Property: no memory allocated
    {
        set{ TheRealValue = value; }  // Sets the value of field TheRealValue
        get{ return TheRealValue; }   // Gets the value of the field
    }
}

class Program
{
    static void Main()
    {
                                    Read from the property as if it were a field
        C1 c = new C1();                              ↓
        Console.WriteLine("MyValue: {0}", c.MyValue);

        c.MyValue = 20;  ←Use assignment to set value of property
        Console.WriteLine("MyValue: {0}", c.MyValue);
    }
}
```

There are several conventions for naming properties and their associated fields. One convention is to use the same string for both names, but use camel casing (in which the first letter is lowercase) for the field and Pascal casing for the property. This violates the general rule that it is bad practice to have different identifiers that differ only in casing, but it has the advantage of tying the two identifiers together in a meaningful way.

Another convention is to use Pascal casing for the property, and for the field, use an underscore in front of the same identifier.

The following code shows both conventions:

```
private int firstField;                    // Camel casing
public  int FirstField                     // Pascal casing
{
   get { return firstField; } set { firstField = value; }
}

private int _SecondField;                   // Underscore
public  int SecondField
{
   get { return _SecondField; } set { _SecondField = value; }
}
```

Performing Other Calculations

Property accessors are not limited to just passing values back and forth from an associated field—the get and set accessors can perform any—or no—computations. The only action *required* is that the get accessor return a value of the property type.

For instance, the following example shows a valid (but probably useless) property that just returns the value 5 when its get accessor is called. When the set accessor is called, it doesn't do anything. The value of implicit parameter value is ignored.

```
public int Useless
{
   set{  /* I'm not setting anything.     */ }
   get{  /* I'm just returning the value 5.   */
      return 5;
   }
}
```

The following code shows a much more useful, realistic property, where the set accessor performs filtering before setting the associated field. The set accessor sets field TheRealValue to the input value—unless the input value is greater than 100. In that case, it sets TheRealValue to 100.

```
int TheRealValue = 10;                  // The field
int MyValue                             // The property
{
   set {                                // Sets the value of the field
      TheRealValue = value > 100        // But makes sure it's not > 100
                        ? 100
                        : value;
   }
   get {                                // Gets the value of the field
      return TheRealValue;
   }
}
```

Note In the preceding code sample, the syntax between the equals sign and the end of the statement might look somewhat strange. That expression uses the *conditional operator*, which will be covered in greater detail in Chapter 8.

The conditional operator is a ternary operator that evaluates the expression before the question mark, and, if the expression evaluates to true, it returns the first expression after the question mark. Otherwise, it returns the expression after the colon.

Read-Only and Write-Only Properties

You can leave one or the other of a property's accessors undefined by omitting its declaration.

- A property with only a get accessor is called a *read-only* property. A read-only property is a safe way of passing an item of data out from a class or class instance without allowing too much access.

- A property with only a set accessor is called a *write-only* property. A write-only property is a safe way of passing an item of data from outside of the class to the class without allowing too much access.

- At least one of the two accessors must be defined; otherwise, the compiler will produce an error message.

Figure 6-10 illustrates read-only and write-only properties.

Read-Only Property   Write-Only Property

Figure 6-10. *A property can have one or the other of its accessors undefined.*

A Computed, Read-Only Property Example

In most of the examples so far, the property has been associated with a field, and the get and set accessors have referenced that field. However, a property does not have to be associated with a field. In the following example, the get accessor *computes* the return value.

In the following example code, class RightTriangle represents, not surprisingly, a right triangle.

- It has two public fields that represent the lengths of the two right-angle sides of the triangle. These fields can be written to and read from.

- The third side is represented by property Hypotenuse, which is a read-only property whose return value is based on the lengths of the other two sides. It is not stored in a field. Instead, it computes the correct value, on demand, for the current values of A and B.

Figure 6-11 illustrates read-only property Hypotenuse.

```
class RightTriangle
{
    public double A = 3;
    public double B = 4;
    public double Hypotenuse                      // Read-only property
    {
        get{ return Math.Sqrt((A*A)+(B*B)); }     // Calculate return value
    }
}

class Program
{
    static void Main()
    {
        RightTriangle c = new RightTriangle();
        Console.WriteLine("Hypotenuse: {0}", c.Hypotenuse);
    }
}
```

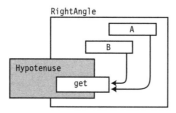

Figure 6-11. *Read-only property Hypotenuse*

Example of Properties and Databases

Another example in which a property is not associated with a field is when the property is associated with a value in a database. In that case, the get accessor makes the appropriate database calls to get the value from the database. The set accessor makes the corresponding calls to the database to set the new value in the database.

For example, the following property is associated with a particular value in some database. The code assumes that there are two other methods in the class to handle the details of the database transactions:

- SetValueInDatabase takes an integer parameter and uses it to set a particular field in a record in some database.

- GetValueFromDatabase retrieves and returns a particular integer field value from a particular record in some database.

```
int MyDatabaseValue
{
   set                                 // Sets integer value in the database
   {
      SetValueInDatabase(value);
   }
   get                                 // Gets integer value from the database
   {
      return GetValueFromDatabase();
   }
}
```

Static Properties

Properties can also be declared static. Accessors of static properties, like all static members

- Cannot access instance members of a class—although they can be accessed by them

- Exist regardless of whether there are instances of the class

- Must be referenced by the class name, rather than an instance name, when being accessed from outside the class

For example, the following code shows a class with a static property called MyValue that is associated with a static field called myValue. In the first three lines of Main, the property is accessed, even though there are no instances of the class. The last line of Main calls an instance method that accesses the property from *inside* the class.

```
class Trivial
{
   static int myValue;
   public static int MyValue
   {
      set { myValue = value; }
      get { return myValue;  }
   }

   public void PrintValue()                  Accessed from inside the class
   {                                                     ↓
      Console.WriteLine("Value from inside: {0}", MyValue);
   }
}

class Program
{
   static void Main()                        Accessed from outside the class
   {                                                     ↓
      Console.WriteLine("Init Value: {0}", Trivial.MyValue);
      Trivial.MyValue = 10;   ← Accessed from outside the class
      Console.WriteLine("New Value : {0}", Trivial.MyValue);

      Trivial tr = new Trivial();
      tr.PrintValue();
   }
}
```

```
Init Value: 0
New Value : 10
Value from inside: 10
```

Instance Constructors

An instance constructor is a special method that is executed whenever a new instance of a class is created.

- A constructor is used to initialize the state of the class instance.

- If you want to be able to create instances of your class from outside the class, you need to declare the constructor `public`.

Figure 6-12 shows the syntax of a constructor. A constructor looks like the other methods in a class declaration, except for the following:

- The name of the constructor is the same as the name of the class.

- A constructor cannot return a value.

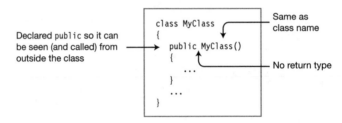

Figure 6-12. *Constructor declaration*

For example, the following class uses its constructor to initialize its fields. In this case, it has a field called `TimeOfInstantiation` that is initialized with the current date and time.

```
class MyClass
{
   DateTime TimeOfInstantiation;                    // Field
   ...
   public MyClass()                                 // Constructor
   {
      TimeOfInstantiation = DateTime.Now;           // Initialize field
   }
   ...
}
```

■Note   Having finished the section on static properties, take a closer look at the line that initializes `TimeOfInstantiation`. The `DateTime` class is from the BCL, and `Now` is a *static property* of the `DateTime` class. The `Now` property creates a new instance of the `DateTime` class, initializes it with the current date and time from the system clock, and returns a reference to the new `DateTime` instance.

Constructors with Parameters

Like other methods, constructors

- Can have parameters. The syntax for the parameters is exactly the same as for other methods.

- Can be overloaded.

When creating an instance of a class with the new operator, you are telling it which constructor to use by supplying the class name, along with any actual parameters for the constructor, as the operand to the new operator.

For example, in the following code, Class1 has three constructors: one that takes no parameters, one that takes an int, and another that takes a string. Main creates an instance using each one.

```
class Class1
{
   int    MyNumber;
   string MyName;

   public Class1()          { MyNumber=28; MyName="Nemo"; } // Constructor 0
   public Class1(int Value){ MyNumber=Value; MyName="Nemo"; } // Constructor 1
   public Class1(String Name) { MyName=Name; }              // Constructor 2

   public void SoundOff()
      {Console.WriteLine("MyName {0}, MyNumber {1}", MyName, MyNumber); }
}

class Program
{
   static void Main()
   {
      Class1 a = new Class1(),              // Call constructor 0.
             b = new Class1(7),             // Call constructor 1.
             c = new Class1("Bill");        // Call constructor 2.

      a.SoundOff();
      b.SoundOff();
      c.SoundOff();
   }
}
```

This code produces the following output:

```
MyName Nemo, MyNumber 28
MyName Nemo, MyNumber 7
MyName Bill, MyNumber 0
```

Default Constructors

If no instance constructor is explicitly supplied in the class declaration, then the compiler supplies an implicit, default constructor with

- No parameters

- An empty body

If the programmer defines any constructor at all, then the compiler does not define any default constructors for the class.

For example, Class2 declares two constructors.

- Because there is at least one explicitly defined constructor, the compiler does not create any additional constructors.

- In Main, there is an attempt to create a new instance using a constructor with no parameters. Since there *is* no constructor with zero parameters, the compiler will produce an error message.

```
class Class2
{
   public Class2(int Value)    { ... }   // Constructor 0
   public Class2(String Value) { ... }   // Constructor 1
}

class Program
{
   static void Main()
   {
      Class2 a = new Class2();   // Error! No constructor with 0 parameters
      ...
   }
}
```

Static Constructors

Constructors can also be declared static. While an instance constructor initializes each new instance of a class, a static constructor initializes items at the class level. Generally, static constructors initialize the static fields of the class.

- Class level items need to be initialized
  - Before any static member is referenced
  - Before any instance of the class is created

- Like instance constructors
  - The name of the static constructor must be the same as the name of the class.
  - The constructor cannot return a value.

- Unlike instance constructors
  - Static constructors use the static keyword in the declaration.
  - There can only be a single static constructor for a class, and it cannot have parameters.
  - Static constructors cannot have accessibility modifiers.

The following is an example of a static constructor. Notice that its form is the same as that of an instance constructor, but with the addition of the static keyword.

```
class Class1
{
   static Class1 ()
   {
      ...                // Do all the static initializations.
   }
   ...
```

Other important things you should know about static constructors are the following:

- A class can have both static and instance constructors.

- As with static methods, a static constructor cannot access non-static members of its class, and therefore cannot use the this accessor.

- Static constructors cannot be called by your program. They are called automatically by the system
  - Before any instance of the class is created
  - Before any static member of the class is referenced

Example of a Static Constructor

The following code uses a static constructor to initialize a private static field named RandomKey of type Random. Random is a class provided by the BCL to produce random numbers. It is in the System namespace.

```
class RandomNumberClass
{
    private static Random RandomKey;          // Private static field

    static RandomNumberClass()                // Static constructor
    {
        RandomKey = new Random();             // Initialize RandomKey
    }

    public int GetRandomNumber()
    {
        return RandomKey.Next();
    }
}

class Program
{
    static void Main()
    {
        RandomNumberClass a = new RandomNumberClass();
        RandomNumberClass b = new RandomNumberClass();

        Console.WriteLine("Next Random #: {0}", a.GetRandomNumber());
        Console.WriteLine("Next Random #: {0}", b.GetRandomNumber());
    }
}
```

One execution of the preceding code produced the following output:

```
Next Random #: 47857058
Next Random #: 1124842041
```

Accessibility of Constructors

Access modifiers can be assigned to constructors just as they can to other members. Notice that in the examples, the constructors have been declared public so that you can create instances from outside the class.

You can also create private constructors, which cannot be called from outside the class, but can be used from within the class, as you shall see in the next chapter (which covers inheritance).

Finalizers

Finalizers perform actions required to clean up or release unmanaged resources before an instance of a class is destroyed. The important things to know about finalizers are the following:

- You can only have a single finalizer per class.

- A finalizer cannot have parameters.

- A finalizer cannot have accessibility modifiers.

- A finalizer has the same name as the class, but is preceded by a tilde character (pronounced *TIL-duh*).

- A finalizer only acts on instances of classes. Hence, there are no static finalizers.

- A finalizer cannot be called explicitly by your code. It is called in the garbage collection process, when your class is no longer accessible.

For example, the following code illustrates the syntax for a finalizer of a class called Class1:

```
Class1
{
   ~Class1()                                        // The finalizer
   {
      CleanupCode
   }
   ...
}
```

Some important guidelines for using finalizers are the following:

- Don't implement a finalizer if you don't need one. They can incur performance costs.

- A finalizer should only release external resources that the object owns. It should not access other objects.

- Since it cannot be called explicitly, make it less visible by not declaring it with public access.

Calling the Finalizer

Unlike the C++ destructor, a C# finalizer is not called immediately when an instance goes out of scope. In fact, there is no way of knowing when the finalizer will be called. Furthermore, as mentioned, you cannot explicitly call a finalizer. If your code needs one, you just provide it for the system, which will call it at some point before the object is destroyed.

If your code contains unmanaged resources that should be released in a timely manner, you should not leave that for the finalizer, since there is no guarantee that the finalizer will run anytime soon. Instead, you should adopt the convention of encapsulating the cleanup code for these resources in a void, parameterless method. By convention, you should call it `Dispose`.

When you're done with the resources and want them released, call `Dispose`. Notice that *you* need to invoke `Dispose`—it is not the finalizer, and the system will not call it for you automatically.

Some guidelines for your `Dispose` method are the following:

- Implement the code in `Dispose` in such a way that it is all right if the method is called more than once. It should not cause an exception to be raised, and it should not do any additional work on subsequent calls.

- Don't assume that `Dispose` will get called. Make sure that the finalizer will release the resources if, for some reason, `Dispose` isn't called.

Comparison of Constructors and Finalizers

Table 6-3 provides a summary of when constructors and finalizers are called.

Table 6-3. *Constructors and Finalizers*

		When and How Often Called
Instance	Constructor	Called once on the creation of each new instance of the class.
	Finalizer	Called for each instance of the class, at some point after the program flow can no longer access the instance.
Static	Constructor	Called only once—either before the first access of any static member of the class, or before any instances of the class are created—whichever is first.
	Finalizer	Does not exist—finalizers only work on instances.

The readonly Modifier

A field can be declared with the readonly modifier. The effect is similar to declaring a field as const, in that once the value is set, it cannot be changed.

- While a const field can only be initialized in the field's declaration statement, a readonly field can have its value set in either of the following:
    - The field declaration statement—like a const.
    - Any of the class constructors. If it is a static field, then it must be done in the static constructor.

- While the value of a const field must be determinable at compile time, the value of a readonly field can be determined at run time. This additional freedom allows you to set different values in different constructors!

- Unlike a const, which always acts like a static, the following is true of a readonly field:
    - It can be either an instance field or a static field.
    - It has a storage location in memory.

For example, the following code declares a class called Shape, with two readonly fields.

- Field PI is initialized in its declaration.

- Field NumberOfSides is set to either 3 or 4, depending on which constructor is called.

```
class Shape
{   Keyword               Initialized
        ↓                     ↓
    readonly double PI = 3.1416;
    readonly int    NumberOfSides;
        ↑                   ↑
    Keyword             Not initialized

    public Shape(double side1, double side2)          // Constructor
    {
        // Shape is a rectangle
        NumberOfSides = 4;
            ↑
        ... Set in constructor
    }

    public Shape(double side1, double side2, double side3)   // Constructor
    {
        // Shape is a triangle
        NumberOfSides = 3;
            ↑
        ... Set in constructor
    }
}
```

The this Keyword

The this keyword, used in a class, is a reference to the current instance. It can only be used in the *blocks* of the following class members:

- Instance constructors
- Instance methods
- Instance accessors of properties and indexers

Clearly, since static members are not part of an instance, you cannot use the this keyword inside the code of any static function member. Rather, it is used for the following:

- To distinguish between class members and local variables or parameters
- As an actual parameter when calling a method

For example, the following code declares class MyClass, with an int field and a method that takes a single int parameter. The method compares the values of the parameter and the field, and returns the greater value. The only complicating factor is that the names of the field and the formal parameter are the same: Var1. The two names are distinguished inside the method by using the this access keyword to reference the field.

```
class MyClass
{
   int Var1 = 10;
           ↑     Both are called "Var1"   ↓
   public int ReturnMaxSum(int Var1)
   {            Parameter    Field
                    ↓         ↓
       return Var1 > this.Var1
                    ? Var1                // Parameter
                    : this.Var1;          // Field
   }
}

class Program
{
   static void Main()
   {
       MyClass mc = new MyClass();
       Console.WriteLine("Max: {0}", mc.ReturnMaxSum(30));
       Console.WriteLine("Max: {0}", mc.ReturnMaxSum(5));
   }
}
```

Indexers

If you were to define class Employee, with three fields of type string (as shown in Figure 6-13), you could access the fields using their names, as shown in the code in Main.

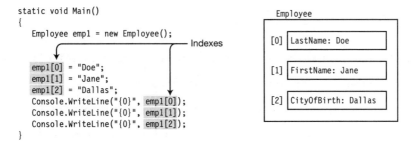

```
class Employee
{
    public string LastName;
    public string FirstName;
    public string CityOfBirth;
}

class Program
{
    static void Main()
    {
        Employee emp1 = new Employee();

        emp1.LastName = "Doe";
        emp1.FirstName = "Jane";
        emp1.CityOfBirth = "Dallas";
        Console.WriteLine("{0}", emp1.LastName);
        Console.WriteLine("{0}", emp1.FirstName);
        Console.WriteLine("{0}", emp1.CityOfBirth);
    }
}
```

Figure 6-13. *Simple class without indexers*

There are times, however, when it would be convenient to be able to access them with an index, as if the instance were an array of fields. This is exactly what *indexers* allow you to do. If you were to write an indexer for class Employee, method Main might look like the code in Figure 6-14. Notice that instead of using dot-syntax notation, indexers use *index notation*, which consists of an index between square brackets.

```
static void Main()
{
    Employee emp1 = new Employee();

    emp1[0] = "Doe";
    emp1[1] = "Jane";
    emp1[2] = "Dallas";
    Console.WriteLine("{0}", emp1[0]);
    Console.WriteLine("{0}", emp1[1]);
    Console.WriteLine("{0}", emp1[2]);
}
```

Figure 6-14. *Using indexed fields*

What Is an Indexer?

An indexer is a set of get and set accessors, similar to those of properties. Figure 6-15 shows representations of an indexer for a class that can get and set values of type string.

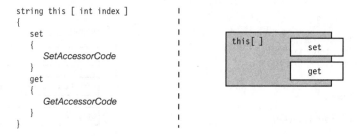

```
string this [ int index ]
{
   set
   {
      SetAccessorCode
   }
   get
   {
      GetAccessorCode
   }
}
```

Figure 6-15. *Representations of an indexer*

Indexers and Properties

Indexers and properties are similar in many ways.

- Like a property, an indexer does not allocate memory for storage.

- Both indexers and properties are used primarily for giving access to *other* data members with which they are associated, and for which they provide set and get access.
  - A property is usually associated with a *single* data member.
  - An indexer is usually associated with *multiple* data members.

Note You can think of an *indexer* as a *property* that gives get and set access to *multiple data members* of the class. You select which of the many possible data members by supplying an index, which itself can be of any type—not just numeric.

Some additional points to be aware of when working with indexers are the following:

- An indexer can have either one or both of the accessors.

- Indexers are always instance members. Hence, an indexer cannot be declared static.

- Like properties, the code implementing the get and set accessors does not have to be associated with any fields or properties. The code can do anything, or nothing, as long as the get accessor returns some value of the specified type.

Declaring an Indexer

The syntax for declaring an indexer is shown following. Notice the following about indexers:

- An indexer *does not have a name.* In place of the name is the keyword `this`.

- The parameter list is between *square brackets.*

- There must be at least one parameter declaration in the parameter list.

```
                    Keyword   Parameter list
                       ↓            ↓
      ReturnType this [ Type param1, ... ]
      {                ↑                 ↑
          get              Square brackets
          {
              ...
          }
          set
          {
              ...
          }
      }
```

Declaring an indexer is similar to declaring a property. Figure 6-16 shows the syntactic similarities and differences.

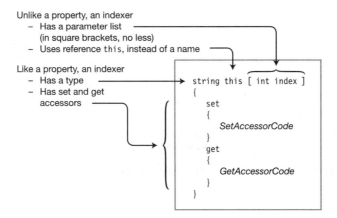

Figure 6-16. *Comparing an indexer declaration to a property declaration*

The set Accessor

When the indexer is the target of an assignment, the `set` accessor is called, and receives two items of data, as follows:

- An implicit parameter, named `value`, where `value` holds the data to be stored

- One or more index parameters that represent where it should be stored

```
emp[0] = "Doe";
   ↑        ↑
 Index    Value
Parameter
```

   Your code in the `set` accessor must examine the index parameters, determine where the data should be stored, and then store it.

   The syntax and meaning of the `set` accessor are shown in Figure 6-17. The left side of the figure shows the actual syntax of the accessor declaration. The right side shows the semantics of the accessor, if it were written using the syntax of a normal method. The figure on the right shows that the `set` accessor has the following semantics:

- It has a `void` return type.

- It uses the same parameter list as that in the indexer declaration.

- It has an implicit value parameter named `value`, of the same type as the indexer.

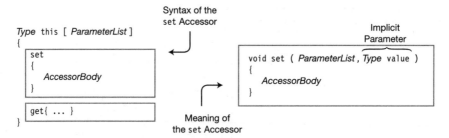

Figure 6-17. *The syntax and meaning of the set accessor declaration*

The get Accessor

When the indexer is used to retrieve a value, the get accessor is called with one or more index parameters. The index parameters represent which value to retrieve.

```
string s = emp[0];
              ↑
        Index parameter
```

Your code in the get accessor body must examine the index parameters, determine which field they represent, and return the value of that field.

The syntax and meaning of the get accessor are shown in Figure 6-18. The left side of the figure shows the actual syntax of the accessor declaration. The right side shows the semantics of the accessor if it were written using the syntax of a normal method. The semantics of the get accessor are as follows:

- It has the same parameter list as in the indexer declaration.

- It returns a value of the same type as the indexer.

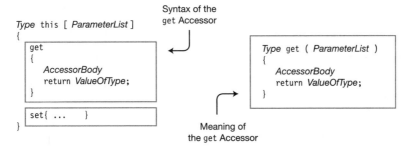

Figure 6-18. *The syntax and meaning of the get accessor declaration*

More About Indexers

As with properties, the get and set accessors cannot be called explicitly. Instead, the get accessor is called automatically when the indexer is used in an expression for a value. The set accessor is called automatically when the indexer is assigned a value with the assignment statement.

When an indexer is "called," the parameters are supplied between the square brackets.

```
  Index      Value
    ↓          ↓
emp1[0] = "Doe";                    // Calls set accessor
string NewName = emp[0];            // Calls get accessor
                      ↑
                    Index
```

Declaring the Indexer for the Employee Example

Now that you know about indexers, let's declare an indexer for the earlier example: class Employee.

- The indexer must read and write values of type string—so you declare that as the type of the indexer.

- You will arbitrarily index the three fields as integers 0 through 2, so the formal parameter between the square brackets will be of type int, and you will name it index.

- The indexer is declared public so that you can access it easily.

- In the body of the set accessor, you determine which field the index refers to, assign value to it, and return.

- In the body of the get accessor, you determine which field the index refers to and return the value of that field.

```
class Employee
{
   public string LastName;                    // Call this field 0.
   public string FirstName;                   // Call this field 1.
   public string CityOfBirth;                 // Call this field 2.

   public string this[int index]             // Indexer declaration
   {
      set                                      // Set accessor declaration
      {
         switch (index)
         {
            case 0: LastName = value;
               break;
            case 1: FirstName = value;
               break;
            case 2: CityOfBirth = value;
               break;
         }
      }

      get                                      // Get accessor declaration
      {
         switch (index)
         {
            case 0: return LastName;
            case 1: return FirstName;
            case 2: return CityOfBirth;
            default:
               return "";
         }
      }
   }
}
```

An Additional Example of an Indexer

The following is an additional example—indexing the two int fields of class Class1.

```
class Class1
{
   int Temp0;                          // Private field
   int Temp1;                          // Private field
   public int this [ int index ]       // The indexer
   {
      get
      {
         return ( 0 == index )          // Return value of either Temp0 or Temp1
                       ? Temp0
                       : Temp1;
      }

      set
      {
         if( 0 == index )
             Temp0 = value;             // Note the implicit variable "value".
         else
             Temp1 = value;             // Note the implicit variable "value".
      }
   }
}

class Example
{
   static void Main()
   {
      Class1 a = new Class1();
      Console.WriteLine("Values -- T0: {0},  T1: {1}", a[0], a[1]);
      a[0] = 15;
      a[1] = 20;
      Console.WriteLine("Values -- T0: {0}, T1: {1}", a[0], a[1]);
   }
}
```

This code produces the following output:

```
Values -- T0: 0,  T1: 0
Values -- T0: 15, T1: 20
```

Indexer Overloading

A class can have more than one indexer, as long as the parameter lists are different. It is not sufficient for the indexer *type* to be different. This is called *indexer overloading*, because all the indexers have the same "name"—the this access reference.

For example, the following class has three indexers: two of type string, and one of type int. Of the two indexers of type string, one has a single int parameter and the other has two int parameters.

```
class MyClass
{
                     ↓        ↓
   public string this [ int index ]
   {
      get { ... }
      set { ... }
   }


                  ↓         ↓
   public string this [ int index1, int index2 ]
   {
      get { ... }
      set { ... }
   }


                ↓       ↓
   public int this [ float index1 ]
   {
      get { ... }
      set { ... }
   }

   ...
}
```

■**Note** Remember that what is important is that the parameter lists be different in each of the overloaded indexers of the class.

Access Modifiers on Accessors

In this chapter, you've seen two types of function members that have get and set accessors: properties and indexers. By default, both a member's accessors have the same access level as the member itself. That is, if a property has an access level of public, then both its accessors have that same access level. The same is true of indexers.

With C# 2.0, the accessors of a member can now, under certain conditions, have different access levels. For example, in the following code, property Name has an access level of public, but the set accessor has an access level of protected.

```
class MyClass
{
    private string _Name = "John Doe";
    public string Name
    {
        get { return _Name; }
        protected set { _Name = value; }
    }       ↑
}
```

There are several restrictions on the access modifiers of accessors. The most important ones are the following:

- An accessor can have an access modifier only if the member (property or indexer) has both a get accessor and a set accessor.

- Although both accessors must be present, only one of them can have an access modifier.

- The access modifier of the accessor must be *strictly more restrictive* than the access level of the member.

Figure 6-19 shows the hierarchy of access levels. The access level of an accessor must be strictly lower in the chart than the access level of the member.

For example, if a property has an access level of public, you can give any of the four lower access levels on the chart to one of the accessors. But if the property has an access level of protected, the only access modifier you can use on one of the accessors is private.

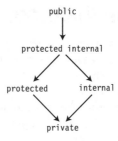

Figure 6-19. *Hierarchy of strictly restrictive accessor levels*

Partial Classes

The declaration of a class can be partitioned among several partial class declarations.

- Each of the partial class declarations contains the declarations of some of the class members.

- The partial class declarations of a class can be in the same file or in different files.

  Each partial declaration must be labeled as partial class, in contrast to the single keyword class. The declaration of a partial class looks the same as the declaration of a normal class, other than the addition of the type modifier partial.

```
Type modifier
   ↓
partial class MyPartClass    // Same class name as following
{
    member1 declaration
    member2 declaration
        ...
}
Type modifier
   ↓
partial class MyPartClass    // Same class name as preceding
{
    member3 declaration
    member4 declaration
        ...
}
```

■**Note** The type modifier `partial` is not a keyword, so in other contexts it can be used as a programmer-defined identifier. But when used immediately before the keywords `class`, `struct`, or `interface`, it signals the use of a partial type.

For example, the box on the left of Figure 6-20 represents a file with a class declaration. The boxes on the right of the figure represent that same class declaration split into two files.

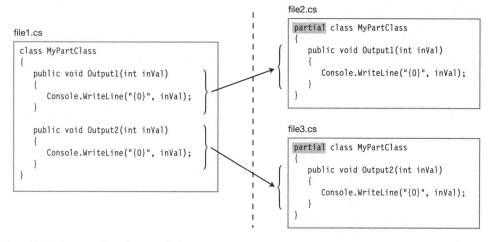

Figure 6-20. *Class split using partial types*

All the partial class declarations comprising a class must be compiled together. A class using partial class declarations has the same meaning as if all the class members were declared within a single class declaration body.

Besides classes, you can also create partial types for structures and interfaces, which are types I will cover in Chapters 12 and 17, respectively.

CHAPTER 7

■■■

Classes and Inheritance

Class Inheritance
Accessing the Inherited Members
Hiding Members of a Base Class
Base Access
Using References to a Base Class
Constructor Execution
Inheritance Between Assemblies
Member Access Modifiers
Abstract Members
Abstract Classes
Sealed Classes
External Methods

Class Inheritance

Inheritance allows you to define a new class that incorporates and extends an already declared class.

- You can use an existing class, called the *base class*, as the basis for a new class, called the *derived class*. The members of the derived class consist of the following:
  - The members in its own declaration
  - The members of the base class

- To declare a derived class, you add a *class-base specification* after the class name. The class-base specification consists of a colon, followed by the name of the class to be used as the base class. The derived class is said to *directly inherit* from the base class listed.

- A derived class is said to *extend* its base class, because it includes the members of the base class plus any additional functionality provided in its own declaration.

- A derived class *cannot delete* any of the members it has inherited.

For example, the following shows the declaration of a class called `OtherClass`, which is derived from a class called `SomeClass`.

```
                  Class-base specification
                          ↓
                  _____
class OtherClass : SomeClass
{                      ↑    ↑
    ...           Colon  Base class
}
```

Figure 7-1 shows an instance of each of the classes. Class `SomeClass`, on the left, has one field and one method. Class `OtherClass`, on the right, is derived from `SomeClass` and contains an additional field and an additional method.

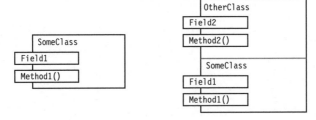

Figure 7-1. *Base class and derived class*

Accessing the Inherited Members

Inherited members are accessed just as if they had been declared in the derived class itself. For example, the following code declares classes SomeClass and OtherClass, which were shown in Figure 7-1. The code shows that all four members of OtherClass can be seamlessly accessed, regardless of whether they are declared in the base class or the derived class.

- Main creates an object of derived class OtherClass.

- The next two lines in Main call Method1 in the *base class*, using Field1 from the base class, and then Field2 from the derived class.

- The subsequent two lines in Main call Method2 in the *derived class*, again using Field1 from the base class and then Field2 from the derived class.

```
class SomeClass {                           // Base class
   public string Field1 = "base class field";
   public void Method1( string value ) {
      Console.WriteLine("Base class -- Method1:    {0}", value);
   }
}

class OtherClass: SomeClass {               // Derived class
   public string Field2 = "derived class field";
   public void Method2( string value ) {
      Console.WriteLine("Derived class -- Method2:  {0}", value);
   }
}

class Program {
   static void Main() {
      OtherClass oc = new OtherClass();

      oc.Method1( oc.Field1 );              // Base method with base field
      oc.Method1( oc.Field2 );              // Base method with derived field
      oc.Method2( oc.Field1 );              // Derived method with base field
      oc.Method2( oc.Field2 );              // Derived method with derived field
   }
}
```

This code produces the following output:

```
Base class -- Method1:    base class field
Base class -- Method1:    derived class field
Derived class -- Method2: base class field
Derived class -- Method2: derived class field
```

All Classes are Derived From Class object

All classes, except special class object, are derived classes, even if they don't have a class-base specification. Class object is the only one that is not derived, since it is the base of the inheritance hierarchy.

Classes without a class-base specification are implicitly derived directly from class object. Leaving off the class-base specification is just shorthand for specifying that object is the base class. The two forms are completely equivalent.

Figure 7-2 shows both forms of declaration for the same class.

```
class SomeClass                    class SomeClass : object
{                                  {
    ...                                ...
}                                  }

Implicitly derives from object     Explicitly derives from object
```

Figure 7-2. *Direct inheritance from object*

Other important facts about class derivation are the following:

- A class declaration can have only a single class listed in its class-base specification. This is called *single inheritance*.

- Although a class can directly inherit from only a single base class, there is no limit to the *level* of derivation. That is, the class listed as the base class might be derived from another class, which is derived from another class, and so forth, until you eventually reach object.

Base class and *derived class* are relative terms. All classes are derived classes, either from object or from another class—so generally when we call a class a derived class, we mean that it is immediately derived from some class other than object. Figure 7-3 shows a simple class hierarchy. After this, I will not show object in the figures, since all classes are ultimately derived from it.

```
class SomeClass                         | MyNewClass |
{ ... }                                 |------------|
                                        | OtherClass |
class OtherClass: SomeClass             |------------|
{ ... }                                 | SomeClass  |
                                        |------------|
class MyNewClass: OtherClass            | object     |
{
    ...
}
```

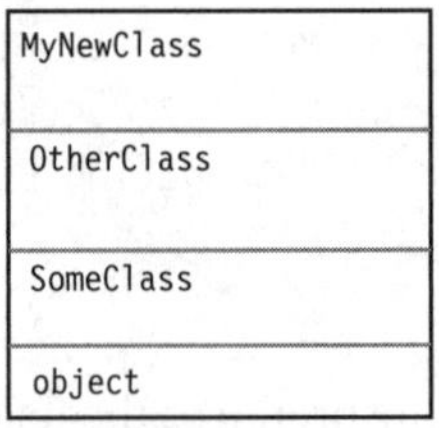

Figure 7-3. *A class hierarchy*

Hiding Members of a Base Class

Although a derived class cannot delete any of the members it has inherited, it can hide them.

- You can *hide*, or *mask*, an inherited function member by declaring a new function member with the same signature. Remember that the *signature* consists of the name and parameter list, but does not include the return type.

- To hide an inherited data member, declare a new member of the same type and with the same *name*.

- To let the compiler know that you are purposely hiding an inherited member, use the new modifier. Without it, the program will compile successfully, but the compiler will give you a warning that you are hiding an inherited member.

The following code declares a base class and a derived class, each with a string member called Field1. The keyword new is used to explicitly tell the compiler to mask the base class member. Figure 7-4 illustrates an instance of each class.

```
class SomeClass                          // Base class
{
      string Field1;
   ...
}

class OtherClass : SomeClass             // Derived class
{
   new string Field1;                    // Mask base member with same name.
     ↑
   Keyword
```

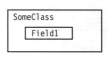
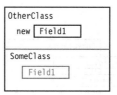

Figure 7-4. *Hiding a member of a base class*

In the following code, OtherClass derives from SomeClass but hides both its inherited members. Note the use of the new modifier. The code is illustrated in Figure 7-5.

```
class SomeClass                                        // Base class
{
   public string Field1 = "SomeClass Field1";
   public void    Method1(string value)
       { Console.WriteLine("SomeClass.Method1:  {0}", value); }
}


class OtherClass : SomeClass                           // Derived class
{ Keyword
  ↓
   new public string Field1 = "OtherClass Field1";   // Mask the base member.
   new public void    Method1(string value)          // Mask the base member.
    ↑   { Console.WriteLine("OtherClass.Method1:  {0}", value); }
} Keyword


class Program
{
   static void Main()
   {
      OtherClass oc = new OtherClass();       // Use the masking member.
      oc.Method1(oc.Field1);                  // Use the masking member.
   }
}
```

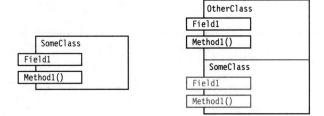

Figure 7-5. *Hiding a field and a method of the base class*

Base Access

Sometimes, your derived class might need to access a hidden inherited member. You can access a hidden base class member by using a *base access* expression. This expression consists of the keyword base, followed immediately by a period and the name of the member, as shown here.

```
Console.WriteLine("{0}", base.Field1);
                              ↑
                         Base access
```

For example, in the following code, derived class OtherClass hides Field1 in its base class but accesses it by using a base access expression.

```
class SomeClass {                                      // Base class
   public string Field1 = "Field1 -- In the base class";
}

class OtherClass : SomeClass {                          // Derived class

   new public string Field1 = "Field1 -- In the derived class";
       ↑                      ↑
   Hides the field in the base class
   public void PrintField1()
   {
      Console.WriteLine("{0}", Field1);        // Access the derived class.
      Console.WriteLine("{0}", base.Field1);   // Access the base class.
   }                                  ↑
}                                Base access

class Program {
   static void Main()
   {
      OtherClass oc = new OtherClass();
      oc.PrintField1();
   }
}
```

This code produces the following output:

```
Field1 -- In the derived class
Field1 -- In the base class
```

Using References to a Base Class

An instance of a derived class consists of an instance of the base class, plus the additional members of the derived class. A reference to the derived class points to the whole class object, including the base class part.

You can get a reference to the base class part of an object by casting an object reference, to the type of the base class. In the next few sections you will look at accessing an object by using a reference to the base class part of the object.

For example, in the following line of code, variable derived contains a reference to an object of type MyDerivedClass. Figure 7-6 illustrates the parts of the object seen by the different variables.

- Casting the reference in derived to the type of the base class gives a reference to the base class part of the object.

- The reference to the base class part is stored in variable mybc, on the left side of the assignment operator.

- The reference to the base class part cannot "see" the rest of the derived class object.

```
MyBaseClass mybc = (MyBaseClass) derived;
```

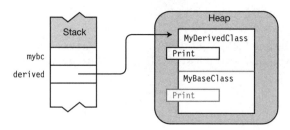

derived is a reference to a MyDerivedClass object, and can see the entire object.

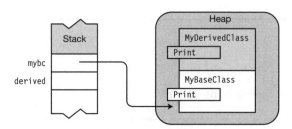

mybc is a reference to a MyBaseClass object, and can only see
the base class portion of the object.

Figure 7-6. *Different views of the same object through a reference to the derived class and a reference to the base class*

For example, the following code shows the declaration and use of these two classes. Figure 7-7 illustrates the object and references in memory.

Main creates an object of type MyDerivedClass and stores its reference in variable derived. Main also creates a variable of type MyBaseClass and uses it to store a reference to the base class portion of the object. When the Print method is called on each reference, the call invokes the implementation of the method that that reference can see, producing different output strings.

```
class MyBaseClass {
   public void Print() {
      Console.WriteLine("This is the base class.");
   }
}

class MyDerivedClass : MyBaseClass {
   new public void Print() {
      Console.WriteLine("This is the derived class.");
   }
}

class Program {
   static void Main() {
      MyDerivedClass derived = new MyDerivedClass();
      MyBaseClass mybc = (MyBaseClass)derived;
                             ↑
                     Cast to base class
      derived.Print();          // Call Print from derived portion.
      mybc.Print();             // Call Print from base portion.
   }
}
```

This code produces the following output:

```
This is the derived class.
This is the base class.
```

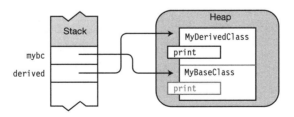

Figure 7-7. *A reference to the derived class and the base class*

Virtual and Override Methods

In the previous section, you saw that when you access an object of a derived class by using a reference to the base class, you get the members from the base class. *Virtual methods* allow a reference to the base class, to access "up into" the derived class.

You can use a reference to a base class to call a method in the *derived class*, if the following are true:

- The method in the derived class and the method in the base class each have the same signature and return type.

- The method in the base class is labeled virtual.

- The method in the derived class is labeled override.

For example, the following code shows the virtual and override modifiers on the methods in the base class and derived class.

```
class MyBaseClass                                // Base class
{
   virtual public void Print()
        ↑

...
class MyDerivedClass : MyBaseClass               // Derived class
{
   override public void Print()
         ↑
```

Figure 7-8 illustrates this set of virtual and override methods. Notice how the behavior differs from the previous case, where I used new to hide the base class members.

- When the Print method is called by using the reference to the base class (mybc), the method call is passed up to the *derived* class and executed, because of the following:
  - The method in the base class is marked as virtual.
  - There is a matching override method in the derived class.

- Figure 7-8 illustrates this by showing the arrow coming out the back of the virtual Print method and pointing at the override Print method.

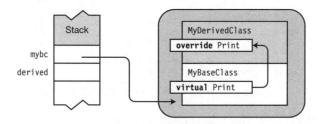

Figure 7-8. *Virtual method and an override method*

The following code is the same as in the previous section, but this time, the methods are labeled `virtual` and `override`. This produces a result that is very different from that of the previous example. In this version, calling the method through the base class invokes the method in the derived class.

```
class MyBaseClass {
   virtual public void Print()
   {
      Console.WriteLine("This is the base class.");
   }
}

class MyDerivedClass : MyBaseClass {
   override public void Print()
   {
      Console.WriteLine("This is the derived class.");
   }
}

class Program {
   static void Main()
   {
      MyDerivedClass derived = new MyDerivedClass();
      MyBaseClass mybc = (MyBaseClass)derived;
                                    ↑
      derived.Print();    Cast to base class
      mybc.Print();
   }
}
```

This code produces the following output:

```
This is the derived class.
This is the derived class.
```

Other important information about the `virtual` and `override` modifiers is the following:

- The overriding and overridden methods must have the same accessibility. In other words, the overridden method cannot be, for example, `private`, and the overriding method `public`.

- You cannot override a method that is `static` or is non-virtual.

- Methods, properties, and indexers (which I covered in the preceding chapter), and another member type, called *events* (which I will cover later in the text), can all be declared `virtual` and `override`.

Overriding a Method Marked override

Overriding methods can occur between any levels of inheritance.

- When you use a reference to the base class part of an object to call an overridden method, the method call is passed up the derivation hierarchy for execution, to the *most-derived* version of the method marked as override.

- If there are other declarations of the method at higher levels of derivation, which are not marked as override—they are not invoked.

For example, the following code shows three classes that form an inheritance hierarchy— MyBaseClass, MyDerivedClass, and SecondDerived. All three classes contain a method named Print, with the same signature. In MyBaseClass, Print is labeled virtual. In MyDerivedClass, it is labeled override. In class SecondDerived, you can declare method Print with either override or new. Let's look at what happens in each case.

```
class MyBaseClass                                   // Base class
{
   virtual public void Print()
   { Console.WriteLine("This is the base class."); }
}

class MyDerivedClass : MyBaseClass                  // Derived class
{
   override public void Print()
   { Console.WriteLine("This is the derived class."); }
}

class SecondDerived : MyDerivedClass                // Most-derived class
{
   ... // Given in the following pages
}
```

Case 1—Declaring Print with override

If you declare the Print method of SecondDerived as override, then it will override *both the less-derived versions* of the method, as shown in Figure 7-9. If a reference to the base class is used to call Print, it gets passed all the way up the chain to the implementation in class SecondDerived.

The following code implements this case. Notice the code in the last two lines of method `Main`.

- The first of the two statements calls the `Print` method by using a reference to the most-derived class—`SecondDerived`. This is not calling through a reference to the base class portion, so it will call the method implemented in `SecondDerived`.

- The second statement, however, calls the `Print` method by using a reference to the base class—`MyBaseClass`.

```
class SecondDerived : MyDerivedClass {
   override public void Print() {
      ↑  Console.WriteLine("This is the second derived class.");
   }
}

class Program {
   static void Main()
   {
      SecondDerived derived = new SecondDerived(); // Use SecondDerived.
      MyBaseClass mybc = (MyBaseClass)derived;     // Use MyBaseClass.

      derived.Print();
      mybc.Print();
   }
}
```

The result is that regardless of whether `Print` is called through the derived class or the base class, the method in the most-derived class is called. When called through the base class, it is passed up the inheritance hierarchy. This code produces the following output:

```
This is the second derived class.
This is the second derived class.
```

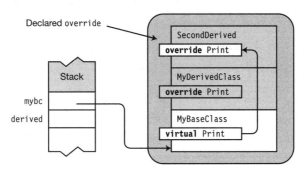

Figure 7-9. *Execution is passed to the top of the chain of multiple levels of override.*

Case 2—Declaring Print with new

If you declare the Print method of SecondDerived as new, the result is as shown in Figure 7-10. Main is the same as in the previous case.

```
class SecondDerived : MyDerivedClass {
   new public void Print() {
      ↑  Console.WriteLine("This is the second derived class.");
   }
}

class Program {
   static void Main()                                      // Main
   {
      SecondDerived derived = new SecondDerived();          // Use SecondDerived.
      MyBaseClass mybc = (MyBaseClass)derived;              // Use MyBaseClass.

      derived.Print();
      mybc.Print();
   }
}
```

The result is that when method Print is called through the reference to SecondDerived, the method in SecondDerived is executed, as you would expect. When the method is called through a reference to MyBaseClass, however, the method call is passed up only one level, to class MyDerived, where it is executed. The only difference between the two cases is whether the method in SecondDerived is declared with modifier override or modifier new.

This code produces the following output:

```
This is the second derived class.
This is the derived class.
```

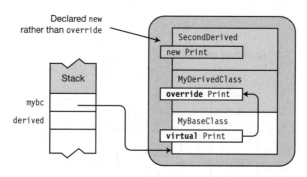

Figure 7-10. *Hiding the overridden methods*

Constructor Execution

In the preceding chapter, you saw that a constructor executes code that prepares a class for use. This includes initializing both the static and instance members of the class. In this chapter, you saw that part of a derived class object is an object of the base class.

- To create the base class part of an object, a constructor for the base class is called as part of the process of creating the instance.

- Each class in the inheritance hierarchy chain executes its base class constructor before it executes its own constructor body.

For example, the following code shows a declaration of class MyDerivedClass and its constructor. When the constructor is called, it calls the parameterless constructor MyBaseClass() before executing its own body.

```
class MyDerivedClass : MyBaseClass
{
    MyDerivedClass()          // Constructor uses base constructor MyBaseClass().
    {
        ...
    }
}
```

The order of construction is shown in Figure 7-11. When an instance is being created, one of the first things that is done is the initialization of all the instance members of the object. After that, the base class constructor is called. Only then is the body of the constructor of the class itself executed.

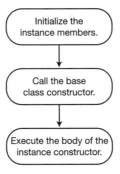

Figure 7-11. *Order of object construction*

For example, in the following code, the values of MyField1 and MyField2 would be set to 5 and 0 respectively, before the base class constructor was called.

```
class MyDerivedClass : MyBaseClass
{
   int MyField1 = 5;                    // 1. Member initialized.
   int MyField2;                        //    Member initialized.

   public MyDerivedClass()              // 3. Body of constructor executed.
   {
      ...
   }
}

class MyBaseClass
{
   public MyBaseClass()                 // 2. Base class constructor called.
   {
      ...
   }
}
```

■**Caution** Calling a virtual method in a constructor is *strongly discouraged*. The virtual method in the base class would call the override method in the derived class while the base class constructor was being executed. But that would be before the derived constructor's body was executed. It would, therefore, be calling up into the derived class before the class was completely initialized.

Constructor Initializers

By default, the parameterless constructor of the base class is called when an object is being constructed. But constructors can be overloaded, so a base class might have more than one. If you want your derived class to use a specific base class constructor other than the parameterless constructor, you must specify it in a *constructor initializer*.

There are two forms of constructor initializer:

- The first form uses the keyword base and specifies which base class constructor to use.

- The second form uses the keyword this and specifies which other constructor from *this* class should be used.

A base class constructor initializer is placed after a colon following the parameter list in a class's constructor declaration. The constructor initializer consists of the keyword base, and the parameter list of the base constructor to call.

For example, the following code shows a constructor for class `MyDerivedClass`.

- The constructor initializer specifies that the base class constructor to use is the one that has two parameters; the first parameter is a `string`, and the second parameter is an `int`.

- The parameters in the base parameter list must match the *intended constructor's* parameter list, in type and order.

```
                                          Constructor initializer
                                                  ↓
public MyDerivedClass( int x, string s ) : base( s, x )
{                                                 ↑
    ...                                        Keyword
```

When you declare a constructor without a constructor initializer, it is a shortcut for the form with a constructor initializer consisting of `base()`, as illustrated in Figure 7-12. The two forms are semantically equivalent.

```
class MyDerived: MyBase                 class MyDerived: MyBase
{                                       {
    MyDerived()                             MyDerived() : base()
    {                                       {
        ...                                     ...
    }                                       }
    ...                                     ...

Constructor implicitly uses base       Constructor explicitly uses base
constructor MyBase().                  constructor MyBase().
```

Figure 7-12. *Equivalent forms of a constructor*

Another form of constructor initializer instructs the constructor to use a different constructor in the same class. For example, the following shows a constructor for class `MyClass`, which uses the constructor from the same class, but with two parameters, supplying a default parameter as the second one.

```
                    Constructor initializer
                            ↓
public MyClass(int x): this(x, "Using Default String")
{                           ↑
    ...                  Keyword
}
```

Class Access Modifiers

A class can be seen and accessed by other classes in the system. This section covers the accessibility of classes. Although I will use classes in the explanations and examples, since that is what you are familiar with at this point in the text, the accessibility rules also apply to the other types I will cover later.

The term *visible* is sometimes used for the term *accessible*. They can be used interchangeably. There are two levels of class accessibility—public and internal.

- A class marked public can be accessed by code from any assembly in the system. To make a class visible to other assemblies, use the public access modifier, as shown here.

```
Keyword
   ↓
public class MyBaseClass
{ ...
```

- A class marked internal can be seen only by classes within its own assembly.
  - This is the default accessibility level, so unless you explicitly specify the modifier public in the class declaration, code outside the assembly cannot access the class.
  - You can explicitly declare a class as internal by using the internal access modifier.

```
Keyword
   ↓
internal class MyBaseClass
{ ...
```

Figure 7-13 illustrates the accessibility of internal and public classes from outside the assembly. Class MyClass is not visible to the classes in the assembly on the left, because it is marked internal. Class OtherClass, however, is visible to the classes on the left, because it is marked public.

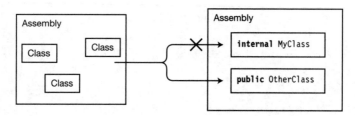

Figure 7-13. *Classes from other assemblies can access public classes but cannot access internal classes.*

Inheritance Between Assemblies

So far, I have been declaring derived classes in the same assembly where the base class is declared. But C# also allows you to derive a class from a base class defined in a different assembly. To do this, the following must be true:

- The base class must be declared `public`, so that it can be accessed from outside its assembly.

- You must include a reference in your Visual Studio project, to the assembly containing the base class.

To make it easier to refer to the classes and types in the other assembly, without using their fully qualified names, place a `using` directive at the top of the source file, with the namespace containing the classes or types you want to access.

■**Note** Adding a reference to the other assembly and adding a `using` directive are two separate things. Adding the reference to the other assembly tells the compiler where the required types are defined. Adding the `using` directive allows you to reference other classes without having to use their fully qualified names. Chapter 10 covers this in detail.

For example, the following two code segments, from different assemblies, show how easy it is to inherit a class from another assembly. The first code listing creates an assembly that contains the declaration of a class called `MyBaseClass`, which has the following characteristics:

- It is declared in a source file called `BaseClass.cs`, and inside a namespace declared as `BaseClassNS`.

- It is declared `public`, so that it can be accessed from other assemblies.

- It contains a single member, a method called `PrintMe`, that just writes out a simple message identifying the class.

```
// Source file name BaseClass.cs
using System;
  Namespace containing declaration of base class
                ↓
namespace BaseClassNS
{
  Declare the class public, so it can be seen outside the assembly.
        ↓
   public class MyBaseClass {
      public void PrintMe() {
         Console.WriteLine("I am MyBaseClass");
      }
   }
}
```

The second assembly contains the declaration of a class called DerivedClass that inherits from MyBaseClass, declared in the first assembly. The source file is named Program.cs. Figure 7-14 illustrates the two assemblies.

- DerivedClass has an empty body but inherits method PrintMe from MyBaseClass.

- Main creates an object of type DerivedClass and calls its inherited method PrintMe.

```
// Source file name Program.cs
using System;
using BaseClassNS;
        ↑
  Namespace containing declaration of base class
namespace UsesBaseClass
{              Base class in other assembly
                        ↓
    class DerivedClass: MyBaseClass {
       // Empty body
    }

    class Program {
       static void Main( )
       {
           DerivedClass mdc = new DerivedClass();
           mdc.PrintMe();
       }
    }
}
```

This code produces the following output:

I am MyBaseClass

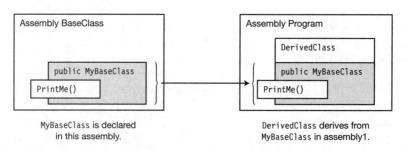

Figure 7-14. *Inheriting across assemblies*

Member Access Modifiers

Class accessibility was covered earlier in the chapter. With class accessibility there are only two modifiers—internal and public. This section covers *member accessibility*. Class accessibility describes the visibility of a class; member accessibility describes the visibility of class members.

Each member declared in a class is visible to various parts of the system, depending on the access modifier assigned to it in the class declaration. You've seen that private members are visible only to other members of the same class, while public members can be visible to classes outside the assembly as well. In this section, you will look again at the public and private access levels, as well as the three other levels of accessibility.

Before looking at the specifics of member accessibility, there are some general things you need to look at first:

- All members explicitly declared in a class's declaration are visible to each other, regardless of their accessibility specification.

- Inherited members are not explicitly declared in a class's declaration, so, as you shall see, inherited members might or might not be visible to members of the derived class.

- There are five member access levels:
  - public
  - private
  - protected
  - internal
  - protected internal

- You must specify member access levels on a per-member basis. If you don't specify an access level for a member, its implicit access level is private.

- A member cannot be more accessible than its class. That is, if a class has an accessibility level limiting it to the assembly, individual members of the class cannot be seen outside the assembly, regardless of their access modifiers.

Regions Accessing a Member

The member access modifiers in a class's declaration specify which other types can and cannot access which members of the class. For example, the following declaration shows members declared with the five access levels.

```
public class MyClass
{
    public             int MyMember1;
    private            int MyMember2;
    protected          int MyMember3;
    internal           int MyMember4;
    protected internal int MyMember5;
    ...
```

The access levels are based on two characteristics with regard to the class being declared:

- Whether the class *is derived from* the class being declared

- Whether a class is *in the same assembly* as the class being declared

These two characteristics yield four groups, as illustrated in Figure 7-15. In relation to the class being declared, another class can be any of the following:

- In the same assembly and derived from it (bottom right)

- In the same assembly but not derived from it (bottom left)

- In a different assembly and derived from it (top right)

- In a different assembly and not derived from it (top left)

These characteristics are used to define the five access levels.

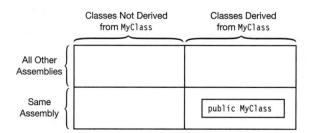

Figure 7-15. *Areas of accessibility*

Public Member Accessibility

The `public` access level is the least restrictive. All classes both inside and outside the assembly have free access to the member. Figure 7-16 illustrates the accessibility of a `public` class member of `MyClass`.

To declare a member public, use the `public` access modifier, as shown.

```
Keyword
  ↓
public int MyMember1;
```

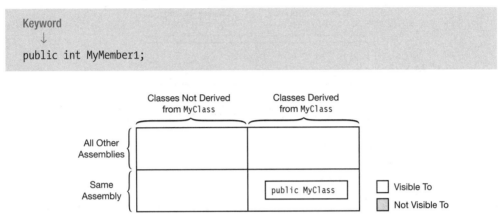

Figure 7-16. *Public member accessibility*

Private Member Accessibility

The `private` access level is the most restrictive.

- A `private` class member can be accessed only by members of its own class. It cannot be accessed by other classes, including classes that are derived from it.

- A private member can, however, be accessed by members of classes nested in its class. *Nested classes* are covered in Chapter 23.

Figure 7-17 illustrates the accessibility of a private member.

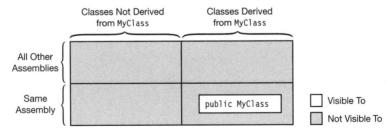

Figure 7-17. *Private member accessibility*

Protected Member Accessibility

The protected access level is like the private access level, except that it allows classes derived from the class to access the member. Figure 7-18 illustrates protected accessibility. Notice that even classes outside the assembly that are derived from the class have access to the member.

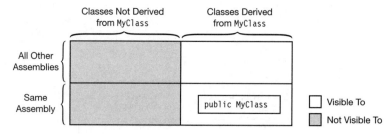

Figure 7-18. *Protected member accessibility*

Internal Member Accessibility

Members marked internal are visible to all the classes in the assembly, but not to classes outside the assembly, as shown in Figure 7-19.

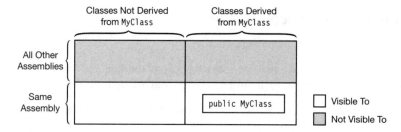

Figure 7-19. *Internal member accessibility*

Protected Internal Member Accessibility

Members marked protected internal are visible to all the classes that inherit from the class, and also to all classes inside the assembly, as shown in Figure 7-20. Notice that the set of classes allowed access is the combined set of classes allowed by the protected modifier plus the set of classes allowed by the internal modifier.

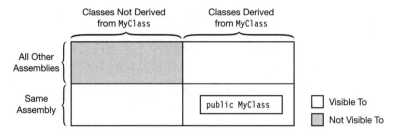

Figure 7-20. *Protected internal member visibility*

Summary of Member Access Modifiers

The following two tables summarize the characteristics of the five member access levels. Table 7-1 lists the modifiers and gives an intuitive summary of the effects of the modifier.

Table 7-1. *Member Access Modifiers*

Modifier	Meaning
private	Accessible only within the class
internal	Accessible to all classes within this assembly
protected	Accessible to all classes derived from this class
protected internal	Accessible to all classes that are either derived from this class or are declared within this assembly
public	Accessible to any class

Table 7-2 lists the access modifiers down the left side of the table, and the categories of classes across the top. *Derived* refers to classes derived from the class declaring the member. *Non-derived* means classes not derived from the class declaring the member. A check in a cell means that that category of class can access members with the corresponding modifier.

Table 7-2. *Summary of Member Accessibility*

	Classes in Same Assembly		Classes in Different Assembly	
	Non-derived	Derived	Non-derived	Derived
private				
internal	✓	✓		
protected		✓		✓
protected internal	✓	✓		✓
public	✓	✓	✓	✓

Abstract Members

An *abstract member* is a function member that is designed to be overridden. An abstract member has the following characteristics:

- It is marked with the `abstract` modifier.

- It does not have an implementation code block. The code blocks of abstract members are replaced with semicolons.

For example, the following code from inside a class declaration declares two abstract members—an abstract method called `PrintStuff` and an abstract property called `MyProperty`. Notice the semicolons in place of the implementation blocks.

```
Keyword                         Semicolon in place of implementation
   ↓                                         ↓
abstract public void PrintStuff(string s);

abstract public int MyProperty
{
   get;   ←Semicolon in place of implementation
   set;   ←Semicolon in place of implementation
}
```

Other important facts about abstract members are the following:

- Abstract methods, although they must be overridden by a corresponding method in a derived class, cannot use the `virtual` modifier in addition to the `abstract` modifier.

- As with virtual methods, the implementation of an abstract method in a derived class must specify the `override` modifier.

- Abstract members can be declared only in *abstract classes*, which you will look at in the next section.

Table 7-3 compares and contrasts virtual members and abstract members.

Table 7-3. *Comparing Virtual and Abstract Members*

	Virtual Member	**Abstract Member**
Keyword	`virtual`	`abstract`
Implementation body	Has an implementation body	No implementation body—semicolon instead
Overridden in a derived class	*Can* be overridden—using `override`	*Must* be overridden—using `override`
Types of members	Methods Properties Events Indexers	Methods Properties Events Indexers

Abstract Classes

An *abstract class* can be used only as the base class of another class. Abstract classes are designed to be inherited from.

- You cannot define variables or create instances of an abstract class.

- An abstract class is declared by using the `abstract` modifier.

```
Keyword
  ↓
abstract class MyClass
{
   ...
}
```

- An abstract class can contain abstract members, but that is not a requirement. The members of an abstract class can be any combination of abstract members and normal members with implementations.

- An abstract class can, itself, be derived from another abstract class. For example, the following code shows one abstract class derived from another.

```
abstract class AbClass                    // Abstract class
{
   ...
}

abstract class MyAbClass : AbClass        // Abstract class derived from
{                                         // an abstract class
   ...
}
```

- Any class derived from an abstract class must implement all the abstract members of the class by using the `override` keyword, unless the derived class is, itself, `abstract`.

Example of an Abstract Class and an Abstract Method

The following code shows an abstract class called AbClass with two methods.

The first method is a normal method with an implementation that prints out the name of the class. The second method is an abstract method that must be implemented in a derived class. Class DerivedClass inherits from AbClass, and implements and overrides the abstract method. Main creates an object of DerivedClass and calls its two methods.

```
Keyword
  ↓
abstract class AbClass                            // Abstract class
{
   public void IdentifyBase()                     // Normal method
   { Console.WriteLine("I am AbClass"); }
     Keyword
       ↓
   abstract public void IdentifyDerived();        // Abstract method
}

class DerivedClass : AbClass                       // Derived class
{   Keyword
      ↓
   override public void IdentifyDerived()          // Implementation of
   { Console.WriteLine("I am DerivedClass"); }     // abstract method
}

class Example
{
   static void Main()
   {
      // AbClass a = new AbClass();               // Error.  Cannot instantiate
      // a.IdentifyDerived();                     // an abstract class.

      DerivedClass b = new DerivedClass();        // Instantiate the derived class.
      b.IdentifyBase();                           // Call the inherited method.
      b.IdentifyDerived();                        // Call the "abstract" method.
   }
}
```

This code produces the following output:

```
I am AbClass
I am DerivedClass
```

Sealed Classes

In the previous section, you saw that an abstract class must be used as a base class—it cannot be instantiated as a stand-alone class. The opposite is true of a *sealed class*.

- A sealed class can be used only as a stand-alone class—it cannot be used as a base class.

- A sealed class is labeled with the `sealed` modifier.

For example, the following class is a sealed class. Any attempt to use it as the base class of another class will produce a compile error.

```
Keyword
  ↓
sealed class MyClass
{
   ...
}
```

External Methods

An *external method* is a method that does not have an implementation in the declaration. Often the implementation is in a language other than C#.

- External methods are marked with the `extern` modifier and do not have an implementation in the class declaration. The implementation is replaced by a semicolon.

```
              Keyword
                 ↓
public static extern int GetCurrentDirectory(int size, StringBuilder buf);
                                                                          ↑
                                                          No implementation
```

- Connecting the declaration with the implementation is implementation-dependent, but is often done using the `DLLImport` attribute. Attributes are covered in detail in Chapter 21.

For example, the following code uses an external method, GetCurrentDirectory, whose implementation is the Win32 system call for getting a string that contains the current directory.

```
using System;
using System.Text;
using System.Runtime.InteropServices;

namespace ExternalMethod
{
   class MyClass
   {
      [DllImport("kernel32", SetLastError=true)]
      public static extern int GetCurrentDirectory(int a, StringBuilder b);
   }

   class Program
   {
      static void Main( )
      {
         const int MaxDirLength = 250;
         StringBuilder sb = new StringBuilder();
         sb.Length = MaxDirLength;

         MyClass.GetCurrentDirectory(MaxDirLength, sb);
         Console.WriteLine(sb);
      }
   }
}
```

This code produces the following output:

```
C:\BookPrograms\ExternalMethod\ExternalMethod\bin\Debug
```

CHAPTER 8

∎∎∎

Expressions and Operators

Expressions
Literals
Order of Evaluation
Simple Arithmetic Operators
The Remainder Operator
Relational and Equality Comparison Operators
Increment and Decrement Operators
Conditional Logical Operators
Logical Operators
Shift Operators
Assignment Operators
The Conditional Operator
Unary Arithmetic Operators
User-Defined Type Conversions
Operator Overloading
The typeof Operator

Expressions

This chapter will define expressions and look at the operators provided by C#. It will also look at how you can define the C# operators to work with your user-defined classes.

An *expression* is a string of operators and operands. Some of the constructs that can act as operands are

- Literals

- Constants

- Variables

- Method calls

- Element accessors, such as array accessors and indexers

- Other expressions

The C# operators take one, two, or three operands. An operator

- Takes its operands as input

- Performs an action

- Returns a value, based on the action

Expressions can be combined, using operators, to create other expressions, as shown in the following illustration:

$$\left.\begin{array}{c} \underbrace{a + b} \\ \underbrace{expr + c} \\ expr \quad + d \end{array}\right\} \quad a + b + c + d$$

Evaluating an expression is the process of applying each operator to its operands, in the proper sequence, to produce a value.

- The value is returned to the position at which the expression was evaluated, where it might, in turn, be an operand in an enclosing expression.

- Besides the value returned, some expressions also have side effects, such as setting a value in memory.

Literals

Literals are numbers or strings typed into the source code that represent a specific, set value of a specific type.

For example, the following code shows literals of six types. Notice, for example, the difference between the double literal and the float literal.

```
static void Main()          Literals
{                              ↓
    Console.WriteLine("{0}", 1024);            // int literal
    Console.WriteLine("{0}", 3.1416);          // double literal
    Console.WriteLine("{0}", 3.1416F);         // float literal
    Console.WriteLine("{0}", true);            // boolean literal
    Console.WriteLine("{0}", 'x');             // character literal
    Console.WriteLine("{0}", "Hi there");      // string literal
}
```

The output of this code is the following:

```
1024
3.1416
3.1416
True
x
Hi there
```

Because literals are written into the source code, their values must be known at compile time.

Several of the predefined types have their own forms of literal:

- Type `bool` has two literals: `true` and `false`.

- For reference type variables, literal `null` means that the variable is not set to a reference in memory.

Integer Literals

Integer literals are the most commonly used of all literals. Integer type literals are written as a sequence of decimal digits, with

- No decimal point

- An optional suffix to specify the type of the integer

For example, the following lines show four literals for the integer 236. Each is interpreted by the compiler as a different type of integer, depending on its suffix.

```
236         // int
236L        // long
236U        // unsigned
236UL       // unsigned long
```

Integer type literals can also be written in hexadecimal (hex) form. The digits must be the hex digits (0 through F), and the string must be prefaced with either 0x or 0X (numeral *0*, letter *x*).

The integer literal formats are shown in Figure 8-1. Components with names in square brackets are optional.

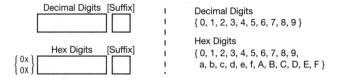

Figure 8-1. *The integer literal formats*

The integer literal suffixes are listed in Table 8-1. For a given suffix, the compiler will inter-pret the string of digits as the smallest of the corresponding integer types that can represent the value without losing data.

For example, take the literals 236 and 5000000000, where neither of them has a suffix. Since 236 can be represented with 32 bits, it will be interpreted by the compiler as an int. The larger number, however, will not fit into 32 bits, so it is interpreted as a long.

Table 8-1. *Integer Literal Suffixes*

Suffix	Integer Type	Notes
None	int, uint, long, ulong	
U, u	uint, ulong	
L, l	long, ulong	Using the lowercase letter *l* is not recommended, as it is easily mistaken for the digit *1*.
ul, uL, Ul, UL lu, Lu, lU, LU	ulong	Using the lowercase letter *l* is not recommended, as it is easily mistaken for the digit *1*.

Real Literals

Literals for real numbers consist of the following:

- Decimal digits

- An optional decimal point

- An optional exponent part

- An optional suffix

For example, the following code shows various formats of literals of the real types:

```
float  f1 = 236F;
double d1 = 236.714;
double d2 = .35192;
double d3 = 6.338e-26;
```

The valid formats for real literals are shown in Figure 8-2. Components with names in square brackets are optional. The real suffixes and their meanings are shown in Table 8-2.

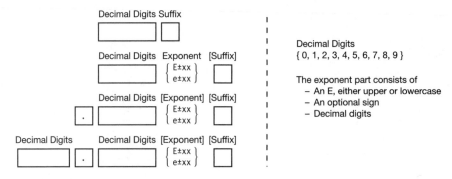

Figure 8-2. *The real literal formats*

Table 8-2. *Suffixes for the Real Literals*

Suffix	Real Type
None	double
F, f	float
D, d	double
M, m	decimal

Note Real literals without a suffix are of type double, not float!

Character Literals

A *character literal* consists of a character representation between two single quote characters. A character representation can be any of the following: a single character, a simple escape sequence, a hex escape sequence, or a Unicode escape sequence.

- The type of a character literal is char.

- A *simple escape sequence* is a backslash followed by a single character.

- A hex escape sequence is a backslash, followed by an upper or lowercase *x*, followed by up to four hex digits.

- A Unicode escape sequence is a backslash, followed by an upper or lowercase *u*, followed by up to four hex digits.

For example, the following code shows various formats of character literals:

```
char c1 = 'd';                   // Single character
char c2 = '\n';                  // Simple escape sequence
char c3 = '\x0061';              // Hex escape sequence
char c4 = '\u005a';              // Unicode escape sequence
```

Some of the important special characters and their encodings are shown in Table 8-3.

Table 8-3. *Important Special Characters*

Name	Escape Sequence	Hex Encoding
Null	\0	0x0000
Alert	\a	0x0007
Backspace	\b	0x0008
Horizontal tab	\t	0x0009
New line	\n	0x000A
Vertical tab	\b	0x000B
Form feed	\f	0x000C
Carriage return	\r	0x000D
Double quote	\"	0x0022
Single quote	\'	0x0027
Backslash	\\	0x005C

String Literals

String literals use double quote marks rather than the single quote marks used in character literals. There are two types of string literals:

- Regular string literals

- Verbatim string literals

A regular string literal consists of a sequence of characters between a set of double quotes. A regular string literal can include the following:

- Characters

- Simple escape sequences

- Hex and Unicode escape sequences

Here's an example:

```
string st1 = "Hi there!";
string st2 = "Val1\t5, Val2\t10";
string st3 = "Add\x000ASome\u0007Interest";
```

The verbatim string literal differs from a regular string literal in that escape sequences are not evaluated.

- A verbatim string literal is written like a regular string literal, but is prefaced with an @ character.

- Everything between the set of double quotes—including what would normally be considered escape sequences—is printed exactly as it is listed in the string.

- The only exception is sets of contiguous double quotes, which are interpreted as a *single* double quote character.

For example, the following code compares some regular and verbatim string literals:

```
string rst1 = "Hi there!";
string vst1 = @"Hi there!";

string rst2 = "It started, \"Four score and seven...\"";
string vst2 = @"It started, ""Four score and seven...""";

string rst3 = "Value 1 \t 5, Val2 \t 10";     // Interprets tab esc sequence
string vst3 = @"Value 1 \t 5, Val2 \t 10";    // Does not interpret tab

string rst4 = "C:\\Program Files\\Microsoft\\";
string vst4 = @"C:\Program Files\Microsoft\";

string rst5 = " Print \x000A Multiple \u000A Lines";
string vst5 = @" Print
 Multiple
 Lines";
```

Printing these strings produces the following output:

```
Hi there!
Hi there!

It started, "Four score and seven..."
It started, "Four score and seven..."

Value 1         5, Val2         10
Value 1 \t 5, Val2 \t 10

C:\Program Files\Microsoft\
C:\Program Files\Microsoft\

 Print
 Multiple
 Lines

 Print
 Multiple
 Lines
```

Note The compiler saves memory by having identical string literals share the same memory location in the heap.

Order of Evaluation

An expression can be made up of many nested sub-expressions. The order in which the sub-expressions are evaluated can make a difference in the final value of the expression.

For example, given the expression 3 * 5 + 2, there are two possible results depending on the order in which the sub-expressions are evaluated, as shown in Figure 8-3.

- If the multiplication is performed first, the result is 17.

- If the 5 and the 2 are added together first, the result is 21.

Figure 8-3. *Simple order of evaluation*

Precedence

You know from your grade school days that in the preceding example, the multiplication must be performed before the addition because multiplication has a *higher precedence* than addition. But unlike grade school days, when you had four operators and two levels of precedence, things are a bit more complex with C#, which has over 45 operators and 14 levels of precedence.

The complete list of operators and their precedences is given in Table 8-4. The table lists the highest precedence operators at the top, and continues down to the lowest precedence operators at the bottom.

Table 8-4. *Operator Precedence: Highest to Lowest*

Category	Operators
Primary	a.x f(x) a[x] x++ x-- new typeof checked unchecked
Unary	+ - ! ~ ++x --x (T)x
Multiplicative	* / %
Additive	+ -
Shift	<< >>
Relational and type	< > <= >= is as
Equality	== !=
Logical AND	&
Logical XOR	^
Logical OR	|
Conditional AND	&&
Conditional OR	||

Category	Operators
Conditional	?:
Assignment	= *= /= %= += -= <<= >>= &= ^= |=

Associativity

If all the operators in an expression have different levels of precedence, then evaluate each sub-expression, starting at the one with the highest level, and work down the precedence scale.

But what if two sequential operators have the same level of precedence? For example, given the expression 2 / 6 * 4, there are two possible evaluation sequences:

$$(2 / 6) * 4 = 4/3$$
or
$$2 / (6 * 4) = 1/12$$

When sequential operators have the same level of precedence, the order of evaluation is determined by *operator associativity*. That is, given two operators of the same level of precedence, one or the other will have precedence, depending on the operators' associativity. Some important characteristics of operator associativity are the following, and are summarized in Table 8-5:

- *Left-associative* operators are evaluated from left to right.

- *Right-associative* operators are evaluated from right to left.

- Binary operators, except the assignment operators, are left-associative.

- The assignment operators and the conditional operator are right-associative.

Therefore, given these rules, the preceding example expression should be grouped left to right, giving

$$(2 / 6) * 4, \text{which yields } 4/3.$$

Table 8-5. *Summary of Operator Associativity*

Type of Operator	Associativity
Assignment operators	Right-associative
Other binary operators	Left-associative
The conditional operator	Right-associative

Parenthesized Expressions

You can explicitly set the order of evaluation of the sub-expressions of an expression by using parentheses. Parenthesized sub-expressions

- Override the precedence and associativity rules

- Are evaluated in order from the innermost nested set to the outermost

Simple Arithmetic Operators

The simple arithmetic operators perform the four basic arithmetic operations, and are listed in Table 8-6. These operators are binary and left-associative.

Table 8-6. *The Simple Arithmetic Operators*

Operator	Name	Description
+	Addition	Adds the two operands.
-	Subtraction	Subtracts the second operand from the first.
*	Multiplication	Multiplies the two operands.
/	Division	Divides the first operand by the second. Integer division rounds the result toward 0 to the nearest integer.

The arithmetic operators perform the standard arithmetic operations on all the predefined simple arithmetic types.

The following are examples of the simple arithmetic operators:

```
int x1 = 5 + 6;        double d1 = 5.0 + 6.0;
int x2 = 12 - 3;       double d2 = 12.0 - 3.0;
int x3 = 3 * 4;        double d3 = 3.0 * 4.0;
int x4 = 10 / 3;       double d4 = 10.0 / 3.0;

byte b1 = 5 + 6;
sbyte sb1 = 6 * 5;
```

The Remainder Operator

The remainder operator (%) divides the first operand by the second operand, ignores the quotient, and returns the remainder. Its description is given in Table 8-7.

The remainder operator is binary and left-associative.

Table 8-7. *The Remainder Operator*

Operator	Name	Description
%	Remainder	Divides the first operand by the second operand and returns the remainder

The following lines show examples of the *integer remainder operator*.

- 0 % 3 = 0, because 0 divided by 3 is 0 with a remainder of 0.

- 1 % 3 = 1, because 1 divided by 3 is 0 with a remainder of 1.

- 2 % 3 = 2, because 2 divided by 3 is 0 with a remainder of 2.

- 3 % 3 = 0, because 3 divided by 3 is 1 with a remainder of 0.

- 4 % 3 = 1, because 4 divided by 3 is 1 with a remainder of 1.

The remainder operator can also be used with real numbers to give *real remainders*.

```
Console.WriteLine("0.0f % 1.5f is {0}", 0.0f % 1.5f);
Console.WriteLine("0.5f % 1.5f is {0}", 0.5f % 1.5f);
Console.WriteLine("1.0f % 1.5f is {0}", 1.0f % 1.5f);
Console.WriteLine("1.5f % 1.5f is {0}", 1.5f % 1.5f);
Console.WriteLine("2.0f % 1.5f is {0}", 2.0f % 1.5f);
Console.WriteLine("2.5f % 1.5f is {0}", 2.5f % 1.5f);
```

This code produces the following output:

```
0.0f % 1.5f is 0        //   0.0 / 1.5 = 0 remainder  0
0.5f % 1.5f is 0.5      //   0.5 / 1.5 = 0 remainder .5
1.0f % 1.5f is 1        //   1.0 / 1.5 = 0 remainder  1
1.5f % 1.5f is 0        //   1.5 / 1.5 = 1 remainder  0
2.0f % 1.5f is 0.5      //   2.0 / 1.5 = 1 remainder .5
2.5f % 1.5f is 1        //   2.5 / 1.5 = 1 remainder  1
```

Relational and Equality Comparison Operators

The relational and equality comparison operators are binary operators that compare their operands and return a value of type bool. These operators are listed in Table 8-8.

The relational and equality operators are binary and left-associative.

Table 8-8. *The Relational and Equality Comparison Operators*

Operator	Name	Description
<	Less than	true if first operand is less than second operand; false otherwise
>	Greater than	true if first operand is greater than second operand; false otherwise
<=	Less than or equal to	true if first operand is less than or equal to second operand; false otherwise
>=	Greater than or equal to	true if first operand is greater than or equal to second operand; false otherwise
==	Equal to	true if first operand is equal to second operand; false otherwise
!=	Not equal to	true if first operand is not equal to second operand; false otherwise

A binary expression with a relational or equality operator returns a value of type bool.

Note Unlike C and C++, numbers in C# do not have a Boolean interpretation.

```
int x = 5;
if( x )            // Wrong.  x is of type int, not type boolean.
   ...
if( x == 5 )       // Fine, since expression returns a value of type boolean
   ...
```

When printed, the Boolean values true and false are represented by the string output values True and False.

```
int x = 5, y = 4;
Console.WriteLine("x == x is {0}", x == x);
Console.WriteLine("x == y is {0}", x == y);
```

The output of this code is the following:

```
x == x is True
x == y is False
```

Comparison and Equality Operations

When comparing most reference types for equality, only the *references* are compared.

- If the references point to the same objects in memory, the equality comparison is true; otherwise it is false. This is true even if *the two separate objects* in memory are *exactly equivalent* in every other respect.

- This is called a *shallow comparison*.

Figure 8-4 illustrates the comparison of reference types.

- On the left of the figure, the references of both a and b are the same, so a comparison would return true.

- On the right of the figure, the references are not the same, so even if the contents of the two AClass objects were exactly the same, the comparison would return false.

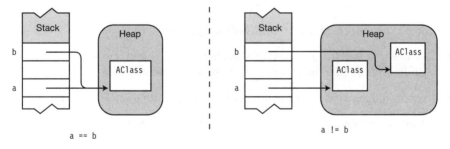

Figure 8-4. *Comparing reference types for equality*

Objects of type string are also reference types, but they are compared differently. When strings are compared for equality, they are compared in length and content, which is case sensitive.

- If two strings have the same length and the same case-sensitive content, the equality comparison returns true, even if they occupy different areas of memory.

- This is called a *deep comparison*.

Delegates are also reference types, and also use deep comparison. When delegates are compared for equality, the comparison returns true if both delegates are null, or if both have the same number of members in their invocation lists, and the invocation lists match.

When comparing numeric expressions, the types and values are compared.

When comparing enum types, the comparisons are done on the underlying values of the operands.

Increment and Decrement Operators

The increment operator adds 1 to the operand. The decrement operator subtracts 1 from the operand. The operators and their descriptions are listed in Table 8-9.

These operators are unary and have two forms, the *pre-* form, and the *post-* form, which act differently.

- In the pre- form, the operator is before the operand; for example, ++x and --y.

- In the post- form, the operator is after the operand; for example, x++ and y--.

Table 8-9. *The Increment and Decrement Operators*

Operator	Name	Description
++	Pre-increment ++*Var*	Increment the value of the variable by one and save it. Return the new value of the variable.
	Post-increment *Var*++	Increment the value of the variable by one and save it. Return the old value of the variable before it was incremented.
--	Pre-decrement --*Var*	Decrement the value of the variable by one and save it. Return the new value of the variable.
	Post-decrement *Var*--	Decrement the value of the variable by one and save it. Return the old value of the variable before it was decremented.

In comparing the pre- and post- forms of the operators

- The saved value of the operand variable after the statement is executed is the same regardless of whether the pre- or post- form of the operator is used.

- The only difference is the value *returned* by the operator to the expression.

An example summarizing the behavior is shown in Table 8-10.

Table 8-10. *Behavior of Pre- and Post- Increment and Decrement Operators*

	Expression: x = 10	Value Returned to the Expression	Value of Variable After Evaluation
Pre-increment	++x	11	11
Post-increment	x++	10	11
Pre-decrement	--x	9	9
Post-decrement	x--	10	9

For example, the following is a simple demonstration of the four different versions of the operators. In order to show the different results on the same input, the value of the operand x is reset to 5 before each assignment statement.

```
int x = 5, y;
y = x++;   // result: y: 5, x: 6
Console.WriteLine("y: {0}, x: {1}", y, x);

x = 5;
y = ++x;   // result: y: 6, x: 6
Console.WriteLine("y: {0}, x: {1}", y, x);

x = 5;
y = x--;   // result: y: 5, x: 4
Console.WriteLine("y: {0}, x: {1}", y, x);

x = 5;
y = --x;   // result: y: 4, x: 4
Console.WriteLine("y: {0}, x: {1}", y, x);
```

This code produces the following output:

```
y: 5, x: 6
y: 6, x: 6
y: 5, x: 4
y: 4, x: 4
```

Conditional Logical Operators

The logical operators are used for comparing or negating the logical values of their operands and returning the resulting logical value. The operators are listed in Table 8-11.

The logical AND and logical OR operators are binary and left-associative. The logical NOT is unary.

Table 8-11. *The Conditional Logical Operators*

Operator	Name	Description
&&	Logical AND	true if both operands are true; false otherwise
||	Logical OR	true if at least one operand is true; false otherwise
!	Logical NOT	true if the operand is false; false otherwise

The syntax for these operators is the following, where *expr1* and *expr2* evaluate to Boolean values.

```
Expr1 && Expr2
Expr1 || Expr2
   !Expr
```

The following are some examples:

```
bool bVal;
bVal = (1 == 1) && (2 == 2);      // True, both operand expressions are true
bVal = (1 == 1) && (1 == 2);      // False, second operand expression is false

bVal = (1 == 1) || (2 == 2);      // True, both operand expressions are true
bVal = (1 == 1) || (1 == 2);      // True, first operand expression is true
bVal = (1 == 2) || (2 == 3);      // False, both operand expressions are false

bVal = true;                      // Set bVal to true.
bVal = !bVal;                     // bVal is now false.
```

The conditional logical operators operate in "short circuit" mode, meaning that, if after evaluating *Expr1* the result can already be determined, then it skips the evaluation of *Expr2*. The following code shows examples of expressions in which the value can be determined after evaluating the first operand:

```
bool bVal;
bVal = (1 == 2) && (2 == 2);    // False, after evaluating first expression

bVal = (1 == 1) || (1 == 2);    // True, after evaluating first expression
```

Because of the short circuit behavior, do not place expressions with side effects (such as changing a value) in *Expr2*, since they might not be evaluated. In the following code, the post-increment of variable iVal would not be executed.

```
bool bVal; int iVal = 10;

bVal = (1 == 2) && (9 == iVal++);          // result:  bVal = False, iVal = 10
```

Logical Operators

The bitwise logical operators are often used to set the bit patterns for parameters to methods. The operators are listed in Table 8-12.

These operators, except for bitwise negation, are binary and left-associative. The bitwise negation operator is unary.

Table 8-12. *The Logical Operators*

Operator	Name	Description
&	Bitwise AND	Produces the bitwise AND of the two operands. The resulting bit is 1 only if both operand bits are 1.
|	Bitwise OR	Produces the bitwise OR of the two operands. The resulting bit is 1 if either operand bit is 1.
^	Bitwise XOR	Produces the bitwise XOR of the two operands. The resulting bit is 1 only if one, but not both, operand bits are 1.
~	Bitwise negation	Each bit in the operand is switched to its opposite. This produces the 1's complement of the operand.

The binary bitwise operators compare the corresponding bits at each position in each of their two operands, and set the bit in the return value according to the logical operation.

Figure 8-5 shows four examples of the bitwise logical operations.

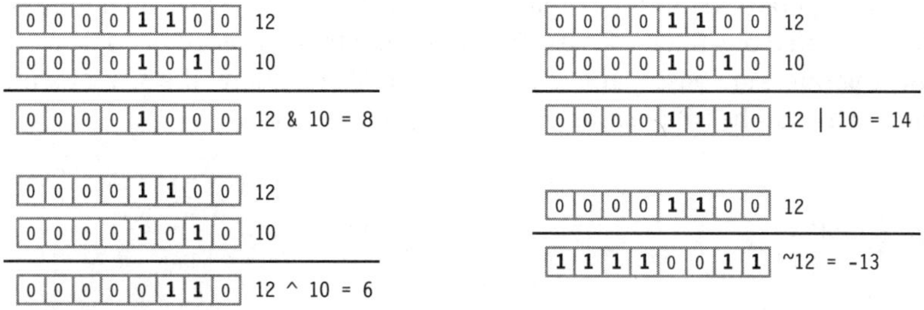

Figure 8-5. *Examples of bitwise logical operators*

The following code implements the preceding examples:

```
const byte x = 12, y = 10;
sbyte a;

a = x & y;              //  a = 8
a = x | y;              //  a = 14
a = x ^ y;              //  a = 6
a = ~x;                 //  a = -13
```

Shift Operators

The bitwise shift operators shift the bit pattern either right or left a specified number of positions, with the vacated bits filled with 0s. The shift operators are listed in Table 8-13.

The shift operators are binary and left-associative. The syntax of the bitwise shift operators is shown here. The number of positions to shift is given by *Count*.

```
Operand << Count                    // Left shift
Operand >> Count                    // Right shift
```

Table 8-13. *The Shift Operators*

Operator	Name	Description
<<	Left shift	Shifts the bit pattern left by the given number of positions. The bits shifted off the left end are lost. Bit positions opening up on the right are filled with 0s.
>>	Right shift	Shifts the bit pattern right by the given number of positions. Bits shifted off the right end are lost. If the left-most bit of the operand is a 1, bit positions opening up on the left are filled with 1s. Otherwise, they are filled with 0s.

Figure 8-6 shows how the expression 14 << 3 would be evaluated in a byte. This operation causes the following:

- Each of the bits in the operand (14) is shifted three places to the left.

- The three bit positions vacated on the right end are filled with 0s.

- The resulting value is 112.

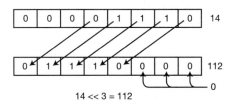

Figure 8-6. *Example of left shift of three bits*

Figure 8-7 illustrates bitwise shift operations.

0	0	0	0	1	1	1	0	14

0	1	1	1	0	0	0	0	14 << 3 = 112

0	0	0	0	1	1	1	0	14

0	0	0	0	0	0	0	1	14 >> 3 = 1

Figure 8-7. *Bitwise shifts*

The following code implements the preceding examples:

```
int a, b, x = 14;

a = x << 3;             // Shift left
b = x >> 3;             // Shift right

Console.WriteLine("{0} << 3 = {1}", x, a);
Console.WriteLine("{0} >> 3 = {1}", x, b);
```

This code produces the following output:

```
14 << 3 = 112
14 >> 3 = 1
```

Assignment Operators

The assignment operators evaluate the expression on the right side of the operator and use that value to set the value of the "variable-type" expression on the left side of the operator. As in C and C++, the value assigned to the left-hand side can be modified if the operator is a compound assignment operator. The assignment operators are listed in Table 8-14.

The assignment operators are binary and left-associative.

Table 8-14. *The Assignment Operators*

Operator	Description
=	Simple assignment; evaluate the expression on the right and assign the returned value to the variable or expression on the left.
*=	Compound assignment; var *= expr is equal to var = var * (expr).
/=	Compound assignment; var /= expr is equal to var = var / (expr).
%=	Compound assignment; var %= expr is equal to var = var % (expr).
+=	Compound assignment; var += expr is equal to var = var + (expr).
-=	Compound assignment; var -= expr is equal to var = var - (expr).
<<=	Compound assignment; var <<= expr is equal to var = var << (expr).
>>=	Compound assignment; var >>= expr is equal to var = var >> (expr).
&=	Compound assignment; var &= expr is equal to var = var & (expr).
^=	Compound assignment; var ^= expr is equal to var = var ^ (expr).
|=	Compound assignment; var |= expr is equal to var = var | (expr).

The syntax is as follows:

```
VariableExpression Operator Expression
```

For simple assignment, the expression to the right of the operator is evaluated and its value is assigned to the variable on the left.

```
int x;
x = 5;
x = y * z;
```

The types of objects that can be on the left side of an assignment operator are the following. They will be discussed later in the text.

- Variables (local variables, fields, parameters)

- Properties

- Indexers

- Events

Compound Assignment

Frequently, you'll want to evaluate an expression and add the results to the current value of a variable, as shown:

```
x = x + expr;
```

The compound assignment operators allow a shorthand method for avoiding the repetition of the left-side variable on the right side under certain common circumstances. For example, the following two statements are exactly equivalent semantically, but the second is shorter and just as easy to understand.

```
x = x + (y - z);
x += y - z;
```

The other compound assignment statements are analogous:

```
                       Notice the parentheses.
                           ↓     ↓
x *= y - z;    // Equivalent to x = x * (y - z)
x /= y - z;    // Equivalent to x = x / (y - z)
   ...
```

The Conditional Operator

The conditional operator is a powerful and succinct way of returning one of two values, based on the result of a condition. The operator is shown is Table 8-15.

The conditional operator is ternary.

Table 8-15. *The Conditional Operator*

Operator	Name	Description
? :	Conditional operator	Evaluates an expression and returns one of two values, depending on whether the expression returns true or false.

The syntax for the conditional operator is shown following. It has a test expression and two result expressions.

- If *Condition* evaluates to true, then *Expression1* is evaluated and returned. Otherwise, *Expression2* is evaluated and returned.

- Expression *Condition* must return a value of type bool.

```
Condition ? Expression1 : Expression2
```

The conditional operator can be compared with the if...else construct. For example, the following if...else construct checks a condition, and if the condition is true, it assigns 5 to variable IntVar. Otherwise it assigns it the value 10.

```
if( x < y )                              // if...else
   IntVar = 5;
else
   IntVar = 10;
```

The conditional operator can perform the same operation in a less verbose form, as shown in the following statement:

```
IntVar = x < y ? 5 : 10;                 // Conditional operator
```

Figure 8-8 compares the two forms shown in the example.

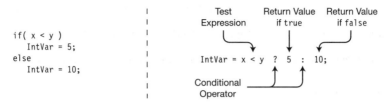

Figure 8-8. *The conditional operator versus if...else*

For example, the following code uses the conditional operator three times—once in each of the WriteLine statements. In the first instance, it returns either the value of x or the value of y. In the second two instances, it returns either the empty string or the string " not."

```
int x = 10, y = 9;
int HighVal = (x > y)                        // Condition
                ? x                          // Expression 1
                : y;                         // Expression 2
Console.WriteLine("HighVal:  {0}\n", HighVal);

Console.WriteLine("x is{0} greater than y",
                  x > y                      // Condition
                  ? ""                       // Expression 1
                  : " not");                 // Expression 2
y = 11;
Console.WriteLine("x is{0} greater than y",
                  x > y                      // Condition
                  ? ""                       // Expression 1
                  : " not");                 // Expression 2
```

This code produces the following output:

```
HighVal:   10

x is greater than y
x is not greater than y
```

■**Note** The if...else statement is a flow-of-control *statement*. It should be used for *doing* one or the other of two *actions*. The conditional expression is an *expression*. It should be used for *returning* one or the other of two *values*.

Unary Arithmetic Operators

The unary operators set the sign of a numeric value. They are listed in Table 8-16.

- The unary positive operator simply returns the value of the operand.

- The unary negative operator returns the value of the operand subtracted from 0.

Table 8-16. *The Unary Operators*

Operator	Name	Description
+	Positive sign	Returns the numeric value of the operand
-	Negative sign	Returns the numeric value of the operand subtracted from 0

For example, the following code shows the use and results of the operators:

```
int x = 10;       // x = 10
int y = -x;       // y = -10
int z = -y;       // z = 10
```

User-Defined Type Conversions

User-defined conversions will be discussed in greater detail in Chapter 18, but I will mention them here as well because they are operators.

- You can define both implicit and explicit conversions for your own classes and structs. This allows you to convert an object of your user-defined type to some other type, and vice versa.

- C# provides implicit and explicit conversions.

  - With an *implicit conversion*, the compiler will automatically make the conversion, if necessary, when it is resolving what types to use in a particular context.

  - With an *explicit conversion*, the compiler will only make the conversion when an explicit cast operator is used.

The syntax for declaring an implicit conversion is the following. The syntax for the explicit conversion is the same, except that explicit is substituted for implicit.

The modifiers public and static are required for all user-defined conversions.

```
              Required                  Target              Source
                 ↓                        ↓                   ↓
public static implicit operator TargetType ( SourceType Identifier )
{
    ...
    return ObjectOfTargetType;
}
```

The following code shows an example of declarations for conversion operators that will convert an object of type LimitedInt to type int, and vice versa.

```
class LimitedInt                    Target    Source
{                                     ↓         ↓
   public static implicit operator int (LimitedInt li)
   {
      return li.TheValue;
   }                                Target      Source
                                      ↓           ↓
   public static implicit operator LimitedInt (int x)
   {
      LimitedInt li = new LimitedInt();
      li.TheValue = x;
      return li;
   }

   private int _TheValue = 0;
   public int TheValue{ ... }
}
```

For example, the following code reiterates and uses the two type conversion operators defined previously. In Main, an int literal is converted into a LimitedInt object, and in the next line, a LimitedInt object is converted into an int.

```
class LimitedInt
{
   const int MaxValue = 100;
   const int MinValue = 0;

   public static implicit operator int(LimitedInt li)      // Convert type
   {
      return li.TheValue;
   }

   public static implicit operator LimitedInt(int x)       // Convert type
   {
      LimitedInt li = new LimitedInt();
      li.TheValue = x;
      return li;
   }

   private int _TheValue = 0;
   public int TheValue                                      // Property
   {
      get { return _TheValue; }
      set
      {
         if (value < MinValue)
            _TheValue = 0;
         else
            _TheValue = value > MaxValue
                           ? MaxValue
                           : value;
      }
   }
}

class Program
{
   static void Main()                              // Main
   {
      LimitedInt li = 5;                           // Convert 5 to LimitedInt
      int Five = li;                               // Convert LimitedInt to int

      Console.WriteLine("li: {0}, Five: {1}", li.TheValue, Five);
   }
}
```

Explicit Conversion and the Cast Operator

The preceding example code showed the implicit conversion of the int to a LimitedInt type and the implicit conversion of a LimitedInt type to an int. If, however, you had declared the two conversion operators as explicit, you would have had to explicitly use cast operators when making the conversions.

A *cast operator* consists of the name of the type to which you want to convert the expression, inside a set of parentheses. For example, the following casts the value 5 to a LimitedInt object.

```
                        Cast operator
                            ↓
                       _____
    LimitedInt li = (LimitedInt) 5;
```

For example, here is the relevant portion of the code, with the changes marked:

```
                    ↓
               _____
public static explicit operator int(LimitedInt li)
{
    return li.TheValue;
}
                    ↓
               _____
public static explicit operator LimitedInt(int x)
{
    LimitedInt li = new LimitedInt();
    li.TheValue = x;
    return li;
}

static void Main()
{                          ↓
                      _____
    LimitedInt li = (LimitedInt) 5;
    int Five = (int) li;
              ⊤
    Console.WriteLine(" li: {0}, Five: {1}", li.TheValue, Five);
}
```

In both versions of the code, the output is the following:

```
li: 5, Five: 5
```

Operator Overloading

The C# operators, as you've seen, are defined to work using the predefined types as operands. If confronted with a user-defined type, the operator simply would not know how to process it. Operator overloading allows you to define how the C# operators should operate on operands of your user-defined types.

- Operator overloading is only available for classes and structs.

- You can overload an operator *x* for use with your class or struct by declaring a method named operator *x* that implements the behavior (e.g., operator +, operator -, etc.).

  - The overload methods for unary operators take a single parameter of the class or struct type.

  - The overload methods for binary operators take two parameters, at least one of which must be of the class or struct type.

```
public static LimitedInt operator -(LimitedInt x)             // Unary
public static LimitedInt operator +(LimitedInt x, double y)   // Binary
```

An operator overload method must be declared as

- Both static and public

- A member of the class or struct for which it is an operand

For example, the following code shows two of the overloaded operators of a class named LimitedInt: the addition operator and the negation operator. You can tell that it is negation and not subtraction because the operator overload method has only a single parameter, and is therefore unary; whereas the subtraction operator is binary.

```
class LimitedInt      Return
{         Required     type    Keyword  Operator
             ↓          ↓         ↓        ↓
    public static LimitedInt operator +(LimitedInt x, double y)
    {
        LimitedInt li = new LimitedInt();
        li.TheValue = x.TheValue + (int)y;
        return li;
    }

    public static LimitedInt operator -(LimitedInt x)
    {
        // In this strange class, negating a value just sets its value to 0.
        LimitedInt li = new LimitedInt();
        li.TheValue = 0;
        return li;
    }
}
```

Restrictions on Operator Overloading

Not all operators can be overloaded, and there are restrictions on the types of overloading that can be done. The important things you should know about the restrictions on operator overloading are described later in the section.

Only the following operators can be overloaded. Prominently missing from the list is the assignment operator.

Overloadable unary operators: +   -   !   ~   ++   --   true   false

Overloadable binary operators: +   -   *   /   %   & | ^   <<   >>   ==   !=   >
<   >=   <=

The increment and decrement operators are overloadable. But unlike the predefined versions, there is no distinction between the pre- and post- usage of the overloaded operator.

You *cannot* do the following things with operator overloading:

- Create a new operator

- Change the syntax of an operator

- Redefine how an operator works on the predefined types

- Change the precedence or associativity of an operator

■**Note** Your overloaded operators should conform to the intuitive meanings of the operators.

Example of Operator Overloading

The following example shows the overloads of three operators for class LimitedInt: negation, subtraction, and addition.

```
class LimitedInt {
   const int MaxValue = 100;
   const int MinValue = 0;

   public static LimitedInt operator -(LimitedInt x)
   {
      // In this strange class, negating a value just sets its value to 0.
      LimitedInt li = new LimitedInt();
      li.TheValue = 0;
      return li;
   }

   public static LimitedInt operator -(LimitedInt x, LimitedInt y)
   {
      LimitedInt li = new LimitedInt();
```

```
            li.TheValue = x.TheValue - y.TheValue;
            return li;
        }


        public static LimitedInt operator +(LimitedInt x, double y)
        {
            LimitedInt li = new LimitedInt();
            li.TheValue = x.TheValue + (int)y;
            return li;
        }

        private int _TheValue = 0;
        public int TheValue
        {
            get { return _TheValue; }
            set
            {
                if (value < MinValue)
                    _TheValue = 0;
                else
                    _TheValue = value > MaxValue
                                    ? MaxValue
                                    : value;
            }
        }
    }
    class Program {
        static void Main() {
            LimitedInt li1 = new LimitedInt();
            LimitedInt li2 = new LimitedInt();
            LimitedInt li3 = new LimitedInt();
            li1.TheValue = 10; li2.TheValue = 26;
            Console.WriteLine(" li1: {0}, li2: {1}", li1.TheValue, li2.TheValue);

            li3 = -li1;
            Console.WriteLine("-{0} = {1}", li1.TheValue, li3.TheValue);

            li3 = li2 - li1;
            Console.WriteLine(" {0} - {1} = {2}",
                        li2.TheValue, li1.TheValue, li3.TheValue);
```

```
      li3 = li1 - li2;
      Console.WriteLine(" {0} - {1} = {2}",
              li1.TheValue, li2.TheValue, li3.TheValue);
   }
}
```

This code produces the following output:

```
li1: 10, li2: 26
-10 = 0
 26 - 10 = 16
 10 - 26 = 0
```

The typeof Operator

The typeof operator returns the System.Type object of any type given as its parameter. From this object, you can learn the characteristics of the type. (There is only one System.Type object for any given type.) The operator's characteristics are listed in Table 8-17.

The typeof operator is unary.

Table 8-17. *The typeof Operator*

Operator	Description
typeof	Returns the System.Type object of a given type.

The following is an example of the syntax of the typeof operator. Type is a class in the System namespace.

```
Type t = typeof ( SomeClass )
```

You cannot overload the typeof operator, as that would defeat the .NET type-safety mechanisms.

For example, the following code uses the typeof operator to get information on a class called SomeClass, and print the names of its public fields and methods.

```
using System.Reflection;

class SomeClass
{
   public int  Field1;
   public int  Field2;

   public void Method1() { }
   public int  Method2() { return 1; }
}

class Program
{
   static void Main()
   {
      Type t = typeof(SomeClass);
      FieldInfo[]  fi = t.GetFields();
      MethodInfo[] mi = t.GetMethods();

      foreach (FieldInfo f in fi)
         Console.WriteLine("Field : {0}", f.Name);
      foreach (MethodInfo m in mi)
         Console.WriteLine("Method: {0}", m.Name);
   }
}
```

The output of this code is the following:

```
Field : Field1
Field : Field2
Method: Method1
Method: Method2
Method: GetType
Method: ToString
Method: Equals
Method: GetHashCode
```

The typeof operator is also called by the GetType method, which is available for every object of every type. For example, the following code retrieves the name of the type of the object:

```
class SomeClass
{
   ...
}

class Program
{
   static void Main()
   {
      SomeClass s = new SomeClass();

      Console.WriteLine("Type s: {0}", s.GetType().Name);
   }
}
```

This code produces the following output:

```
Type s: SomeClass
```

CHAPTER 9

Statements

What are Statements?

Expression Statements

Flow-of-Control Statements

The if Statement

The if...else Statement

The switch Statement

The while Loop

The do Loop

The for Loop

Jump Statements

The break Statement

The continue Statement

Labeled Statements

The goto Statement

The using Statement

Other Statements

What Are Statements?

The statements in C# are very similar to those of C and C++. This chapter will cover the characteristics of a C# statement, as well as the flow-of-control statements provided by the language.

- A *statement* is a source code instruction describing a type or telling the program to perform an action.

- There are three major categories of statements, as follows:
    - *Declaration statements*: Statements that declare types or variables
    - *Labeled statements*: Statements to which control can jump
    - *Embedded statements*: Statements that perform actions or manage flow of control

Previous chapters have covered a number of different declaration statements, including declarations of local variables, classes, and class members. This chapter will cover the embedded statements, which do not declare types, variables, or instances. Instead, they use expressions and flow-of-control constructs to work with the objects and variables that have been declared by the declaration statements.

- A *simple statement* consists of an expression followed by a semicolon.

- A *block* is a sequence of statements enclosed by matching curly braces. The enclosed statements can include the following:
    - Declaration statements
    - Labeled statements
    - Embedded statements
    - Nested blocks

The following code gives examples of each:

```
int x = 10;             // Simple declaration
int z;                  // Simple declaration

{                       // Block
   int y = 20;          // Simple declaration
   z = x + y;           // Embedded statement
top: y = 30;            // Labeled statement
      ...
   {                    // Nested block
      ...
   }
}
```

> **■Note** A block counts syntactically as a single embedded statement. Anywhere that an embedded statement is required syntactically, you can use a block.

An *empty statement* consists of just a semicolon. You can use an empty statement at a position where the syntax of the language requires an embedded statement, but your program logic does not require any action.

For example, the following code is an example of using the empty statement:

- The second line in the code is an empty statement. It is required because there must be an embedded statement between the `if` part and the `else` part of the construct.

- The fourth line is a simple statement, as shown by the terminating semicolon.

```
if( x < y )
    ;                  // Empty statement
else
    z = a + b;         // Simple statement
```

Expression Statements

The last chapter looked at expressions. Expressions return values, but they can also have *side effects*.

- A side effect is an action that affects the state of the program.

- Many expressions are evaluated only for their side effects.

You can create a statement from an expression by placing a statement terminator (semicolon) after it. Any value returned by the expression is discarded. For example, the following code shows an expression statement. It consists of the assignment expression (an assignment operator and two operands) followed by a semicolon. This does the following two things:

- The expression assigns the value on the right of the operator to the memory location referenced by variable x. In fact this is probably the main reason for the statement, *this is considered the side effect*.

- After setting the value of x, the expression returns with the new value of x. But there is nothing to receive this return value, so it is ignored.

```
x = 10;
```

The whole reason for evaluating the expression was to achieve the side effect.

Flow-of-Control Statements

C# provides the flow-of-control constructs common to modern programming languages.

- *Conditional execution* executes or skips a section of code depending on a condition. The conditional execution statements are the following:
  - if
  - if...else
  - switch

- *Looping constructs* execute a section of code multiple times, where the number of times depends on the changing state of the program. The looping statements are the following:
  - while
  - do
  - for
  - foreach

- *Jump statements* change the flow of control from one section of code to a specific statement in another section of code. The jump statements are the following:
  - break
  - continue
  - return
  - goto
  - throw

Conditional execution and looping constructs (other than foreach) require a test expression, or *condition*, to determine where the program should continue execution.

■**Note** Unlike C and C++, test expressions must return a value of type bool. Numbers do not have a Boolean interpretation in C#.

The if Statement

The if statement implements conditional execution. The syntax for the if statement is shown here, and is illustrated in Figure 9-1.

- If *TestExpr* evaluates to true, *Statement* is executed.

- If it evaluates to false, *Statement* is skipped.

- *TestExpr* must evaluate to a value of type bool.

```
if( TestExpr )
    Statement
```

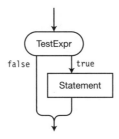

Figure 9-1. *The if statement*

The following code shows examples of if statements:

```
// With a simple statement
if( x <= 10 )
    z = x - 1;                  // Single statement, no curly braces needed


// With a block
if( x >= 20 )
{
    x = x - 5;                  // Block--braces needed
    y = x + z;
}


int x = 5;
if( x )             // Error: test expression must be a bool, not int
{
    ...
}
```

The if...else Statement

The if...else statement implements a two-way branch. The syntax for the if...else statement is shown here, and is illustrated in Figure 9-2.

- If *TestExpr* evaluates to true, *Statement1* is executed.

- If it evaluates to false, *Statement2* is executed instead.

```
if( TestExpr )
    Statement1
else
    Statement2
```

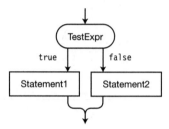

Figure 9-2. *The if...else statement*

The following is an example of the if...else statement:

```
if( x <= 10 )
    z = x - 1;                 // Single statement--no braces needed
else
{                              // Multiple statements--block
    x = x - 5;
    y = x + z;
}
```

The switch Statement

The switch statement implements multi-way branching. The syntax and structure of the switch statement are shown in Figure 9-3.

- The switch statement contains zero or more *switch sections*.

- Each *switch section* starts with one or more *switch labels*.

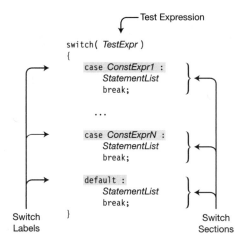

Figure 9-3. *Structure of a switch statement*

Switch labels have the following form:

```
case ConstantExpression :
     ↑                    ↑
  Keyword        Switch label terminator
```

The flow of control through the structure in Figure 9-3 is the following:

- Test expression *TestExpr* is evaluated at the top of the construct.

- If the value of *TestExpr* is equal to the value *ConstExpr1*, the constant expression in the first switch label, then the statements in the *statement list* following the switch label are executed, until the break statement is encountered.

- Each switch section must end with a break statement (or a goto statement, as discussed later).

- The break statement branches execution to the end of the switch statement.

- The default case is optional.

The general flow of control through a switch statement is illustrated in Figure 9-4. You can modify the flow through a switch statement with a goto statement or a return statement.

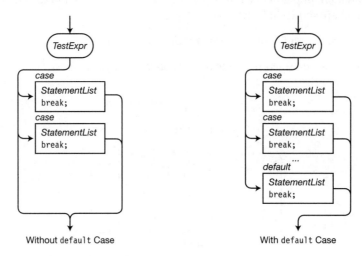

Without `default` Case   With `default` Case

Figure 9-4. *The flow of control through a switch statement*

■**Note** Unlike C and C++, each switch section must end with a break or return statement. In C#, there is no *falling through* from one switch section to the next.

A Switch Example

The following code executes the switch statement five times, with the value of x ranging from 1 to 5. From the output, you can tell which case section was executed on each cycle through the loop.

```
for( int x=1; x<6; x++ )
{
   switch( x )                              // Evaluate the value of variable x.
   {
      case 2:                               // If x equals 2
         Console.WriteLine
            ("x is {0} -- In Case 2", x);
         break;                             // Go to end of switch.

      case 5:                               // If x equals 5
         Console.WriteLine
            ("x is {0} -- In Case 5", x);
         break;                             // Go to end of switch.

      default:
                                            // If x is neither 2 nor 5
         Console.WriteLine
            ("x is {0} -- In Default case", x);
         break;
                                            // Go to end of switch.
   }
}
```

The output of the preceding code is the following:

```
x is 1 -- In Default case
x is 2 -- In Case 2
x is 3 -- In Default case
x is 4 -- In Default case
x is 5 -- In Case 5
```

More on the switch Statement

A switch statement can have any number of switch sections, including none. The default section is not required, as shown in the following example. It is, however, generally considered good practice to include it, since it can catch potential errors.

For example, the switch statement in the following code has no default case. The switch statement is inside a for loop, which executes the statement five times, with the value of x starting at 1 and ending at 5.

```
for( int x=1; x<6; x++ )
{
    switch( x )
    {
        case 5:
            Console.WriteLine("x is {0} -- In Case 5", x);
            break;
    }
}
```

The output of this code is the following:

```
x is 5 -- In Case 5
```

The following code has *only* the default case:

```
for( int x=1; x<4; x++ )
{
    switch( x )
    {
        default:
            Console.WriteLine("x is {0} -- In Default case", x);
            break;
    }
}
```

This code produces the following output:

```
x is 1 -- In Default case
x is 2 -- In Default case
x is 3 -- In Default case
```

Switch Labels

The expression following the keyword case, in a switch label

- Must be a constant expression, and therefore must be completely evaluable by the compiler at *compile* time

- Must be of the same type as the test expression

For example, Figure 9-5 shows three sample switch statements.

```
const string YES = "yes";        const char LetterB = 'b';        const int Five = 5;

string s = "no";                 char c = 'a';                    int x = 5;
switch (s)                       switch (c)                      switch (x)
{                                {                               {
   case YES:                        case 'a':                       case Five:
      PrintOut("Yes");                 PrintOut("a");                  PrintOut("5");
      break;                           break;                          break;

   case "no":                       case LetterB:                   case 10:
      PrintOut("No");                  PrintOut("b");                  PrintOut("10");
      break;                           break;                          break;
}                                }                               }
```

Figure 9-5. *Switch statements with different types of switch labels*

Although C# does not allow falling through from one switch section to another.

- You can attach multiple switch labels to any switch section.

- Following the statement list associated with a case, there must be a break or goto statement before the next switch label, unless there are *no intervening executable statements* between the switch labels.

For example, in the following code there are no executable statements between the first three switch labels, so it is perfectly fine to have one follow the other. In cases 5 and 6, however, there is an executable statement between them, so there must be a break or goto statement.

```
switch( x )
{
   case 1:                    // Acceptable
   case 2:
   case 3:
      ...                     // Execute this code if x equals 1, 2 or 3
      break;

   case 5:
      y = x + 1;
   case 6:                    // Not acceptable because there is no break
      ...
```

The while Loop

The while loop is a simple loop construct in which the test expression is performed at the top of the loop. The syntax of the while loop is shown here, and is illustrated in Figure 9-6.

- First, *TestExpr* is evaluated.

- If *TestExpr* evaluates to false, then execution continues after the end of the while loop.

- Otherwise, when *TestExpr* evaluates to true, then *Statement* is executed, and *TestExpr* is evaluated again. Each time *TestExpr* evaluates to true, *Statement* is executed another time. The loop ends when *TestExpr* evaluates to false.

```
while( TestExpr )

    Statement
```

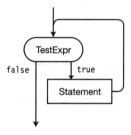

Figure 9-6. *The while loop*

The following code shows an example of the while loop, where the test expression variable starts with a value of 3 and is decremented at each iteration. The loop exits when the value of the variable becomes 0.

```
int x = 3;
while( x > 0 )
{
    Console.WriteLine("x: {0}", x);
    x--;
}
Console.WriteLine("Out of loop");
```

The output from this code is the following:

```
x:   3
x:   2
x:   1
Out of loop
```

The do Loop

The do loop is a simple loop construct in which the test expression is performed at the bottom of the loop. The syntax for the do loop is shown here and illustrated in Figure 9-7.

- First, *Statement* is executed.

- *TestExpr* is then evaluated.

- If *TestExpr* returns true, then *Statement* is executed again.

- Each time *TestExpr* returns true, *Statement* is executed again.

- When *TestExpr* returns false, control passes to the statement following the end of the loop construct.

```
do
    Statement
while( TestExpr );                          // End of do loop
```

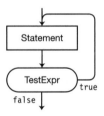

Figure 9-7. *The do loop*

The do loop has several characteristics that set it apart from other flow-of-control constructs. They are the following:

- The body of the loop, *Statement*, will always be executed at least once, even if *TestExpr* is initially false.

- The semicolon is required after the closing parenthesis of the test expression.

The following code shows an example of a do loop:

```
int x = 0;
do
    Console.WriteLine("x is {0}", x++);
while (x<3);
       ↑
       Required
```

This code produces the following output:

```
x is 0
x is 1
x is 2
```

The for Loop

The for loop construct executes the body of the loop, as long as the test expression returns true when it is evaluated at the top of the loop. The syntax of the for loop is shown here and illustrated in Figure 9-8.

- At the beginning of the for loop, *Initializer* is executed once.

- *TestExpr* is then evaluated.

- If it returns true, *Statement* is executed, followed by *Iterator*.

- Control then returns to the top of the loop, and *TestExpr* is evaluated again.

- As long as *TestExpr* returns true, *Statement*, followed by *Iterator*, will be executed.

- As soon as *TestExpr* returns false, execution continues at the statement following *Statement*.

Separated by semicolons
↓   ↓

```
for( Initializer ; TestExpr ; Iterator )
    Statement
```

Initializer, *TestExpr*, and *Iterator* are all optional. Their positions can be left blank.

- The semicolons are required.

- If the *TestExpr* position is left blank, the test is *assumed to return* true. Therefore, there must be some other method of exiting the statement if the program is to avoid going into an infinite loop.

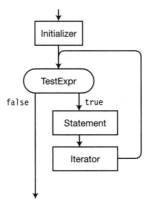

Figure 9-8. *The for loop*

Figure 9-8 illustrates the flow of control through the for statement. You should also know the following about its components:

- *Initializer* is executed only once, before any other part of the for construct. It is usually used to declare and initialize local values to be used in the loop.

- *TestExpr* is evaluated to determine whether *Statement* should be executed or skipped. It must evaluate to a value of type bool.

- *Iterator* is executed immediately after *Statement*, and before returning to the top of the loop to *TestExpr*.

For example, in the following code:

- Before anything else, the initializer (int i=0) defines a variable called i, and initializes its value to 0.

- The condition (i<3) is then evaluated. If it is true, then the body of the loop is executed.

- At the bottom of the loop, after all the loop statements have been executed, the iterator statement is executed—in this case incrementing the value of i.

```
// The body of this for loop is executed three times.
for( int i=0 ; i<3 ; i++ )
    Console.WriteLine("Inside loop.  i:  {0}", i);

Console.WriteLine("Out of Loop");
```

The output from this code is the following:

```
Inside loop.  i:  0
Inside loop.  i:  1
Inside loop.  i:  2
Out of Loop
```

Scope of Variables in a for Statement

Any variables declared in the *initializer* are visible *only within the* for *statement.*

- This is different than C and C++.

- The following example illustrates this point:

```
Type is needed here for declaration
    ↓
for( int i=0; i<10; i++ ) // Variable i is in scope here, and also
    Statement;            // here within the statement.
                          // Here, after the statement, i no longer exists.


Type is needed here again because previous variable has gone out of existence
    ↓
for( int i=0; i<10; i++ ) // We need to define a new variable i here, since
    Statement;            // the previous one has gone out of existence.
```

The local variables declared within the body of the loop are known only within the loop.

■**Note** Unlike C and C++, the scope of variables declared in the initializer lasts only for the length of the loop.

Multiple Expressions in the Initializer and Iterator

Both the initializer and the iterator can contain multiple expressions as long as they are separated by commas.

For example, the following code has two variable declarations in the initializer and two expressions in the iterator:

```
static void Main( )
{
    const int MaxI = 5;
            Two declarations              Two expressions
            ─────────────               ─────────────
                  ↓                           ↓
    for (int i = 0, j = 10; i < MaxI; i++, j += 10)
    {
        Console.WriteLine("{0}, {1}", i, j);
    }
}
```

The output from this code is the following:

```
0, 10
1, 20
2, 30
3, 40
4, 50
```

Jump Statements

When the flow of control reaches *jump statements*, program execution is unconditionally transferred to another part of the program. The jump statements are the following:

- break

- continue

- return

- goto

- throw

This chapter covers the first four of these statements. The throw statement is discussed in Chapter 11.

The break Statement

You have already seen the break statement earlier in this chapter—used in the switch statement. But it can also be used in the following statement types as well:

- for

- foreach

- while

- do

- switch

In the body of one of these statements, break causes execution to exit the *innermost enclosing statement*.

For example, the following while loop would be an infinite loop if it relied only on its test expression, which is always true. But instead, after three iterations of the loop, the break statement is encountered and the loop is exited.

```
int x = 0;
while( true )
{
    x++;
    if( x >= 3 )
        break;
}
```

The continue Statement

The continue statement causes program execution to go to the *top* of the *innermost enclosing loop* of the following types:

- while

- do

- for

- foreach

For example, the following for loop is executed five times. In the first three iterations, it encounters the continue statement and goes directly back to the top of the loop, missing the WriteLine statement at the bottom of the loop. Execution only reaches the WriteLine statement during the last two iterations.

```
for( int x=0; x<5; x++ )              // Execute loop five times
{
   if( x < 3 )                        // The first three times
      continue;                       // Go directly back to the top of loop.

   // This line is only reached when x is 3 or greater.
   Console.WriteLine("Value of x is {0}", x);
}
```

The output of this code is the following:

```
Value of x is 3
Value of x is 4
```

The following code shows an example of a continue statement in a while loop. This code has the same output as the preceding for loop example.

```
int x = 0;
while( x < 5 )
{
   if( x < 3 )
   {
      x++;
      continue;                       // Go back to top of loop
   }

   // This line is reached only when x is 3 or greater.
   Console.WriteLine("Value of x is {0}", x);
   x++;
}
```

Labeled Statements

A *labeled statement* consists of an identifier, followed by a colon, followed by a statement. It has the following form:

```
Identifier: Statement
```

A labeled statement is executed exactly as if the label were not there and consisted of just the *Statement* part.

- Adding a label to a statement allows control to be transferred to the statement from another part of the code.

- Labeled statements are only allowed inside blocks.

Labels

Labels have their own declaration space, so the identifier in a labeled statement can be any valid identifier—including those that might be declared in an overlapping scope, such as local variables or parameter names.

For example, the following code shows the valid use of a label with the same identifier as a local variable:

```
{
    int xyz = 0;                              // Variable xyz
       ...
    xyz: Console.WriteLine("No problem.");    // Label xyz
}
```

There are restrictions, however. The identifier cannot be either

- The same as another label identifier with an overlapping scope

- A keyword

The Scope of Labeled Statements

Labeled statements cannot be seen (or accessed) from *outside* the block in which they are declared.

The scope of a labeled statement is

- The block in which it is declared

- Any blocks nested inside that block

For example, the code on the left of Figure 9-9 contains several nested blocks, with their scopes marked. There are two labeled statements declared in Scope B of the program: increment and end.

- The shaded portions on the right of the figure show the areas of the code in which the labeled statements are in scope.

- Code in Scope B, and all the nested blocks, can see and access the labeled statements.

- Code from any of the inner scopes can jump *out* to the labeled statements.

- Code from outside (Scope A, in this case) *cannot jump into* a block with a labeled statement.

```
static void Main( )
{ // Scope A

    { // Scope B

    increment:  x++;
        { // Scope C

            { // Scope D
              ...
            }
            { // Scope E
              ...
            }
            ...
        }
    end: Console.WriteLine("Exiting");
    }
}
```

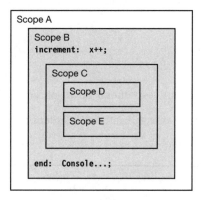

Figure 9-9. *The scope of labels includes nested blocks.*

The goto Statement

The goto statement unconditionally transfers control to a *labeled statement*. Its general form is the following, where *Identifier* is the identifier of a labeled statement:

```
goto Identifier ;
```

For example, the following code shows the simple use of a goto statement:

```
bool ThingsAreFine;
while (true)
{
   ThingsAreFine = MonitorNuclearReactor();

   if ( ThingsAreFine )
      Console.WriteLine("Things are fine.");
   else
      goto NotSoGood;
}

NotSoGood: Console.WriteLine("We have a problem.");
```

The goto statement must be *within* the scope of the labeled statement.

- A goto statement can jump to any labeled statement within its own block, or *out* to any block in which it is nested.

- A goto statement cannot jump *into* any blocks nested within its own block.

■**Caution** Using the goto statement is strongly discouraged, as it can lead to code that is poorly structured, and difficult to debug and maintain. Edsger Dijkstra's 1968 letter to the Communications of the ACM, entitled "Go To Statement Considered Harmful," was an important point in the history of computer science; it was one of the first published descriptions of the pitfalls of using the goto statement.

The goto Statement Inside a switch Statement

There are also two other forms of the goto statement, for use inside switch statements. These goto statements transfer control to the correspondingly named switch label in the switch statement.

```
goto case ConstantExpression;
goto default;
```

The using Statement

It is imperative that certain types of objects be allowed to clean up and free the unmanaged resources they are holding. The using statement is used to simplify the process and ensure that these resources are properly disposed of.

A *resource* is a class or struct that implements the System.IDisposable interface. Interfaces are covered in detail in Chapter 17—but in short, an interface is a collection of unimplemented function members that classes and structs can choose to implement. The IDisposable interface contains a single method named Dispose.

The phases of using a resource are shown in Figure 9-10, and consist of the following:

- Allocating the resource

- Using the resource

- Disposing of the resource

If an unexpected runtime error occurs during the portion of the code using the resource, the code disposing of the resource might not get executed.

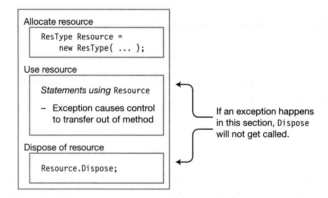

Figure 9-10. *Components of using a resource*

■**Note** The using statement is different than the using directives. The using directives are covered in Chapter 10.

Packaging Use of the Resource

The using statement helps reduce the potential problem of an unexpected runtime error by neatly packaging the use of a resource.

There are two forms of the using statement. The first form is the following, and is illustrated in Figure 9-11.

- The code between the parentheses allocates the resource.

- The *Statement* is the code that uses the resource.

- The using statement *implicitly generates* the code to dispose of the resource.

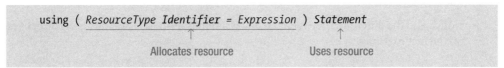

Unexpected runtime errors are called *exceptions*, and are covered in Chapter 11. The standard way of handling the possibility of exceptions is to place the code that might cause an exception in a try block, and place any code that *must* be executed, whether or not there is an exception, into a finally block.

This form of the using statement does exactly that. It performs the following:

- Allocates the resource

- Places the *Statement* in a try block

- Creates a call to the resource's Dispose method and places it in a finally block.

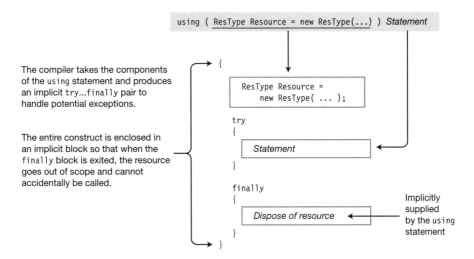

Figure 9-11. *The effect of the using statement*

Example of the using Statement

The following code uses the using statement twice—once with a class called TextWriter, and once with a class called TextReader, both from the System.IO namespace. Both classes implement the IDisposable interface, as required by the using statement.

- The TextWriter resource opens a text file for writing and writes a line to the file.

- The TextReader resource then opens the same text file, and reads and displays the contents, line by line.

- In both cases, the using statement makes sure that the objects' Dispose methods are called.

- Notice also the difference between the using statements in Main and the using directives on the first two lines.

```
using System;                    // using DIRECTIVE; not using statement
using System.IO;                 // using DIRECTIVE; not using statement

namespace UsingStatement
{
    class Program
    {
        static void Main( )
        {
            // using statement
            using (TextWriter tw = File.CreateText("Lincoln.txt") )
            {
                tw.WriteLine("Four score and seven years ago, ...");
            }

            // using statement
            using (TextReader tr = File.OpenText("Lincoln.txt"))
            {
                string InputString;
                while (null != (InputString = tr.ReadLine()))
                    Console.WriteLine(InputString);
            }
        }
    }
}
```

This code produces the following output:

```
Four score and seven years ago, ...
```

Multiple Resources and Nesting

The using statement can also be used with multiple resources of the same type, with the resource declarations separated with commas. The syntax is the following:

```
         Only one type
             ↓              ↓           ↓
using ( ResourceType Id1 = Expr1,  Id2 = Expr2, ... ) EmbeddedStatement
```

For example, in the following code, each using statement allocates and uses two resources.

```
static void Main()
{
   using (TextWriter tw1 = File.CreateText("Lincoln.txt"),
                    tw2 = File.CreateText("Franklin.txt"))
   {
      tw1.WriteLine("Four score and seven years ago, ...");
      tw2.WriteLine("Early to bed; Early to rise ...");
   }

   using (TextReader tr1 = File.OpenText("Lincoln.txt"),
                    tr2 = File.OpenText("Franklin.txt"))
   {
      string InputString;
      while (null != (InputString = tr1.ReadLine()))
         Console.WriteLine(InputString);
      while (null != (InputString = tr2.ReadLine()))
         Console.WriteLine(InputString);
   }
}
```

Another characteristic of using statements is that they can be nested. For example, in the following code, there are two things to notice—besides the nesting of the using statements, also note that it is not necessary to use a block with the second using statement because it consists of only a single, simple statement.

```
using (TextWriter tw1 = File.CreateText("Lincoln.txt"))
{
   tw1.WriteLine("Four score and seven years ago, ...");

   using( TextWriter tw2 = File.CreateText("Franklin.txt")) // Nested
      tw2.WriteLine("Early to bed; Early to rise ...");       // Single
}
```

Another Form of the using Statement

Another form of the using statement is the following:

```
Keyword   Resource      Uses resource
   ↓          ↓              ↓
using ( Expression ) EmbeddedStatement
```

In this form, the resource is declared before the using statement.

```
TextWriter tw = File.CreateText("Lincoln.txt");          // Resource declared

using ( tw )                                             // using statement
    tw.WriteLine("Four score and seven years ago, ...");
```

Although this form still ensures that the Dispose method will always be called after you use the resource, it does not protect you from attempting to use the resource after the using statement has deallocated it. It therefore gives less protection and is discouraged. This form is illustrated in Figure 9-12.

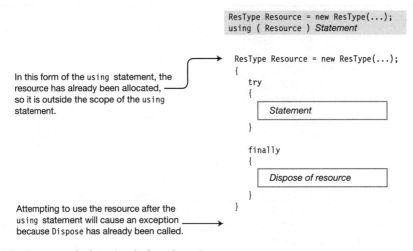

Figure 9-12. *Resource declaration before the using statement*

Other Statements

There are other statements that are associated with particular features of the language. These statements are covered in the sections dealing with those features. The statements covered in other chapters are shown in Table 9-1.

Table 9-1. *Statements Covered in Other Chapters*

Statement	Description	Relevant Chapter
checked, unchecked	These statements control the overflow-checking context.	Chapter 18
foreach	This statement iterates through each member of a collection.	Chapter 20
try, throw	These statements are associated with exceptions.	Chapter 11
return	This statement returns control to the calling function member, and can also return a value.	Chapter 5
yield	This statement is used with iterators.	Chapter 20

CHAPTER 10

Namespaces and Assemblies

Referencing Other Assemblies
Namespaces
The using Directives
The Structure of an Assembly
The Identity of an Assembly
Strongly Named Assemblies
Private Deployment of an Assembly
Shared Assemblies and the GAC
Configuration Files
Delayed Signing

Referencing Other Assemblies

In Chapter 1, you took a high-level look at the compilation process. You saw that the compiler takes the source code file and produces an output file called an *assembly*. In this chapter, you will take a closer look at assemblies and how they are produced and deployed. You will also look at how namespaces help organize types.

All the programs you've seen so far have, for the most part, declared and used their own classes. In many projects, however, you will want to use classes or types from other assemblies. These other assemblies might come from the BCL, a third-party vendor, or you might have created them yourself. These are called *class libraries*, and the names of their assembly files generally end with the `.dll` extension rather than the `.exe` extension.

For example, suppose that you want to create a class library that contains classes and types that can be used by other assemblies. The source code for a simple library is shown in the following example and is contained in a file called `SuperLib.cs`. The library contains a single public class called `SquareWidget`. Figure 10-1 illustrates the production of the DLL.

```
public class SquareWidget
{
    public double SideLength = 0;
    public double Area
    {
        get { return SideLength * SideLength; }
    }
}
```

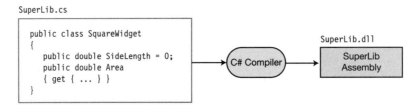

Figure 10-1. *The SuperLib source code and the resulting assembly*

Suppose also that you are writing a program called MyWidgets, and you want to use the SquareWidget class. The code for the program is in a file called MyWidgets.cs and is shown in the following example. The code simply creates an object of type SquareWidget and uses the object's members.

```
using System;

class WidgetsProgram
{
   static void Main( )
   {
      SquareWidget sq = new SquareWidget();   // From class library.
             ↑
   Not declared in this assembly
      sq.SideLength = 5.0;                     // Set the side length.
      Console.WriteLine(sq.Area);             // Print out the area.
   }      ↑
}   Not declared in this assembly
```

Notice that the code doesn't declare class SquareWidget. Instead, you use the class defined in SuperLib. When you compile the MyWidgets program, however, the compiler must be aware that your code uses assembly SuperLib so it can get the information about class SquareWidget. To do this, you need to give the compiler a *reference* to the assembly, by giving its name and location.

In Visual Studio, you can add references to a project in the following way:

- Select the Solution Explorer and find the References folder underneath the project name. The References folder contains a list of the assemblies used by the project.

- Right-click the References folder and select Add Reference. There are five tab pages from which to choose, allowing you to find the class library in different ways.

- For our program, select the Browse tab and browse to the DLL file and select it.

- Click the OK button, and the reference is added to the project.

After you've added the reference, you can compile MyWidgets. The full compilation process is illustrated in Figure 10-2.

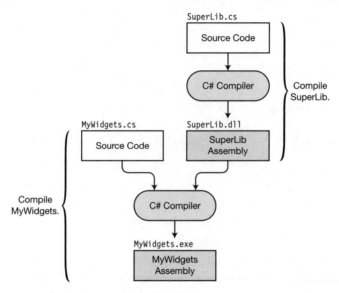

Figure 10-2. *Referencing another assembly*

The mscorlib Library

There's a class library that I've been using in almost every example in the book so far. It is the one that contains the Console class. The Console class is defined in an assembly called mscorlib in a file called mscorlib.dll. You won't find this assembly listed in the References folder, however. Assembly mscorlib contains the definitions of the C# types, and the basic types for most .NET languages. It must always be referenced when compiling a C# program, so Visual Studio does not show it in the References folder.

When you take into account mscorlib, the compilation process for MyWidgets looks more like the representation shown in Figure 10-3. After this, I will assume the use of the mscorlib assembly, without representing it again.

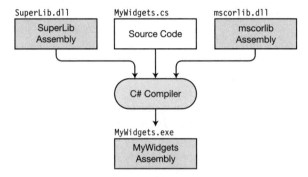

Figure 10-3. *Referencing class libraries*

Now suppose that your program has been working fine with the SquareWidget class, but you want to expand its capabilities to use a class called CircleWidget, which is defined in a different assembly called UltraLib. The MyWidgets source code now looks like the following. It creates a SquareWidget object as defined in SuperLib, and a CircleWidget object as defined in UltraLib.

```
class WidgetsProgram
{
   static void Main( )
   {
      SquareWidget sq = new SquareWidget();       // From SuperLib
      ...

      CircleWidget circle = new CirclWidget();    // From UltraLib
      ...
   }
}
```

The source code for class library UltraLib is shown in the following example. Notice that besides class CircleWidget, like library SuperLib, it also declares a class called SquareWidget. You can compile UltraLib to a DLL and add it to the list of references in project MyWidgets.

```
public class SquareWidget
{
   ...
}

public class CircleWidget
{
   public double Radius = 0;
   public double Area
   {
      get { ... }
   }
}
```

When you attempt to compile program MyWidgets, however, the compiler produces an error message, because it doesn't know which version of class SquareWidget to instantiate. This *name clash* is illustrated in Figure 10-4.

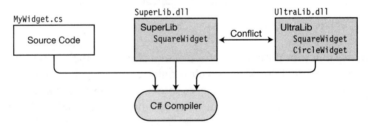

Figure 10-4. *Since assemblies SuperLib and UltraLib both contain declarations for a class called SquareWidget, the compiler doesn't know which one to instantiate.*

Namespaces

In the MyWidgets example, since you have the source code, you can solve the name clash by just changing the name of the SquareWidget class in either the SuperLib source code or the UltraLib source code. But what if these libraries had been developed by separate companies, and you didn't have the source code? Suppose that SuperLib was produced by a company called MyCorp, and UltraLib was produced by the ABCCorp company. In that case, you wouldn't be able to use them together if you used any classes or types where there was a clash.

As you can imagine, with your development machine containing assemblies produced by dozens of different companies, there is likely to be a certain amount of duplication in the names of classes. It would be a shame if you couldn't use two assemblies in the same program just because they happened to have type names in common. The *namespace* feature helps you avoid this problem.

Namespaces group a set of types together and give them a name, called the *namespace name*. The namespace name should be descriptive of the contents of the namespace and be distinctive from other namespace names.

The following shows the syntax for declaring a namespace. The names of all the classes and other types declared between the curly braces are *members* of the namespace.

```
Keyword      Namespace name
   ↓             ↓
namespace SimpleNamespace
{
    TypeDeclarations
}
```

Now suppose that the programmers at MyCorp have modified the source code as shown in the following example. It now has a namespace that surrounds the class declarations. Notice two interesting things about the namespace name:

- The company name is at the beginning of the namespace name.

- Namespaces can contain periods.

```
   Company name  Period
             ↓ ↓
   namespace MyCorp.SuperLib
   {
       public class SquareWidget
       {
           public double SideLength = 0;
           public double Area
           {
               get { return SideLength * SideLength; }
           }
       }
   }
```

When the MyCorp company ships you the new updated assembly, you can use it by modifying the MyWidgets program as shown here. Notice that instead of just using the class name (since it's ambiguous between the two class libraries), you preface the namespace name to the class name and separate the two with a period. The entire string, with the namespace name and the class name, is called the *fully qualified name*.

```
class WidgetsProgram {
   static void Main( )
   {              Fully qualified name                     Fully qualified name
                         ↓                                        ↓

      MyCorp.SuperLib.SquareWidget sq = new MyCorp.SuperLib.SquareWidget();
                 ↑            ↑
          Namespace name   Class name


      CircleWidget circle = new CircleWidget();
      ...
```

Now that you have explicitly specified the SuperLib version of SquareWidget in your code, the compiler will no longer have a problem distinguishing the classes. The fully qualified name is a bit long to type, but at least you can now use both libraries. A little later in the chapter, you'll use the using alias directive to solve the inconvenience of having to repeatedly type in the fully qualified name.

If the UltraLib assembly is also updated with a namespace by the company that produces it, the ABCCorp company, the compile process would be as shown in Figure 10-5.

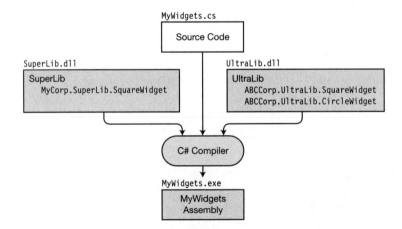

Figure 10-5. *Class libraries with namespaces*

Namespace Names

As you saw, the name of a namespace can contain the name of the company that created the assembly. The name is also used to help programmers get a quick idea of the kinds of types defined in the namespace.

Some important points about the names of namespaces are the following:

- A namespace name can be any valid identifier.

- A namespace name can include the period character, which is used to organize types into hierarchies.

For example, the following are the names of some of the namespaces in the .NET BCL:

System	System.IO
System.Data	Microsoft.CSharp
System.Drawing	Microsoft.VisualBasic
System.Drawing.Drawing2D	Microsoft.VisualBasic.IO

Namespace naming guidelines suggest the following:

- Start namespace names with the company name.

- Follow the company name with the technology name.

- Do not name a namespace with the same name as a class or type.

For example, the software development department of the Acme Widget Company develops software in the following three namespaces, as shown in the following code:

- AcmeWidgets.SuperWidget

- AcmeWidgets.Media

- AcmeWidgets.Games

```
namespace AcmeWidgets.SuperWidget.SPDComponent
{
   class SPDBase ...
   ...
}
```

More About Namespaces

There are several other important points you should know about namespaces:

- Every type name in a namespace must be different from all the others.

- The types in a namespace are called *members* of the namespace.

- A source file can contain any number of namespace declarations, either sequentially or nested.

Figure 10-6 shows a source file on the left that declares two namespaces sequentially, with several types in each one. Notice that even though the namespaces contain several class names in common, they are differentiated by their namespace names, as shown in the assembly at the right of the figure.

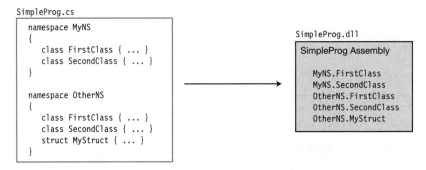

Figure 10-6. *Multiple namespaces in a source file*

The .NET Framework BCL offers thousands of defined classes and types to choose from in building your programs. To help organize this array of available functionality, types with related functionality are declared in the same namespace. The BCL uses more than 100 namespaces to organize its types.

Namespaces Spread Across Files

A namespace is not closed. This means that you can add more type declarations to it by declaring it again either later in the source file or in another source file.

For example, Figure 10-7 shows the declaration of three classes, all in the same namespace, but declared in separate source files. The source files can be compiled into a single assembly, as shown in Figure 10-7, or into separate assemblies, as shown in Figure 10-8.

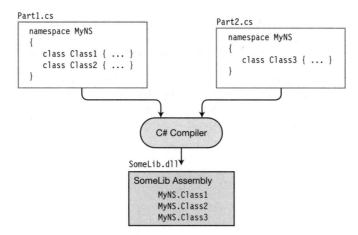

Figure 10-7. *A namespace can be spread across source files and compiled to a single assembly.*

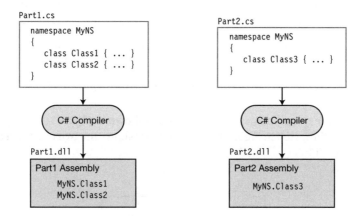

Figure 10-8. *A namespace can be spread across source files and compiled to separate assemblies.*

Nesting Namespaces

A namespace can be a member of another namespace. The member is called a *nested namespace*. Nesting namespaces allows you to create a conceptual hierarchy of types.

The nested namespace is a member of the enclosing namespace. However, the members of the nested namespace are not members of the enclosing namespace. That is, members of the enclosing namespace cannot automatically "see" the members of the nested namespace.

There are two ways of declaring a nested namespace:

- *Textual nesting*: You can create a nested namespace by placing its declaration inside the declaration body of the enclosing namespace. This is illustrated on the left in Figure 10-9. In this example, namespace OtherNS is nested in namespace MyNamespace.

- *Separate declaration*: You can also create a separate declaration for the nested namespace, but you must use its fully qualified name in the declaration. This is illustrated on the right in Figure 10-9. Notice that in the declaration of nested namespace OtherNS, the fully qualified name MyNamespace.OtherNS is used.

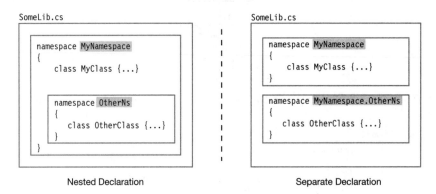

Figure 10-9. *The two forms of declaring a nested namespace are equivalent.*

Both forms of the nested namespace declarations shown in Figure 10-9 produce the same assembly, as illustrated in Figure 10-10. The figure shows the two classes declared in file SomeLib.cs, with their fully qualified names.

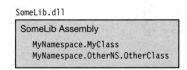

Figure 10-10. *Nested namespace structure*

The using Directives

Fully qualified names can be quite long, and using them throughout the code could become quite tedious. There are two compiler directives, however, that allow you to avoid having to use fully qualified names—the *using namespace directive* and the *using alias directive*.

Two important points about the using directives are the following:

- They must be placed at the top of the source file, *before any type declarations*.

- They apply for all the namespaces in the current source file.

The using Namespace Directive

You saw in the MyWidgets example several sections back that you can specify a class by using the fully qualified name. You can avoid having to use the long name by placing *using namespace* directives at the top of the source file.

The using namespace directive instructs the compiler that you will be using classes from certain specific namespaces. You can then use the simple class names without having to fully qualify them.

When the compiler encounters a name that is not in the current namespace, it checks the list of namespaces given in the using namespace directives and appends the unknown name to the first namespace in the list. If the resulting fully qualified name matches a class in this assembly or a referenced assembly, the compiler uses that class. If it does not match, it tries the next namespace in the list.

The using namespace directive consists of the keyword using, followed by a namespace identifier.

```
Keyword
   ↓
using System ;
            ↑
   Name of namespace
```

One method I have been using throughout the text is the WriteLine method, which is a member of class Console, in the System namespace. Rather than use its fully qualified name throughout the code, I simplified our work just a bit, by the use of the using namespace directive at the top of the code.

For example, the following code uses the using namespace directive in the first line to state that the code uses classes or other types from the System namespace.

```
using System;                                // using namespace directive
    ...
System.Console.WriteLine("This is text 1");  // Use fully qualified name.
Console.WriteLine("This is text 2");         // Use directive.
```

The using Alias Directive

The *using alias directive* allows you to assign an alias for either of the following:

- A namespace

- A type in a namespace

For example, the following code shows the use of two using alias directives. The first directive instructs the compiler that identifier Syst is an alias for namespace System. The second directive says that identifier SC is an alias for class System.Console.

```
Keyword  Alias   Namespace
   ↓       ↓         ↓
  using Syst = System;
  using SC   = System.Console;
    ↑    ↑
Keyword Alias            Class
```

The following code uses these aliases. All three lines of code in Main call the System.Console.WriteLine method.

- The first statement in Main uses the alias for a *namespace*—System.

- The second statement uses the *fully qualified name* of the method.

- The third statement uses the alias for a *class*—Console.

```
using Syst = System;                  // using alias directive
using SC   = System.Console;          // using alias directive

namespace MyNamespace
{
   class SomeClass
   {
      static void Main()
      { Alias for namespace
           ↓
         Syst.Console.WriteLine  ("Using the namespace alias.");
         System.Console.WriteLine("Using fully qualified name.");
         SC.WriteLine            ("Using the type alias");
          ↑
      } Alias for class
   }
}
```

The Structure of an Assembly

As you saw in Chapter 1, an assembly does not contain native machine code, but Common Intermediate Language (CIL) code. It also contains everything needed by the Just-In-Time (JIT) compiler to convert the CIL into native code at run time, including references to other assemblies it references. The file extension for an assembly is generally .exe or .dll.

Most assemblies are composed of a single file. Figure 10-11 illustrates the four main sections of an assembly.

- The assembly *manifest* contains the following:
  - The components of the assembly name
  - A list of the files that make up the assembly
  - A map of where things are in the assembly
  - Information about other assemblies that are referenced

- The *type metadata* section contains the information about all the types defined in the assembly. This information contains everything there is to know about each type.

- The *CIL* section contains all the intermediate code for the assembly.

- The *resources* section is optional, but can contain graphics or language resources.

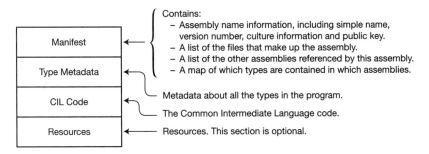

Figure 10-11. *The structure of a single-file assembly*

Although most assemblies comprise a single file, some have more. For an assembly with multiple modules, one file is the *primary module* and the others are *secondary modules*.

- The primary module contains the manifest of the assembly, and references to the secondary modules.

- The filenames of secondary modules end with the extension `.netmodule`.

- Multiple-file assemblies are considered a single unit. They are deployed together and versioned together.

Figure 10-12 illustrates a multi-file assembly with secondary modules.

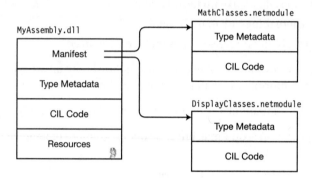

Figure 10-12. *A multi-file assembly*

The Identity of an Assembly

In the .NET Framework, the filenames of assemblies are not as important as in other operating systems and environments. What is much more important is the *identity* of an assembly.

The identity of an assembly has four components that together should uniquely identify it. These four components are the following:

- *Simple name*: This is just the filename without the file extension. Every assembly has a simple name. It is also called the *assembly name*, or the *friendly name*.

- *Version number*: This consists of a string of four period-separated integers, in the form `MajorVersion.MinorVersion.Build.Revision`. For example, `2.0.35.9`.

- *Culture information*: This is a string that consists of two to five characters representing a language, or a language and a country or region. For example, the culture name for English as used in the United States is `en-US`. For German as used in Germany, it is `de-DE`.

- *Public key*: This 128-byte string should be unique to the company producing the assembly.

The public key is part of a public/private key pair, which is a set of two very large, specially chosen numbers that can be used to create secure digital signatures. The public key, as its name implies, can be made public. The private key must be guarded by the owner. The public key is part of the assembly's identity. You will look at the use of the private key later in the chapter.

The components of an assembly's name are embedded in the assembly's manifest. Figure 10-13 illustrates this section of the manifest.

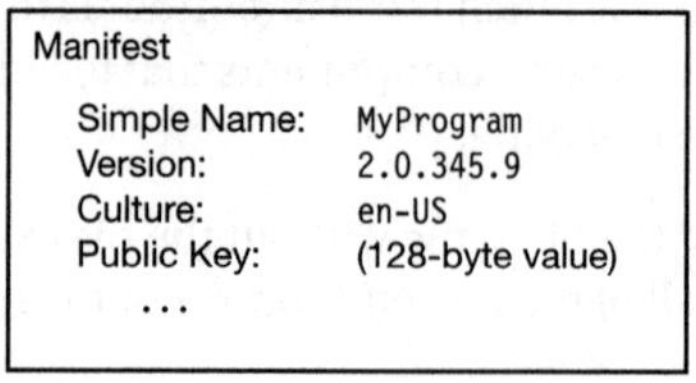

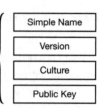

```
Manifest
    Simple Name:    MyProgram
    Version:        2.0.345.9
    Culture:        en-US
    Public Key:     (128-byte value)
        . . .
```

Figure 10-13. *The components of an assembly identity in the manifest*

Figure 10-14 shows some of the terms used in the .NET documentation and literature regarding the identity of an assembly.

Identity – All four of the components listed at the right together constitute the identity of an assembly.

Fully Qualified Name – A textual listing of the simple name, version, culture, and the public key, represented by a 16-byte public key token.

Display Name – Same as fully qualified name.

| Simple Name |
| Version |
| Culture |
| Public Key |

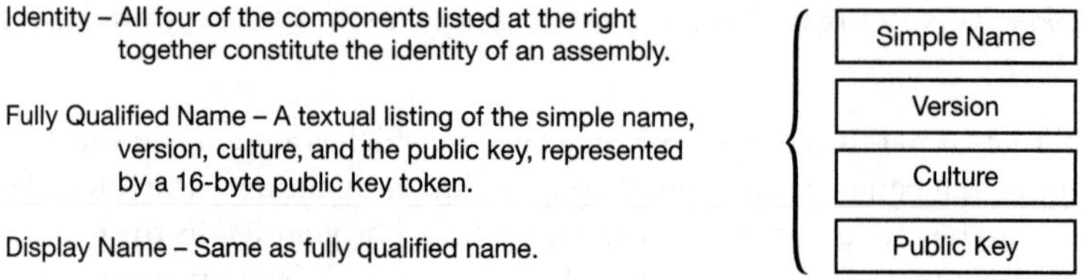

Figure 10-14. *Terms for an assembly's identity*

Strongly Named Assemblies

A *strongly named* assembly is one that has a unique digital signature attached to it. Strongly named assemblies are much more secure than assemblies that do not have strong names, for the following reasons:

- Uniqueness of the assembly. No one else can create an assembly with the same strong name, so the user can be sure that the assembly came from the claimed source.

- The contents of an assembly with a strong name cannot be altered without the security components of the CLR catching the modification.

A *weakly named* assembly is one that is not strongly named. Since a weakly named assembly does not have a digital signature, it is inherently insecure. Because a chain is only as strong as its weakest link, strongly named assemblies can access only other strongly named assemblies.

The programmer does not produce the strong name. The compiler produces it by taking information about the assembly and hashing it to create a unique digital signature that it attaches to the assembly. The information components it uses in the hash process are the following:

- The sequence of bytes composing the assembly

- The simple name

- The version number

- The culture information

- The public/private key pair

Creating a Strongly Named Assembly

To strongly name an assembly by using Visual Studio 2005, you must have a copy of the public/private key pair file. If you don't have a key file, you can have Visual Studio generate one for you. You can then do the following:

- Open the Properties of the project.

- Select the Signing tab.

- Select the Sign the Assembly check box and enter the location of the key file.

When you compile, the compiler will produce a strongly named assembly. The inputs and output of the compiler are illustrated in Figure 10-15.

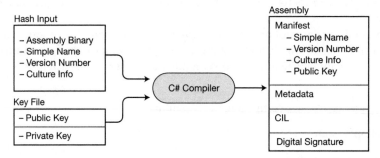

Figure 10-15. *Creating a strongly named assembly*

Private Deployment of an Assembly

To deploy a program on a target machine can be as simple as creating a directory on the machine and copying the application to it. If the application doesn't need any other assemblies such as DLLs, or the required DLLs are in the same directory, the program should work just fine where it is. Programs deployed this way are called *private assemblies*, and this method of deployment is called *xcopy* deployment.

Private assemblies can be placed in almost any directory, and are self-sufficient as long as all the files on which they depend are in the same directory or a subdirectory. As a matter of fact, you could have several directories in various parts of the file system, each with the identical set of assemblies, and they would all work fine in their various locations.

Some important things to know about private assembly deployment are the following:

- The directory in which the private assemblies are placed is called the *application directory*.

- A private assembly can be either strongly named or weakly named.

- There is no need to register components in the registry.

- To uninstall a private assembly, just delete it from the file system.

Shared Assemblies and the GAC

Private assemblies are very useful, but sometimes you will want to put a DLL in a central place so that a single copy can be shared by other assemblies on the system. .NET has such a repository, called the *global assembly cache* (GAC). An assembly placed into the GAC is called a *shared assembly*.

Some important facts about the GAC are the following:

- Only strongly named assemblies can be added to the GAC.

- Although earlier versions of the GAC accepted only files with the .dll extension, you can now add assemblies with the .exe extension as well.

- The GAC is located in a subdirectory named Assembly, of the Windows system directory.

Installing Assemblies into the GAC

When you attempt to install an assembly into the GAC, the security components of the CLR must first verify that the digital signature on the assembly is valid. If there is no digital signature, or if it is invalid, the system will not install the assembly into the GAC.

This is a one-time check, however. After an assembly is in the GAC, no further checks are required when it is referenced by a running program.

The gacutil.exe command-line utility allows you to add and delete assemblies from the GAC, and to list the assemblies it contains. The three most useful flags are the following:

- /i: Inserts an assembly into the GAC

- /u: Uninstalls an assembly from the GAC

- /l: Lists the assemblies in the GAC

Side-by-Side Execution in the GAC

After an assembly is deployed to the GAC, it can be used by other assemblies in the system. Remember, however, that an assembly's identity consists of all four parts of the fully qualified name. So, if the version number of a library changes, or if it has a different public key, these differences specify different assemblies.

The result is that there can be many different assemblies in the GAC that have the same filename. Although they have the same filename, *they are different assemblies* and coexist perfectly fine together in the GAC. This makes it easy for different applications to use different versions of the same DLL at the same time, since they are different assemblies with different identities. This is called *side-by-side execution*.

Figure 10-16 illustrates four different DLLs in the GAC that all have the same filename— MyLibrary.dll. Looking at the figure, you can see that the first three come from the same company, because they have the same public key, and the fourth comes from a different source, since it has a different public key. These versions differ as follows:

- An English version 1.0.0.0, from company A

- An English version 2.0.0.0, from company A

- A German version 1.0.0.0, from company A

- An English version 1.0.0.0, from company B

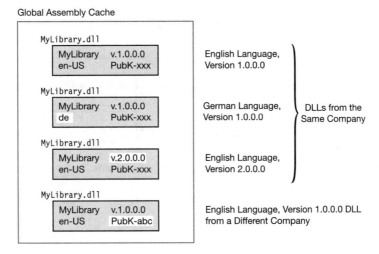

Figure 10-16. *Four different side-by-side DLLs in the GAC*

Configuration Files

Configuration files contain information about the application, for use by the CLR at run time. They can instruct the CLR to do such things as use a different version of a DLL, or to look in additional directories when searching for a DLL referenced by the program.

Configuration files consist of XML code and don't contain C# code. The details of writing the XML code are beyond the scope of this text, but you should understand the purpose of configuration files and how they are used. One way they are used is to update an application assembly to use the new version of a DLL.

Suppose, for example, that you have an application that references a DLL in the GAC. The identity of the reference in the application's manifest must exactly match the identity of the DLL assembly in the GAC. If a new version of the DLL is released, it can be added to the GAC, where it can happily coexist with the old version.

The application, however, still has embedded in its manifest the identity of the old version of the DLL. Unless you recompile the application and make it reference the new version of the DLL, it will continue to use the old version. That's fine, if that's what you want.

If, however, you do not want to recompile the application but want it to use the new DLL, then you can create a configuration file telling the CLR to use the new version rather than the old version. The configuration file is placed in the application directory.

Figure 10-17 illustrates objects in the runtime process. The MyProgram.exe application on the left calls for version 1.0.0.0 of the MyLibrary.dll, as indicated by the dashed arrow. But the application has a configuration file, which instructs the CLR to load version 2.0.0.0 instead. Notice that the name of the configuration file consists of the full name of the executable file including the extension, plus the additional extension .config.

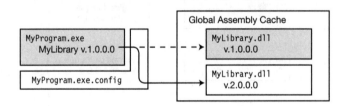

Figure 10-17. *Using a configuration file to bind to a new version*

Delayed Signing

It is important that companies carefully guard the private key of their official public/private key pair. Otherwise, if untrustworthy people were to obtain it, they could publish code masquerading as the company's code. To avoid this, companies clearly cannot allow free access to the file containing their public/private key pair. In large companies, the final strong naming of an assembly is often performed at the very end of the development process, by a special group with access to the key pair.

This can cause problems, though, in the development and testing processes, for several reasons. First, since the public key is one of the four components of an assembly's identity, it can't be set until the public key is supplied. Also, a weakly named assembly cannot be deployed to the GAC. Both the developers and testers need to be able to compile and test the code in the way it will be deployed on release, including its identity and location in the GAC.

To allow for this, there is a modified form of assigning a strong name, called *delayed signing*, or *partial signing*, that overcomes these problems, but without releasing access to the private key.

In delayed signing, the compiler uses only the public key of the public/private key pair. The public key can then be placed in the manifest to complete the assembly's identity. Delayed signing also uses a block of zeros to reserve space for the digital signature.

To create a delay-signed assembly, you must do two things. First, create a copy of the key file that has only the public key, rather than the public/private key pair. Next, add an additional attribute called `DelaySignAttribute` to the assembly scope of the source code and set its value to `true`.

Figure 10-18 shows the input and output for producing a delay-signed assembly. Notice the following in the figure:

- In the input, the DelaySignAttribute is located in the source files, and the key file contains only the public key.

- In the output, there is space reserved for the digital signature at the bottom of the assembly.

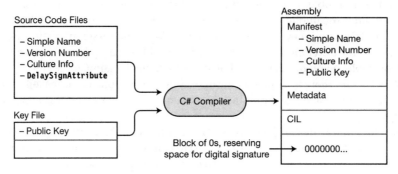

Figure 10-18. *Creating a delay-signed assembly*

If you try to deploy the delay-signed assembly to the GAC, the CLR will not allow it, because it is not strongly named. You must first issue a command-line command that disables the GAC's signature verification on this machine, for this assembly only, and allows it to be installed in the GAC. To do this, issue the following command from the Visual Studio command prompt.

```
sn -vr MyAssembly.dll
```

You've now looked at unsigned assemblies, delay-signed assemblies, and strongly named assemblies. Figure 10-19 summarizes the differences in their structures.

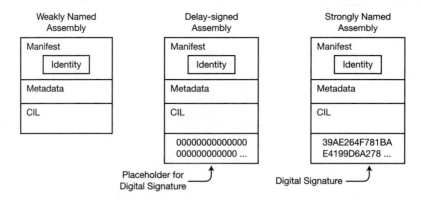

Figure 10-19. *The structures of different assembly signing stages*

CHAPTER 11

■ ■ ■

Exceptions

What Are Exceptions?
The try Statement
The Exception Classes
The catch Clause
Examples Using Specific catch Clauses
The catch Clauses Section
The finally Block
Finding a Handler for an Exception
Searching Further
Throwing Exceptions
Throwing Without an Exception Object

What Are Exceptions?

An *exception* is a runtime error in a program that violates a system or application constraint, or a condition that is not expected to occur during normal operation. Examples are when a program tries to divide a number by zero or tries to write to a read-only file. When these occur, the system catches the error and *raises* an exception.

If the program has not provided code to handle the exception, the system will halt the program.

For example, the following code raises an exception when it attempts to divide by zero:

```
static void Main()
{
    int x = 10, y = 0;
    x /= y;                  // Attempt to divide by zero--raises an exception
}
```

When this code is run, the system displays the following error message:

```
Unhandled Exception: System.DivideByZeroException: Attempted to divide by zero.   at
Exceptions_1.Program.Main() in C:\Progs\Exceptions\Program.cs:line 12
```

The try Statement

The try statement allows you to designate blocks of code to be guarded for exceptions, and to supply code to handle those exceptions. The try statement consists of three sections, as shown in Figure 11-1.

- The try *block* contains the code that is being guarded for exceptions.

- The catch *clauses section* contains one or more catch *clauses*. These are blocks of code to handle the exceptions. They are also known as *exception handlers*.

- The finally *block* contains code to be executed under all circumstances, whether or not an exception is raised.

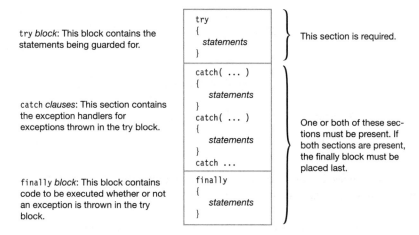

Figure 11-1. *Structure of the try statement*

Handling the Exception

The previous example showed that attempting to divide by zero causes an exception. You can modify the program to handle that exception by placing the code inside a try block and supplying a simple catch clause. When the exception is raised, it is caught and handled in the catch block.

```
static void Main()
{
   int x = 10;

   try
   {
      int y = 0;
      x /= y;                        // Raises an exception
   }
   catch
   {
      ...                            // Code to handle the exception

      Console.WriteLine("Handling all exceptions - Keep on Running");
   }
}
```

This code produces the following message. Notice that, other than the output message, there is no indication that an exception has occurred.

```
Handling all exceptions - Keep on Running
```

The Exception Classes

There are many different types of exceptions that can occur in a program. The BCL defines a number of exception classes, each representing a specific type of exception. When an exception occurs, the CLR

- Creates an exception object for the type of the exception that occurred

- Looks for an appropriate `catch` clause to handle the exception

All exception classes are ultimately derived from the `System.Exception` class. A portion of the exception inheritance hierarchy is shown in Figure 11-2.

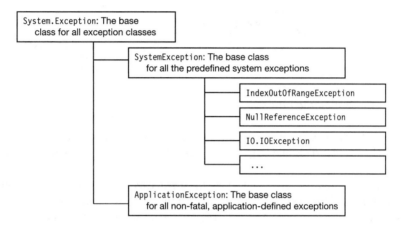

Figure 11-2. *Structure of the exception hierarchy*

An exception object contains read-only properties with information about the exception that caused it. Some of these properties are shown in Table 11-1.

Table 11-1. *Selected Properties of an Exception Object*

Property	Type	Description
Message	string	This property contains an error message explaining the cause of the exception.
StackTrace	string	This property contains information describing where the exception occurred.
InnerException	Exception	If the current exception was raised by another exception, this property contains a reference to the previous exception.
HelpLink	string	This property can be set by application-defined exceptions to give a URN or URL for information on the cause of the exception.
Source	string	If not set by an application-defined exception, this property contains the name of the assembly where the exception originated.

The catch Clause

The catch clause handles exceptions. There are three forms of the catch clause, allowing different levels of processing. The forms are shown in Figure 11-3.

```
catch                              General catch Clause
{                                    – Does not have a parameter list after the catch keyword.
   Statements                        – Matches any type of exception raised in the try block.
}
- - - - - - - - - - - - - - - - - - - - - - - - - - - - - - - - - - - - - -
catch( ExceptionType )             Specific catch Clause
{                                    – Takes the name of an exception class as a single parameter.
   Statements                        – Matches any exception of the named type.
}
- - - - - - - - - - - - - - - - - - - - - - - - - - - - - - - - - - - - - -
                                   Specific catch Clause with ID
catch( ExceptionType  InstID )       – Includes an identifier after the name of the exception class.
{                                    – The identifier acts as a local variable in the block of the catch
   Statements                          clause, and is called the exception variable.
}                                    – The exception variable references the exception object, and
                                       can be used to access information about the object.
```

Figure 11-3. *The three forms of the catch clause*

The *general* catch *clause* can accept any exception, but cannot determine the type of exception that caused it. This allows general processing and cleanup for whatever exception might occur.

The *specific* catch *clause* form takes the name of an exception class as a parameter. It matches exceptions of the specified class or exception classes derived from it.

The *specific* catch *clause with ID* form gives you the most information about the exception. It matches exceptions of the specified class, or exception classes derived from it. It also gives you an exception instance ID, called the *exception variable*, which is a reference to the exception object created by the CLR. You can access the exception variable's properties within the block of the catch clause to get specific information about the exception raised.

For example, the following code handles exceptions of type IndexOutOfRangeException. When one occurs, a reference to the actual exception object is passed into the code with parameter name e. The three WriteLine statements each read a string field from the exception object.

```
          Exception type      Exception variable
               ↓                     ↓
catch ( IndexOutOfRangeException  e )
{                                    Accessing the exception variable
                                             ↓
    Console.WriteLine( "Message: {0}", e.Message );
    Console.WriteLine( "Source:  {0}", e.Source );
    Console.WriteLine( "Stack:   {0}", e.StackTrace );
```

Examples Using Specific catch Clauses

In the following code, the catch clause of a previous example has been modified to specifically handle exceptions of the DivideByZeroException class. While in the other example, the catch clause would handle any exception raised in the try block, the current example will only handle those of the DivideByZeroException class.

```
int x = 10;
try
{
   int y = 0;
   x /= y;                    // Raises an exception
}                Exception type
                     ↓
catch ( DivideByZeroException )
{
     ...
   Console.WriteLine("Handling an exception.");
}
```

For example, you could further modify the catch clause to use an exception variable. This allows you to access the exception object inside the catch block.

```
int x = 10;
try
{
   int y = 0;
   x /= y;                      // Raises an exception
}          Exception type        Exception variable
                 ↓                       ↓
catch ( DivideByZeroException  e )
{                              Accessing the exception variable
                                          ↓
   Console.WriteLine("Message: {0}", e.Message );
   Console.WriteLine("Source: {0}", e.Source );
   Console.WriteLine("Stack:   {0}", e.StackTrace );
}
```

This produces the following output:

```
Message: Attempted to divide by zero.
Source:  Exceptions 1
Stack:      at Exceptions_1.Program.Main() in C:\Progs\Exceptions 1\Exceptions 1\
Program.cs:line 14
```

The catch Clauses Section

The catch clauses section can contain multiple catch clauses. Figure 11-4 shows a summary of the catch clauses section.

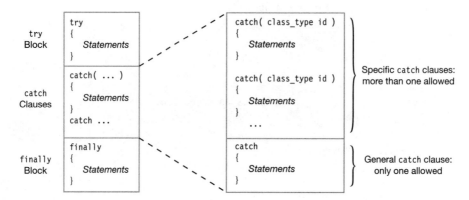

Figure 11-4. *Structure of the catch clauses section of a try statement*

When an exception is raised, the list of catch clauses is searched in order, and the first catch clause that matches the type of the exception object is executed. Because of this, there are two important rules in ordering the catch clauses. They are the following:

- The specific catch clauses must be ordered with the most specific exception types first, progressing to the most general. For example, if you declare an exception class derived from NullReferenceException, the catch clause for your derived exception type should be listed before the catch clause for NullReferenceException.

- If there is a general catch clause, it must be the last clause—after all specific catch clauses.

The finally Block

If a program's flow of control enters a try statement that has a finally block, the finally block is *always* executed. The flow of control is illustrated in Figure 11-5.

- If no exception occurs inside the try block, then at the end of the try block, control goes to the finally block—skipping over any catch clauses.

- If an exception occurs inside the try block, then any appropriate catch clauses in the catch clauses section are executed, followed by the finally block.

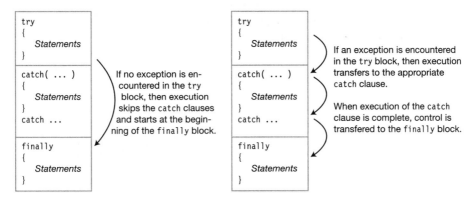

Figure 11-5. *Execution of the finally block*

Even if a try block has a return statement, the finally block will still always be executed before returning to the calling code. For example, in the following code, there is a return statement in the middle of the try block that is executed under certain conditions. This does not allow it to bypass the finally statement.

```
try
{
    if (inVal < 10) {
        Console.Write("First Branch  - ");
        return;
    }
    else
        Console.Write("Second Branch - ");
}
finally
{ Console.WriteLine("In finally statement"); }
```

This code produces the following output when variable inVal has the value 5.

```
First Branch  - In finally statement
```

Finding a Handler for an Exception

When a program raises an exception, the system checks to see whether the program has provided an exception handler for it. The flow of control is illustrated in Figure 11-6.

- If the exception occurred inside a try block, the system will check to see whether any of the catch clauses can handle the exception.

- If an appropriate catch clause is found
  - The catch clause is executed.
  - If there is a finally block, it is executed.
  - Execution continues after the end of the try statement (i.e., after the finally block, or after the last catch clause if there is no finally block).

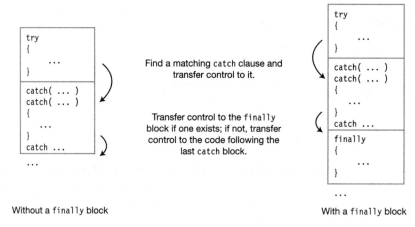

Find a matching catch clause and transfer control to it.

Transfer control to the finally block if one exists; if not, transfer control to the code following the last catch block.

Without a finally block

With a finally block

Figure 11-6. *Exception with handler in current try statement*

Searching Further

If the exception was raised in a section of code that was not guarded by a try statement, or if the try statement did not have a matching exception handler—the system will have to look further for a matching handler. It will do this by searching down the call stack, in sequence, to see whether there is an enclosing try block with a matching handler.

Figure 11-7 illustrates the search process. On the left of the figure is the calling structure of the code, and on the right is the call stack. The figure shows that Method2 is called from inside the try block of Method1. If an exception occurs inside the try block of Method2, the system performs the following steps:

- First, the system checks to see whether Method2 was called from an enclosing try statement.
  - If so, Method2's catch clauses are checked to see whether any of them match the exception.
  - If not, the system continues down the call stack to Method1, searching for an appropriate handler.

- If Method1 has an appropriate catch clause
  - The system goes back to the top of the call stack—which is Method2.
  - The system executes Method2's finally block, and pops Method2 off the stack.
  - It then executes Method1's catch clause and its finally block.

- If Method1 does not have an appropriate catch clause, it will continue searching down the call stack.

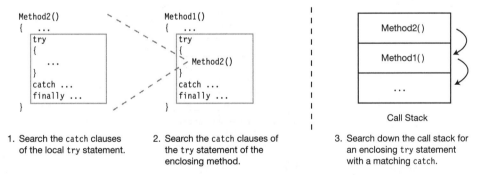

1. Search the catch clauses of the local try statement.

2. Search the catch clauses of the try statement of the enclosing method.

3. Search down the call stack for an enclosing try statement with a matching catch.

Figure 11-7. *Searching down the call stack*

General Algorithm

The general algorithm for handling an exception is shown in Figure 11-8.

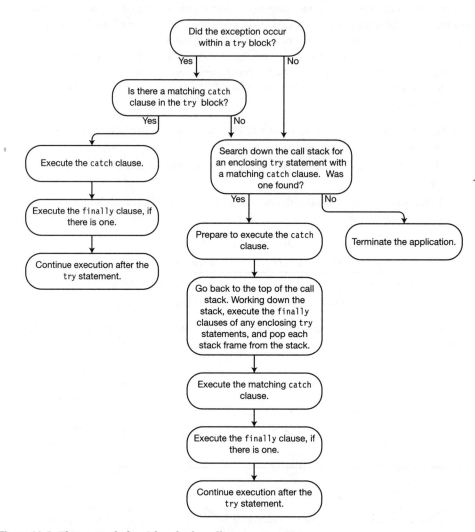

Figure 11-8. *The general algorithm for handling an exception*

Example of Searching Down the Call Stack

In this program, Main starts execution and calls method A, which calls method B. A description and diagram of the process are given in the following code and in Figure 11-9.

```
class Program
{
    static void Main()
    {
        MyClass MCls = new MyClass();
        try
            { MCls.A(); }
        catch (DivideByZeroException e)
            { Console.WriteLine("catch clause in Main()"); }
        finally
            { Console.WriteLine("finally clause in Main()"); }
        Console.WriteLine("After try statement in Main.");
        Console.WriteLine("          -- Keep running.");
    }
}

class MyClass
{
    public void A()
    {
        try
            { B(); }
        catch (System.NullReferenceException)
            { Console.WriteLine("catch clause in A()"); }
        finally
            { Console.WriteLine("finally clause in A()"); }
    }

    void B()
    {
        int x = 10, y = 0;
        try
            { x /= y; }
        catch (System.IndexOutOfRangeException)
            { Console.WriteLine("catch clause in B()"); }
        finally
            { Console.WriteLine("finally clause in B()"); }
    }
}
```

This code produces the following output:

```
finally clause in B()
finally clause in A()
catch clause in Main()
finally clause in Main()
After try statement in Main.
            -- Keep running.
```

1. Main calls A, which calls B, which encounters a DivideByZeroException exception.

2. The system checks B's catch section for a matching catch clause. Although it has one for IndexOutOfRangeException, it does not have one for DivideByZeroException.

3. The system then moves down the call stack and checks A's catch section, where it finds that A also does not have a matching catch clause.

4. The system continues down the call stack, and checks Main's catch clause section, where it finds that Main *does* have a DivideByZeroException catch clause.

5. Although the matching catch clause has now been located, it is not executed yet. Instead, the system goes back to the top of the stack, executes B's finally clause, and pops B from the call stack.

6. The system then moves to A, executes its finally clause, and pops A from the call stack.

7. Finally, Main's matching catch clause is executed, followed by its finally clause. Execution then continues after the end of Main's try statement.

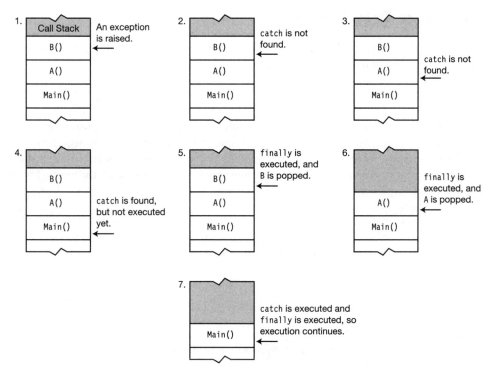

Figure 11-9. *Searching the stack for an exception handler*

Throwing Exceptions

You can make your code explicitly raise an exception by using the throw statement. The syntax for the throw statement is the following:

```
throw ExceptionObject;
```

For example, the following code defines a method called PrintArg that takes a string argument and prints it out. Inside the try block, it first checks to make sure that the argument is not null. If it is, it creates an ArgumentNullException instance and throws it. The exception instance is caught in the catch statement, and the error message is printed. Main calls the method twice: once with a null argument, and then with a valid argument.

```
class MyClass
{
   public static void PrintArg(string arg)
   {
      try
      {
         if (arg == null)
         {
            ArgumentNullException MyEx = new ArgumentNullException();
            throw MyEx;
         }
         Console.WriteLine(arg);
      }
      catch (ArgumentNullException e)
      {
         Console.WriteLine("Message:  {0}", e.Message);
      }
   }
}
```

```
class Program
{
   static void Main()
   {
      string s = null;
      MyClass.PrintArg(s);
      MyClass.PrintArg("Hi there!");
   }
}
```

This code produces the following output:

```
Message:  Value cannot be null.
Hi there!
```

Throwing Without an Exception Object

The throw statement can also be used without an exception object, inside a catch block.

- This form rethrows the current exception, and the system continues its search for additional handlers for it.

- This form can only be used inside a catch statement.

For example, the following code rethrows the exception from inside the first catch clause:

```
class MyClass
{
   public static void PrintArg(string arg)
   {
      try
      {
         try
         {
            if (arg == null)
            {
               ArgumentNullException MyEx = new ArgumentNullException();
               throw MyEx;
            }
            Console.WriteLine(arg);
         }
         catch (ArgumentNullException e)
         {
            Console.WriteLine("Inner Catch: {0}", e.Message);
            throw;
         }    ↑
      }    Rethrow the exception—no additional parameters
      catch
      {
         Console.WriteLine("Outer Catch:  Handling an Exception.");
      }
   }
}

class Program {
   static void Main() {
      string s = null;
      MyClass.PrintArg(s);
   }
}
```

This code produces the following output:

```
Inner Catch:  Value cannot be null.
Outer Catch:  Handling an Exception.
```

CHAPTER 12

■ ■ ■

Structs

What Are Structs?
Structs Are Value Types
Assigning to a Struct
Constructors and Finalizers
Field Initializers
Inheritance
Boxing and Unboxing
Structs As Return Values and Parameters
Additional Information About Structs

What Are Structs?

Structs are programmer-defined data types, very similar to classes. They have data members and function members. Although similar to classes, there are a number of important differences. The most important ones are the following:

- Classes are reference types and structs are value types.

- Structs are implicitly sealed, which means that they cannot be derived from.

The syntax for declaring a struct is similar to that of declaring a class.

```
Keyword
   ↓
struct StructName
{
    MemberDeclarations
}
```

For example, the following code declares a struct named Point. It has two public fields, named X and Y. In Main, three variables of the struct type Point are declared, and their values are assigned and printed out.

```
struct Point
{
    public int X;
    public int Y;
}

class Program
{
    static void Main()
    {
        Point First, Second, Third;

        First.X  = 10; First.Y  = 10;
        Second.X = 20; Second.Y = 20;
        Third.X = First.X + Second.X;
        Third.Y = First.Y + Second.Y;

        Console.WriteLine("First:   {0}, {1}", First.X, First.Y);
        Console.WriteLine("Second:  {0}, {1}", Second.X, Second.Y);
        Console.WriteLine("Third:   {0}, {1}", Third.X, Third.Y);
    }
}
```

Structs Are Value Types

As with all value types, a variable of a struct type contains its own data. Consequently

- A variable of a struct type cannot be null.

- Two structs cannot refer to the same object.

For example, the following code declares a class called CSimple, and a struct called Simple, and a variable of each. Figure 12-1 shows how the two would be arranged in memory.

```
class CSimple
{
   public int x;
   public int y;
}

struct Simple
{
   public int x;
   public int y;
}

class Program
{
   static void Main()
   {
      CSimple cs = new CSimple();
      Simple  ss = new Simple();
         ...
```

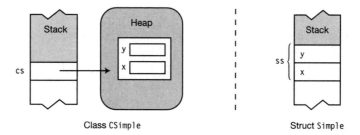

Figure 12-1. *Memory arrangement of a class versus a struct*

Assigning to a Struct

Assigning one struct to another copies the values from one to the other. This is quite different from copying from a class variable, where only the reference is copied.

Figure 12-2 shows the difference between the assignment of a class variable and a struct variable. Notice that after the class assignment, cs2 is pointing at the same object in the heap as cs1. But after the struct assignment, the values of ss2's members are the same as those of ss1.

```
class CSimple
{ public int x; public int y; }

struct Simple
{ public int x; public int y; }

class Program
{
   static void Main()
   {
      CSimple cs1 = new CSimple(), cs2 = null;         // Class instances
      Simple ss1 =  new Simple(),  ss2 = new Simple(); // Struct instances

      cs1.x = ss1.x = 5;                   // Assign 5 to ss1.x and cs1.x
      cs1.y = ss1.y = 10;                  // Assign 10 to ss1.y and cs1.y

      cs2 = cs1;                           // Assign class instance
      ss2 = ss1;                           // Assign struct instance
```

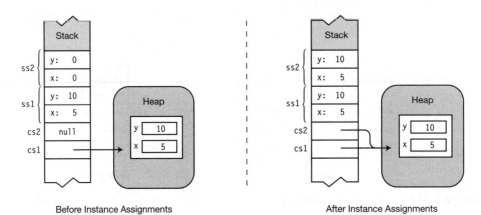

Figure 12-2. *Assigning a class variable and a struct variable*

Constructors and Finalizers

Structs can have instance and static constructors, but finalizers are not allowed.

Instance Constructors

The language implicitly supplies a parameterless constructor for every struct. This constructor sets each of the struct's members to the default value for that type. Value members are set to their default values. Reference members are set to null.

The predefined parameterless constructor exists for every struct—and you cannot delete or redefine it. You can, however, create additional constructors, as long as they have parameters. Notice that this is different from classes. For classes, the compiler will only supply an implicit parameterless constructor if no other constructors are declared.

To call a constructor, including the implicit parameterless constructor, use the new operator. Notice that the new operator is used even though the memory is not allocated from the heap.

For example, the following code declares a simple struct with a constructor that takes two int parameters. Main creates two instances of the struct—one using the implicit parameterless constructor, and the second with the declared two-parameter constructor.

```
struct Simple
{
   public int x;
   public int y;

   public Simple(int a, int b)              // Constructor with parameters
   {
      x = a;
      y = b;
   }
}

class Program
{
   static void Main()
   {                   Call implicit constructor
                              ↓
      Simple s1 = new Simple();
      Simple s2 = new Simple(5, 10);
                              ↑
                    Call constructor
      Console.WriteLine("{0},{1}", s1.x, s1.y);
      Console.WriteLine("{0},{1}", s2.x, s2.y);
   }
}
```

You can also create an instance of a struct without using the new operator. If you do this, however, there are several restrictions—you *cannot*

- Use the value of a data member until you have explicitly set it

- Call *any* function member until *all* the data members have been assigned

For example, the following code shows two instances of struct Simple created without using the new operator. When there is an attempt to access s1 without explicitly setting the data member values, the compiler produces an error message. There are no problems reading from s2 after assigning values to its members.

```
struct Simple
{
   public int x;
   public int y;
}

class Program
{
   static void Main()
   {               No constructor calls
                        ↓

      Simple s1, s2;
      Console.WriteLine("{0},{1}", s1.x, s1.y);            // Compiler error
                                    ⊤    ⊤
                              Not yet assigned
      s2.x = 5;
      s2.y = 10;
      Console.WriteLine("{0},{1}", s2.x, s2.y);            // OK
   }
}
```

Static Constructors

As with classes, the static constructors of structs create and initialize the static data members, and cannot reference instance members. Static constructors for structs follow the same rules as those for classes.

A static constructor is called before the first of either of the following two actions:

- A call to an explicitly declared constructor

- A reference to a static member of the struct

Summary of Constructors and Finalizers

Table 12-1 summarizes the use of constructors and finalizers with structs.

Table 12-1. *Summary of Constructors and Finalizers*

Type	Description
Instance constructor (parameterless)	Cannot be declared in the program. An implicit constructor is supplied by the system for all structs. It cannot be deleted or redefined by the program.
Instance constructor (with parameters)	Can be declared in the program.
Static constructor	Can be declared in the program.
Finalizer	Cannot be declared in the program. Finalizers are not allowed.

Field Initializers

Field initializers are not allowed in structs.

```
struct Simple
{              Not allowed
                   ↓
    public int x = 0;                          // Compile error
    public int y = 10;                         // Compile error
}                  ↑
           Not allowed
```

Inheritance

Structs are always implicitly sealed, and hence, you cannot derive other structs from them.

Since structs do not support inheritance, the use of several of the class member modifiers with struct members would not make sense; thus, they cannot be used in their declarations. The modifiers that cannot be used with structs are the following:

- protected

- internal

- abstract

- virtual

Structs themselves are, under the covers, derived from System.ValueType, which is derived from object.

The one inheritance-associated keyword you *can* use with a struct member is the new modifier, to override the implementation of a member of base class System.ValueType.

Boxing and Unboxing

As with other value type data, if you want to use a struct instance as a reference type object, you must make a boxed copy. Boxing and unboxing are covered in detail in Chapter 18.

Structs As Return Values and Parameters

Structs can be used as return values and parameters.

- *Return value*: When a struct is a return value, a copy is created and returned from the function member.

- *Value parameter*: When a struct is used as a value parameter, a copy of the actual parameter struct is created. The copy is used in the execution of the method.

- ref *and* out *parameters*: If you use a struct as a ref or out parameter, a reference to the struct is passed into the method.

Additional Information About Structs

Allocating structs requires less overhead than creating instances of a class, so using structs instead of classes can sometimes improve performance—but beware of the costs of boxing and unboxing.

Finally, some last things you should know about structs are the following:

- The predefined simple types (int, short, long, etc.), although considered primitives in .NET and C#, are all actually implemented in .NET as structs.

- Structs, like classes, can implement interfaces.

■ ■ ■

Enumerations

Enumerations
Underlying Types and Values
Bit Flags
More About Enums

Enumerations

An enumeration, or enum, is a programmer-defined type, like a class or a struct.

- Like structs, enums are value types, and therefore store their data directly, rather than separately, with a reference and data.

- Enums have only one type of member: named constants.

For example, the following code shows the declaration of a new enum type called `TrafficLight`, which contains three members. Notice that the list of member declarations is a comma-separated list; there are no semicolons in an enum declaration.

```
Keyword   Enum name
   ↓          ↓
enum TrafficLight
{
    Green,   ←Comma separated--no semicolons
    Yellow,  ←Comma separated--no semicolons
    Red
}
```

The following code shows the declaration of three variables of the enum type `TrafficLight`, which was just defined in the preceding code. Notice that you can assign member literals to variables, or you can copy the value from another variable of the same type.

```
class Program {
    static void Main()
    {       Type     Variable     Member
             ↓         ↓             ↓
        TrafficLight t1 = TrafficLight.Red;      // Assign from member
        TrafficLight t2 = TrafficLight.Green;    // Assign from member
        TrafficLight t3 = t2;                    // Assign from variable

        Console.WriteLine(t1);
        Console.WriteLine(t2);
        Console.WriteLine(t3);
    }
}
```

This code produces the following output. Notice that the member names are printed as strings.

```
Red
Green
Green
```

Underlying Types and Values

Every enum type has an underlying integral type. By default, the underlying type is `int`.

- Each enum member is assigned a constant value of the underlying type.

- Unless a member is initialized at its declaration, the compiler assigns each member a value, starting with 0, and incrementing by 1.

For example, in the enum type `TrafficLight` declared previously, the compiler performed the default actions, including setting the underlying type to `int`, and assigning the `int` values 0, 1, and 2 to members `Green`, `Yellow`, and `Red`, respectively. In the output of the following code, you can see the underlying member values by casting them to type `int`. Their arrangement on the stack is illustrated in Figure 13-1.

```
TrafficLight t1 = TrafficLight.Green;
TrafficLight t2 = TrafficLight.Yellow;
TrafficLight t3 = TrafficLight.Red;

Console.WriteLine("{0},\t{1}",    t1, (int) t1);
Console.WriteLine("{0},\t{1}",    t2, (int) t2);
Console.WriteLine("{0},\t{1}\n",  t3, (int) t3);
```
                                       Cast to int

This code produces the following output:

```
Green,  0
Yellow, 1
Red,    2
```

```
static void Main( )
{
    TrafficLight t1 = TrafficLight.Green;
    TrafficLight t2 = TrafficLight.Yellow;
    TrafficLight t3 = TrafficLight.Red;
}
```

Figure 13-1. *The member constants of an enum are represented by underlying integral values.*

Setting the Underlying Type

To explicitly set the type associated with an enum, place a colon and the type name after the enum name. The type can be any integral type except char. All the member constants are of the enum's underlying type.

```
                    Colon
                      ↓
 enum TrafficLight : ulong
 {                         ↑
    ...           Underlying type
```

Setting Explicit Values for the Members

The values of the member constants can be any values of the underlying type. To explicitly set the value of a member, use an initializer after its name in the enum declaration. There can be duplicate values, although not duplicate names, as shown here:

```
enum TrafficLight
{
   Green  = 10,
   Yellow = 15,            // Duplicate values
   Red    = 15             // Duplicate values
}
```

For example, when enum TrafficLight was declared in the preceding code, the compiler defaults for the underlying type and numbering of the members were accepted. Now that you know how to set these factors, you can create a declaration explicitly setting both characteristics. Figure 13-2 shows the declarations.

- The code on the left accepts the default type and numbering.

- The code on the right explicitly sets the underlying type to int and the members to values corresponding to the default values.

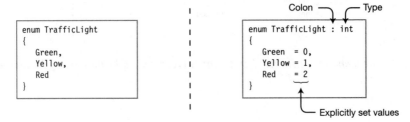

Figure 13-2. *Equivalent enum declarations*

Implicit Member Numbering

You can explicitly assign the values for any of the member constants. If you do not initialize a member constant, the compiler implicitly assigns it a value. The rules the compiler uses for assigning values to those members are the following:

- If the first member does not have an explicit value, the compiler assigns it the value 0.

- For every other member without an initializer, the compiler assigns it the value one greater than the previous member.

- The values associated with the member names do not need to be distinct.

For example, the following code declares two enumerations. CardSuit accepts the implicit numbering of the members, as shown in the right column. FaceCards sets some members explicitly and accepts implicit numbering of the others.

```
enum CardSuit
{
    Hearts,                     // 0--since this is first
    Clubs,                      // 1--one more than the previous one
    Diamonds,                   // 2--one more than the previous one
    Spades,                     // 3--one more than the previous one
    MaxSuits                    // 4--this is a common way to assign a constant
                                //    to the count of the listed items.

}

enum FaceCards
{
    // Member                   // Value assigned
    Jack              = 11,     // 11--explicitly set
    Queen,                      // 12--one more than the previous one
    King,                       // 13--one more than the previous one
    Ace,                        // 14--one more than the previous one
    NumberOfFaceCards = 4,      // 4--explicitly set
    SomeOtherValue,             // 5--one more than the previous one
    HighestFaceCard   = Ace     // 14--Ace is defined above
}
```

Bit Flags

Programmers have long used the different bits in a single word as a compact way to represent a set of on/off flags for options. Enums offer a convenient way to implement this.

The general steps are the following:

1. Determine how many bit flags you need, and choose an unsigned integral type with enough bits to hold them.

2. Determine what each bit represents, and declare an enum of the chosen integral type, with members representing each bit.

3. Use the bitwise OR operator to set the appropriate bits in a word holding the bit flags.

4. Unpack the bit flags by using the bitwise AND operator.

For example, the following code shows the enum declaration representing the options for a card deck in a card game. The underlying type, uint, is more than sufficient to hold the four bit flags needed. Notice the following about the code:

- The members have names that represent the options and are set to the value representing the value of a particular bit.

- Decorating the enum with the Flags attribute is not actually necessary, but gives some additional convenience, which I will discuss shortly.

```
[Flags]
enum CardDeckSettings : uint
{
    SingleDeck    = 0x01,        // Bit 0
    LargePictures = 0x02,        // Bit 1
    FancyNumbers  = 0x04,        // Bit 2
    Animation     = 0x08         // Bit 3
}
```

■**Note** Hexadecimal representation is often used when working with bits because there is a more direct correlation between the hex representation of a number and its bit pattern than with the decimal representation.

To create a word with the appropriate bit flags, declare a variable of the enum type, and use the bitwise OR operator to set the required bits. For example, the following code sets three of the four options:

```
       Enum type    Flag word          Bit flags ORed together
          ↓            ↓                         ↓
CardDeckSettings ops = CardDeckSettings.SingleDeck
                          | CardDeckSettings.FancyNumbers
                          | CardDeckSettings.Animation ;
```

To determine whether a particular bit is set, use the bitwise AND operator with the flag word and the bit flag.

For example, the following code checks to see whether the SingleDeck bit flag is set. The AND operation is performed, and the result is compared to the value of the SingleDeck bit flag.

```
UseSingleDeck =
      (ops & CardDeckSettings.SingleDeck) == CardDeckSettings.SingleDeck;
       ↑                   ↑
   Flag word           Bit flag
```

The Flags Attribute

I will cover attributes in Chapter 21, but it's worth mentioning the Flags attribute here. The attribute does not change the calculations at all. It does, however, provide several convenient features.

First, it informs object browsers looking at the code that the members of the enum are meant to be combined as bit flags, rather than only used as separate values. This allows the browsers to interpret variables of the enum type more appropriately.

Second, it allows the ToString method of an enum to provide more appropriate formatting for the values of bit flags. The ToString method takes an enum value and compares it to the values of the constant members of the enum. If it matches one of the members, ToString returns the string name of the member.

Suppose, for example, that you have used the enum declaration for CardDeckSettings (given in the preceding code), and have *not* used the Flags attribute. The first line of the following code creates a variable (named ops) of the enum type, and sets the value of a single flag bit. The second line uses ToString to get the string name of the member represented by that value.

```
CardDeckSettings ops = CardDeckSettings.SingleDeck;    // Set the bit flag.
Console.WriteLine( ops.ToString() );                   // Print its name.
```

This code produces the following output:

```
SingleDeck
```

Suppose, however, that you set two bit flags instead of one, as in the following code:

```
// Set two bit flags.
ops = CardDeckSettings.SingleDeck | CardDeckSettings.Animation;
Console.WriteLine( ops.ToString() );          // Print what?
```

The resulting value of ops is 9, where 1 is from the SingleDeck flag, and 8 is from the Animation flag. In the second line, when ToString attempts to look up the value in the list of enum members, it finds that there is no member with the value 9—so it just returns the string representing 9. The resulting output is the following:

```
9
```

If, however, you use the Flags attribute before the declaration of the enum, that tells the ToString method that the bits can be considered separately. In looking up the value, it would find that 9 corresponds to the two bit flag members SingleDeck and Animation. It would then return the string containing their names, separated by a comma and space, as shown here:

```
SingleDeck, Animation
```

Example Using Bit Flags

The following code puts together all the pieces of using bit flags:

```
[Flags]
enum CardDeckSettings : uint {
   SingleDeck   = 0x01,          // Bit 0
   LargePictures = 0x02,         // Bit 1
   FancyNumbers = 0x04,          // Bit 2
   Animation    = 0x08           // Bit 3
}

class MyClass {
   bool UseSingleDeck = false, UseBigPics   = false,
        UseFancyNums  = false, UseAnimation = false;

   public void SetOptions2(CardDeckSettings ops) {
      UseSingleDeck = (ops & CardDeckSettings.SingleDeck)
                               == CardDeckSettings.SingleDeck;
      UseBigPics    = (ops & CardDeckSettings.LargePictures)
                               == CardDeckSettings.LargePictures;
      UseFancyNums  = (ops & CardDeckSettings.FancyNumbers)
                               == CardDeckSettings.FancyNumbers;
      UseAnimation  = (ops & CardDeckSettings.Animation)
                               == CardDeckSettings.Animation;
   }

   public void PrintOptions() {
      Console.WriteLine("Option settings:");
      Console.WriteLine("   Use Single Deck    - {0}", UseSingleDeck);
      Console.WriteLine("   Use Large Pictures - {0}", UseBigPics);
      Console.WriteLine("   Use Fancy Numbers  - {0}", UseFancyNums);
      Console.WriteLine("   Show Animation     - {0}", UseAnimation);
   }
}

class Program {
   static void Main() {
      MyClass mc = new MyClass();
      CardDeckSettings ops = CardDeckSettings.SingleDeck
                          | CardDeckSettings.FancyNumbers
                          | CardDeckSettings.Animation;
      mc.SetOptions2(ops);
      mc.PrintOptions();
   }
}
```

This code produces the following output:

```
Option settings:
   Use Single Deck    - True
   Use Large Pictures - False
   Use Fancy Numbers  - True
   Show Animation     - True
```

More About Enums

Enums only have a single member type: the declared member constants.

- There are no modifiers that can be used with the members. They all implicitly have the same accessibility as the enum.

- Since the members are constants, they are accessible even if there are no variables of the enum type. Use the enum type name, followed by a dot and the member name.

For example, the following code does not create any variables of the enum type TrafficLight, but the members are accessible, and can be printed out using WriteLine.

```
static void Main()
{
   Console.WriteLine("{0}", TrafficLight.Green);
   Console.WriteLine("{0}", TrafficLight.Yellow);
   Console.WriteLine("{0}", TrafficLight.Red);
}                                ↑          ↑
                          Enum name   Member name
```

An enum is a distinct type. Comparing enum members of different enum types results in a compile-time error. For example, the following code declares two enum types.

- The first if statement is fine because it compares different members from the same enum type.

- The second if statement produces an error because it compares members from different enum types.

```
enum ET1                         // First enum type
{
   mem1,
   mem2
}

enum ET2                         // Second enum type
{
   mem1,
   mem2
}

class Program
{
   static void Main()
   {
      if (ET1.mem1 < ET1.mem2)  // OK--comparing members of same enum type
         Console.WriteLine("True");

      if (ET1.mem1 < ET2.mem1)  // Error--different enum types
         Console.WriteLine("True");
   }
}
```

■ ■ ■

CHAPTER 14

Arrays

Arrays

Types of Arrays

An Array As an Object

One-Dimensional and Rectangular Arrays

Instantiating a One-Dimensional or Rectangular Array

Accessing Array Elements

Initializing an Array

Jagged Arrays

Comparing Rectangular and Jagged Arrays

The foreach Statement

Array Covariance

Useful Inherited Array Members

Comparing Array Types

Arrays

An array is a set of uniform data elements, represented by a single variable name. The individual elements are accessed using the variable name and one or more indexes between square brackets, as shown here:

```
Array name   Index
     ↓     ↓
   MyArray[4]
```

Definitions

Let's start with some important definitions having to do with arrays in C#.

   Elements: The individual data items of an array are called *elements*. All elements of an array must be of the same type.

   Rank/dimensions: Arrays can have any positive number of *dimensions*. The number of dimensions an array has is called its *rank*.

   Dimension length: Each dimension of an array has a *length*, which is the number of positions in that direction.

   Array length: The total number of elements contained in an array, in *all* dimensions, is called the *length* of the array.

Important Details

Besides the preceding definitions, there are several high-level facts about C# arrays that I should mention before launching into a discussion of arrays.

- Once an array is created, its size is fixed. C# does not support dynamic arrays.

- Array indexes are *0-based*. That is, if the length of a dimension is *n*, the index values range from 0 to *n* - 1. For example, Figure 14-1 shows the dimensions and lengths of two example arrays. Notice that for each dimension, the indexes range from 0 to *length* - 1.

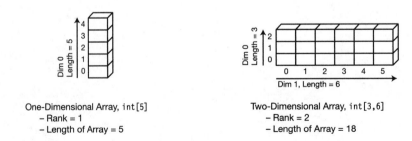

One-Dimensional Array, `int[5]`
– Rank = 1
– Length of Array = 5

Two-Dimensional Array, `int[3,6]`
– Rank = 2
– Length of Array = 18

Figure 14-1. *Dimensions and sizes*

Types of Arrays

C# provides two types of arrays:

- One-dimensional arrays can be thought of as a single line, or *vector*, of elements.

- Multidimensional arrays are composed such that each position in the primary vector is itself an array, called a *sub-array*. Positions in the sub-array vectors can themselves be sub-arrays.

In addition, there are two types of multidimensional arrays, rectangular arrays and jagged arrays, which have the following characteristics:

- Rectangular arrays
  - Are multidimensional arrays where all the sub-arrays in a particular dimension have the same length
  - Always use a single set of square brackets, regardless of the number of dimensions

```
int x = myArray2[4, 6, 1]              // One set of square brackets
```

- Jagged arrays
  - Are multidimensional arrays where each sub-array is an independent array
  - Can have sub-arrays of *different* lengths
  - Use a separate set of square brackets for each dimension of the array

```
jagArray1[2][7][4]                     // Three sets of square brackets
```

Figure 14-2 shows the kinds of arrays available in C#.

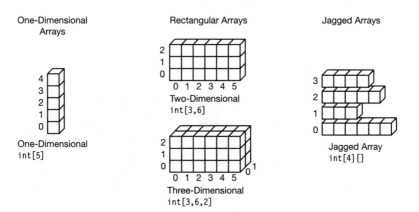

Figure 14-2. *One-dimensional, rectangular, and jagged arrays*

An Array As an Object

An array instance is an object whose type derives from class System.Array. Since arrays are derived from this BCL base class, they inherit a number of useful members from it, such as

- Rank: A property that returns the number of dimensions of the array

- Length: A property that returns the length of the array (the total number of elements in the array)

Arrays are reference types, and as with all reference types, have both a reference to the data and the data object itself. The reference is in either the stack or the heap, and the data object itself will always be in the heap. Figure 14-3 shows the memory configuration and components of an array.

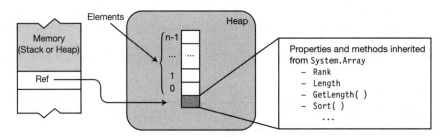

Figure 14-3. *Structure of an array*

Although an array is always a reference type, the elements of the array can be either value types or reference types.

- An array is called a *value type array* if the elements stored are value types.

- An array is called a *reference type array* if the elements stored in the array are *references* of reference type objects.

Figure 14-4 shows a value type array and a reference type array.

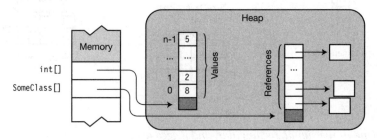

Figure 14-4. *Elements can be values or references.*

One-Dimensional and Rectangular Arrays

Syntactically, one-dimensional arrays and rectangular arrays are very similar, so they will be treated together. Jagged arrays will be treated separately.

Declaring a One-Dimensional Array or a Rectangular Array

To declare a one-dimensional or rectangular array, use a single set of square brackets between the type and the variable name.

The *rank specifiers* are commas between the brackets. They specify the number of dimensions the array will have. The rank is the number of commas, plus one. For example, no commas indicates a one-dimensional array, one comma indicates a two-dimensional array, and so forth.

The base type, together with the rank specifiers, is the *type* of the array. For example, the following line of code declares a one-dimensional array of longs. The type of the array is long[], which is read as "an array of longs."

```
Rank specifiers = 1
       ↓
long[ ] secondArray;
 ↑
Array type
```

The following code shows examples of declarations of rectangular arrays. Notice that

- You can have as many rank specifiers as you need.

- You cannot place array dimension lengths in the array type section. The rank is part of the array's type, but the lengths of the dimensions are *not* part of the type.

- When an array is declared, the *number* of dimensions is fixed. The *length* of the dimensions, however, is not determined until the array is instantiated.

```
Rank specifiers
      ↓
int[,,]   firstArray;              // Array type: 3-D array of int
int[,]    arr1;                    // Array type: 2-D array of int
long[,,]  arr3;                    // Array type: 3-D array of long
   ↑
Array type

long[3,2,6] SecondArray;           // Wrong!  Compile error
   ↑
Dimension lengths not allowed!
```

■Note Unlike C/C++, the brackets follow the base type, not the variable name.

Instantiating a One-Dimensional or Rectangular Array

To instantiate an array, you use an *array creation expression*. An array creation expression consists of the new operator, followed by the base type, followed by a pair of square brackets. The length of each dimension is placed in a comma-separated list between the brackets.

The following are examples of one-dimensional array declarations:

- Array arr2 is a one-dimensional array of four ints.

- Array mcArr is a one-dimensional array of four MyClass references.

- Their layouts in memory are shown in Figure 14-5.

```
                        Four elements
                             ↓
    int[]      arr2  = new int[4];
    MyClass[] mcArr  = new MyClass[4];
                        ─────────────
                             ↑
                 Array creation expression
```

The following is an example of a rectangular array. Array arr3 is a three-dimensional array.

- The length of the array is 3 * 6 * 2 = 36.

- Its layout in memory is shown in Figure 14-5.

```
                   Lengths of the dimensions
                             ↓
                           ────
    int[,,] arr3 = new int[3,6,2] ;
```

At the time of instantiation, each element is automatically initialized to the default initialization value for the type of the element.

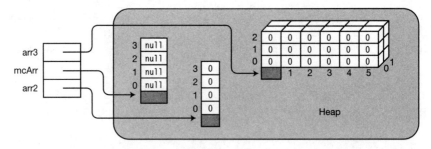

Figure 14-5. *Declaring and instantiating arrays*

Note Array creation expressions do not contain parentheses—even for reference type arrays.

Accessing Array Elements

An array element is accessed using an integer value as an index into the array.

- Each dimension uses 0-based indexing.

- The index is placed between square brackets following the array name.

The following code shows examples of declaring, writing to, and reading from a one-dimensional and a two-dimensional array:

```
int[]  intArr1 = new int[15];      // 1-D example
intArr1[2]     = 10;               // Write to element 2 of the array.
int var1       = intArr1[2];       // Read from element 2 of the array.


int[,] intArr2 = new int[5,10];    // 2-D example
intArr2[2,3]   = 7;                // Write to the array.
int var2       = intArr2[2,3];     // Read from the array.
```

The following code shows the full process of creating and accessing a one-dimensional array:

```
int[] myIntArray;                          // Declare the array.

myIntArray = new int[4];                   // Instantiate the array.

for( int i=0; i<4; i++ )                   // Set the values.
   myIntArray[i] = i*10;

// Read and display the values of each element.
for( int i=0; i<4; i++ )
   Console.WriteLine("Value of element {0} = {1}", i, myIntArray[i]);
```

This code produces the following output:

```
Value of element 0 is 0
Value of element 1 is 10
Value of element 2 is 20
Value of element 3 is 30
```

Initializing an Array

Array elements are always initialized. If they are not explicitly initialized, the system will automatically initialize them to default values.

Automatic Initialization

When any type of array is created, each of the elements is automatically initialized to the default value for the type. The default values for the predefined types are 0 for integer types, 0.0 for floating point types, false for Booleans, and null for reference types.

For example, the following code creates an array and initializes its four elements to the value 0. Figure 14-6 illustrates the layout in memory.

```
int[] intArr = new int[4];
```

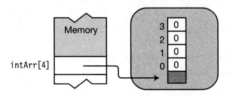

Figure 14-6. *Automatic initialization of a one-dimensional array*

Explicit Initialization of One-Dimensional Arrays

For a one-dimensional array, you can set explicit initial values by including an *initialization list* immediately after the array creation expression of an array instantiation.

- The initialization values must be separated by commas and enclosed in a set of curly braces.

- Notice, however, that nothing separates the array creation expression and the initialization list. That is, there is no equals sign or other connecting operator.

For example, the following code creates an array and initializes its four elements to the values between the curly braces. Figure 14-7 illustrates the layout in memory.

```
                              Initialization list
                                     ↓
int[] intArr = new int[4] { 10, 20, 30, 40 };
                         ↑
                No connecting operator
```

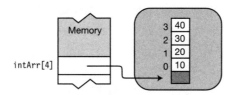

Figure 14-7. *Explicit initialization of a one-dimensional array*

Explicit Initialization of Rectangular Arrays

To explicitly initialize a rectangular array:

- Each *vector of initial values* must be enclosed in curly braces.

- Each *dimension* must also be nested and enclosed in curly braces.

- In addition to the initial values, the initialization lists and components of each dimension must also be separated by commas.

For example, the following code shows the declaration of a two-dimensional array with an initialization list. Figure 14-8 illustrates the layout in memory.

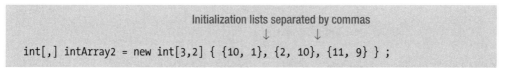

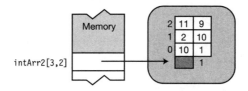

Figure 14-8. *Initializing a rectangular array*

Syntax Points for Initializing Rectangular Arrays

Rectangular arrays are initialized with nested, comma-separated initialization lists. The initialization lists are nested in curly braces. This can sometimes be confusing, so to get the nesting, grouping, and commas right, the following tips can be helpful:

- Commas are used as *separators* between all *elements* and *groups*.

- Commas are *not* placed between left curly braces.

- Commas are *not* placed before a right curly brace.

- Read the rank specifications from left to right, designating the last number as "elements" and all the others as "groups."

For example, read the following declaration as "intArray has four groups of three groups of two elements."

```
                                  Initialization lists, nested and separated by commas
int[,,] intArray = new int[4,3,2] {        ↓        ↓        ↓
                          { {8, 6},  {5,  2}, {12, 9} },
                          { {6, 4},  {13, 9}, {18, 4} },
                          { {7, 2},  {1, 13}, {9,  3} },
                          { {4, 6},  {3,  2}, {23, 8} }
                        };
```

Shortcut Syntax

When combining declaration, array creation, and initialization in a single statement, the array creation expression part of the syntax can be left out. This shortcut syntax is shown in Figure 14-9.

```
int[] arr1 = new int[3] {10, 20, 30};  ⎫
int[] arr1 =              {10, 20, 30};  ⎬ Equivalent

int[,] arr = new int[2,3] {{0, 1, 2}, {10, 11, 12}};  ⎫
int[,] arr =              {{0, 1, 2}, {10, 11, 12}};  ⎬ Equivalent
```

Figure 14-9. *Shortcut for array declaration, creation, and initialization*

Putting It All Together

Now that you have all the pieces, they can be put together in a full example. The following code creates, initializes, and uses a rectangular array.

```
// Declare, create, and initialize the array.
int[,] arr = new int[2,3] {{0, 1, 2}, {10, 11, 12}};

// Print the values.
for( int i=0; i<2; i++ )
   for( int j=0; j<3; j++ )
      Console.WriteLine("Element [{0},{1}] is {2}", i, j, arr[i,j]);
```

This code produces the following output:

```
Element [0,0] is 0
Element [0,1] is 1
Element [0,2] is 2
Element [1,0] is 10
Element [1,1] is 11
Element [1,2] is 12
```

Jagged Arrays

A jagged array is an array of arrays. Unlike rectangular arrays, the sub-arrays of a jagged array can have different numbers of elements.

For example, the following code declares a two-dimensional jagged array. The array's layout in memory is shown in Figure 14-10.

- The length of the first dimension is 3.

- The declaration can be read as "jagArr is an array of three arrays of ints."

- Notice that the figure shows *four* array objects—one for the top-level array, and three for the sub-arrays.

```
int[][] jagArr = new int[3][];    // Declare and create top-level array.
          ...                     // Declare and create sub-arrays.
```

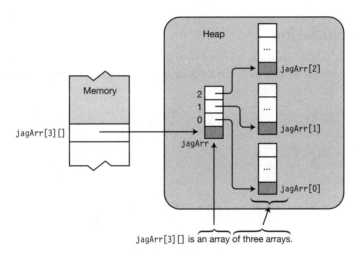

Figure 14-10. *A jagged array is an array of arrays.*

Declaring a Jagged Array

The declaration syntax for jagged arrays requires a separate set of square brackets for each dimension. The number of sets of square brackets in the declaration of the array variable determines the rank of the array.

- A jagged array can be of any number of dimensions greater than one.

- As with rectangular arrays, dimension lengths cannot be included in the array type section of the declaration.

```
Rank specifiers
       ↓
int[][]   SomeArr;          // Rank = 2
int[][][] OtherArr;         // Rank = 3
       ↑         ↑
   Array type  Array name
```

Shortcut Instantiation

You can combine the jagged array declaration with the creation of the first-level array using an array creation expression, such as in the following declaration. The result is shown in Figure 14-11.

```
                   Three sub-arrays
                          ↓
    int[][] jagArr = new int[3][];
```

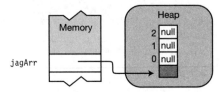

Figure 14-11. *Shortcut first-level instantiation*

You cannot instantiate more than the first-level array in the declaration statement.

```
                   Allowed
                      ↓
    int[][] jagArr = new int[3][4];          // Wrong! Compile error
                          ↑
                   Not allowed
```

Instantiating a Jagged Array

Unlike other types of arrays, you cannot fully instantiate a jagged array in a single step. Since a jagged array is an array of independent arrays—each array must be created separately. Instantiating a full jagged array requires the following steps:

1. First, instantiate the top-level array.

2. Next, instantiate each sub-array separately, assigning the reference to the newly created array to the appropriate element of its containing array.

For example, the following code shows the declaration, instantiation, and initialization of a two-dimensional jagged array. Notice in the code that the reference to each sub-array is assigned to an element in the top-level array. The progression of steps 1 through 4 in the code correspond to the numbered representations in Figure 14-12.

```
int[][] Arr = new int[3][];                 // 1. Instantiate top level

Arr[0] = new int[] {10, 20, 30};            // 2. Instantiate sub-array
Arr[1] = new int[] {40, 50, 60, 70};        // 3. Instantiate sub-array
Arr[2] = new int[] {80, 90, 100, 110, 120}; // 4. Instantiate sub-array
```

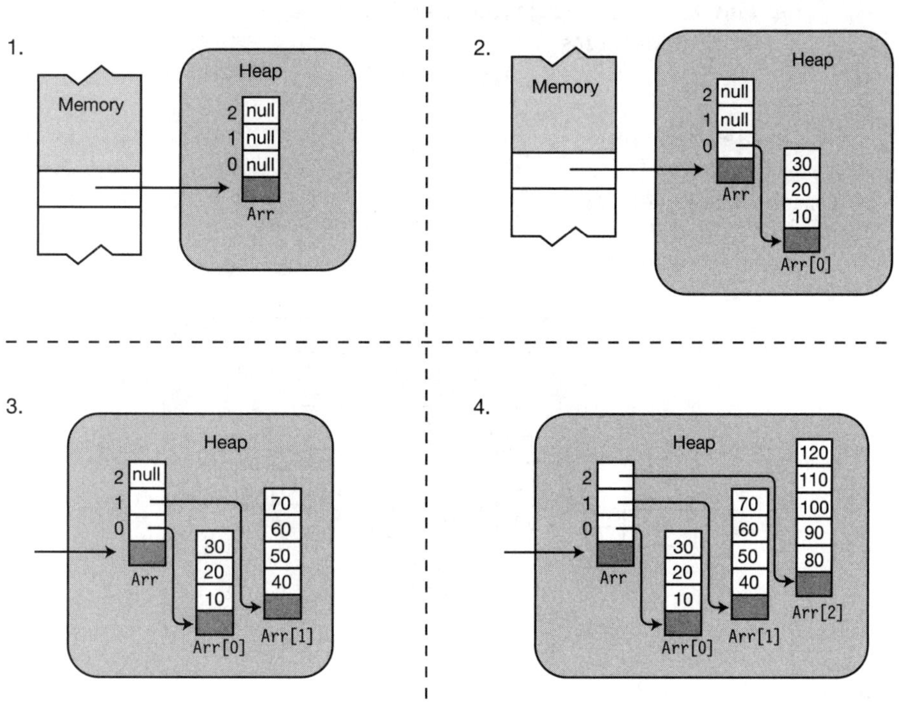

Figure 14-12. *Creating a two-dimensional jagged array*

Sub-Arrays in Jagged Arrays

Since the sub-arrays in a jagged array are themselves arrays, it is possible to have rectangular arrays inside jagged arrays. For example, the following code creates a jagged array of three two-dimensional rectangular arrays and initializes them with values. It then displays the values.

- The structure is illustrated in Figure 14-13.

- The code also uses the GetLength(int n) method of arrays, inherited from System.Array, to get the length of the specified dimension of the array.

```
int[][,] Arr;          // An array of 2-D arrays
Arr = new int[3][,];   // Instantiate an array of three 2-D arrays.

Arr[0] = new int[,] { { 10, 20 },          { 100, 200 }              };
Arr[1] = new int[,] { { 30, 40, 50 },      { 300, 400, 500 }         };
Arr[2] = new int[,] { { 60, 70, 80, 90 }, { 600, 700, 800, 900 } };

            Get length of dimension 0 of Arr ↓
for (int i = 0; i < Arr.GetLength(0); i++)
{              Get length of dimension 0 of Arr[ i ] ↓
   for (int j = 0; j < Arr[i].GetLength(0); j++)
   {                  Get length of dimension 1 of Arr[ i ] ↓
      for (int k = 0; k < Arr[i].GetLength(1); k++) {
         Console.WriteLine
                   ("[{0}][{1},{2}] = {3}", i, j, k, Arr[i][j, k]);
      }
      Console.WriteLine("");
   }
   Console.WriteLine("");
}
```

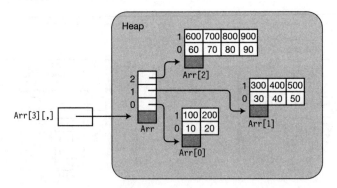

Figure 14-13. *Jagged array of three two-dimensional arrays*

Comparing Rectangular and Jagged Arrays

The structure of rectangular and jagged arrays is significantly different. For example, Figure 14-14 shows the structure of a rectangular three-by-three array, and a jagged array of three one-dimensional arrays of length 3.

- Both arrays hold nine integers, but as you can see, their structures are quite different.

- The rectangular array has a single array object, while the jagged array has four array objects.

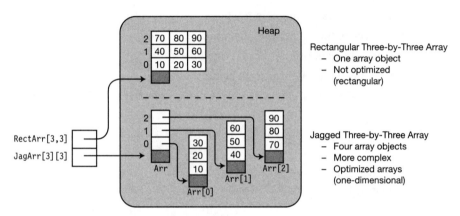

Figure 14-14. *Comparing the structure of rectangular and jagged arrays*

One-dimensional arrays have specific instructions in the CIL that allow them to be optimized for performance. Rectangular arrays do not have these instructions, and are not optimized to the same level. Because of this, it can sometimes be more efficient to use jagged arrays of one-dimensional arrays—which can be optimized—than rectangular arrays, which cannot.

On the other hand, the programming complexity can be less for a rectangular array because it can be treated as a single unit, rather than an array of arrays.

The foreach Statement

The foreach statement allows you to sequentially access each element in an array. It is actually a more general construct in that it also works with other collection types—but this section will only discuss its use with arrays. Chapter 20 will cover its use with other collection types.

The important points of the foreach statement are the following:

- The *iteration variable* is a temporary, read-only variable of the same type as the elements of the array. The foreach statement uses the iteration variable to sequentially represent each element in the array.

- The syntax of the foreach statement is where

  – *Type* is the type of the elements of the array.
  – *Identifier* is the name of the *iteration variable.*
  – *ArrayName* is the name of the array to be processed.
  – *Statement* is a simple statement or a block that is executed once for each element in the array.

```
              Iteration variable declaration
                          ↓
foreach( Type Identifier in ArrayName )
        Statement
```

The way the foreach statement works is the following:

- It starts with the first element of the array and assigns that value to the *iteration variable*.

- It then executes the body of the statement. Inside the body, you can use the iteration variable as a read-only alias for the array element.

- After the body is executed, the foreach statement selects the next element in the array and repeats the process.

In this way, it cycles through the array, allowing you to access each element one by one. For example, the following code shows the use of a foreach statement with a one-dimensional array of four integers:

- The WriteLine statement, which is the body of the foreach statement, is executed once for each of the elements of the array.

- The first time through the loop, iteration variable item has the value of the first element of the array. Each successive time, it will have the value of the next element in the array.

```
int[] arr1 = {10, 11, 12, 13};
        Iteration variable declaration
                 ↓                              Iteration variable use
              _____                                      ↓
foreach( int item in arr1 )
    Console.WriteLine("Item Value: {0}", item);
```

The Iteration Variable Is Read-Only

Since the value of the iteration variable is read-only, clearly, it cannot be changed. But this has different effects on value type arrays and reference type arrays.

For value type arrays, this means that you cannot change the data of the array. For example, in the following code, the attempt to change the data in the iteration variable produces a compile-time error message:

```
int[] arr1 = {10, 11, 12, 13};

foreach( int item in arr1 )
   item++;                      // Wrong. Changing variable value is not allowed
```

For reference type arrays, you still cannot change the iteration variable, but the iteration variable only holds the reference to the data, not the data itself. You *can*, therefore, change the data through the iteration variable.

The following code creates an array of four MyClass objects and initializes them. In the first foreach statement, the data in each of the objects is changed. In the second foreach statement, the changed data is read from the objects.

```
class MyClass
{
   public int MyField = 0;
}

class Program {
   static void Main() {
      MyClass[] mcArray = new MyClass[4];           // Create array
      for (int i = 0; i < 4; i++)
      {
         mcArray[i] = new MyClass();                // Create class objects
         mcArray[i].MyField = i;                    // Set field
      }
      foreach (MyClass item in mcArray)
         item.MyField += 10;                        // Change the data.

      foreach (MyClass item in mcArray)
         Console.WriteLine("{0}", item.MyField);    // Read the changed data.
   }
}
```

This code produces the following output:

```
10
11
12
13
```

The foreach Statement with Multidimensional Arrays

In a multidimensional array, the elements are processed in the order in which the rightmost index is incremented fastest. When the index has gone from 0 to *length* - 1, the next index to the left is incremented, and the indexes to the right are reset to 0.

Example with a Rectangular Array

The following example shows the foreach statement used with a rectangular array:

```
class Sample
{
    static void Main()
    {
        int nTotal = 0;
        int[,] arr1 = { {10, 11}, {12, 13} };

        foreach( int element in arr1 )
        {
            nTotal += element;
            Console.WriteLine
                    ("Element: {0}, Current Total: {1}", element, nTotal);
        }
    }
}
```

The output is the following:

```
Element: 10, Current Total: 10
Element: 11, Current Total: 21
Element: 12, Current Total: 33
Element: 13, Current Total: 46
```

Example with a Jagged Array

Since jagged arrays are arrays of arrays, separate foreach statements must be used for each dimension in the jagged array. The foreach statements must be nested properly to make sure that each nested array is processed properly.

For example, in the following code, the first foreach statement cycles through the top-level array—arr1—selecting the next sub-array to process. The inner foreach statement processes the elements of that sub-array.

```
static void Main()
{
   int nTotal = 0;
   int[][] arr1 = new int[2][];
   arr1[0] = new int[] { 10, 11 };
   arr1[1] = new int[] { 12, 13, 14 };

   foreach (int[] array in arr1)        // Process the top level.
   {
      Console.WriteLine("Starting new array");
      foreach (int item in array)       // Process the second level.
      {
         nTotal += item;
         Console.WriteLine("  Item: {0}, Current Total: {1}", item, nTotal);
      }
   }
}
```

The output is the following:

```
Starting new array
  Item: 10, Current Total: 10
  Item: 11, Current Total: 21
Starting new array
  Item: 12, Current Total: 33
  Item: 13, Current Total: 46
  Item: 14, Current Total: 60
```

Array Covariance

Under certain conditions, you can assign an object to an array element even if the object is not of the array's base type. This property is called *covariance*. You can use covariance if

- The array is a reference type array.

- There is an implicit or explicit conversion between the type of the object you are assigning and the array's base type.

Since there is always an implicit conversion between a derived class and its base class, you can always assign an object of a derived class to an array declared for the base class.

For example, the following code declares two classes, A and B, where class B derives from class A. The last line shows covariance by assigning objects of type B to array elements of type A. The memory layout for the code is shown in Figure 14-15.

```csharp
class A { ... }                                    // Base class
class B : A { ... }                                // Derived class

class Program {
   static void Main() {
      // Two arrays of type A[]
      A[] AArray1 = new A[3];
      A[] AArray2 = new A[3];

      // Normal--assigning objects of type A to an array of type A
      AArray1[0] = new A(); AArray1[1] = new A(); AArray1[2] = new A();

      // Covariant--assigning objects of type B to an array of type A
      AArray2[0] = new B(); AArray2[1] = new B(); AArray2[2] = new B();
   }
}
```

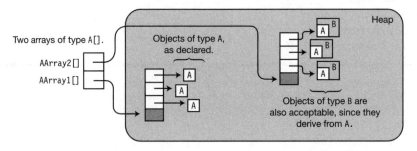

Figure 14-15. *Arrays showing covariance*

■Note There is no covariance for value type arrays.

Useful Inherited Array Members

I mentioned earlier that C# arrays are derived from class System.Array. From that base class, they inherit a number of useful properties and methods. Some of the most useful ones are listed in Table 14-1.

Table 14-1. *Some Useful Members Inherited by Arrays*

Member	Type	Lifetime	Meaning
Rank	Property	Instance	Gets the number of dimensions of the array
Length	Property	Instance	Gets the total number of elements in all the dimensions of the array
GetLength	Method	Instance	Returns the length of a particular dimension of the array
Clear	Method	Static	Sets a range of elements to 0 or null
Sort	Method	Static	Sorts the elements in a one-dimensional array
BinarySearch	Method	Static	Searches a one-dimensional array for a value, using binary search
Clone	Method	Instance	Performs a shallow copy of the array—copying only the elements, both for arrays of value types and reference types
IndexOf	Method	Static	Returns the index of the first occurrence of a value in a one-dimensional array
Reverse	Method	Static	Reverses the order of the elements of a range of a one-dimensional array
GetUpperBound	Method	Instance	Gets the upper bound at the specified dimension

For example, the following code uses some of these properties and methods:

```
public static void PrintArray(int[] a)
{
    foreach (int x in a)
        Console.Write("{0}  ", x);
    Console.WriteLine("");
}

static void Main()
{
    int[] arr = new int[] { 15, 20, 5, 25, 10 };  PrintArray(arr);
    Array.Sort(arr);                               PrintArray(arr);
    Array.Reverse(arr);                            PrintArray(arr);

    Console.WriteLine("Rank = {0}, Length = {1}",arr.Rank, arr.Length);
    Console.WriteLine("GetLength(0) = {0}",arr.GetLength(0));
    Console.WriteLine("GetType()    = {0}",arr.GetType());
}
```

The Clone Method

The Clone method performs a shallow copy of an array. This means that it only creates a clone of the array itself. If it is a reference type array, it does *not* copy the objects referenced by the elements. This has different results for value type arrays and reference type arrays.

- Cloning a value type array results in two independent arrays.

- Cloning a reference type array results in two arrays pointing at the same objects.

The Clone method returns a reference of type object, which must be cast to the array type.

```
int[] intArr1 = { 1, 2, 3 };
                   Array type     Returns object
                       ↓               ↓
int[] intArr2 = ( int[] ) intArr1.Clone();
```

For example, the following code shows an example of cloning a value type array, producing two independent arrays. Figure 14-16 illustrates the steps shown in the code.

```
static void Main()
{
    int[] intArr1 = { 1, 2, 3 };                          // Step 1
    int[] intArr2 = (int[]) intArr1.Clone();              // Step 2

    intArr2[0] = 100; intArr2[1] = 200; intArr2[2] = 300; // Step 3
}
```

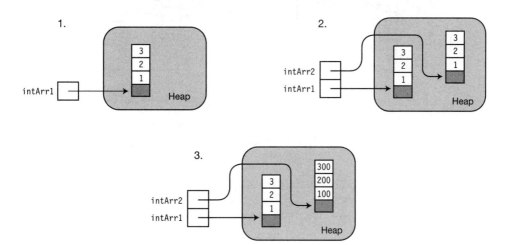

Figure 14-16. *Cloning a value type array produces two independent arrays.*

Cloning a reference type array results in two arrays *pointing at the same objects*. The following code shows an example. Figure 14-17 illustrates the steps shown in the code.

```
class A
{
   public int Value = 5;
}

class Program
{
   static void Main()
   {
      A[] AArray1 = new A[3] { new A(), new A(), new A() };      // Step 1
      A[] AArray2 = (A[]) AArray1.Clone();                        // Step 2

      AArray2[0].Value = 100;
      AArray2[1].Value = 200;
      AArray2[2].Value = 300;                                     // Step 3
   }
}
```

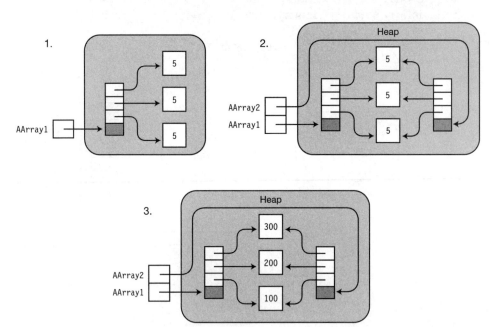

Figure 14-17. *Cloning a reference type array produces two arrays referencing the same objects.*

Comparing Array Types

Table 14-2 summarizes some of the important similarities and differences between the three types of arrays.

Table 14-2. *Summary Comparing Array Types*

Array Type	Array Objects	Syntax Brackets	Syntax Commas	Shape
One-dimensional • Has optimizing instructions in CIL.	1	Single set	No	One-Dimensional `int[3]`
Rectangular • Multidimensional • All sub-arrays in a multidimensional array must be the same length.	1	Single set	Yes	Two-Dimensional `int[3,6]` Three-Dimensional `int[3,6,2]`
Jagged • Multidimensional • Sub-arrays can be of different lengths.	Multiple	Multiple sets	No	Jagged `int[4][]`

CHAPTER 15

■■■

Delegates

What Is a Delegate?
Declaring the Delegate Type
Creating the Delegate Object
Assigning Delegates
Combining Delegates
Adding Methods to Delegates
Deleting Methods from a Delegate
Invoking a Delegate
Delegate Example
Invoking Delegates with Return Values
Invoking Delegates with Reference Parameters
Anonymous Methods

What Is a Delegate?

A *delegate* can be thought of as an object that contains an ordered list of methods with the same signature and return type.

- The list of methods is called the *invocation list.*

- When a delegate is invoked, it calls each method in its invocation list.

Figure 15-1 represents a delegate with four methods in its invocation list.

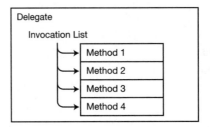

Figure 15-1. *A delegate as a list of methods*

A delegate with a single method is similar to a function pointer in C++. Unlike function pointers, however, delegates are object oriented and type-safe.

Methods in the Invocation List

Methods held by a delegate *can be from any class or struct*, as long as they match *both* the delegate's

- Return type

- Signature

Methods in the invocation list can be either instance methods or static methods.

Declaring the Delegate Type

Delegates are types, just as classes are types. And as with classes, a *delegate type* must be declared before you can create variables and objects of the type. The following example code declares a delegate type.

- The delegate type declaration, as with all type declarations, does not need to be declared inside a class.

The declaration of a delegate type looks much like the declaration of a method, in that it has both a *return type* and a *signature*. The return type and signature specify the form of the methods that the delegate will accept.

For example, the following code declares delegate type `MyDel`. The declaration specifies that objects of this type will accept only methods that return no value and have a single `int` parameter. Figure 15-2 shows a representation of the delegate type on the left, and the object on the right.

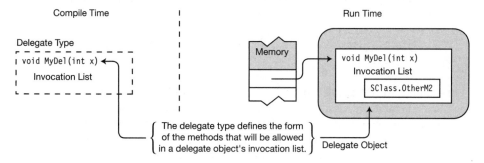

Figure 15-2. *Delegate type and object*

The delegate type declaration differs from a method declaration in two ways. The delegate type declaration

- Is prefaced with the keyword `delegate`

- Does not have a method body

Creating the Delegate Object

A delegate is a reference type, and therefore has both a reference and an object. After a delegate type is declared, you can declare variables and create objects of the type. The following code shows the declaration of a variable of a delegate type:

```
Delegate type   Variable
      ↓            ↓
    MyDel   delVar;
```

You can create a delegate object by using the new operator, as shown in the following code. The operand of the new operator consists of the following:

- The delegate type name

- A set of parentheses containing the name of a method to use as the first member in the invocation list. The method can be either an instance method or a static method.

```
                        Instance method
                             ↓
    delVar = new MyDel( MyInstObj.MyM1 );   // Create delegate and save ref.
    dVar   = new MyDel( SClass.OtherM2 );   // Create delegate and save ref.
                             ↑
                        Static method
```

You can also use the shortcut syntax, which consists of just the method specifier, as shown in the following code. This code and the preceding code are equivalent. Using the shortcut syntax works, because there is an implicit conversion between a method name and a compatible delegate type.

```
    delVar = MyInstObj.MyM1;        // Create delegate and save reference.
    dVar   = SClass.OtherM2;        // Create delegate and save reference.
```

For example, the following code creates two delegate objects—one with an instance method, and the other with a static method. Figure 15-3 shows the instantiations of the delegates. This code assumes that there is a class object called MyInstObj, which has a method called MyM1 that returns no value and takes an int as a parameter. It also assumes that there is a class called SClass, which has a static method OtherM2 with a return type and signature matching those of delegate MyDel.

```
delegate void MyDel(int x);                    // Declare delegate type.
MyDel delVar, dVar;                            // Create delegate variables.
                         Instance method
                              ↓
delVar = new MyDel( MyInstObj.MyM1 );  // Create delegate and save ref.
dVar   = new MyDel( SClass.OtherM2 );  // Create delegate and save ref.
                              ↑
                         Static method
```

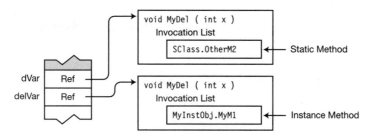

Figure 15-3. *Instantiating the delegates*

Besides allocating the memory for the delegate, creating a delegate object also places the first method in the delegate's invocation list. You can also create the variable and instantiate the object in the same statement, using the initializer syntax. For example, the following statements produce the same configuration shown earlier, in Figure 15-3.

```
MyDel delVar = new MyDel( MyInstObj.MyM1 );
MyDel dVar   = new MyDel( SClass.OtherM2 );
```

The following statements use the shortcut syntax, but again, produce the results shown in Figure 15-3.

```
MyDel delVar = MyInstObj.MyM1;
MyDel dVar   = SClass.OtherM2;
```

Assigning Delegates

Because delegates are reference types, you can change the reference contained in a delegate variable, by assigning to it. The old delegate object is disposed of by the Garbage Collector (GC).

For example, the following code sets and then changes the value of delVar. Figure 15-4 illustrates the code.

```
MyDel delVar;
delVar = MyInstObj.MyM1;    // Create and assign the delegate object.

   ...
delVar = SClass.OtherM2;    // Create and assign the new delegate object.
```

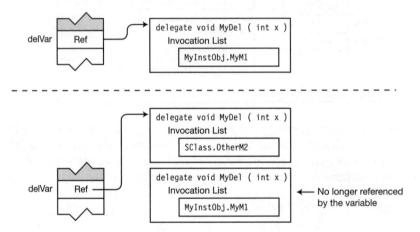

Figure 15-4. *Assigning to a delegate variable*

Combining Delegates

All the delegates you've seen so far have had only a single method in their invocation lists. Delegates can be "combined" by using the addition operator. The result of the operation is the creation of a new delegate, with an invocation list that is the concatenation of copies of the invocation lists of the two operand delegates.

For example, the following code creates three delegates. The third delegate is created from the combination of the first two.

```
MyDel DelA = MyInstObj.MyM1;
MyDel DelB = SClass.OtherM2;

MyDel DelC = DelA + DelB;                // Has combined invocation list
```

Although the term *combining delegates* might give the impression that the operand delegates are modified, they are not changed at all. As a matter of fact, *delegates are immutable.* After a delegate object is created, it cannot be changed.

Figure 15-5 illustrates the results of the preceding code. Notice that the operand delegates remain unchanged.

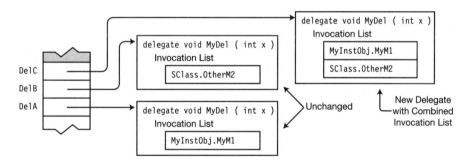

Figure 15-5. *Combining delegates*

Adding Methods to Delegates

Although you saw in the previous section that delegates are, in reality, immutable, C# provides syntax for making it appear that you can add a method to a delegate—and it's perfectly fine to think of it that way. You can add a method, or another delegate, to a delegate by using the += operator.

For example, the following code "adds" two methods to the invocation list of the delegate. The methods are added to the bottom of the invocation list. Figure 15-6 shows the result.

```
MyDel delVar  = Inst.MyM1;      // Create and initialize.
delVar        += SC1.m3;        // Add a method.
delVar        += X.Act;         // Add a method.
```

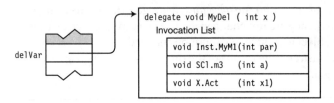

Figure 15-6. *Result of adding methods to a delegate*

What is actually happening, of course, is that when the += operator is used, a new delegate is created, with an invocation list that is the combination of the delegate on the left plus the method listed on the right.

Deleting Methods from a Delegate

You can also delete a method from a delegate, using the -= operator.

The following code shows the use of the -= operator. Figure 15-7 shows the result of this code when applied to the delegate illustrated in Figure 15-6.

```
delVar -= SC1.m3;                // Delete the method from the delegate.
```

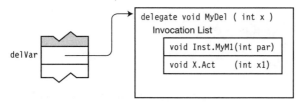

Figure 15-7. *Result of subtracting a method from a delegate*

As with adding a method to a delegate, the resulting delegate is actually a new delegate. The new delegate is a copy of the old delegate—but without the reference to the method that was removed.

The following are some things to remember when removing methods:

- If there are multiple entries for a method in the invocation list, the -= operator starts searching at the bottom of the list and removes the first instance it finds of the matching method.

- Attempting to delete a method that is not in the delegate has no effect.

- Attempting to invoke an empty delegate throws an exception.

- You can check whether a delegate's invocation list is empty by comparing the delegate to null. If the invocation list is empty, the delegate is null.

Invoking a Delegate

You invoke a delegate by calling it, as if it were simply a method. The parameters used to invoke the delegate are used to invoke each of the methods on the invocation list (unless one of the parameters is an output parameter, which I will explain shortly).

For example, the delegate delVar, as shown in the following code, takes a single integer input value. Invoking the delegate with a parameter causes it to invoke each of the members in its invocation list with the same parameter value (55, in this case). The invocation is illustrated in Figure 15-8.

```
MyDel delVar   = Inst.MyM1;
delVar        += SC1.m3;
delVar        += X.Act;
   ...
delVar( 55 );                                  // Invoke the delegate.
   ...
```

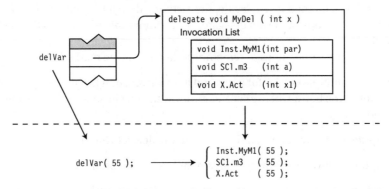

Figure 15-8. *When the delegate is invoked, it invokes each of the methods in its invocation list, with the same parameters with which it was called.*

A method can be in the invocation list more than once. If that is the case, then when the delegate is invoked, the method will be called each time it is encountered in the list.

Delegate Example

The following code defines and uses a delegate with no parameters and no return value. Note the following about the code:

- Class Test defines two print functions.

- Method Main creates an instance of the delegate and then adds three more methods.

- The program then invokes the delegate, which calls its methods.

- Note the test for the null delegate, before attempting to invoke it.

```
// Define a delegate with no return value and no parameters.
delegate void PrintFunction();

class Test
{
    public void Print1()
    { Console.WriteLine("Print1 -- instance"); }

    public static void Print2()
    { Console.WriteLine("Print2 -- static"); }
}

class Program
{
    static void Main()
    {
        Test t = new Test();       // Create a test class instance.
        PrintFunction pf;          // Create a null delegate.

        pf = t.Print1;             // Instantiate and initialize the delegate.

        // Add three more methods to the delegate.
        pf += Test.Print2;
        pf += t.Print1;
        pf += Test.Print2;

        // The delegate now contains four methods.
        if( null != pf )           // Make sure the delegate has methods.
            pf();                  // Invoke the delegate.
        else
            Console.WriteLine("Delegate is empty");
    }
}
```

This code produces the following output:

```
Print1 -- instance
Print2 -- static
Print1 -- instance
Print2 -- static
```

Invoking Delegates with Return Values

If a delegate has a return value and more than one method in its invocation list, the following occurs:

- The value returned by the last method in the invocation list will be the value returned from the delegate invocation.

- The return values from all the other methods in the invocation list are ignored.

For example, the following code declares a delegate that returns an int value. Main creates an object of the delegate and adds two additional methods. It then calls the delegate in the WriteLine statement and prints its return value. Figure 15-9 shows a graphical representation of the code.

```
delegate int MyDel( );                    // Declare method with return value.
class MyClass {
    int IntValue = 5;
    public int Add2() { IntValue += 2; return IntValue;}
    public int Add3() { IntValue += 3; return IntValue;}
}

class Program {
    static void Main( )
    {
        MyClass mc = new MyClass();
        MyDel mDel = mc.Add2;             // Create and initialize the delegate.
        mDel += mc.Add3;                  // Add a method.
        mDel += mc.Add2;                  // Add a method.
        Console.WriteLine("Value: {0}", mDel() );
    }                                            ↑
}                          Invoke the delegate and use the return value.
```

This code produces the following output:

```
Value: 12
```

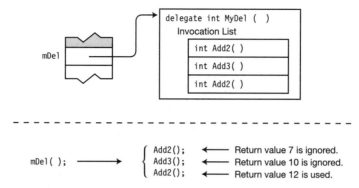

Figure 15-9. *The return value of the last method executed is the value returned by the delegate.*

Invoking Delegates with Reference Parameters

If a delegate has a reference parameter, the value of the parameter can change upon return from one or more of the methods in the invocation list.

- When calling the next method in the invocation list, the *new value of the parameter* is the one passed to the next method.

For example, the following code invokes a delegate with a reference parameter. Figure 15-10 illustrates the code.

```
delegate void MyDel( ref int X );

class MyClass {
    public void Add2(ref int x) { x += 2; }
    public void Add3(ref int x) { x += 3; }
    static void Main(string[] args)
    {
        MyClass mc = new MyClass();

        MyDel mDel = mc.Add2;
        mDel += mc.Add3;
        mDel += mc.Add2;

        int x = 5;
        mDel(ref x);

        Console.WriteLine("Value: {0}", x);
    }
}
```

This code produces the following output:

Value: 12

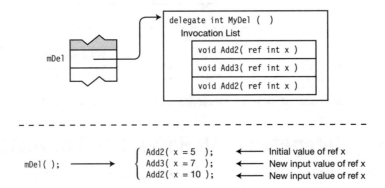

Figure 15-10. *The value of a reference parameter can change between calls.*

Anonymous Methods

So far, you've seen that you can use either static methods or instance methods to instantiate a delegate. In either case, the method itself can be called explicitly from other parts of the code, and, of course, must be a member of some class or struct.

What if, however, the method is used only one time—to instantiate the delegate? In that case, other than the syntactic requirement for creating the delegate, there is no real need for a separate, named method. C# 2.0 introduces the anonymous method, which allows you to dispense with the separate, named method.

- An *anonymous method* is a method that is declared in-line, at the point of instantiating a delegate.

For example, Figure 15-11 shows two versions of the same class. The version on the left declares and uses a method named Add20. The version on the right uses an anonymous method instead. The nonshaded code of both versions is identical.

```
class Program                                        class Program
{                                                    {
  public static int Add20(int x)
  {
    return x + 20;
  }

  delegate int OtherDel(int InParam);                  delegate int OtherDel(int InParam);
  static void Main()                                   static void Main()
  {                                                    {
    OtherDel del = Add20;                                OtherDel del = delegate(int x)
                                                                        {
                                                                          return x + 20;
                                                                        };
    Console.WriteLine("{0}", del(5));                    Console.WriteLine("{0}", del(5));
    Console.WriteLine("{0}", del(6));                    Console.WriteLine("{0}", del(6));
  }                                                    }
}                                                    }
          Named Method                                      Anonymous Method
```

Figure 15-11. *Comparing a named method and an anonymous method*

Both sets of code in Figure 15-11 produce the following output:

```
25
26
```

Using Anonymous Methods

You can use an anonymous method in the following places:

- As an initializer expression when declaring a delegate variable.

- On the right-hand side of an assignment statement when combining delegates.

- On the right-hand side of an assignment statement adding a delegate to an event. Chapter 16 covers events.

Syntax of Anonymous Methods

The syntax of an anonymous method expression includes the following components:

- The type keyword `delegate`.

- The *parameter list* can be omitted if the statement block doesn't use any parameters.

- The *statement block* contains the code of the anonymous method.

```
             Parameter
  Keyword      list            Statement block
    ↓           ↓                    ↓
  delegate ( Parameters )  { ImplementationCode }
```

Return Type

An anonymous method does not explicitly declare a return type. The behavior of the implementation code itself, however, must match the delegate's return type, by returning a value of that type. If the delegate has a return type of `void`, then the anonymous method code cannot return a value.

For example, in the following code the delegate's return type is `int`. The implementation code of the anonymous method must therefore return an `int` on all pathways through the code.

```
Return type of delegate type
            ↓
delegate int OtherDel(int InParam);

static void Main()
{
    OtherDel del = delegate(int x)
                   {
                       return x + 20 ;                  // Returns an int
                   };
        ...
}
```

Parameters

Except in the case of array parameters, the parameter list of an anonymous method must match that of the delegate in the following three characteristics:

- Number of parameters

- Types of the parameters

- Modifiers

You can simplify the parameter list of an anonymous method by leaving the parentheses empty or omitting them altogether, if *both* of the following are true:

- The delegate's parameter list does not contain any out parameters.

- The anonymous method does not use *any* parameters.

For example, the following code declares a delegate that does not have any out parameters, and an anonymous method that does not use any parameters. Since both conditions are met, you can omit the parameter list from the anonymous method.

```
delegate void SomeDel ( int X );          // Declare the delegate type.

SomeDel SDel = delegate                   // Parameter list omitted
               {
                   PrintMessage();
                   Cleanup();
               };
```

params Parameters

If the delegate declaration's parameter list contains a params parameter, then the params keyword is omitted from the parameter list of the anonymous method. For example, in the following code:

- The delegate type declaration specifies the last parameter as a params type parameter.

- The anonymous method parameter list, however, must omit the params keyword.

```
                    Params keyword used in delegate type declaration
                                       ↓
    delegate void SomeDel( int X, params int[] Y);


                    Params keyword omitted in matching anonymous method
                                       ↓
    SomeDel mDel = delegate (int X, int[] Y)
                   {
                         ...
                   };
```

Scope of Variables and Parameters

The scopes of parameters and local variables declared in an anonymous method are limited to the body of the implementation code, as illustrated in Figure 15-12.

For example, the following anonymous method defines parameter y and local variable z. After the close of the body of the anonymous method, y and z are no longer in scope. The last line of the code would produce a compile error.

```
delegate void MyDel( int x );
...

MyDel mDel = delegate ( int y )
             {
                 int z = 10;
                 Console.WriteLine("{0}, {1}", y, z);
             };                                         Scope of y and z

Console.WriteLine("{0}, {1}", y, z);    // Compile error.
                              ↑
                         Out of Scope
```

Figure 15-12. *Scope of variables and parameters*

Outer Variables

Unlike the named methods of a delegate, anonymous methods have access to the local variables and environment of the scope surrounding them.

- Variables from the surrounding scope are called *outer variables*.

- An outer variable used in the implementation code of an anonymous method is said to be *captured* by the method.

For example, the code in Figure 15-13 shows variable x defined outside the anonymous method. The code in the method, however, has access to x and can print its value.

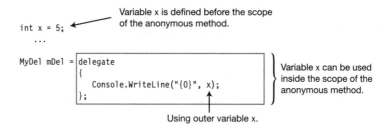

```
                              Variable x is defined before the scope
    int x = 5;  ←             of the anonymous method.
    ...

MyDel mDel = delegate
             {
                 Console.WriteLine("{0}", x);          Variable x can be used
             };                                        inside the scope of the
                                                       anonymous method.
                        ↑
             Using outer variable x.
```

Figure 15-13. *Using an outer variable*

Extension of Captured Variable's Lifetime

A captured outer variable remains alive, as long as its capturing method is part of the delegate, even if the variable would have normally gone out of scope.

For example, the code in Figure 15-14 illustrates the extension of a captured variable's lifetime.

- Local variable x is declared and initialized inside a block.

- Delegate mDel is then instantiated, using an anonymous method that captures outer variable x.

- When the block is closed, x goes out of scope.

- If the WriteLine statement following the close of the block were to be uncommented, it would cause a compile error, because it references x, which is now out of scope.

- The anonymous method inside delegate mDel, however, maintains x in its environment and prints its value, when mDel is invoked.

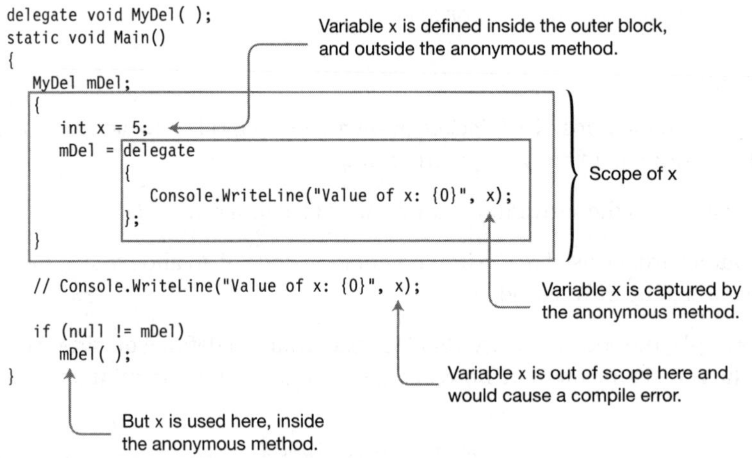

```
delegate void MyDel( );
static void Main()                        Variable x is defined inside the outer block,
{                                         and outside the anonymous method.
    MyDel mDel;
    {
        int x = 5;
        mDel = delegate
        {
            Console.WriteLine("Value of x: {0}", x);
        };                                                   Scope of x
    }

    // Console.WriteLine("Value of x: {0}", x);        Variable x is captured by
                                                       the anonymous method.
    if (null != mDel)
        mDel( );                              Variable x is out of scope here and
}                                             would cause a compile error.

        But x is used here, inside
        the anonymous method.
```

Figure 15-14. *Variable captured in an anonymous method*

This code produces the following output:

Value of x: 5

CHAPTER 16

■■■

Events

Events Are Like Delegates
Overview of Source Code Components
Declaring an Event
Raising an Event
Subscribing to an Event
Standard Event Usage
The MyTimerClass Code
Event Accessors

Events Are Like Delegates

The preceding chapter covered delegates. Many aspects of events are similar to those of delegates. In fact, an event is like a simpler delegate that is specialized for a particular use. Figure 16-1 illustrates that, like a delegate, an event has methods registered with it, and invokes those methods when it is invoked.

The following are some important terms related to events:

- *Raising* an event: The term for *invoking* or *firing* an event. When an event is raised, all the methods registered with it are invoked—in order.

- *Publisher*: A class or struct that makes an event available to other classes or structs for their use.

- *Subscriber*: A class or struct that registers methods with a publisher.

- *Event handler*: A method that is registered with an event. It can be declared in the same class or struct as the event, or in a different class or struct.

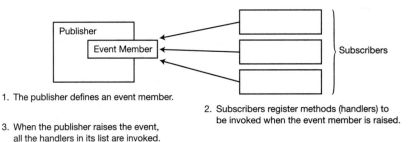

1. The publisher defines an event member.

2. Subscribers register methods (handlers) to be invoked when the event member is raised.

3. When the publisher raises the event, all the handlers in its list are invoked.

Figure 16-1. *Publishers and subscribers*

An Event Has a Private Delegate

There's good reason for the similarities in the behaviors of delegates and events. An event contains a private delegate, as illustrated in Figure 16-2. The important things to know about an event's private delegate are the following:

- An *event* gives structured access to its privately controlled delegate.

- Unlike the many operations available with a delegate, with an event, you can only add, remove, and invoke event handlers.

- When an event is raised, it invokes the delegate, which sequentially calls the methods in the invocation list.

Notice in Figure 16-2 that only the += and -= operators are sticking out to the left of the event. This is because they are the only operations allowed on an event.

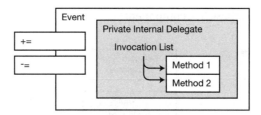

Figure 16-2. *An event as an encapsulated delegate*

Figure 16-3 illustrates the runtime view of a publisher class with an event called Elapsed. ClassA and ClassB, on the right, each have an event handler registered with Elapsed. Inside the event you can see the delegate referencing the two event handlers. Besides the event, the publisher also contains the code that raises the event.

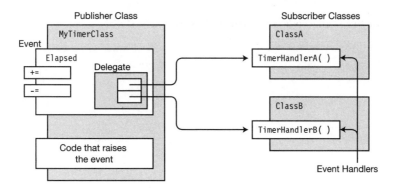

Figure 16-3. *Structure and terminology of a class with a timer event*

Overview of Source Code Components

There are five portions of code that need to be in place to use events:

- *Delegate type declaration*: The event and the event handlers must have a common signature and return type, which is described by the delegate type declaration.

- *Event handler declarations*: The declarations in the subscriber classes, of the methods (the event handlers) to be executed when the event is raised.

- *Event declaration*: The declaration in the publisher class, of the event that holds and invokes the event handlers.

- *Event registration*: The code that connects the event handlers to the event.

- *Code that raises the event*: The code in the publisher that calls the event, causing it to invoke its event handlers.

Figure 16-4 illustrates these five components.

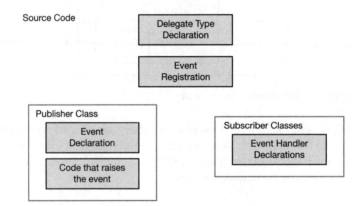

Figure 16-4. *The five source code components of using an event*

Declaring an Event

The publisher must provide the event and the code to raise the event.

Creating an event is simple—it requires only a delegate type and a name. The syntax for an event declaration is shown in the following code, which declares an event called `Elapsed`. Notice the following about event `Elapsed`:

- It is declared inside a class called `MyTimerClass`.

- It accepts event handlers with the return type and signature matching the delegate type `EventHandler`.

- It is declared public so that other classes and structs can register event handlers with it.

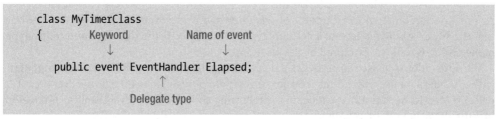

```
class MyTimerClass
{
    public event EventHandler Elapsed;
}
```

You can declare more than one event in a declaration statement by using a comma-separated list. For example, the following statement declares three events.

```
public event EventHandler MyEvent1, MyEvent2, OtherEvent;
```

Events can also be static, by including the `static` keyword in the declaration, as shown in the following code.

```
public static event EventHandler Elapsed;
```

An Event Is a Member

A common error is to think of an event as a type, which it is not. An event is a *member*, and there are several important ramifications to this:

- Because an event is a member
  - It must be declared in a class or struct, with the other members.
  - You cannot declare an event in a block of executable code.

- Because a member is not a type, you do not use a new expression to create its object. That is done automatically when its class or struct object is created.

The Delegate Type and EventHandler

An event declaration requires the name of a *delegate type*. You can either declare one or use one that already exists. If you declare a delegate type, it must specify the signature and return type of the methods that will be stored by the event.

A better idea is to use the predefined delegate type used by the .NET BCL and designated as the standard for use with events. You are strongly encouraged to use it. It is the EventHandler delegate, and its declaration is shown in the following code. Delegate EventHandler is covered in more detail later in this chapter.

```
public delegate void EventHandler(object sender, EventArgs e);
```

Raising an Event

The event member itself just holds the event handlers that need to be invoked. Nothing happens with them unless the event is raised. You need to make sure there is code to do just that, at the appropriate times.

For example, the following code raises event Elapsed. Notice the following about the code:

- Before raising the event, it is compared to null, to see whether it contains any event handlers. If the event is null, it is empty.

- Raising the event itself is like invoking a function.
  - Use the name of the event, followed by the parameter list enclosed in parentheses.
  - The parameter list must match the delegate type of the event.

```
      if (Elapsed != null)        // Make sure there are methods to execute.
          Elapsed(obj, e);        // Raise the event.
             ↑        ↑
      Event name   Parameter list
```

Putting together the event declaration and the code to raise the event gives the following class declaration for the publisher. The code contains two members: the event, and a method called OnOneSecond, which raises the event.

```
public class MyTimerClass
{
   public event EventHandler Elapsed;    // Declare the event.

   private void OnOneSecond(object obj, EventArgs e)
   {
      if (Elapsed != null)              // Make sure there are methods to execute.
         Elapsed(obj, e);
   }            ↑
       Raise the event.

   // The following code makes sure that method OnOneSecond is called every
   // 1,000 milliseconds.
      ...
}
```

For now, I'll let method OnOneSecond be somehow, mysteriously, called once every second. Later in the chapter I'll show you how to make this happen. But for now, remember these important points:

- The class has an event.

- The class has the code to raise the event.

Subscribing to an Event

To add an event handler to an event, the handler must have the same return type and signature as the event's delegate.

- Use the += operator to add an event handler to an event, as shown in the following code.

- The method can be either an instance method or a static method.

For example, the following code adds three methods to event Elapsed.

```
   Class              Instance method
     ↓                    ↓
   mc.Elapsed += ca.TimerHandlerA;                      // Method reference form
   mc.Elapsed += ClassB.TimerHandlerB;                  // Method reference form
         ↑                  ↑
   Event member        Static method
   mc.Elapsed += new EventHandler(cc.TimerHandlerC); // Delegate form
```

The following program uses the MyTimerClass class declared in the previous section. The code performs the following:

- It registers two event handlers from two different class instances.

- After registering the event handlers, it sleeps for 2 seconds. During that time, the timer class raises the event two times, and both event handlers are executed each time.

```
public class MyTimerClass { ... }

class ClassA {
   public void TimerHandlerA(object obj, EventArgs e)      // Event handler
   { Console.WriteLine("Class A handler called"); }
}

class ClassB {
   public static void TimerHandlerB(object obj, EventArgs e)   // Static
   { Console.WriteLine("Class B handler called"); }
}

class Program {
   static void Main( )
   {
      ClassA ca = new ClassA();                // Create the class object.
      MyTimerClass mc = new MyTimerClass();    // Create the timer object.

      mc.Elapsed += ca.TimerHandlerA;          // Add handler A -- instance.
      mc.Elapsed += ClassB.TimerHandlerB;      // Add handler B -- static.

      Thread.Sleep(2000);
   }
}
```

This code produces the following output:

```
Class A handler called
Class B handler called
Class A handler called
Class B handler called
```

Removing Event Handlers

You can remove an event handler from an event by using the -= operator, as shown here.

```
mc.Elapsed -= ca.TimerHandlerA;          // Remove handler A.
```

For example, in the following code, you remove the event handler for ClassB after the first two times the event is raised, and then let the program run for another 2 seconds.

```
...
mc.Elapsed += ca.TimerHandlerA;          // Add instance handler A.
mc.Elapsed += ClassB.TimerHandlerB;      // Add static handler B.
Thread.Sleep(2250);                      // Sleep more than 2 seconds.

mc.Elapsed -= ClassB.TimerHandlerB;      // Remove static handler B.
Thread.Sleep(2250);                      // Sleep more than 2 seconds.
```

This code produces the following output. The first four lines are the result of both handlers being called twice, in the first two seconds. After you removed the handler for ClassB, only the handler for the instance of ClassA was called, during the last 2 seconds.

```
Class A handler called
Class B handler called
Class A handler called
Class B handler called
Class A handler called          ←The event handler for ClassB has been removed.
Class A handler called
```

Adding Anonymous Method Event Handlers

You can also add anonymous method event handlers, just as with delegates.

For example, the following code adds an anonymous method to the event and then sleeps for a little more than 2 seconds. The event is raised twice in that time.

```
                              Anonymous method
                                     ↓
    mc.Elapsed += delegate(object obj, EventArgs e)
           {
               Console.WriteLine("This is the anonymous method.");
           };
           ↑
    Semicolon required

    Thread.Sleep(2250);
}
```

This code produces the following output:

```
This is the anonymous method.
This is the anonymous method.
```

Standard Event Usage

GUI programming is event driven, which means that while the program is running, it can be interrupted at any time by events such as button clicks, key presses, or system timers. When this happens, the program needs to handle the event and then continue on its course.

Clearly, this asynchronous handling of program events is the perfect situation to use C# events. Windows GUI programming uses events so extensively that there is a standard .NET Framework pattern for using them, which you are strongly encouraged to follow.

The foundation of the standard pattern for event usage is the EventHandler delegate type, which is declared in the System namespace. The declaration of the EventHandler delegate type is shown in the following code.

- The first parameter is meant to hold a reference to the object that raised the event. It is of type object and can, therefore, match any instance of any type.

- The second parameter is meant to hold state information of whatever type is appropriate for the application.

- The return type is void.

```
public delegate void EventHandler(object sender, EventArgs e);
```

Using the EventArgs Class

The second parameter in the EventHandler delegate type is an object of class EventArgs, which is declared in the System namespace. You might be tempted to think that, since the second parameter is meant for passing data, an EventArgs class object would be able to store data of some sort. You would be wrong.

- The EventArgs class is designed to carry no data. It is used for event handlers that do *not* need to pass data—and is generally ignored by them.

- If you want to pass data, you must declare a class *derived* from EventArgs, with the appropriate fields to hold the data you want to pass.

Even though the EventArgs class does not actually pass data, it is an important part of the pattern of using the EventHandler delegate. Class object and class EventArgs are the base classes of whatever actual types are used as the parameters. This allows EventHandler to provide a signature that is the lowest common denominator for all events and event handlers, allowing them to have exactly two parameters, rather than having different signatures for each case.

Passing Data by Extending EventArgs

To pass data in the second parameter of your event handler, and adhere to the standard conventions, you need to declare a custom class derived from EventArgs that can store the data you need passed. The name of the class should end in *EventArgs*. For example, the following code declares a custom class that can store a string in a field called Message.

```
           Custom class name     Base class
                    ↓                  ↓
public class MyTCEventArgs: EventArgs
{
   public string Message;                 // Stores a message
   public MyTCEventArgs(string s)         // The constructor sets the message.
   {
      Message = s;
   }
}
```

Using the Custom Delegate

Now that you have a custom class for passing data in the second parameter of your event handlers, you need a delegate type that uses the new custom class. There are two ways you can do this:

- The first way is to use the nongeneric method:
  - Create a new custom delegate, using your custom class type, as shown in the following code.
  - Use the new delegate name throughout the four other sections of the event code.

```
             Custom delegate name             Custom class
                      ↓                            ↓
   public delegate void MyTCEventHandler(object sender, MyTCEventArgs e);
```

- The second way is new with C# 2.0, and uses the generic delegate EventHandler<>, which is also declared in the namespace System. To use the generic delegate, follow these steps:
  - Place the name of the custom class between the angle brackets.
  - Use the entire string, wherever you would have used the name of your custom delegate type. For example, this is what the event declaration would look like.

```
            Generic delegate using custom class
                           ↓
   public event EventHandler< MyTCEventArgs > Elapsed;
                                                  ↑
                                             Event name
```

Use the custom class and the custom delegate, either nongeneric or generic, in the other four sections of code dealing with the event.

For example, the following code updates the MyTimerClass code to use a custom EventArgs class called MyTCEventArgs and the generic EventHandler<> delegate.

```
public class MyTCEventArgs: EventArgs            ┐
{                                                │
   public string Message;                        │   Declaration of custom class
                                                 │
   public MyTCEventArgs(string s) {              │
      Message = s;                               │
   }                                             │
}                                                ┘

public class MyTimerClass    Event declaration
{                                   ↓
   public event EventHandler<MyTCEventArgs> Elapsed;    // Event declaration

   private void OnOneSecond(object obj, EventArgs e)
   {
      if (Elapsed != null)                                         ┐
      {                                                            │
         MyTCEventArgs mtcea =                                     │
            new MyTCEventArgs("Message from OnOneSecond");         │  Code to raise event
         Elapsed(obj, mtcea);                                      │
      }                                                            │
   }                                                               │
   ...                                                             ┘
}

class ClassA
{                                                                  ┐
   public void TimerHandlerA(object obj, MyTCEventArgs e)          │
   {                                                               │
      Console.WriteLine("Class A Message:  {0}", e.Message);       │  Event handler
   }                                                               │
}                                                                  ┘

class Program
{
   static void Main()
   {
      ClassA ca = new ClassA();
      MyTimerClass mc = new MyTimerClass();
                    Register event handler
      mc.Elapsed +=          ↓                            // Register handler.
         new EventHandler<MyTCEventArgs>(ca.TimerHandlerA);

      Thread.Sleep(3250);
   }
}
```

This code produces the following output:

```
Class A Message:  Message from OnOneSecond
Class A Message:  Message from OnOneSecond
Class A Message:  Message from OnOneSecond
```

The MyTimerClass Code

Now that you've seen all five areas of code that need to be implemented to use an event, I can show you the full MyTimerClass class that I have been using.

Most things about the class have been pretty clear—it has an event called Elapsed that can be subscribed to, and a method called OnOneSecond that is called every second and raises the event. The one question remaining about it is, what causes OnOneSecond to be called every second?

The answer is that OnOneSecond is, itself, an event handler that is subscribed to an event in a class called Timer, in the System.Timers namespace. The event in Timer is raised every 1,000 milliseconds and calls event handler OnOneSecond, which in turn raises event Elapsed in class MyTimerClass. Figure 16-5 shows the structure of the code.

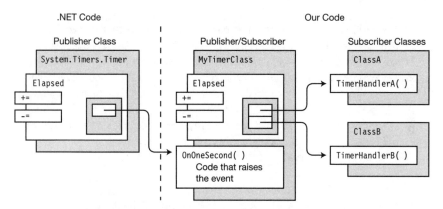

Figure 16-5. *The code structure of MyTimerClass*

The Timer class is a useful tool, so I'll mention a little more about it. First, it has a public event called Elapsed. If that sounds familiar, it's because I named the event in MyTimerClass after it. The names have no other connection than that. I could have named the event anything.

One of the properties of Timer is Interval, which is of type double, and specifies the number of milliseconds between raising the event. The other property I use is Enabled, which is of type bool, and starts and stops the timer.

The actual code is the following. The only things I haven't shown previously are the private timer field, called MyPrivateTimer, and the constructor for the class. The constructor does the work of setting up the internal timer and attaching it to event handler OnOneSecond.

```csharp
public class MyTimerClass
{
    public event EventHandler Elapsed;

    private void OnOneSecond(object obj, EventArgs e)
    {
        if (Elapsed != null)
            Elapsed(obj, e);
    }


    //------------
    private System.Timers.Timer MyPrivateTimer;     // Private timer.

    public MyTimerClass()                           // Constructor
    {
        MyPrivateTimer = new System.Timers.Timer(); // Create the private timer.


        // The following statement sets our OnOneSecond method above as an event
        // handler to the Elapsed event of class Timer.  It is completely
        // unrelated to our event Elapsed, declared above.
        MyPrivateTimer.Elapsed += OnOneSecond;      // Attach our event handler.


        // Property Interval is of type double, and specifies the number of
        // milliseconds between when its event is raised.
        MyPrivateTimer.Interval = 1000;             // 1 second interval.


        // Property Enabled is of type bool, and turns the timer on and off.
        MyPrivateTimer.Enabled = true;              // Start the timer.
    }
}
```

Event Accessors

The last topic to cover in this chapter is event accessors. I mentioned earlier that the += and -= operators were the only operations allowed for an event. These operators have the well-defined behavior that you have seen so far in this chapter.

You can, however, change these operators' behavior and have the event perform whatever custom code you like when they ar
e used. You can do this by defining event accessors for
the event.

- There are two accessors: add and remove.

- The declaration of an event with accessors looks similar to the declaration of a property.

The following example shows the form of an event declaration with accessors. Both accessors have an implicit value parameter called value, which takes a reference to either an instance method or a static method.

```
public event EventHandler Elapsed
{
    add
    {
        ...                              // Code to implement the =+ operator
    }
    remove
    {
        ...                              // Code to implement the -= operator
    }
}
```

When event accessors are declared, the event does not contain an embedded delegate object. You must implement your own storage mechanism for storing and removing the methods registered with the event.

The event accessors act as void methods, meaning that they cannot use return statements that return a value.

CHAPTER 17

■ ■ ■

Interfaces

What Is an Interface?

Declaring an Interface

Implementing an Interface

An Interface Is a Reference Type

Implementing Multiple Interfaces

Implementing Interfaces with Duplicate Members

References to Multiple Interfaces

An Inherited Member As an Implementation

Explicit Interface Member Implementations

Interfaces Can Inherit Interfaces

Using the as Operator with Interfaces

What Is an Interface?

An *interface* is a reference type that represents a set of function members, but does not implement them. Other types—classes or structs—can implement interfaces.

To get a feeling for interfaces, I'll start by showing one that is already defined. The BCL declares an interface called IComparable, which is shown in the code that follows. Notice that the interface body contains the declaration of a single method, CompareTo, which takes a single parameter of type object. Although the method has a name, parameters, and a return type, there is no implementation. Instead, the implementation is replaced by a semicolon.

```
          Keyword    Interface name
              ↓            ↓
    public interface IComparable
    {
        int CompareTo( object obj );
    }                              ↑
                  Semicolon in place of method implementation
```

Figure 17-1 illustrates interface IComparable. The CompareTo method is shown in gray to illustrate that it doesn't contain an implementation.

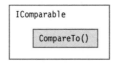

Figure 17-1. *Representation of interface IComparable*

Although the interface declaration does not provide an implementation for the method, the .NET documentation of interface IComparable describes what the method should do, in case you decide to create a class or struct that implements the interface. It says that when the method is called, it should return one of the following values:

- A negative value, if the current object is less than the parameter object.

- A positive value, if the current object is greater than the parameter object.

- Zero, if the two objects are considered equal in the comparison.

Example Using the IComparable Interface

To understand what this means and why it's useful, let's start by taking a look at the following code, which takes an unsorted array of integers and sorts them in ascending order.

- The first line creates an array of five integers that are in no particular order.

- The second line uses the static Sort method of the Array class to sort the elements.

- The foreach loop prints them out, showing that the integers are now in ascending order.

```
int[] MyInt = new int[5] { 20, 4, 16, 9, 2 }; // Create an array of ints.

Array.Sort(MyInt);                             // Sort elements by magnitude.

foreach (int i in MyInt)                       // Print them out.
   Console.Write("{0} ", i);
```

This code produces the following output:

```
2 4 9 16 20
```

The Sort method works great on an array of ints, but what would happen if you were to try to use it on one of your own classes, as shown here?

```
class MyClass                   // Declare a simple class.
{
   public int TheValue;
}
   ...
MyClass[] mc= new MyClass[5];   // Create an array of five elements.
   ...                          // Create and initialize the elements.

Array.Sort(mc);                 // Try to use Sort--raises exception
```

When you try to run this code, it raises an exception. So why did it work for an array of ints, but not for an array of MyClass objects?

The reason Sort doesn't work with the array of user-defined objects is that it relies on the objects in the array to implement interface IComparable. When Sort is running, it compares one element of the array to another by calling the element's CompareTo method and passing in as a parameter a reference to the other element.

The int type implements IComparable, but MyClass does not, so when Sort tries to call the nonexistent CompareTo method of MyClass, it raises an exception.

So how can you make the Sort method work with objects of type MyClass? To implement an interface, a class or struct must do two things:

- It must list the interface name in its base class list.

- It must provide an implementation for each of the interface's members.

For example, the following code updates MyClass to implement interface IComparable. Notice the following about the code:

- The name of the interface is listed in the base class list of the class declaration.

- The class implements a method called CompareTo, whose parameter type and return type match those of the interface member.

- Method CompareTo is implemented following the definition given in the interface's documentation. That is, it returns a negative 1, positive 1, or 0, depending on its value compared to the object passed into the method.

```
                Interface name in base class list
                              ↓
class MyClass : IComparable
{
    public int TheValue;

    public int CompareTo(object obj)    // Implementation of interface method
    {
        MyClass mc = (MyClass)obj;
        if (this.TheValue < mc.TheValue) return -1;
        if (this.TheValue > mc.TheValue) return  1;
        return 0;
    }
}
```

Figure 17-2 illustrates the updated class. The arrow from the grayed interface method to the class method indicates that the interface method does not contain code, but is implemented by the class-level method.

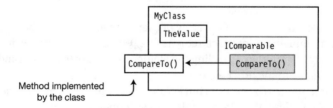

Figure 17-2. *Implementing IComparable in MyClass*

Now that MyClass implements IComparable, Sort will work on it as well. It would not, by the way, have been sufficient to just declare the CompareTo method—it must be part of implementing the interface, which means placing the interface name in the base class list.

The following shows the complete updated code, which can now use the Sort method to sort an array of MyClass objects. Main creates and initializes an array of MyClass objects and then prints them out. It then calls Sort and prints them out again to show that they have been sorted.

```csharp
class MyClass: IComparable                        // Class implements interface
{
   public int TheValue;
   public int CompareTo(object obj)               // Implement the method.
   {
      MyClass mc = (MyClass)obj;
      if (this.TheValue < mc.TheValue) return -1;
      if (this.TheValue > mc.TheValue) return 1;
      return 0;
   }
}

class Program
{
   static void PrintOut( string s, MyClass[] ma)
   {
      Console.Write(s);
      foreach (MyClass i in ma)
         Console.Write("{0} ", i.TheValue);
      Console.WriteLine("");
   }

   static void Main()
   {
      int[] MyInt = new int[5] { 20, 4, 16, 9, 2 };

      MyClass[] MyMc    = new MyClass[5];          // Create array of MyClass objs
      for (int i = 0; i < 5; i++)                  // Initialize the array.
      {
         MyMc[i] = new MyClass();
         MyMc[i].TheValue = MyInt[i];
      }
```

```
        PrintOut("Initial Order:  ", MyMc);      // Print the initial array.
        Array.Sort( MyMc );                      // Sort the array.
        PrintOut("Sorted Order:   ", MyMc);      // Print the sorted array.
    }
}
```

This code produces the following output:

```
Initial Order:   20 4 16 9 2
Sorted Order:    2 4 9 16 20
```

Declaring an Interface

The previous section used an interface that was already declared in the BCL. In this section, you'll see how to declare interfaces.

The important things to know about declaring an interface are the following:

- An interface declaration can only contain declarations of the following kinds of function members:
    - Methods
    - Properties
    - Events
    - Indexers

- The declarations of these function members cannot contain any implementation code. Instead, a semicolon must be used for the body of each member declaration.

- An interface declaration cannot contain data members.

- By convention, interface names begin with an uppercase *I* (e.g., ISaveable).

For example, the following code shows the declaration of an interface with two method members:

```
Keyword      Interface name
   ↓             ↓
interface IMyInterface1              Semicolon in place of body
{                                        ↓
    int    DoStuff     ( int nVar1, long lVar2 );
    double DoOtherStuff( string s, long x );
}                                    ↑
                            Semicolon in place of body
```

There is an important difference between the accessibility of an interface and the accessibility of interface members.

- An interface declaration can have any of the access modifiers public, protected, internal, or private.

- *Members* of an interface, however, are implicitly public, and *no* access modifiers, including public, are allowed.

```
Access modifiers are allowed on interfaces.
   ↓
public interface IMyInterface2
{
    private int Method1( int nVar1, long lVar2 );          // Error
}    ↑
Access modifiers are NOT allowed on interface members.
```

Implementing an Interface

An interface can only be implemented by either a class or a struct. As shown in the Sort example, to implement an interface, a class or struct must

- Include the name of the interface in its base class list.

- Supply implementations for each of the interface's members.

For example, the following code shows a new declaration for class MyClass, which implements interface IMyInterface1, declared in the previous section. Notice that the interface name is listed in the base class list after the colon, and that the class provides the actual implementation code for the interface members.

```
            Colon   Interface name
              ↓         ↓
class MyClass: IMyInterface1
{
    int    DoStuff     ( int nVar1, long lVar2 )
    { ... }                                              // Implementation code

    double DoOtherStuff( string s, long x )
    { ... }                                              // Implementation code
}
```

Some important things to know about implementing interfaces are the following:

- If a class implements an interface, it must implement *all* the members of that interface.

- If a class is derived from a base class and also implements interfaces, the name of the base class must be listed in the base class list *before* any interfaces, as shown here:

```
            Base class must be first        Interface names
                     ↓                           ↓
class Derived : MyBaseClass, IIfc1, IEnumerable, IEnumerator
{
    ...
}
```

Example with a Simple Interface

The following code declares an interface named IIfc1, which contains a single method named PrintOut. Class MyClass implements interface IIfc1 by listing it in its base class list and supplying a method named PrintOut that matches the signature and return type of the interface member. Main creates an object of the class and calls the method from the object.

```
interface IIfc1    Semicolon in place of body                  // Declare interface
{                        ↓
    void PrintOut(string s);
}
            Implement interface
                    ↓
class MyClass : IIfc1                                          // Declare class
{
    public void PrintOut(string s)                            // Implementation
    {
        Console.WriteLine("Calling through:  {0}", s);
    }
}

class Program
{
    static void Main()
    {
        MyClass mc = new MyClass();                           // Create instance
        mc.PrintOut("object.");                               // Call method
    }
}
```

This code produces the following output:

```
Calling through:  object.
```

An Interface Is a Reference Type

An interface is more than just a list of members for a class or struct to implement. It is a reference type.

You cannot access an interface directly through the class object's members. You can, however, get a *reference to the interface* by casting the class object reference to the type of the interface. Once you have a reference to the interface, you can use dot-syntax notation with the reference to call interface members.

For example, the following code shows an example of getting an interface reference from a class object reference.

- In the first statement, variable mc is a reference to a class object that implements interface IIfc1. The statement casts that reference to a reference to the interface and assigns it to variable ifc.

- The second statement uses the reference to the interface to call the implementation method.

```
Interface     Cast to interface
   ↓               ↓
IIfc1 ifc = (IIfc1) mc;                 // Get ref to interface
     ↑              ↑
 Interface ref   Class object ref

ifc.PrintOut ("interface");             // Use ref to interface to call member
       ↑
Use dot-syntax notation to call through the interface reference.
```

For example, the following code declares an interface and a class that implements it. The code in Main creates an object of the class, and calls the implementation method through the class object. It also creates a variable of the interface type, casts the reference of the class object to the interface type, and calls the implementation method through the reference to the interface.

```
interface IIfc1
{
   void PrintOut(string s);
}

class MyClass: IIfc1
{
   public void PrintOut(string s)
   {
      Console.WriteLine("Calling through:  {0}", s);
   }
}

class Program
{
   static void Main()
   {
      MyClass mc = new MyClass();   // Create class object
      mc.PrintOut("object.");       // Call class object implementation method

      IIfc1 ifc = (IIfc1)mc;        // Cast class object ref to interface ref
      ifc.PrintOut("interface.");   // Call interface method
   }
}
```

Figure 17-3 illustrates the class and the reference to the interface.

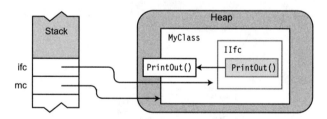

Figure 17-3. *A reference to the class object and a reference to the interface*

Implementing Multiple Interfaces

In the examples shown so far, the classes have implemented a single interface.

- A class or struct can implement any number of interfaces.

- All the interfaces implemented must be listed in the base class list and separated by commas (following the base class name, if there is one).

For example, the following code shows class MyData, which implements two interfaces: IDataRetrieve and IDataStore. Figure 17-4 illustrates the implementation of the multiple interfaces in the class shown in the preceding code.

```
interface IDataRetrieve { int GetData(); }              // Declare interface
interface IDataStore { void SetData( int x ); }         // Declare interface

                   Interface        Interface
                      ↓                ↓
class MyData: IDataRetrieve, IDataStore                 // Declare class
{
    int mem1;                                           // Declare field
    public int  GetData()       { return mem1; }
    public void SetData( int x ){ mem1 = x; }
}

class Program {
    static void Main() {                                // Main
        MyData data = new MyData();
        data.SetData( 5 );
        Console.WriteLine("Value = {0}", data.GetData());
    }
}
```

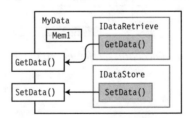

Figure 17-4. *Class implementing multiple interfaces*

Implementing Interfaces with Duplicate Members

Since a class can implement any number of interfaces, it is possible that two or more of the interface members might have the same signature and return type. How does the compiler handle that situation?

For example, suppose you had two interfaces—IIfc1 and IIfc2—as shown following. Each interface has a method named PrintOut, with the same signature and return type. If you were to create a class that implemented both interfaces, how should you handle these duplicate interface methods?

```
interface IIfc1
{
   void PrintOut(string s);
}

interface IIfc2
{
   void PrintOut(string t);
}
```

The answer is that if a class implements multiple interfaces, where several of the interfaces have members with the same signature and return type, the class can implement a single member that satisfies all the interfaces containing that duplicated member.

For example, the following code shows the declaration of class MyClass, which implements both IIfc1 and IIfc2. Its implementation of method PrintOut satisfies the requirement for both interfaces.

```
class MyClass : IIfc1, IIfc2              // Implement both interfaces
{
   public void PrintOut(string s)         // Single implementation for both
   {
      Console.WriteLine("Calling through: {0}", s);
   }
}

class Program
{
   static void Main()
   {
      MyClass mc = new MyClass();
      mc.PrintOut("object.");
   }
}
```

This code produces the following output:

```
Calling through:  object.
```

Figure 17-5 illustrates the duplicate interface methods being implemented by a single class-level method implementation.

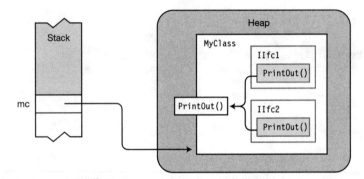

Figure 17-5. *Multiple interfaces implemented by the same class member*

References to Multiple Interfaces

You saw previously that interfaces are reference types, and that you can get a reference to an interface by casting an object reference to the interface type. If a class implements multiple interfaces, you can get separate references for each one.

For example, the following class implements two interfaces with the single method PrintOut. The code in Main calls method PrintOut in three ways:

- Through the class object

- Through a reference to the IIfc1 interface

- Through a reference to the IIfc2 interface

```
interface IIfc1 { void PrintOut(string s); }    // Declare interface
interface IIfc2 { void PrintOut(string s); }    // Declare interface

class MyClass : IIfc1, IIfc2 {                   // Declare class
   public void PrintOut(string s)
   {
      Console.WriteLine("Calling through: {0}", s);
   }
}

class Program {
   static void Main() {
      MyClass mc = new MyClass();
      IIfc1 ifc1 = (IIfc1) mc;                   // Get ref to IIfc1
      IIfc2 ifc2 = (IIfc2) mc;                   // Get ref to IIfc2

      mc.PrintOut("object.");                    // Call through class object
      ifc1.PrintOut("interface 1.");             // Call through IIfc1
      ifc2.PrintOut("interface 2.");             // Call through IIfc2
   }
}
```

This code produces the following output:

```
Calling through:  object.
Calling through:  interface 1.
Calling through:  interface 2.
```

Figure 17-6 illustrates the class object with references to the class object, to IIfc1, and to IIfc2.

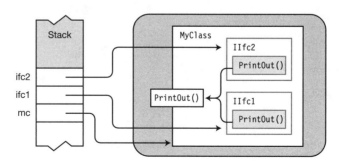

Figure 17-6. *Separate references to different interfaces in the class*

An Inherited Member As an Implementation

A class implementing an interface can inherit the code for an implementation from one of its base classes. For example, the following code illustrates a class inheriting implementation code from a base class.

- IIfc1 is an interface with a method member called PrintOut.

- MyBaseClass contains a method called PrintOut that matches IIfc1's method.

- Class Derived has an empty declaration body, but derives from class MyBaseClass and contains IIfc1 in its base class list.

- Even though Derived's declaration body is empty, the code in the base class satisfies the requirement to implement the interface.

```csharp
interface IIfc1 { void PrintOut(string s); }

class MyBaseClass                                // Declare base class
{
   public void PrintOut(string s)                // Declare the method.
   {
      Console.WriteLine("Calling through: {0}", s);
   }
}

class Derived : MyBaseClass, IIfc1               // Declare class
{
}
```

```
class Program {
   static void Main()
   {
      Derived d = new Derived();            // Create class object
      d.PrintOut("object.");                // Call method
   }
}
```

Figure 17-7 illustrates the preceding code. Notice that the arrow from IIfc1 goes down to the code in the base class.

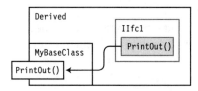

Figure 17-7. *Implementation in the base class*

Explicit Interface Member Implementations

You saw in a previous section that you can use a single class implementation to implement multiple interfaces. This was illustrated in Figures 17-5 and 17-6.

But what if you want separate implementations for each interface? In this case, you can create what are called *explicit interface member implementations*. An explicit interface member implementation has the following characteristics:

- Like all interface implementations, it is placed in the class or struct implementing the interface.

- It is declared using a *qualified interface name*, which consists of the interface name and member name, separated by a dot.

For example, the following code shows the syntax for declaring explicit interface member implementations. Each of the two interfaces implemented by MyClass implements its own version of method PrintOut.

```
class MyClass : IIfc1, IIfc2
{          Qualified interface name
                    ↓
   void IIfc1.PrintOut (string s)            // Explicit implementation
   { ... }

   void IIfc2.PrintOut (string s)            // Explicit implementation
   { ... }
}
```

Figure 17-8 illustrates the class and interfaces. Notice that the boxes representing the explicit interface member implementations are not shown in gray, since they now represent actual code.

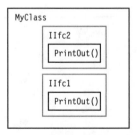

Figure 17-8. *Explicit interface member implementations*

For example, in the following code, class MyClass declares explicit interface member implementations for the members of the two interfaces. Notice that in this example there are only explicit interface member implementations. There is no class-level implementation.

```
interface IIfc1 { void PrintOut(string s); }    // Declare interface
interface IIfc2 { void PrintOut(string t); }    // Declare interface

class MyClass : IIfc1, IIfc2
{          Qualified interface name
                    ↓

   void IIfc1.PrintOut(string s)                 // Explicit interface member
   {                                             //    Implementation
      Console.WriteLine("IIfc1: {0}", s);
   }

           Qualified interface name
                    ↓

   void IIfc2.PrintOut(string s)                 // Explicit interface member
   {                                             //    Implementation
      Console.WriteLine("IIfc2: {0}", s);
   }
}

class Program
{
   static void Main()
   {
      MyClass mc = new MyClass();                // Create class object

      IIfc1 ifc1 = (IIfc1) mc;                   // Get reference to IIfc1
      ifc1.PrintOut("interface 1.");             // Call explicit implementation

      IIfc2 ifc2 = (IIfc2) mc;                   // Get reference to IIfc2
      ifc2.PrintOut("interface 2.");             // Call explicit implementation
   }
}
```

This code produces the following output:

```
IIfc1:  interface 1.
IIfc2:  interface 2.
```

Figure 17-9 illustrates the code. Notice in the figure that the interface methods are not pointing at class-level implementations, but contain their own code.

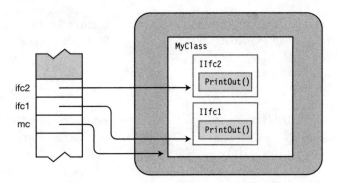

Figure 17-9. *References to interfaces with explicit interface member implementations*

When there is an explicit interface member implementation, a class-level implementation is allowed, but not required. The explicit implementation satisfies the requirement that the class or struct must implement the method. You can therefore have any of the following three implementation scenarios:

- A class-level implementation

- An explicit interface member implementation

- Both a class-level and an explicit interface member implementation

Accessing Explicit Interface Member Implementations

An explicit interface member implementation can only be accessed through a reference to the interface. This means that even other class members can't directly access them.

For example, the following code shows the declaration of class MyClass, which implements interface IIfc1 with an explicit implementation. Notice that even Method1, which is also a member of MyClass, can't directly access the explicit implementation.

- The first two lines of Method1 produce compile errors because the method is trying to access the implementation directly.

- Only the last line in Method1 will compile, because it casts the reference to the current object (this) to a reference to the interface type, and uses that reference to the interface to call the explicit interface implementation.

```csharp
class MyClass : IIfc1
{
    void IIfc1.PrintOut(string s)          // Explicit interface implementation
    {
        Console.WriteLine("IIfc1");
    }

    public void Method1()
    {
        PrintOut("...");                   // Compile error
        this.PrintOut("...");              // Compile error

        ((IIfc1)this).PrintOut("...");     // OK, call method
    }                      ↑
} Cast to a reference to the interface
```

This restriction has an important ramification for inheritance. Since explicit interface member implementations can't even be accessed by other fellow class members directly, they clearly can't be directly accessed by classes derived from the class implementing them either. They must always be accessed through a reference to the interface.

Interfaces Can Inherit Interfaces

You saw earlier that interface implementations can be inherited from base classes. But an interface itself can inherit from one or more other interfaces.

- To specify that an interface should inherit from other interfaces, place the names of the base interfaces in a comma-separated list after a colon, following the interface name in the interface declaration, as follows:

```
                      Colon              Base interface list
                        ↓          ↓
interface IDataIO : IDataRetrieve, IDataStore, IDataRestore
{ ...
```

- Unlike a class, which can only have a single class name in its base class list, an interface can have any number of interfaces in its base interface list.
  - The interfaces in the list can themselves have inherited interfaces.
  - The resulting interface contains all the members it declares, as well as all those of its base interfaces.

The code in Figure 17-10 shows the declaration of three interfaces. Interface IDataIO is derived from the first two. The figure on the right shows IDataIO encompassing the other two interfaces.

```
interface IDataRetrieve
{ int GetData( ); }

interface IDataStore
{ void SetData( int x ); }

// Derives from the first two interfaces
interface IDataIO: IDataRetrieve, IDataStore
{
}

class MyData: IDataIO {
   int nPrivateData;
   public int GetData( )
        { return nPrivateData; }
   public void SetData( int x )
        { nPrivateData = x; }
}

class Program {
   static void Main( ) {
      MyData data = new MyData ();
      data.SetData( 5 );
      Console.WriteLine("{0}", data.GetData());
   }
}
```

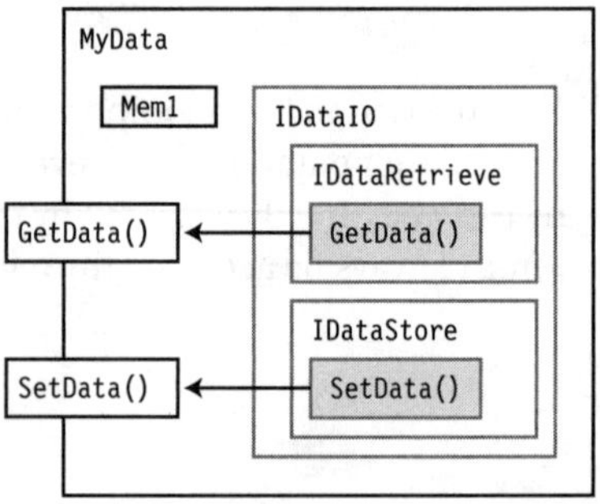

Figure 17-10. *Class with interface inheriting multiple interfaces*

Using the as Operator with Interfaces

The as operator will be covered in detail in Chapter 18, but I will mention it here as well, since it is commonly used with interfaces.

You saw earlier that you can cast a class object reference to a reference to an interface that it implements. If, however, you attempt the cast on a class object that does not implement the interface, the cast operation will raise an exception. You can avoid this problem by using the as operator instead. It works as follows:

- If the class implements the interface, the expression returns a reference to the interface.

- If the class does not implement the interface, the expression returns null rather than raising an exception.

The following code shows the use of the as operator. The first line uses the as operator to obtain an interface reference from a class object. The result of the expression sets the value of b either to null or to a reference to an ILiveBirth interface.

The second line checks the value of b, and if it is not null, executes the command that calls the interface member method.

```
       Class object ref    Interface name
              ↓               ↓
   ILiveBirth b = a as ILiveBirth;              // Similar to cast: (ILiveBirth)a
                 ↑     ↑
       Interface ref   Operator


if (b != null)
    Console.WriteLine("Baby is called: {0}", b.BabyCalled());
```

Example of Different Classes Implementing an Interface

The following code illustrates several aspects of interfaces that have been covered. The program declares a class called Animal, which is used as a base class for several other classes that represent various types of animals. It also declares an interface named ILiveBirth.

Classes Cat, Dog, and Bird all derive from base class Animal. Cat and Dog both implement the ILiveBirth interface, but class Bird does not.

In Main, the program creates an array of Animal objects and populates it with a class object of each of the three types of animal classes. Finally, the program iterates through the array, and using the as operator, retrieves references to the ILiveBirth interface of each object that has one, and calls its BabyCalled method.

```csharp
interface ILiveBirth                      // Declare interface
{
    string BabyCalled();
}

class Animal { }                          // Base class Animal

class Cat : Animal, ILiveBirth            // Declare class Cat
{
    string ILiveBirth.BabyCalled()
    { return "kitten"; }
}

class Dog : Animal, ILiveBirth            // Declare class Dog
{
    string ILiveBirth.BabyCalled()
    { return "puppy"; }
}

class Bird : Animal                       // Declare class Bird
{
}
```

```
class Program
{
   static void Main()
   {
      Animal[] AnimalArray = new Animal[3];// Create Animal array
      AnimalArray[0] = new Cat();          // Insert Cat class object
      AnimalArray[1] = new Bird();         // Insert Bird class object
      AnimalArray[2] = new Dog();          // Insert Dog class object
      foreach( Animal a in AnimalArray )   // Cycle through array
      {
         ILiveBirth b = a as ILiveBirth;// if implements ILiveBirth...
         if (b != null)
            Console.WriteLine("Baby is called: {0}", b.BabyCalled());
      }
   }
}
```

This code produces the following output:

```
Baby is called: kitten
Baby is called: puppy
```

Figure 17-11 illustrates the array and the objects in memory.

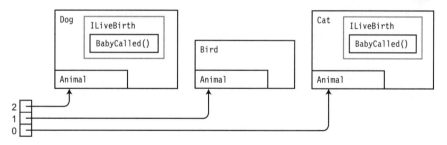

Figure 17-11. *Different object types of base class Animal are interspersed in the array.*

CHAPTER 18

■■■

Conversions

What Are Conversions?
Implicit Conversions
Explicit Conversions and Casting
Types of Conversions
Numeric Conversions
Reference Conversions
Boxing Conversions
Unboxing Conversions
User-Defined Conversions
The is Operator
The as Operator

What Are Conversions?

Consider the simple case in which you declare two variables of different types, and then assign the value of one (*the source*) to the other (*the target*). Before the assignment can occur, the source value must be converted to a value of the target type. Figure 18-1 illustrates type conversion.

- *Conversion* is the process of taking a value of one type and *using it as* the equivalent value of another type.

- The value resulting from the conversion should be the same as the source value—but in the target type.

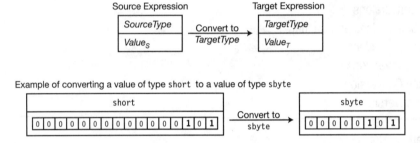

Figure 18-1. *Type conversion*

For example, the code in Figure 18-2 shows the declaration of two variables of different types.

- Var1 is of type short, a 16-bit signed integer that is initialized to 5. Var2 is of type sbyte, an 8-bit signed integer that is initialized to the value 10.

- The third line of the code assigns the value of Var1 to Var2. Since these are two different types, the value of Var1 must be converted to a value of the same type as Var2 before the assignment can be performed. This is performed using the *cast expression*, which you will see shortly.

- Notice also that the value and type of Var1 are unchanged. Although it is called a *conversion*, this only means that the source value is *used as* the target type.

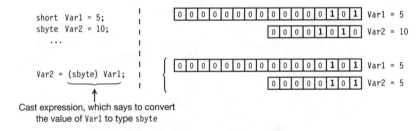

Figure 18-2. *Converting from a short to an sbyte*

Implicit Conversions

For certain types of conversions, there is no possibility of loss of data or precision. For example, it's easy to stuff an 8-bit value into a 16-bit type with no loss of data.

- The language will do these conversions for you automatically. These are called *implicit conversions.*

- When converting from a source type with fewer bits to a target type with more bits, the extra bits in the target need to be filled with either 0s or 1s.

- When converting from a smaller unsigned type to a larger unsigned type, the extra, most significant bits of the target are filled with 0s. This is called *zero extension.*

Figure 18-3 shows an example of the zero extension of an 8-bit value of 10 converted to a 16-bit value of 10.

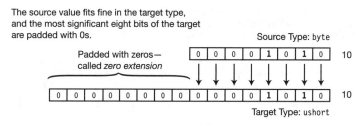

Figure 18-3. *Zero extension in unsigned conversions*

For conversion between signed types, the extra most significant bits are filled with the sign bit of the source expression.

- This maintains the correct sign and magnitude for the converted value.

- This is called *sign extension,* and is illustrated in Figure 18-4, first with 10, and then with -10.

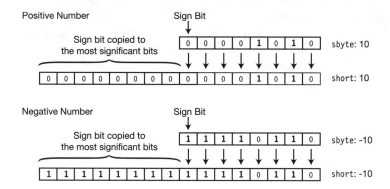

Figure 18-4. *Sign extension in signed conversions*

Explicit Conversions and Casting

When converting from a shorter type to a longer type, it is easy for the longer type to hold all the bits of the shorter type. In other situations, however, the target type might not be able to accommodate the source value without loss of data.

For example, suppose you want to convert a ushort value to a byte.

- A ushort can hold any value between 0 and 65,535.

- A byte can only hold a value between 0 and 255.

- As long as the ushort value you want to convert is less than 256, there won't be any loss of data. If it is greater, however, the most significant bits will be lost.

For example, Figure 18-5 shows an attempt to convert a ushort with a value of 1,365 to a byte, resulting in a loss of data.

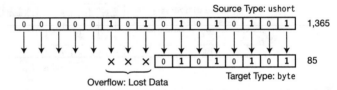

Figure 18-5. *Attempting to convert a ushort to a byte*

Clearly, only a relatively small number (0.4 percent) of the possible unsigned 16-bit ushort values can be safely converted to an unsigned 8-bit byte type without loss of data. The rest result in data *overflow*, yielding a different value.

Casting

For the predefined types, C# will automatically convert from one data type to another—but only between those types for which there is no possibility of data loss between the source type and the target type. That is, the language does not provide automatic conversion between two types if there is *any* value of the source type that would lose data if it were converted to the target type. If you want to make a conversion of this type, it must be an *explicit conversion*, using a *cast expression*.

The following code shows an example of a cast expression. It converts the value of Var1 to type sbyte. A cast expression consists of

- A set of matching parentheses containing the name of the target type

- The source expression, following the parentheses

```
Target type
    ↓
( sbyte ) Var1;
         ↑
    Source expression
```

In using a cast expression, you are explicitly taking responsibility for performing the operation that might lose data. Essentially, you are saying, "In spite of the possibility of data loss, I know what I'm doing, so make this conversion anyway." (Make sure, however, that you *do* know what you're doing.)

For example, Figure 18-6 shows cast expressions converting two values of type ushort to type byte. In the first case, there is no loss of data. In the second case, the most significant bits are lost, giving a value of 85—which is clearly not equivalent to the source value, 1,365.

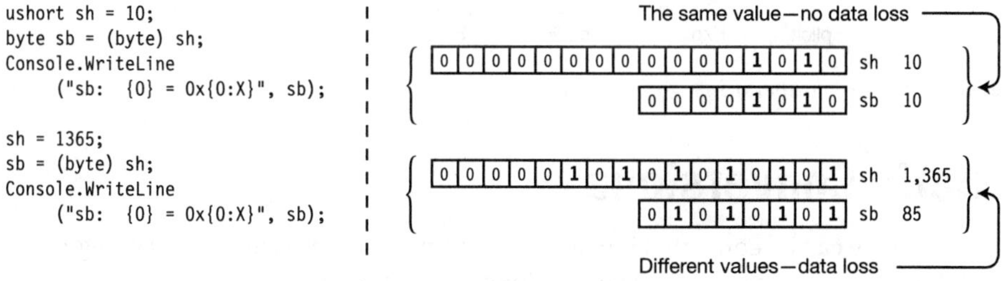

Figure 18-6. *Casting a ushort to a byte*

The output of the code in the figure is the following:

```
sb:  10 = 0xA
sb:  85 = 0x55
```

Types of Conversions

There are a number of standard, predefined conversions for the numeric and reference types. The categories are illustrated in Figure 18-7.

- Beyond the standard conversions, you can also define both implicit and explicit conversions for your user-defined types.

- There is also a predefined type of conversion called *boxing*, which converts any value type to either
  - Type object
  - Type System.ValueType

- Unboxing converts a boxed value back to its original type.

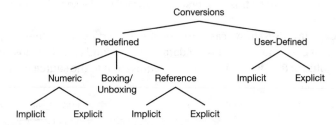

Figure 18-7. *Types of conversions*

Numeric Conversions

Any numeric type can be converted into any other numeric type, as illustrated in Figure 18-8. Some of the conversions are implicit conversions, and others are explicit.

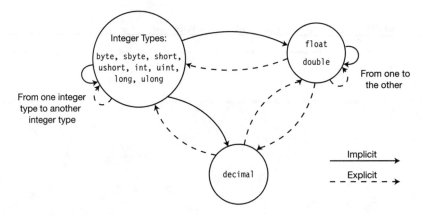

Figure 18-8. *Numeric conversions*

Implicit Numeric Conversions

The implicit numeric conversions are shown in Figure 18-9.

- There is an *implicit conversion* from the source type to the target type if there is a path, following the arrows, from the source type to the destination type.

- Any numeric conversion for which there is not a path following the arrows from the source type to the destination type must be an *explicit conversion*.

The figure demonstrates that, as you would expect, there is an implicit conversion between numeric types that occupy fewer bits to those that occupy more bits.

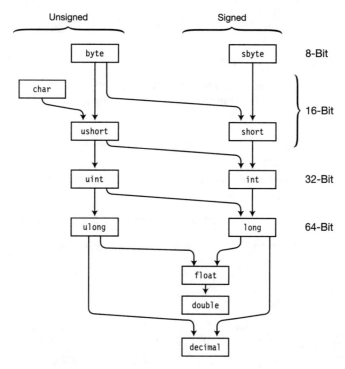

Figure 18-9. *The implicit numeric conversions*

Overflow Checking Context

You've seen that explicit conversions have the possibility of losing data and not being able to represent the source value equivalently in the target type. C# provides you with the ability to choose whether the runtime should check the result for overflow when making these types of conversions. It does this through the checked operator and statement.

- Whether a segment of code is checked or not is called its *overflow checking context*.
  - If you designate an expression or segment of code as checked, the CLR will raise an OverflowException exception if the conversion produces an overflow.
  - If the code is not checked, the conversion will proceed regardless of whether there is an overflow.
- The default overflow checking context is *not* checked.

The checked and unchecked Operators

The checked and unchecked operators control the overflow checking context of an expression, which is placed between a set of parentheses. The syntax is the following:

```
checked ( Expression )
unchecked ( Expression )
```

For example, the following code executes the same conversion—first in a checked operator and then in an unchecked operator.

- In the unchecked context, the overflow is ignored, resulting in the value 208.
- In the checked context, an OverflowException exception is raised.

```
ushort sh = 2000;
byte    sb;

sb = unchecked ( (byte) sh );        // Most significant bits lost
Console.WriteLine("sb: {0}", sb);
sb =   checked ( (byte) sh );        // OverflowException raised
Console.WriteLine("sb: {0}", sb);
```

This code produces the following output:

```
sb: 208

Unhandled Exception: System.OverflowException: Arithmetic operation resulted
 in an overflow. at Test1.Test.Main() in C:\Programs\Test1\Program.cs:line 21
```

The checked and unchecked Statements

The checked and unchecked *operators*, which you just looked at in the previous section, act on the single expression between the parentheses. The checked and unchecked *statements* perform the same function, but control all the conversions in a block of code, rather than in a single expression.

The checked and unchecked statements can be nested to any level.

For example, the following code uses checked and unchecked statements, and produces the same results as the previous example, which uses checked and unchecked expressions. In this case, however, blocks of code are affected, rather than just expressions.

```
byte   sb;
ushort sh = 2000;

unchecked                                   // Set unchecked
{
   sb = (byte) sh;
   Console.WriteLine("sb: {0}", sb);

   checked                                  // Set checked
   {
      sb = (byte) sh;
      Console.WriteLine("sb: {0}", sh);
   }
}
```

Explicit Numeric Conversions

You've seen that the implicit conversions automatically convert from the source expression to the target type because there is no possible loss of data. With the explicit conversions, however, there is the possibility of losing data—so it is important for you as the programmer to know how a conversion will handle that loss if it occurs.

In this section, you will look at each of the various types of explicit numeric conversions. Figure 18-10 shows the subset of explicit conversions shown in Figure 18-8.

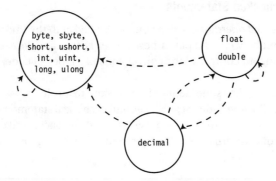

Figure 18-10. *The explicit numeric conversions*

Integral to Integral

Figure 18-11 shows the behavior of the integral-to-integral explicit conversions. In the checked case, if the conversion loses data, the operation raises an OverflowException exception. In the unchecked case, any lost bits go unreported.

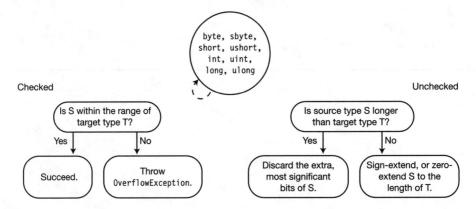

Figure 18-11. *Integer type to integer type explicit conversions*

float or double to Integral

When converting a floating point type to an integer type, the value is rounded toward zero to the nearest integer. Figure 18-12 illustrates the conversion conditions. If the rounded value is not within the range of the target type, then

- The CLR raises an `OverflowException` exception if the overflow checking context is checked.

- C# does not define what its value should be if the context is unchecked.

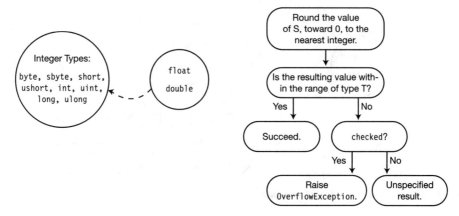

Figure 18-12. *Converting a float or a double to an integral type*

decimal to Integral

When converting from `decimal` to the integer types, the CLR raises an `OverflowException` exception if the resulting value is not within the target type's range. Figure 18-13 illustrates the conversion conditions.

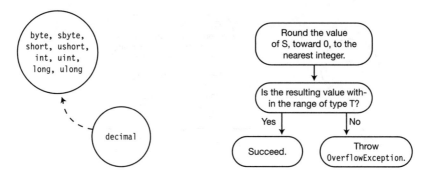

Figure 18-13. *Converting a decimal to an integral*

double to float

Values of type float occupy 32 bits, and values of type double occupy 64 bits. The double type value is rounded to the nearest float type value. Figure 18-14 illustrates the conversion conditions.

- If the value is too small to be represented by a float, the value is set to either positive or negative 0.

- If the value is too large to be represented by a float, the value is set to either positive or negative infinity.

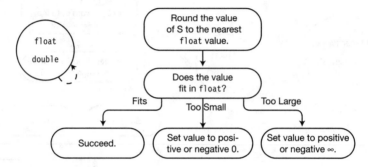

Figure 18-14. *Converting a double to a float*

float or double to decimal

Figure 18-15 shows the conversion conditions for converting from floating point types to decimal.

- If the value is too small to be represented by the decimal type, the result is set to 0.

- If the value is too large, the CLR raises an OverflowException exception.

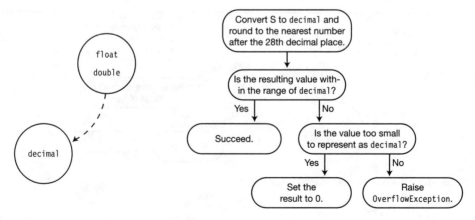

Figure 18-15. *Converting a float or double to a decimal*

decimal to float or double

Conversions from decimal to the floating point types always succeed. There might, however, be a loss of precision. Figure 18-16 shows the conversion conditions.

Figure 18-16. *Converting a decimal to a float or double*

Reference Conversions

As you well know by now, reference type objects comprise two parts in memory: the reference and the data.

- Part of the information held by the reference is the *type of the data it is pointing at.*

- A reference conversion takes a source reference and returns a reference pointing at the same place in the heap, but "labels" it as a different type.

For example, the following code shows two reference variables, MyVar1 and MyVar2, that point to the same object in memory. The code is illustrated in Figure 18-17.

- To MyVar1, the object it references looks like an object of type B—which it is.

- To MyVar2, the same object looks like an object of type A.
  - Even though it is actually pointing at an object of type B, it cannot see the parts of B that extend A, and therefore cannot see Field2.
  - The second WriteLine statement would, therefore, cause a compile error.

Notice that the "conversion" does not change MyVar1.

```
class A     { public int Field1; }

class B: A { public int Field2; }

class Program {
   static void Main( )
   {
      B MyVar1 = new B();
   Return the reference to MyVar1 as a reference to a class A.
                        ↓

      A MyVar2 = (A) MyVar1;

      Console.WriteLine("{0}", MyVar2.Field1);        // Fine
      Console.WriteLine("{0}", MyVar2.Field2);        // Compile error!
   }                                     ↑
}                            MyVar2 can't see Field2.
```

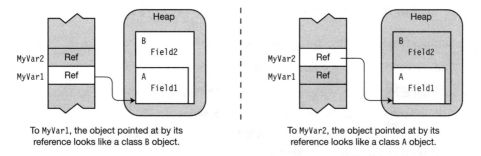

To MyVar1, the object pointed at by its
reference looks like a class B object.

To MyVar2, the object pointed at by its
reference looks like a class A object.

Figure 18-17. *A reference conversion returns a different type associated to the object.*

Implicit Reference Conversions

Just as there are implicit numeric conversions that the language will perform for you automatically, there are also implicit reference conversions. These are illustrated in Figure 18-18.

- All reference types can implicitly be converted to type object.

- Any interface can be implicitly converted to an interface from which it is derived.

- A class can be implicitly converted to
  - Any class in the chain from which it is derived
  - Any interface that it implements

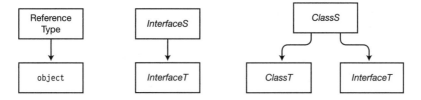

Figure 18-18. *Implicit conversions for classes and interfaces*

A delegate can be implicitly converted to the .NET BCL classes and interfaces shown in Figure 18-19.

An array, *ArrayS*, with elements of type *Ts*, can be implicitly converted to

- The .NET BCL class and interfaces shown in Figure 18-19.

- Another array, *ArrayT*, with elements of type *Tt*, if *all* of the following are true:

  - Both arrays have the same number of dimensions.

  - The element types, *Ts* and *Tt*, are reference types—*not* value types.

  - There is an *implicit* conversion between types *Ts* and *Tt*.

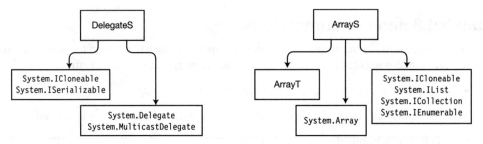

Figure 18-19. *Implicit conversions for delegates and arrays*

Explicit Reference Conversions

Explicit reference conversions are reference conversions from a general type to a more specialized type.

- Explicit conversions include
  - Conversions from an object to any reference type
  - Conversions from a base class to a class derived from it

- The explicit reference conversions are illustrated by reversing each of the arrows in Figures 18-18 and 18-19.

If this type of conversion were allowed without restriction, you could easily attempt to reference members of a class that are not actually in memory. The compiler, though, *does* allow these types of conversions. When encountered at run time, however, the system raises an exception.

For example, the code in Figure 18-20 converts the reference of base class A to its derived class B, and assigns it to variable MyVar2.

- If MyVar2 were to attempt to access Field2, it would be attempting to access a field in the "B part" of the object, which is not in memory—causing a memory fault.

- The runtime will catch this inappropriate cast and raise an InvalidCastException exception. Notice, however, that it does *not* cause a compile error.

```
class A {
    public int Field1 }

class B: A {
    public int Field2 }

class Program {
    static void Main( )
    {
        A MyVar1 = new A();
        B MyVar2 = (B)MyVar1;
    }
}
```

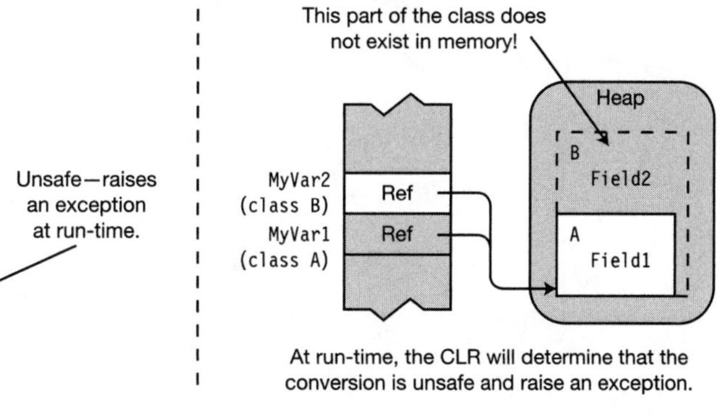

Unsafe—raises
an exception
at run-time.

This part of the class does
not exist in memory!

Heap

MyVar2
(class B)   Ref

MyVar1
(class A)   Ref

B
Field2

A
Field1

At run-time, the CLR will determine that the
conversion is unsafe and raise an exception.

Figure 18-20. *Invalid casts raise runtime exceptions.*

Valid Explicit Reference Conversions

There are three situations in which an explicit reference conversion will succeed at run time—that is, not raise an InvalidCastException exception.

The first case is where the explicit conversion is unnecessary—that is, where the language would have performed an implicit conversion for you anyway. For example, in the code that follows, the explicit conversion is unnecessary because there is always an implicit conversion from a derived class to one of its base classes.

```
class A { }
class B: A { }
   ...
B MyVar1 = new B();
A MyVar2 = (A) MyVar1;// Cast is unnecessary; A is the base class of B.
```

The second case is where the source reference is null. For example, in the following code, even though it would normally be unsafe to convert a reference of a base class to that of a derived class, the conversion is allowed because the value of the source reference is null.

```
class A { }
class B: A { }
   ...
A MyVar1 = null;
B MyVar2 = (B) MyVar1;    // Allowed because MyVar1 is null
```

The third case is where the *actual data* pointed to by the source reference could safely be converted implicitly. The following code shows an example, and Figure 18-21 illustrates the code.

- The implicit conversion in the second line makes `MyVar2` "think" that it is pointing to data of type A, while it is actually pointing to a data object of type B.

- The explicit conversion in the third line is casting a reference of a base class to a reference of one of its derived classes. Normally this would raise an exception. In this case, however, the object being pointed to is actually a *data item of type* B.

```
B MyVar1 = new B();
A MyVar2 = MyVar1;      // Implicitly cast MyVar1 to type A.
B MyVar3 = (B)MyVar2;   // This cast is fine because the data is of type B.
```

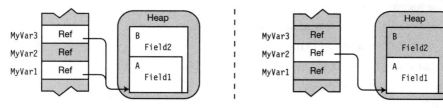

Figure 18-21. *Casting to a safe type*

Boxing Conversions

All C# types, including the value types, are derived from type object. Value types, however, are efficient, lightweight types that do not, by default, include their object component in the heap. When the object component is needed, however, you can use *boxing*, which is an implicit conversion that takes a value type value, creates from it a full reference type object in the heap, and returns a reference to the object.

For example, Figure 18-22 shows three lines of code.

- The first two lines of code declare and initialize value type variable i and reference type variable oi.

- In the third line of code, you want to assign the value of variable i to oi. But oi is a reference type variable, and must be assigned a reference to an object in the heap. Variable i, however, is a value type, and does not *have* a reference to an object in the heap.

- The system therefore *boxes* the value of i by
  - Creating an object of type int in the heap
  - Copying the value of i to the int object
  - Returning the reference of the int object to oi to store as its reference

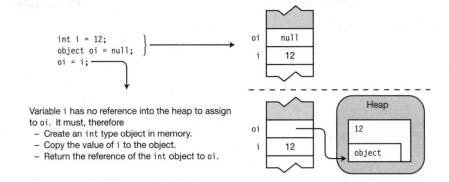

Figure 18-22. *Boxing creates a full reference type object from a value type*

Boxing Creates a Copy

A common misunderstanding about boxing is that it somehow acts upon the item being boxed. It doesn't. It returns a reference type *copy* of the value. After the boxing procedure, there are two copies of the value—the value type original and the reference type copy—each of which can be manipulated separately.

For example, the following code shows the separate manipulation of each copy of the value. Figure 18-23 illustrates the code.

- The first line defines value type variable i and initializes its value to 10.

- The second line creates reference type variable oi and initializes it with the boxed copy of variable i.

- The last three lines of code show i and oi being manipulated separately.

```
int i = 10;                      // Create and initialize value type
  Box i and return the reference to oi.
         ↓
object oi = i;                   // Create and initialize reference type
Console.WriteLine("i: {0}, io: {1}", i, oi);

i  = 12;
oi = 15;
Console.WriteLine("i: {0}, io: {1}", i, oi);
```

This code produces the following output:

```
i: 10, io: 10
i: 12, io: 15
```

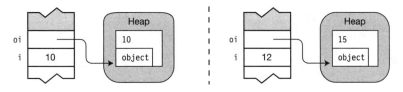

Figure 18-23. *Boxing creates a copy that can be manipulated separately*

The Boxing Conversions

Figure 18-24 shows the boxing conversions. Any value type *ValueTypeS* can be implicitly converted to any of types object, System.ValueType, or *InterfaceT*, if *ValueTypeS* implements *InterfaceT*.

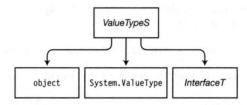

Figure 18-24. *Boxing is the implicit conversion of value types*

Unboxing Conversions

Unboxing is the process of converting a boxed object back to its value type.

- Unboxing is an explicit conversion.

- The system performs the following steps when unboxing a value to *ValueTypeT*:
    - It checks that the object being unboxed is actually a boxed value of type *ValueTypeT*.
    - It copies the value of the object to the variable.

 For example, the following code shows an example of unboxing a value.

- Value type variable i is boxed and assigned to reference type variable oi.

- Variable oi is then unboxed, and its value assigned to value type variable j.

```
static void Main()
{
    int i = 10;
   Box i and assign its reference to oi.
              ↓
    object oi = i;
   Unbox oi and assign its value to j.
              ↓
    int j = (int) oi;
    Console.WriteLine("i: {0},   oi: {1},   j: {2}", i,  oi, j);
}
```

This code produces the following output:

```
i: 10,   oi: 10,   j: 10
```

Attempting to unbox a value to a type other than the original type raises an `InvalidCastException` exception.

The Unboxing Conversions

Figure 18-25 shows the unboxing conversions.

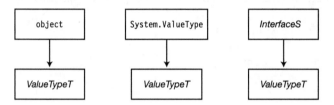

Figure 18-25. *The unboxing conversions*

User-Defined Conversions

Besides the standard conversions, you can also define both implicit and explicit conversions for your own classes and structs.

The syntax for user-defined conversions is shown following.

- The syntax is the same for both implicit and explicit conversion declarations, except for the keywords implicit or explicit.

- The modifiers public and static are required.

```
     Required                        Target              Source
        ↓                              ↓                   ↓
public static implicit operator TargetType ( SourceType Identifier )
{                       ↑
              Implicit or explicit
   ...
   return ObjectOfTargetType;
}
```

For example, the following shows an example of the syntax of a conversion method that converts an object of type Person to an int.

```
public static implicit operator int(Person p)
{
    return p.Age;
}
```

Constraints on User-Defined Conversions

There are some important constraints on user-defined conversions. The most important are the following:

- You can only define user-defined conversions for classes and structs.

- You cannot redefine standard implicit or explicit conversions.

- The following is true for source type *S* and target type *T*:
  - *S* and *T* must be different types.
  - *S* and *T* cannot be related by inheritance. That is, *S* cannot be derived from *T*, and *T* cannot be derived from *S*.
  - Neither *S* nor *T* can be an interface type or the type object.
  - The conversion operator must be a member of either *S* or *T*.

- You cannot declare two conversions, one implicit, and the other explicit, with the same source and target types.

Example of a User-Defined Conversion

The following code defines a class called Person that contains a person's name and age in years. The class also defines two implicit conversions. The first converts a Person object to an int value. The target int value is the age of the person. The second converts an int to a Person object.

```
class Person
{
    public string Name;
    public int Age;
    public Person(string name, int age) {
        Name = name;
        Age = age;
    }

    public static implicit operator int(Person p) { // Convert Person to int
        return p.Age;
    }

    public static implicit operator Person(int i) { // Convert int to Person
        return new Person("Nemo", i);
    }
}


class Program {
    static void Main( )
    {
        Person Bill = new Person( "Bill", 25);

    Convert a Person object to an int.
                   ↓
        int age = Bill;
        Console.WriteLine("Person Info: {0}, {1}", Bill.Name, age);

        Convert an int to a Person object.
                   ↓
        Person Anon = 35;
        Console.WriteLine("Person Info: {0}, {1}", Anon.Name, Anon.Age);
    }
}
```

This code produces the following output:

```
Person Info: Bill, 25
Person Info: Nemo, 35
```

If you had defined the same conversion operators as explicit rather than implicit, then you would have needed to use cast expressions to perform the conversions, as shown here:

```
      ...                 ↓
   public static explicit operator int( Person p ) {
      return p.Age;
   }

...

   static void Main( )
   {
            ... Requires cast expression
                    ↓
      int age = (int) Bill;
            ...
```

Evaluating User-Defined Conversions

The user-defined conversions discussed so far have directly converted the source type to an object of the target type in a single step, as shown in Figure 18-26.

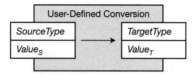

Figure 18-26. *Single-step user-defined conversion*

But user-defined conversions can have up to three steps in the full conversion. Figure 18-27 illustrates these stages, which include

- The preliminary standard conversion

- The user-defined conversion

- The following standard conversion

There is *never* more than a single user-defined conversion in the chain.

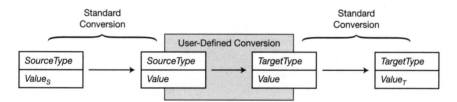

Figure 18-27. *Multi-step user-defined conversion*

Example of a Multi-Step User-Defined Conversion

The following code declares class `Employee`, which is derived from class `Person`.

- Since there is a user-defined conversion from class `Person` to int, then if there is a standard conversion from `Employee` to `Person` and one from int to float, you can convert from `Employee` to float.

  - There is a standard conversion from `Employee` to `Person`, since `Employee` is derived from `Person`.

  - There is a standard conversion from int to float, since that is an implicit numeric conversion.

- Since all three parts of the chain exist, you can convert from `Employee` to float.

```
class Employee : Person { }

class Person
{
   public string Name;
   public int Age;

   // Convert a Person object to an int
   public static implicit operator int(Person p) {
      return p.Age;
   }
}

class Program
{
   static void Main( )
   {
      Employee Bill = new Employee();
      Bill.Name = "William"; Bill.Age = 25;

         Convert an Employee to a float.
                      ↓
      float FVar1 = Bill;

      Console.WriteLine("Person Info: {0}, {1}", Bill.Name, FVar1);
   }
}
```

Figure 18-28 illustrates the conversion.

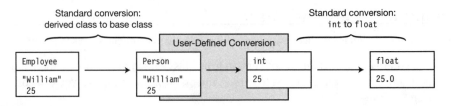

Figure 18-28. *Conversion of Employee to float*

The is Operator

As shown previously, some conversion attempts are not successful, and raise an InvalidCastException exception at run time. Instead of blindly attempting a conversion, you can use the is operator to check whether a conversion would complete successfully.

The syntax of the is operator is the following, where *Expr* is the source expression:

```
Returns a bool
      ↓
Expr is TargetType
```

The operator returns true if *Expr* can be successfully converted to the target type through any of the following:

- A reference conversion

- A boxing conversion

- An unboxing conversion

For example, in the following code, you use the is operator to check whether variable Bill of type Employee can be converted to type Person, and then take the appropriate action.

```
class Employee : Person { }
class Person {
   public string Name = "Anonymous";
   public int Age      = 25;
}

class Program {
   static void Main()
   {
      Employee Bill = new Employee();
      Person p;

      // Check if variable Bill can be converted to type Person
      if( Bill is Person ) {
         p = Bill;
         Console.WriteLine("Person Info: {0}, {1}", p.Name, p.Age);
      }
   }
}
```

The is operator can only be used for reference conversions and boxing and unboxing conversions. It *cannot* be used for user-defined conversions.

The as Operator

The as operator is like the cast operator, except that it does not raise an exception. If the conversion fails, rather than raising an exception, it sets the target reference to null.

The syntax of the as operator is the following, where

- *Expr* is the source expression.

- *TargetType* is the target type, which must be a reference type.

```
                  Returns a reference
                          ↓
                  ─────────────────
                  Expr  as  TargetType
```

Since the as operator returns a reference expression, it can be used as the source for an assignment.

For example, variable Bill of type Employee is converted to type Person, using the as operator, and assigned to variable p of type Person. You then check to see whether p is null before using it.

```
class Employee : Person { }
class Person {
   public string Name = "Anonymous";
   public int Age    = 25;
}

class Program {
   static void Main()
   {
      Employee Bill = new Employee();
      Person p;

      p = Bill as Person;
      if( p != null )
      {
         Console.WriteLine("Person Info: {0}, {1}", p.Name, p.Age);
      }
   }
}
```

The as operator can only be used for reference conversions and boxing conversions. It *cannot* be used for user-defined conversions or conversions to a value type.

CHAPTER 19

■ ■ ■

Generics

What Are Generics?
Generics in C#
Generic Classes
Declaring a Generic Class
Creating a Constructed Type
Creating Variables and Instances
Constraints on Type Parameters
Generic Structs
Generic Interfaces
Generic Delegates
Generic Methods

What Are Generics?

With the language constructs you've learned so far, you can build powerful objects of many different types. You do this mostly by declaring classes that encapsulate the behavior you want, and then creating instances of those classes.

All the types used in the class declarations so far have been specific types—either programmer-defined, or supplied by the language or the BCL. There are times, however, when a class would be more useful if you could "distill" or "refactor" out its actions and apply them not just to the data types for which they are coded, but for other types as well.

Generics allow you to do just that. You can refactor your code and add an additional layer of abstraction so that, for certain kinds of code, the data types are not hard-coded. This is particularly designed for cases in which there are multiple sections of code performing the same instructions, but on different data types.

That might sound pretty abstract, so we'll start with an example that should make things clearer.

A Stack Example

Suppose first that you have created the following code, which declares a class called MyIntStack, which implements a stack of ints. It allows you to push ints onto the stack and pop them off.

```
class MyIntStack                        // Stack for ints
{
   int    StackPointer = 0;
   int[] StackArray;                    // Array of int


   public void Push( int x )            // Input type: int
   {
      ...
   }

   public int Pop()                     // Return type: int
   {
      ...
   }

      ...
}
```

Suppose now that you would like the same functionality for values of type float. There are several ways you could achieve this. One way is to perform the following steps to produce the subsequent code:

- Cut and paste the code for class MyIntStack.

- Change the class name to MyFloatStack.

- Change the appropriate int declarations to float declarations throughout the class declaration.

```
class MyFloatStack                      // Stack for floats
{
    int   StackPointer = 0;
    float[] StackArray;                 // Array of float


    public void Push( float x )         // Input type: float
    {
        ...
    }


    public float Pop()                  // Return type: float
    {
        ...
    }

    ...
}
```

This method works, but is error-prone, and has the following drawbacks:

- You need to inspect every part of the class carefully to determine which type declarations need to be changed, and which should be left alone.

- You need to repeat the process for each new type of stack class you need (long, double, string, etc.).

- After the process, you end up with multiple copies of nearly identical code, taking up additional space.

- Debugging and maintaining the parallel implementations is inelegant and error-prone.

Generics in C#

With C# 2.0, Microsoft introduced the *generics* features, which offer more elegant ways of using a set of code with more than one type. Generics allow you to declare *type-parameterized* code, which you can instantiate with different types. What this means is that you can write the code with "placeholders for types," and then supply the *actual* types when you create an instance of the class.

By this point in the text, you should be very familiar with the concept that a type is not an object, but a template for an object. In the same way, a generic type is not a type, but a template for a type. Figure 19-1 illustrates this point.

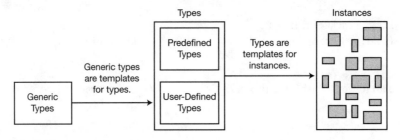

Figure 19-1. *Generic types are templates for types.*

C# provides five kinds of generics: classes, structs, interfaces, delegates, and methods. Notice that the first four are types, and methods are members.

Figure 19-2 shows how generic types fit in with the other types covered.

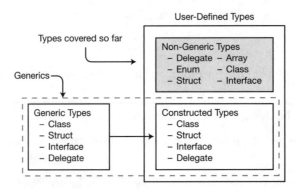

Figure 19-2. *Generics and user-defined types*

Continuing with the Example

In the stack example just shown, with classes `MyIntStack` and `MyFloatStack`, the bodies of the declarations of the classes are identical except at the positions dealing with the type of the value held by the stack.

- In `MyIntStack`, these positions are occupied by type `int`.

- In `MyFloatStack`, they are occupied by `float`.

You can create a generic class from `MyIntStack` by doing the following:

- Take the `MyIntStack` class declaration, and instead of substituting `float` for `int`, substitute the placeholder `T`.

- Change the class name to `MyStack`.

- Place the string `<T>` after the class name.

The result is the following generic class declaration. The string consisting of the angle brackets with the `T` means that `T` is a placeholder for a type. (It doesn't have to be the letter `T`—it could be any identifier.) Everywhere throughout the body of the class declaration where `T` is located, an actual type will need to be substituted by the compiler.

```
class MyStack <T>
{
    int StackPointer = 0;
    T [] StackArray;

    public void Push(T x ) {...}

    public T Pop() {...}
        ...
}
```

Generic Classes

Now that you've seen a generic class, let's look at generic classes in more detail and see how they are created and used.

When you are creating and using your own regular, non-generic classes, there are two steps in the process: declaring the class and creating instances of the class. But generic classes are templates for classes, not actual classes—so you must first construct actual class types from them. You can then create references and instances from these constructed class types.

Figure 19-3 illustrates the process at a high level. If it's not all completely clear yet, don't worry—each part will be covered in the sections that follow.

1. Declare a class, using placeholders for some of the types.

2. Provide *actual* types to substitute in for the placeholders. This gives you an actual class definition, with all the "blanks" filled in.

3. Create instances from the "filled-in" class definition.

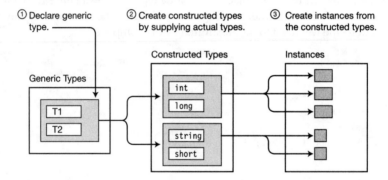

Figure 19-3. *Creating instances from a generic type*

Declaring a Generic Class

Declaring a simple generic class is much like declaring a regular class, with the following differences:

- Place a matching set of angle brackets after the class name.

- Between the angle brackets, place a comma-separated list of the placeholder strings that represent the types, to be supplied on demand. These are called *type parameters*.

- Use the type parameters throughout the body of the declaration of the generic class to represent the types that should be substituted in.

For example, the following code declares a generic class called SomeClass. The type parameters are listed between the angle brackets, and then used throughout the body of the declaration as if they were real types.

```
                    Type parameters
                         ↓
  class SomeClass < T1, T2 >
  {    Normally, types would be used in these positions.
                  ↓                     ↓
     public T1 SomeVar  = new T1();
     public T2 OtherVar = new T2();
  }             ↑                   ↑
       Normally, types would be used in these positions.
```

There is no special keyword that flags a generic class declaration. The presence of the type parameter list distinguishes a generic class declaration from a regular class declaration.

Creating a Constructed Type

You cannot create class objects directly from a generic class. First, you need to tell the compiler what *actual* types should be substituted for the placeholders (the type parameters). The compiler takes those actual types and creates a template from which it creates actual class objects.

To construct a class type from a generic class, list the class name and supply real types between the angle brackets, in place of the type parameters. The real types being substituted for the type parameters are called *type arguments*.

```
               Type arguments
                    ↓
  SomeClass< short, int >
```

The compiler takes the type arguments and substitutes them for their corresponding type parameters throughout the body of the generic class, producing the *constructed type*—from which actual class instances are created.

Figure 19-4 shows the declaration of generic class SomeClass on the left. On the right, it shows the constructed class created by using the type arguments short and int.

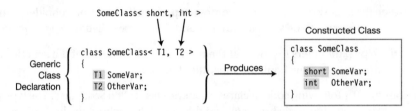

Figure 19-4. *Supplying type arguments for all the type parameters of a generic class produces a constructed class from which actual class objects can be created.*

Figure 19-5 illustrates the difference between *type parameters* and *type arguments*.

- Generic class declarations have type parameters.

- Type arguments are the actual types you supply when creating a constructed type.

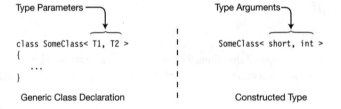

Figure 19-5. *Type parameters versus type arguments*

Creating Variables and Instances

A constructed class type is used just like a regular type in creating references and instances. For example, the following code shows the creation of two class objects.

- The first line shows the creation of an object from a regular, non-generic class. This is a form that you should be completely familiar with by now.

- The second line shows the creation of an object from generic class SomeClass, instantiated with types short and int. The form is exactly analogous to the line above it, with the constructed class forms in place of a regular class name.

```
MyNonGenClass        MyNGC = new MyNonGenClass        ();
SomeClass<short, int> MySc  = new SomeClass<short, int>();
```
        ↑   ↑
    Constructed class   Constructed class

As with non-generic classes, the reference and the instance can be created separately, as shown in Figure 19-6. The figure also shows that what is going on in memory is the same as for a non-generic class.

- The first line below the generic class declaration allocates a reference in the stack for variable MyClass. Its value is null.

- The second line allocates an instance in the heap, and assigns its reference to the variable.

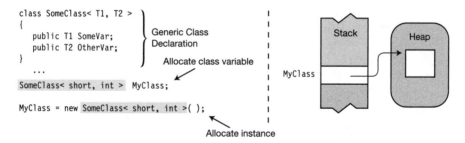

Figure 19-6. *Using a constructed type to create a reference and an instance*

Many different class types can be constructed from the same generic class. Each one is a separate class type, just as if it had its own separate non-generic class declaration.

For example, the following code shows the creation of two types from generic class SomeClass. The code is illustrated in Figure 19-7.

- One type is constructed with types short and int.

- The other is constructed with types int and long.

```
class SomeClass< T1, T2 >                        // Generic class
{
    ...
}

class Program                                    // Program
{
    static void Main()                           // Main
    {
        SomeClass<short, int> First =            // Constructed type
                new SomeClass<short, int>();

        SomeClass<int, long> Second =            // Constructed type
                new SomeClass<int, long>();

        ...
```

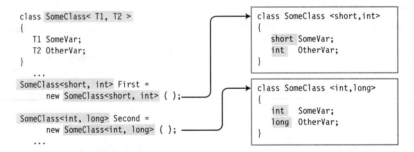

Figure 19-7. *Two constructed classes created from a generic class*

The Stack Example Using Generics

The following code shows the stack example implemented using generics. Method `Main` defines two variables: `StackInt` and `StackString`. The two constructed types are created using `int` and `string` as the type arguments.

```
class MyStack<T>
{
   T[] StackArray;
   int StackPointer = 0;

   public void Push(T x) {
      if ( !IsStackFull )
         StackArray[StackPointer++] = x;
   }

   public T Pop() {
      return ( !IsStackEmpty )
         ? StackArray[--StackPointer]
         : StackArray[0];
   }

   const int MaxStack = 10;
   bool IsStackFull  { get{ return StackPointer >= MaxStack; } }
   bool IsStackEmpty { get{ return StackPointer <= 0; } }

   public MyStack() {
      StackArray = new T[MaxStack];
   }

   public void Print() {
      for (int i = StackPointer -1; i >= 0 ; i--)
         Console.WriteLine("   Value: {0}", StackArray[i]);
   }
}
```

```
class Program {
   static void Main() {
       MyStack<int>    StackInt = new MyStack<int>();
       MyStack<string> StackString = new MyStack<string>();

       StackInt.Push(3); StackInt.Push(5); StackInt.Push(7);
       StackInt.Print();
       StackString.Push("This is fun");
       StackString.Push("Hi there!  ");
       StackString.Print();
   }
}
```

This code produces the following output:

```
Value: 7
Value: 5
Value: 3
Value: Hi there!
Value: This is fun
```

Comparing the Generic and Non-Generic Stack

Table 19-1 summarizes some of the differences between the initial non-generic version of the stack and the final generic version of the stack. Figure 19-8 illustrates some of these differences.

Table 19-1. *Differences Between the Non-Generic and Generic Stacks*

	Non-Generic	Generic
Source Code Size	Larger: you need a new implementation for each type.	Smaller: you only need one implementation regardless of the number of constructed types.
Executable Size	The compiled version of each stack will be present, regardless of whether it is used.	Only types for which there is a constructed type are present in the executable.
Ease of Writing	Easier to write.	Harder to write.
Difficulty to Maintain	More error-prone to maintain, since all changes need to be applied for each applicable type.	Easier to maintain, because modifications are only needed in one place.

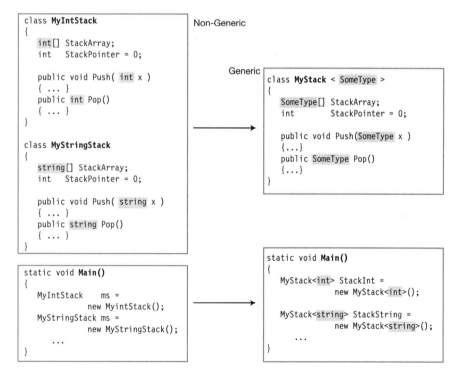

Figure 19-8. *Non-generic stack versus generic stack*

Constraints on Type Parameters

In the generic stack example, the stack did not do anything with the items it contained other than store them and pop them. It did not try to add them, compare them, or do anything else that would require using operations of the items themselves. There's good reason for that. Since the generic stack doesn't know the type of the items it will be storing, it cannot know what members that type implements.

All C# objects, however, are ultimately derived from class object, so the one thing the stack can be sure of about the items it is storing is that they implement the members of class object. These include methods ToString, Equals, and GetType. Other than that, it can't know what members are available.

As long as your code does not access the objects of the types it handles (or as long as it sticks to the members of type object), your generic class can handle *any* type. Type parameters that meet this constraint are called *unbounded type parameters*. If, however, your code tries to use any other members, the compiler will produce an error message.

For example, the following code declares a class called Simple with a method called LessThan that takes two generic type variables. LessThan attempts to return the result of using the less-than operator. But not all classes implement the less-than operator, so the compiler produces an error message.

```
class Simple<T>
{
    static public bool LessThan(T i1, T i2)
    {
        return i1 < i2;                              // Error
    }
    ...
}
```

To make generics more useful, you need to be able to supply additional information to the compiler about what kinds of types are acceptable as arguments. These additional bits of information are called *constraints*. Only arguments that meet the constraints can be substituted for the type parameters.

Where Clauses

Constraints are listed as where clauses.

- Each type parameter that has constraints has its own where clause.

- If a parameter has multiple constraints, they are listed in the where clause, separated by commas.

The syntax of a where clause is the following:

```
        Type parameter              Constraint list
              ↓           _____↓_____
where TypeParam : constraint, constraint, ...
                      ↑
                    Colon
```

The important points about where clauses are the following:

- They are listed after the closing angle bracket of the type parameter list.

- They are not separated by commas, or any other token.

- They can be listed in any order.

- The token where is not a keyword, so you can use it in other contexts.

For example, the following generic class has three type parameters. T1 is unbounded. For T2, only classes of type Customer, or classes derived from Customer, can be used as type arguments. For T3, only classes that implement interface IComparable can be used as type arguments.

```
            Unbounded   With constraints
                ↓    _____↓____  No separators
class MyClass < T1, T2, T3 >        ↓
                  where T2: Customer          // Constraint for T2
                  where T3: IComparable        // Constraint for T3
{                                   ↑
    ...                    No separators
}
```

Constraint Types and Order

There are five types of constraints. These are listed in Table 19-2.

Table 19-2. *Types of Constraints*

Constraint Type	Description
ClassName	Only classes of this type, or classes derived from it, can be used as the type argument.
class	Any reference type, including classes, arrays, delegates, and interfaces, can be used as the type argument.
struct	Any value type can be used as the type argument.
InterfaceName	Only this interface, or types that implement this interface, can be used as the type argument.
new()	Any type with a parameterless public constructor can be used as the type argument. This is called the *constructor constraint*.

The where clauses can be listed in any order. The constraints in a where clause, however, must be placed in a particular order, as shown in Figure 19-9.

- There can be at most one primary constraint, and if there is one, it must be listed first.

- There can be any number of *InterfaceName* constraints.

- If the constructor constraint is present, it must be listed last.

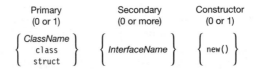

Figure 19-9. *If a type parameter has multiple constraints, they must be in this order.*

The following declarations show examples of where clauses:

```
class SortedList<S>
      where S: IComparable<S> { ... }

class LinkedList<M,N>
      where M : IComparable<M>
      where N : ICloneable    { ... }

class MyDictionary<KeyType, ValueType>
      where KeyType : IEnumerable,
      new()                   { ... }
```

Generic Structs

Like generic classes, generic structs can have type parameters and constraints. The rules and conditions for generic structs are the same as those for generic classes.

For example, the following code declares a generic struct called `PieceOfData`, which stores and retrieves a piece of data, the type of which is determined when the type is constructed. `Main` creates objects of two constructed types—one using `int` and the other using `string`.

```
struct PieceOfData<T>                                    // Generic struct
{
   public PieceOfData(T value) { _Data = value; }
   private T _Data;
   public  T Data
   {
      get { return _Data; }
      set { _Data = value; }
   }
}

class Program
{
   static void Main()                        Constructed type
   {                                                ↓
      PieceOfData<int> IntData       = new PieceOfData<int>(10);
      PieceOfData<string> StringData = new PieceOfData<string>("Hi there.");
                                                ↑
                                         Constructed type
      Console.WriteLine("IntData    = {0}", IntData.Data);
      Console.WriteLine("StringData = {0}", StringData.Data);
   }
}
```

This code produces the following output:

```
IntData    = 10
StringData = Hi there.
```

Generic Interfaces

Generic interfaces allow you to write interfaces where the parameters and return types of interface members are generic type parameters. Generic interface declarations are similar to non-generic interface declarations, but have the type parameter list in angle brackets after the interface name.

For example, the following code declares a generic interface called IMyIfc that declares a single method.

- Generic class Trivial implements the generic interface.

- Main instantiates two objects of the generic class: one with type int, and the other with type string.

```
                  Type parameter
                       ↓
    interface IMyIfc<T>                              // Generic interface
    {
        T ReturnIt(T inValue);
    }
            Type parameter   Generic interface
                  ↓               ↓
    class Trivial<S> : IMyIfc<S>                     // Generic class
    {
        public S ReturnIt(S inValue)                 // Implement interface
        {
            return inValue;
        }
    }

    class Program
    {
        static void Main()
        {
            Trivial<int>    TrivInt    = new Trivial<int>();
            Trivial<string> TrivString = new Trivial<string>();

            Console.WriteLine("{0}", TrivInt.ReturnIt(5));
            Console.WriteLine("{0}", TrivString.ReturnIt("Hi there."));
        }
    }
```

The output of this code is the following:

```
5
Hi there.
```

An Example Using Generic Interfaces

The following example illustrates two additional capabilities of generic interfaces:

- Like other generics, instances of a generic interface instantiated with different type parameters are different interfaces.

- You can implement a generic interface in a *non-generic type*.

For example, the following code is similar to the last example, but in this case, Trivial is a *non-generic* class that implements a generic interface. In fact, it implements two instances of IMyIfc. One instance is instantiated with type int, and the other with type string.

```
interface IMyIfc<T>                          // Generic interface
{
   T ReturnIt(T inValue);
}
        Two different interfaces from the same generic interface
               ↓            ↓
class Trivial : IMyIfc<int>, IMyIfc<string>  // Non-generic class
{
   public int ReturnIt(int inValue)          // Implement int interface
   {
      return inValue;
   }

   public string ReturnIt(string inValue)    // Implement string interface
   {
      return inValue;
   }
}

class Program
{
   static void Main()
   {
      Trivial TrivInt    = new Trivial();
      Trivial TrivString = new Trivial();

      Console.WriteLine("{0}", TrivInt.ReturnIt(5));
      Console.WriteLine("{0}", TrivString.ReturnIt("Hi there."));
   }
}
```

This code produces the following output:

```
5
Hi there.
```

Generic Interface Implementations Must Be Unique

When implementing an interface in a generic type, there must be no possible combination of type arguments that would create a duplicate interface in the type.

For example, in the following code, class Trivial uses two instantiations of interface IMyIfc.

- The first one is a constructed type, instantiated with type int.

- The second one has a type parameter rather than an argument.

This causes a conflict because a class must implement all its declared interfaces. But if int is used as the type argument to replace S in the second interface, then Trivial would have two interfaces of the same type—which is not allowed.

```
interface IMyIfc<T>
{
   T ReturnIt(T inValue);
}
                          Two interfaces
                        ──────── ────────
                            ↓        ↓
class Trivial<S> : IMyIfc<int>, IMyIfc<S>      // Error!
{
   public int ReturnIt(int inValue)       // Implement first interface
   {
      return inValue;
   }

   public S ReturnIt(S inValue)           // Implement second interface,
   {                                      // but if it's int, it would be
      return inValue;                     // the same as the one above.
   }
}
```

Generic Delegates

Generic delegates are very much like non-generic delegates, except that the type parameters determine the characteristics of what methods will be accepted.

- To declare a generic delegate, place the type parameter list in angle brackets after the delegate name, and before the delegate parameter list.

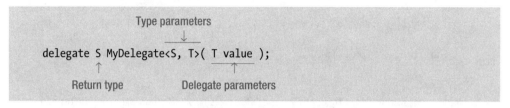

- Notice that there are two parameter lists: the delegate parameter list and the type parameter list.

- The scope of the type parameters includes
  - The return type
  - The formal parameter list
  - The constraint clauses

The following code shows an example of a generic delegate. In Main, generic delegate MyDelegate is instantiated with an argument of type string and initialized with method PrintString.

```
delegate void MyDelegate<T>(T value);              // Generic delegate

class Trivial
{
   static public void PrintString(string s)        // Method matches delegate
   {
      Console.WriteLine(s);
   }

   static public void PrintUpperString(string s)   // Method matches delegate
   {
      Console.WriteLine("{0}", s.ToUpper());
   }
}

class Program
{
   static void Main()
   {
      MyDelegate<string> MyDel =                    // Create inst of delegate
         new MyDelegate<string>(Trivial.PrintString);
      MyDel += Trivial.PrintUpperString;            // Add a method.

      MyDel("Hi There.");                           // Call delegate
   }
}
```

This code produces the following output:

```
Hi There.
HI THERE.
```

Generic Methods

Unlike the other generics, a method is a member, not a type.

Generic methods can be declared in both generic and non-generic classes, structs, and interfaces, as shown in Figure 19-10.

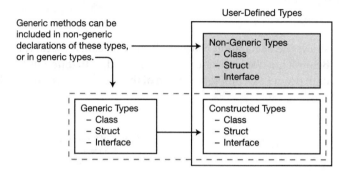

Figure 19-10. *Generic methods can be declared in generic and non-generic types.*

Declaring a Generic Method

Generic methods, like the other generics, have a type parameter list and optional constraints.

- Generic methods, like generic delegates, have two parameter lists, as follows:
    - The *method parameter list*, enclosed in parentheses.
    - The *type parameter list*, enclosed in angle brackets.

- To declare a generic method, do the following:
    - Place the type parameter list immediately after the method name and before the method parameter list.
    - Place the optional constraint clauses after the method parameter list.

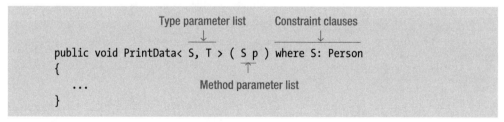

■**Note** Remember that the type parameter list goes *after* the method name and *before* the method parameter list.

Invoking a Generic Method

To invoke a generic method, supply type arguments with the method invocation, as shown here.

```
       Type parameters
              ↓
  MyMethod<short, int>();
  MyMethod<int, long >();
```

Figure 19-11 shows the declaration of a generic method called DoStuff, which takes two type parameters. Below it are two invocations of the method, with different sets of type parameters. Each invocation produces a different version of the method, as shown on the right of the figure.

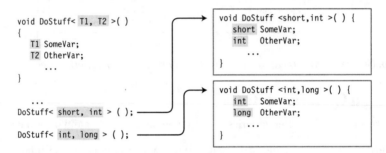

Figure 19-11. *A generic method with two instantiations*

Inferring Types

If you are passing parameters into a method, the compiler can sometimes infer from the types of the *method parameters* the types that should be used as the *type parameters* of the generic method. This can make the method calls simpler and easier to read.

For example, the following code declares MyMethod, which takes a method parameter of the same type as the type parameter.

```
public void MyMethod <T> (T myVal) { ... }
                     ↑    ↑
              Both are of type T
```

If you invoke MyMethod with a variable of type int, as shown in the following code, the information in the type parameter of the method invocation is redundant, since the compiler can see from the method parameter that it is an int.

```
int MyInt = 5;
MyMethod <int> (MyInt);
         ↑       ↑
      Both are ints
```

Since the compiler can infer the type parameter from the method parameter, you can omit the type parameter (and its angle brackets) from the invocation, as shown here:

```
MyMethod(MyInt);
```

Example of a Generic Method

The following code declares a generic method called ReverseAndPrint in a non-generic class called Trivial. The method takes as its parameter an array of any type. Main declares three different array types. It then calls the method twice with each array. The first time it calls the method with a particular array, it explicitly uses the type parameter. The second time, the type is inferred.

```
class Trivial                                          // Non-generic class
{
   static public void ReverseAndPrint<T>(T[] arr)      // Generic method
   {
      Array.Reverse(arr);
      foreach (T item in arr)                          // Use type argument T.
         Console.Write("{0}, ", item.ToString());
      Console.WriteLine("");
   }
}

class Program
{
   static void Main()
   {
      // Create arrays of various types.
      int[] IntArray       = new int[]    { 3, 5, 7, 9, 11 };
      string[] StringArray = new string[] { "first", "second", "third" };
      double[] DoubleArray = new double[] { 3.567, 7.891, 2.345 };

      Trivial.ReverseAndPrint<int>(IntArray);         // Invoke method
      Trivial.ReverseAndPrint(IntArray);              // Infer type and invoke

      Trivial.ReverseAndPrint<string>(StringArray);   // Invoke method
      Trivial.ReverseAndPrint(StringArray);           // Infer type and invoke

      Trivial.ReverseAndPrint<double>(DoubleArray);   // Invoke method
      Trivial.ReverseAndPrint(DoubleArray);           // Infer type and invoke
   }
}
```

This code produces the following output:

```
11 9 7 5 3
3 5 7 9 11
third second first
first second third
2.345 7.891 3.567
3.567 7.891 2.345
```

■ ■ ■

Enumerators and Iterators

Enumerators and Enumerable Types
Using the IEnumerator Interface
The IEnumerable Interface
The Non-Interface Enumerator
The Generic Enumeration Interfaces
The IEnumerator<T> Interface
The IEnumerable<T> Interface
Iterators
Producing Enumerables and Enumerators
Using an Iterator to Produce an Enumerable
Using an Iterator to Produce an Enumerator

Enumerators and Enumerable Types

In Chapter 14, you saw that you can use a foreach statement to cycle through the elements of an array. In this chapter, you'll take a closer look at arrays and see why they can be processed by foreach statements. You'll also look at how you can add this capability to you own user-defined classes. Later, I'll discuss the use of iterators.

Using the foreach Statement

When you use the foreach statement with an array, the statement presents you with each element in the array, one by one, allowing you to read its value.

For example, the following code declares an array with four elements, and then uses a foreach loop to print out the values of the items.

```
int[] Arr1 = { 10, 11, 12, 13 };                    // Define the array.

foreach (int item in Arr1)                          // Enumerate the elements.
   Console.WriteLine("Item value:  {0}", item);
```

This code produces the following output:

```
Item value:  10
Item value:  11
Item value:  12
Item value:  13
```

Why does this work, apparently magically, with arrays? The reason is that an array can produce, upon request, an object called an *enumerator*. The enumerator can return the elements of the array, one by one, in order, as they are requested. The enumerator "knows" the order of the items, and keeps track of where it is in the sequence. It then returns the current item when it is requested.

For types that have enumerators, there must be a way of retrieving them. The standard way of retrieving an object's enumerator in .NET is to call the object's GetEnumerator method. Types that implement a GetEnumerator method are called *enumerable types*, or just *enumerables*. Arrays are enumerables.

Figure 20-1 illustrates the relationship between enumerables and enumerators.

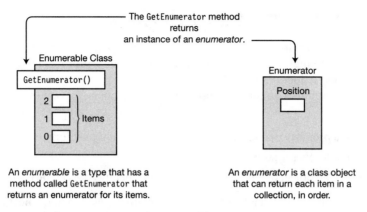

Figure 20-1. *Overview of enumerators and enumerables*

The foreach construct is designed to work with enumerables. As long as the object it is given to iterate over is an enumerable type, such as an array, it will perform the following actions:

- Getting the object's enumerator by calling the GetEnumerator method

- Requesting each item from the enumerator and making it available to your code as the *iteration variable*, which your code can read, but not change

```
                        Must be enumerable
                               ↓
foreach( Type VarName in EnumerableObject )
{
   ...
}
```

Types of Enumerators

There are three variations on enumerators. They all work essentially the same way, with only slight differences. I will discuss all three types. You can implement enumerators using

- The IEnumerator/IEnumerable interfaces—called the *non-generic interface* form

- The IEnumerator<T>/IEnumerable<T> interfaces—called the *generic interface* form

- No interfaces

Using the IEnumerator Interface

This section will start by looking at the first in the preceding list: the non-generic interface form. This form of enumerator is a class that implements the IEnumerator interface. It is called *non-generic* because it does not use C# generics.

The IEnumerator interface contains three function members: Current, MoveNext, and Reset.

- Current is a property that returns the item at the current position in the sequence.
    - It is a read-only property.
    - It returns an object of type object, so an object of any type can be returned.

- MoveNext is a method that advances the enumerator's position to the next item in the collection. It also returns a Boolean value, indicating whether the new position is a valid position or is beyond the end of the sequence.
    - If the new position is valid, the method returns true.
    - If the new position is not valid (i.e., it's at the end), the method returns false.
    - The initial position of the enumerator is *before* the first item in the sequence. MoveNext must be called *before* the first access of Current.

- Reset is a method that resets the position to the initial state.

Figure 20-2 illustrates a collection of three items, which are shown on the left of the figure, and its enumerator, which is shown on the right. In the figure, the enumerator is an instance of a class called ArrEnumerator.

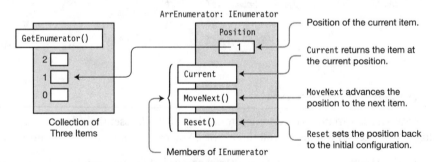

Figure 20-2. *The enumerator for a small collection*

The enumerator class is usually declared as a nested class of the class for which it is an enumerator. A *nested class* is one that is declared inside the declaration of another class.

The way the enumerator keeps track of the current item in the sequence is entirely implementation-dependent. It might be implemented as a reference to an object, an index value, or something else entirely. In the case of an array, it is simply the index of the item.

Figure 20-3 illustrates the states of an enumerator for a collection of three items.

- Notice that the initial position of the enumerator is -1 (i.e., before the first element of the collection).

- Each transition between states is caused by a call to MoveNext, which advances the position in the sequence. Each call to MoveNext between states 1 and 4 returns true. In the transition between states 4 and 5, however, the position ends up beyond the last item in the collection, so the method returns false.

- In the final state, any further calls to MoveNext return false.

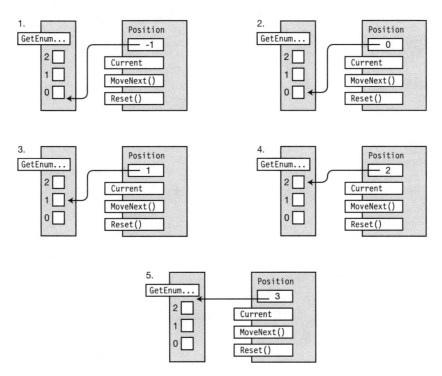

Figure 20-3. *The states of an enumerator*

Given a collection's enumerator, you should be able to simulate a foreach loop by cycling through the items in the collection using the MoveNext and Current members. For example, you know that arrays are enumerable, so the following code does *manually* what the foreach statement does *automatically*. The output is the same as if it were in a foreach loop.

```
static void Main()
{
    int[] MyArray = { 10, 11, 12, 13 };    // Create an array.

    IEnumerator ie = MyArray.GetEnumerator();    // Get its enumerator.
    while (ie.MoveNext() == true)                // Move to the next item.
    {
        int i = (int) ie.Current;            // Get the current item.
        Console.WriteLine("{0}", i);         // Write it out.
    }
}
```

Declaring an IEnumerator Enumerator

To create a non-generic interface enumerator class, you must declare a class that implements the IEnumerator interface. The IEnumerator interface

- Is a member of the System.Collections namespace

- Contains the three members Current, MoveNext, and Reset

The following code shows the outline of a non-generic enumerator class. It does not show how the position is maintained. Notice that Current returns a reference to an object.

```csharp
using System.Collections;                        // Include the namespace.

class MyEnumerator: IEnumerator
{
    public object Current  { get; }              // Current
    public bool MoveNext() { ... }               // MoveNext
    public void Reset()    { ... }               // Reset
        ...
}
```

For example, the following code implements an enumerator class that lists an array of color names:

```
using System.Collections;

class ColorEnumerator: IEnumerator
{
   string[] Colors;
   int Position = -1;

   public object Current {                        // Current
      get { return Colors[Position]; }
   }

   public bool MoveNext() {                       // MoveNext
      if (Position < Colors.Length - 1)
         { Position++; return true; }
      else
         return false;
   }

   public void Reset(){                           // Reset
      Position = -1;
   }

   public ColorEnumerator(string[] theColors)     // Constructor
   {
      Colors = new string[theColors.Length];
      for (int i = 0; i < theColors.Length; i++)
         Colors[i] = theColors[i];
   }
}
```

The IEnumerable Interface

The IEnumerable interface has only a single member, method GetEnumerator, which returns an enumerator for the object.

Figure 20-4 shows class MyClass, which has three items to enumerate, and implements the IEnumerable interface by implementing the GetEnumerator method.

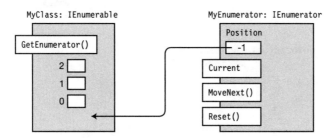

Figure 20-4. *The GetEnumerator method returns an enumerator object for the class.*

The following code shows the form for the declaration of an enumerable class.

```
using System.Collections;
        Implements the IEnumerable interface
                    ↓
class MyClass : IEnumerable
{
    public IEnumerator GetEnumerator { ... }
    ...          ↑
}   Returns an object of type IEnumerator
```

The following code gives an example of an enumerable class that uses enumerator class ColorEnumerator from the previous example. Remember that ColorEnumerator derives from IEnumerator.

```
using System.Collections;

class MyColors: IEnumerable
{
    string[] Colors = { "Red", "Yellow", "Blue" };

    public IEnumerator GetEnumerator()
    {
        return new ColorEnumerator(Colors);
    }                        ↑
}
```

Example Using IEnumerable and IEnumerator

Putting the MyColors and ColorEnumerator examples together, you can add a class called Program with a Main method that creates an instance of MyColors and uses it in a foreach loop.

```csharp
using System;
using System.Collections;

namespace ColorCollectionEnumerator
{
    class ColorEnumerator: IEnumerator
    {
        string[] Colors;
        int Position = -1;

        public ColorEnumerator(string[] theColors)          // Constructor
        {
            Colors = new string[theColors.Length];
            for (int i = 0; i < theColors.Length; i++)
                Colors[i] = theColors[i];
        }

        public object Current                                // Current
        { get { return Colors[Position]; } }

        public bool MoveNext()                               // MoveNext
        {
            if (Position < Colors.Length - 1)
                { Position++; return true; }
            else
                return false;
        }
```

```
      public void Reset()                                    // Reset
      { Position = -1; }
   }

   class MyColors: IEnumerable {
      string[] Colors = { "Red", "Yellow", "Blue" };

      public IEnumerator GetEnumerator()
      { return new ColorEnumerator(Colors); }
   }

   class Program {
      static void Main() {
         MyColors mc = new MyColors();
         foreach (string color in mc)
            Console.Write("{0}  ", color);
         Console.WriteLine("");
      }
   }
}
```

This code produces the following output:

```
Red   Yellow   Blue
```

The Non-Interface Enumerator

You've just seen how to use the IEnumerable and IEnumerator interfaces to create useful enumerables and enumerators. But there are drawbacks to this method.

First, remember that the object returned by Current is of type object. This is fine for reference types, but for value types, this means that before they are returned by Current, they must be boxed to turn them into objects. They must then be unboxed again after they have been received from Current. This can exact a substantial performance penalty if it needs to be done on large amounts of data.

Another drawback of the non-generic interface method is that you've lost type safety. The values being enumerated are being handled as objects, and so can be of any type. This eliminates the safety of compile-time type checking.

You can solve these problems by making the following changes to the enumerator/enumerable class declarations.

- For the enumerator class

  - Do *not* derive the class from IEnumerator.

  - Implement MoveNext just as before.

  - Implement Current just as before, but have as its return type the type of the items being enumerated.

  - You do not have to implement Reset.

- For the enumerable class

  - Do not derive the class from IEnumerable.

  - Implement GetEnumerator as before, but have its return type be the type of the enumerator class.

Figure 20-5 shows the differences. The non-generic interface code is on the left, and the non-interface code is on the right. With these changes, the foreach statement will be perfectly happy to process your collection, but without the drawbacks just listed.

```
class SibEnumerator : IEnumerator        │    class SibEnumerator
{                                        │    {
   ...                                   │       ...
   public object Current                 │       public string Current
      { get { ... } }                    │          { get { ... } }
                                         │
   public bool MoveNext()                 │       public bool MoveNext()
   { ... }                               │       { ... }
                                         │
   public void Reset()                   │
   { ... }                               │
}                                        │    }

class Siblings : IEnumerable             │    class Siblings
{                                        │    {
   ...                                   │       ...
   public IEnumerator GetEnumerator()     │       public SibEnumerator GetEnumerator()
   { ... }                               │       { ... }
}                                        │    }
```

Figure 20-5. *Comparing interface-based and non-interface-based enumerators*

One possible problem with the non-interface enumerator implementation is that types from other assemblies might expect enumeration to be implemented using the interface method. If these objects attempt to get an enumeration of your class objects using the interface conventions, they will not be able to find them.

To solve this problem, you can implement both forms in the same classes. That is, you can create implementations for Current, MoveNext, Reset, and GetEnumerator at the class level, and also create *explicit* interface implementations for them. With both sets of implementations, the type-safe, more efficient implementation will be called by foreach and other constructs that can use the non-interface implementations, while the other constructs will call the explicit interface implementations.

The Generic Enumeration Interfaces

The third form of the enumerator uses the generic interfaces IEnumerable<T> and IEnumerator<T>. They are called generic because they use C# generics. Using them is very similar to using the non-generic forms. Essentially, the differences between the two are the following:

- With the non-generic interface form
  - The GetEnumerator method of interface IEnumerable returns an enumerator class instance that implements IEnumerator.
  - The class implementing IEnumerator implements property Current, which returns an object.

- With the generic interface form
  - The GetEnumerator method of interface IEnumerable<T> returns an enumerator class instance that implements IEnumerator<T>.
  - The class implementing IEnumerator<T> implements property Current, which returns a derived type.

Notice that, with the *generic interfaces*, the items you receive from the enumeration are a specific derived type, whereas with the non-generic interfaces, you get back the more "generic" object from the enumerations.

The IEnumerator<T> Interface

The IEnumerator<T> interface uses generics to return an actual derived type, rather than an object of type object.

The IEnumerator<T> interface derives from two other interfaces: the non-generic IEnumerator interface and the IDisposable interface. It must therefore implement their members.

- You have already seen the non-generic IEnumerator interface and its three members.

- The IDisposable interface has a single, void, parameterless method called Dispose, which can be used to free unmanaged resources being held by the class.

- The IEnumerator<T> interface itself has a single method, Current, which returns an item of a derived type—*not* an item of type object.

- Since both IEnumerator<T> and IEnumerator have a member named Current, you should explicitly implement the IEnumerator version, and implement the generic version in the class itself, as shown in Figure 20-6.

Figure 20-6 illustrates the implementation of the interface.

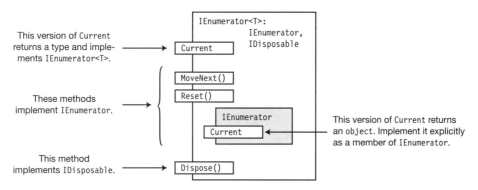

Figure 20-6. *Implementing the IEnumerator<T> interface*

The declaration of the class implementing the interface should look something like the pattern in the following code, where T is the type returned by the enumerator.

```
using System.Collections;
using System.Collections.Generic;

class MyGenEnumerator: IEnumerator< T >
{
   public T Current  { get; }                      // IEnumerator<T>--Current
            Explicit implementation
                        ↓
   object IEnumerator.Current { get { ... } }     // IEnumerator--Current
   public bool MoveNext() { ... }                 // IEnumerator--MoveNext
   public void Reset()    { ... }                 // IEnumerator--Reset

   public void Dispose()  { ... }                 // IDisposable--Dispose
      ...
}
```

For example, the following code implements the `ColorEnumerator` example using the generic enumerator interface:

```
using System.Collections;
using System.Collections.Generic;   Substitute type for T
                                          ↓
class ColorEnumerator : IEnumerator<string>
{
    string[] Colors; int Position = -1;
        Returns a derived type
              ↓
    public string Current                             // Current--generic
    { get { return Colors[Position]; } }
            Explicit implementation
                    ↓
    object IEnumerator.Current                        // Current--non-generic
    { get { return Colors[Position]; } }

    public bool MoveNext()                            // MoveNext
    {
        if (Position < Colors.Length - 1)
            { Position++; return true; }
        else
            return false;
    }

    public void Reset()                               // Reset
    { Position = -1; }

    public void Dispose() { }

    public ColorEnumerator(string[] colors)           // Constructor
    {
        Colors = new string[colors.Length];
        for (int i = 0; i < colors.Length; i++)
            Colors[i] = colors[i];
    }
}
```

The IEnumerable<T> Interface

The generic IEnumerable<T> interface is very similar to the non-generic version, IEnumerable. The generic version derives from IEnumerable, so it must also implement the IEnumerable interface.

- Like IEnumerable, the generic version also contains a single member, a method called GetEnumerator. This version of GetEnumerator, however, returns a class object implementing the generic IEnumerator<T> interface.

- Since the class must implement two GetEnumerator methods, you should explicitly implement the non-generic version, and implement the generic version in the class itself, as shown in Figure 20-7.

Figure 20-7 illustrates the implementation of the interface.

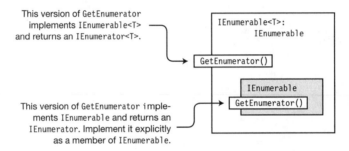

Figure 20-7. *Implementing the IEnumerable<T> interface*

The following code shows a pattern for implementing the generic interface. T is the type returned by the enumerator.

```
using System.Collections;
using System.Collections.Generic;

class MyGenEnumerable: IEnumerable<T>
{
   public IEnumerator<T> GetEnumerator() { ... }      // IEnumerable<T> version


                    Explicit implementation
                             ↓
   IEnumerator IEnumerable.GetEnumerator() { ... }   // IEnumerable version
   ...
}
```

For example, the following code shows the use of the generic enumerable interface:

```
using System.Collections;
using System.Collections.Generic;
                     Substitute actual type for T
                             ↓
class MyColors : IEnumerable<string>
{
   string[] Colors = { "Red", "Yellow", "Blue" };

                  Substitute actual type for T
                             ↓
   public IEnumerator<string> GetEnumerator()        // IEnumerable<T> version
   {
      return new ColorEnumerator(Colors);
   }
                     Explicit implementation
                             ↓
   IEnumerator IEnumerable.GetEnumerator()           // IEnumerable version
   {
      return new ColorEnumerator(Colors);
   }
}
```

Iterators

Enumerable classes and enumerators are used extensively in the .NET collection classes, so it's important that you know how they work. But now that you know how to create you own enumerable classes and enumerators, you might be pleased to learn that, with C# 2.0, the language now has a much simpler way of creating enumerators. In fact, the compiler will create them for you. The construct producing this is called an *iterator*.

Before I explain the details, let's take a look at two examples. The following method declaration implements an iterator.

- The iterator returns a generic enumerator that returns three items of type `string`.

- The `yield return` statements declare that *this is the next item in the enumeration*.

```
Return a generic enumerator.
           ↓
IEnumerator<string> BlackAndWhite()                     // Version 1
{
    yield return "black";                               // yield return
    yield return "gray";                                // yield return
    yield return "white";                               // yield return
}
```

The following method declaration is another version that produces the same end result:

```
Return a generic enumerator.
           ↓
IEnumerator<string> BlackAndWhite()                     // Version 2
{
    string[] TheColors = { "black", "gray", "white" };

    for (int i = 0; i < TheColors.Length; i++)
        yield return TheColors[i];                      // yield return
}
```

I haven't explained the `yield return` statement yet, but on inspecting these code segments, you might have the feeling that something is different about this code. It doesn't seem quite right. What exactly does the `yield return` statement do?

For example, in the first version, if the method returns on the first `yield return` statement, then the last two statements can never be reached. If it doesn't return on the first statement, but continues through to the end of the method, then what happens to the values? And in the second version, if the `yield return` statement in the body of the loop returns on the first iteration, then the loop will *never* get to any subsequent iterations.

And besides all that, an enumerator doesn't just return all the elements in one shot—it returns a new value with each access of the `Current` property. So how does this give you an enumerator? Clearly this code is different than anything shown before.

Iterator Blocks

A code block with one or more `yield` statements is an *iterator block*. Any of the following three types of code blocks can be iterator blocks:

- A method body

- An accessor body

- An operator body

Iterator blocks are treated differently than other blocks. Other blocks contain sequences of statements that are treated *imperatively*. That is, the first statement in the block is executed, followed by the subsequent statements, and eventually control leaves the block.

An iterator block, on the other hand, is not a sequence of imperative commands to be executed at one time. Instead, it describes the behavior of an enumerator class that you want the compiler to build for you. The code in the iterator block describes how to enumerate the elements.

Iterator blocks have two special statements:

- The `yield return` statement specifies the next item in the sequence to return.

- The `yield break` statement specifies that there are no more items in the sequence.

The compiler takes this description of how to enumerate the items and uses it to build the enumerator class, including all the required method and property implementations. The resulting class is nested inside the class where the iterator is declared. Figure 20-8 shows the code on the left and the resulting objects on the right. Notice how much is built for you automatically by the compiler.

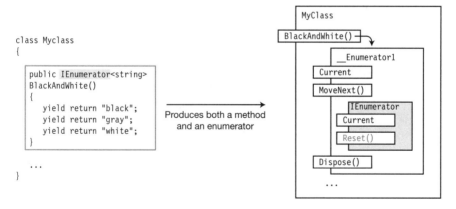

Figure 20-8. *An iterator that produces an enumerator*

More about Iterators

Some other important things to know about iterators are the following:

- Iterators require the System.Collections.Generic namespace, so you should include it with a using directive.

- In the compiler-generated enumerators, the Reset method is not supported. It is implemented, since it is required by the interface, but the implementation throws a System.NotSupportedException exception if it is called. Notice that the Reset method is shown grayed out in Figure 20-8.

Behind the scenes, the enumerator class generated by the compiler is a state machine with four states:

Before: The initial state before the first call to MoveNext.

Running: The state entered when MoveNext is called. While in this state, the enumerator determines and sets the position for the next item. It exits the state when it encounters a yield return, a yield break, or the end of the iterator body.

Suspended: The state where the state machine is waiting for the next call to MoveNext.

After: The state where there are no more items to enumerate.

If the state machine is in either the *before* or *suspended* states, and there is a call to the MoveNext method, it goes into the *running* state. In the running state, it determines the next item in the collection, and sets the position.

If there are more items, the state machine goes into the *suspended* state. If there are no more items, it goes into the *after* state, where it remains. Figure 20-9 shows the state machine.

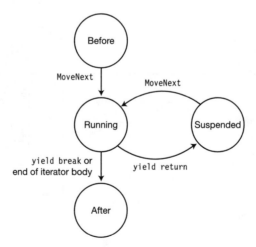

Figure 20-9. *An iterator state machine*

Producing Enumerables and Enumerators

The previous example used a return type of IEnumerator<string>, which caused the compiler to produce an enumerator class using generics. But you can specify other return types as well. The return types you can specify are the following:

- IEnumerator (non-generic)

- IEnumerator<T> (generic—substitute an actual type for T)

- IEnumerable (non-generic)

- IEnumerable<T> (generic—substitute an actual type for T)

For the enumerator types, the compiler generates a nested class that contains the implementation of either the non-generic or generic enumerator, with the behavior specified by the iterator block. It also produces the method that returns the enumerator.

For the enumerable types, it does even more. It produces a nested class that is both enumerable and the enumerator. The class, therefore, implements the GetEnumerator method. Notice that this method is implemented as part of the *nested* class—*not* as part of the *enclosing* class.

Figure 20-10 illustrates the generic enumerable produced by an enumerable iterator.

- The iterator's code is shown on the left side of the figure, and shows that its return type is IEnumerable<string>.

- On the right side of the figure, the diagram shows that the nested class implements both IEnumerator<string> and IEnumerable<string>.

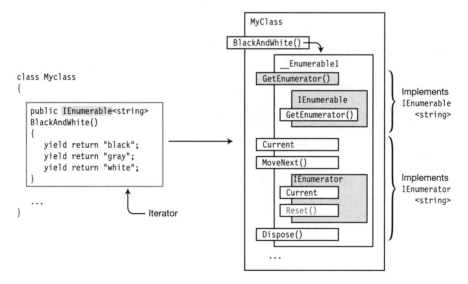

Figure 20-10. *The compiler produces a class that is both an enumerable and an enumerator. It also produces the method that returns the class object.*

Using an Iterator to Produce an Enumerable

You can use the enumerators and enumerables generated by iterators wherever you would use manually coded enumerators or enumerables.

In the following example, iterators are used to produce an enumerable class. Class ColorCollection has two enumerable iterators—one enumerating the items in forward order and the other enumerating them in reverse order.

```
using System;
using System.Collections.Generic;                    // You need this namespace.

namespace ColorCollectionIterator {
   class ColorCollection {
      string[] Colors={"Red", "Orange", "Yellow", "Green", "Blue", "Purple"};

      public IEnumerable<string> Forward() {        // Enumerable iterator
         for (int i = 0; i < Colors.Length; i++)
            yield return Colors[i];
      }

      public IEnumerable<string> Reverse() {        // Enumerable iterator
         for (int i = Colors.Length - 1; i >= 0; i--)
            yield return Colors[i];
      }
   }

   class Program {
      static void Main() {
         ColorCollection cc = new ColorCollection();
                        Return enumerable to the foreach statement
                                       ↓
         foreach (string color in cc.Forward())
            Console.Write("{0} ", color);
         Console.WriteLine("");
                           Return enumerable to the foreach statement
                                       ↓
         foreach (string color in cc.Reverse())
            Console.Write("{0} ", color);
         Console.WriteLine("");
```

```
            // Skip the foreach and manually use the enumerable and enumerator.
            IEnumerable<string> ieable = cc.Reverse();
            IEnumerator<string> ieator = ieable.GetEnumerator();
            while (ieator.MoveNext())
               Console.Write("{0} ", ieator.Current);
            Console.WriteLine("");
         }
      }
   }
```

Using an Iterator to Produce an Enumerator

In the previous example, iterators were used to produce an enumerable class. In this example, iterators are used to produce an enumerator class. Additionally, it shows the iterators implemented as *properties* that return the enumerators, rather than methods.

The code declares two properties that define two different enumerators. The GetEnumerator method returns one of the two enumerators, depending on the value of the Boolean variable ColorFlag. If ColorFlag is true, the Colors enumerator is returned. Otherwise, the BlackAndWhite enumerator is returned.

```
class MyClass: IEnumerable<string>
{
   bool ColorFlag = true;

   public MyClass(bool flag)                // Constructor
   { ColorFlag = flag; }

   IEnumerator<string> BlackAndWhite        // Property--enumerator iterator
   {
      get {
         yield return "black";
         yield return "gray";
         yield return "white";
      }
   }
```

```
      IEnumerator<string> Colors                    // Property--enumerator iterator
      {
         get {
            string[] TheColors = { "blue", "red", "yellow" };
            for (int i = 0; i < TheColors.Length; i++)
               yield return TheColors[i];
         }
      }

      public IEnumerator<string> GetEnumerator()  // GetEnumerator
      {
         return ColorFlag
                   ? Colors                         // Return Colors enumerator
                   : BlackAndWhite;                 // Return BlackAndWhite enumerator
      }

      System.Collections.IEnumerator
      System.Collections.IEnumerable.GetEnumerator()
      {
         return ColorFlag
                   ? Colors                         // Return Colors enumerator
                   : BlackAndWhite;                 // Return BlackAndWhite enumerator
      }
   }
   class Program
   {
      static void Main()
      {
         MyClass mc1 = new MyClass( true );         // Call constructor with true
         foreach (string s in mc1)
            Console.Write("{0} ", s);
         Console.WriteLine("");

         MyClass mc2 = new MyClass( false );        // Call constructor with false
         foreach (string s in mc2)
            Console.Write("{0} ", s);
         Console.WriteLine("");
      }
   }
}
```

This code produces the following output:

```
blue  red  yellow
black  gray  white
```

CHAPTER 21

Attributes

What Is an Attribute?
Applying an Attribute
Using Custom Attributes
Accessing an Attribute
Using Reserved Attributes

What Is an Attribute?

C# is an *imperative language*, which loosely means that you write instructions that tell the program what to do and how to do it. But it also has aspects of *declarative programming*, which means that you *declare* the characteristics of a component, rather than producing a detailed algorithm to implement those characteristics.

A good example of the declarative aspect of the language is the member access modifiers. You can apply the modifiers `public`, `private`, `protected`, and so forth on a member to *declare* its level of access. The compiler stores this information in the assembly, and the compiler and the CLR take care of the details.

Besides these declarative aspects of the language itself, C# also allows you to store user-defined declarative information about the constructs of a program's source code, in the program's assembly. You can do this by using *attributes*. The information stored is not data used *by* the program—it is data *about* the program and is called *metadata*.

An *attribute* is a special type of class, designed specifically for storing information about the program constructs. You can apply attributes to a construct of a program's source code, to declare something about the construct.

- The program construct to which you apply an attribute is called its *target*.

- Programs designed to retrieve and use the metadata, are said to be *consumers* of the attributes.

Figure 21-1 is an overview of the components involved in using attributes, and illustrates the following points about attributes:

- You *apply* attributes to program constructs in the source code.

- The compiler takes the source code and produces metadata from the attributes, and places that metadata in the assembly.

- Other programs, called *consumers*, can access the metadata of the attributes along with the metadata for the rest of the components of the program. Notice that the compiler both produces the assembly and is also a consumer of attributes.

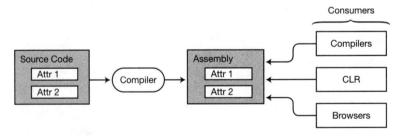

Figure 21-1. *The components involved with creating and using attributes*

A Quick Preview

As a quick preview of attributes, take a look at the following code. In class `Program`, a predefined attribute named `Obsolete` is applied to method `PrintOut`. This attribute declares that the method is obsolete and gives information about what method should be used in its place.

```
using System;
using System.Diagnostics;

namespace AttrObs
{
    class Program        Apply attribute.
    {                         ↓
        [Obsolete("Use method SuperPrintOut")]    // Apply attribute to method.
        static void PrintOut(string str)
        {
            Console.WriteLine(str);
        }

        static void Main(string[] args)
        {
            PrintOut("Start of Main");                // Invoke obsolete method.
        }
    }
}
```

Notice that method `Main` calls `PrintOut`, even though it is marked as obsolete. In spite of this, the code compiles and runs fine, and produces the following output when executed.

```
Start of Main
```

But during compilation, the compiler produces the following warning message to inform you that you are using an obsolete construct.

```
AttrObs.Program.PrintOut(string)' is obsolete: 'Use method SuperPrintOut
```

The Stages of an Attribute

There are three stages in the process of using an attribute—declaring the attribute, applying the attribute, and consuming the attribute. These stages are illustrated in Figure 21-2.

1. Before an attribute can be used, it must be declared.

   – *Predefined attributes* are declared in the .NET Framework.

   – *Custom attributes* are user-defined attributes.

2. The next step is *applying* an attribute to the target construct. You do this by placing the attribute in the source code above the target construct.

3. The last step is *consuming*, or using, an attribute. This is done from a running program, which accesses the metadata stored by the attribute.

Figure 21-2. *The stages of an attribute*

In the preview program you just looked at, the three phases of using the Obsolete attribute are the following:

- *Declare the attribute*: The Obsolete attribute is predefined in the .NET Framework, so this step was unnecessary.

- *Apply the attribute*: The attribute was applied to method PrintOut, in the square braces construct, immediately before the declaration of the method.

- *Use the attribute*: In this case, the compiler was the consumer that used the attribute and took the action of producing the warning message.

Applying an Attribute

The purpose of an attribute is to tell the compiler to emit a certain set of metadata about a program construct, to the assembly. You do this by *applying* the attribute to the construct.

- You apply an attribute by placing an *attribute section* immediately before the construct.

- An *attribute section* consists of square brackets enclosing an attribute name and sometimes a parameter list.

For example, the following code shows the headings of two classes. The first few lines of code show an attribute named Serializable applied to a class called MyClass. Notice that Serializable has no parameter list. The second class declaration has an attribute called MyAttribute, which has a parameter list with two string parameters.

```
[ Serializable ]                                    // Attribute
public class MyClass
{ ...

[ MyAttribute("Simple class", "Version 3.57") ]   // Attribute with parameters
public class MyOtherClass
{ ...
```

Some important things to know about attributes are the following:

- Most attributes apply only to the construct immediately following the attribute section or sections.

- A construct with an attribute applied to it is sometimes said to be *decorated*, or *adorned*, with the attribute. Both terms are common.

Multiple Attributes

You can apply multiple attributes to a single construct.

- Multiple attributes can be listed in either of the following formats:
    - Separate attribute sections stacked on top of each other
    - A single attribute section, with the attributes separated by commas
- You can list the attributes in any order.

For example, the following two sections of code show the two ways of applying multiple attributes. The sections of code are equivalent.

```
[ Serializable ]                                              // Stacked
[ MyAttribute("Simple class", "Version 3.57") ]

[ MyAttribute("Simple class", "Version 3.57"), Serializable ]    // Commas
                        ↑                              ↑
                    Attribute                      Attribute
```

Other Targets

Besides classes, you can also apply attributes to other program constructs such as fields and properties. The following declaration shows an attribute on a field, and multiple attributes on a method.

```
[MyAttribute("Holds a value", "Version 3.2")]                // On a field
public int MyField;

[Obsolete]                                                   // On a method
[MyAttribute("Prints out a message.", "Version 3.6")]
public void PrintOut()
{
    ...
```

You can also explicitly label attributes to apply to a particular construct. To use an explicit target, place the target type, followed by a colon, at the beginning of the attribute section. For example, the following code adorns the *method* with an attribute, and also applies an attribute to the *return value*.

Explicit target
↓
```
[method: MyAttribute("Prints out a message.", "Version 3.6")]
[return: MyAttribute("This value represents ...", "Version 2.3")]
public long ReturnSetting()
{
    ...
```

The C# language defines 10 standardized attribute targets, which are listed in Table 21-1. Most of the target names are self-explanatory, but type covers classes, structs, delegates, enums, and interfaces. The typevar target name specifies type parameters to constructs that use generics.

Table 21-1. *Attribute Targets*

event	field
method	param
property	return
type	typevar
assembly	module

Global Attributes

You can also use an explicit target to set attributes at the assembly and module level, by using the assembly and module target names. Some important points about assembly-level attributes are the following:

- Assembly-level attributes must be placed outside any namespace scope and are usually placed in the AssemblyInfo.cs file.

- The AssembyInfo.cs file usually contains metadata about the company, product, and copyright information.

The following are lines from an AssemblyInfo.cs file.

```
[assembly: AssemblyTitle("SuperWidget")]
[assembly: AssemblyDescription("Implements the SuperWidget product.")]
[assembly: AssemblyConfiguration("")]
[assembly: AssemblyCompany("McArthur Widgets, Inc.")]
[assembly: AssemblyProduct("Super Widget Deluxe")]
[assembly: AssemblyCopyright("Copyright © McArthur Widgets 2006")]
[assembly: AssemblyTrademark("")]
[assembly: AssemblyCulture("")]
```

Predefined Attributes

The .NET Framework predefines a number of attributes that are understood and interpreted by the compiler and the CLR. Table 21-2 lists some of these attributes.

Table 21-2. *Important Attributes Defined in .NET*

CLSCompliant	Declares that the publicly exposed members should be checked by the compiler for compliance with the CLS. Compliant assemblies can be used by any .NET-compliant language.
Serializable	Declares that the construct can be serialized.
NonSerialized	Declares that the construct cannot be serialized.
Obsolete	Declares that the construct should not be used. The compiler also produces a compile time warning or error message, if the construct is used.
DLLImport	Declares that the implementation is unmanaged code.
WebMethod	Declares that the method should be exposed as part of an XML web service.
AttributeUsage	Declares what types of program constructs the attribute can be applied to. This attribute is applied to attribute declarations.

Using Custom Attributes

Now that you've seen how attributes are applied, you've probably noticed that the syntax is very different from anything else you've seen so far. From that, you might get the impression that attributes are an entirely different type of construct. They're not—they are just a special kind of class.

Some important points about attribute classes are the following:

- User-defined attribute classes are called *custom attributes*.

- Attribute classes are derived from class System.Attribute.

Attribute names, by convention, use Pascal casing, and end with the suffix Attribute. When applying an attribute to a target, you can leave off the suffix. For example, if you were to look at the declarations of attributes Serializable and MyAttribute, which I used in previous examples, you would find that they are actually named SerializableAttribute and MyAttributeAttribute.

Declaring a Custom Attribute

Declaring an attribute class is, for the most part, the same as declaring any other class. There are, however, several things to be aware of.

- To declare a custom attribute, do the following:
  - Declare a class derived from System.Attribute.
  - Give it a name ending with the suffix Attribute.

- For security, it is a generally suggested that you declare your attribute classes as sealed.

For example, the following code shows the beginning of the declaration of attribute MyAttributeAttribute.

```
                          Attribute name
                          ↓
public sealed class MyAttributeAttribute : System.Attribute
{                                           ↑         ↑
    ...                                    Suffix   Base class
```

Since an attribute holds information about the target, the public members of an attribute class generally consist only of the following:

- Fields

- Properties

- Constructors

Using Attribute Constructors

Attributes, like other classes, have constructors. Every attribute must have at least one public constructor.

- As with other classes, if you don't declare a constructor, the compiler will produce an implicit, public, parameterless constructor for you.

- Attribute constructors, like other constructors, can be overloaded.

- When declaring the constructor, you must use the full class name, including the suffix. You can use the shortened name only when *applying* an attribute.

For example, with the following code, the compiler would produce an error message if the constructor name did not include the suffix.

```
                        Suffix
                          ↓
                      _____
public MyAttributeAttribute(string desc, string ver)
{
    Description = desc;
    VersionNumber = ver;
}
```

Specifying the Constructor

When you apply an attribute to a target, you are specifying which attribute constructor should be used to create the instance of the attribute. The parameters listed in the attribute application are the actual parameters for the constructor.

For example, in the following code, `MyAttribute` is applied to a field and to a method. For the field, the declaration specifies a constructor with a single `string` parameter. For the method, it specifies a constructor with two `string` parameters.

```
[MyAttribute("Holds a value")]            // Constructor with one string
public int MyField;

[MyAttribute("Version 1.3", "Sal Martin")]    // Constructor with two strings
public void MyMethod()
{ ...
```

Other important points about attribute constructors are the following:

- When applying an attribute, the actual parameters for the constructor must be constant expressions whose values can be determined at compile time.

- If you are applying an attribute constructor with no parameters, you can leave off the parentheses. For example, both classes in the following code use the parameterless constructor for the attribute MyAttr. The meaning of the two forms is the same.

```
[MyAttr]
class SomeClass ...

[MyAttr()]
class OtherClass ...
```

Using the Constructor

As with other classes, you cannot call the constructor explicitly. An instance of an attribute is created, and a constructor called, only when an attribute consumer accesses the attribute.

This is very different from other classes, which are created at the position where you used an object-creation expression. Applying an attribute is a declarative statement that does not determine when an object of the attribute class should be constructed.

Figure 21-3 compares the use of a constructor for a regular class and the use of a constructor with attributes.

- The imperative statement says, in effect, "Create a new class object here."

- The declarative statement says, "This attribute is associated with this target, and in case the attribute needs to be constructed—use this constructor."

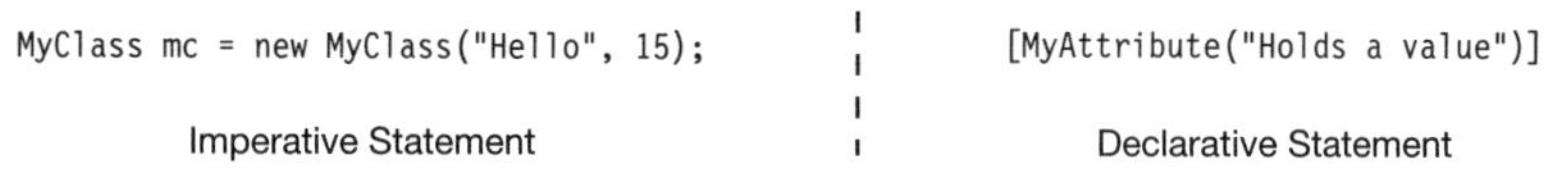

```
MyClass mc = new MyClass("Hello", 15);          [MyAttribute("Holds a value")]

        Imperative Statement                        Declarative Statement
```

Figure 21-3. *Comparing the use of constructors*

Positional and Named Parameters in Constructors

So far, the parameters you've seen with attribute constructors have been like the parameters for regular class constructors. As with regular constructors, the actual parameters of attribute constructors must be placed in the correct order, matching the formal parameters in the class declaration. These are called *positional parameters*, because the compiler knows which actual parameter goes with which formal parameter by its *position* in the parameter list.

But attribute constructors can also have another type of actual parameter, called a *named parameter*.

- A named parameter consists of the name of a field or property, followed by an equals sign, followed by an initializing value.

- A named parameter sets the value of an attribute's field or property.

Named parameters are *actual* parameters. There is nothing different in the declaration of the formal parameters of the constructor. The only difference is in the list of actual parameters that is supplied when the attribute is applied.

The following code shows the application of an attribute using a positional parameter and two named parameters.

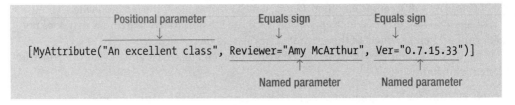

The following code shows the declaration of the attribute class, as well as its application on class MyClass. Notice that the constructor *declaration* lists only a single formal parameter. And yet by using named parameters, you can give the constructor three actual parameters. The two named parameters set the values of fields Ver and Reviewer.

```
public sealed class MyAttributeAttribute : System.Attribute
{
    public string Description;
    public string Ver;
    public string Reviewer;

    public MyAttributeAttribute(string desc)  // Single formal parameters.
    { Description = desc; }
}
                                        // Three actual parameters
[MyAttribute("An excellent class", Reviewer="Amy McArthur", Ver="7.15.33")]
class MyClass
{ ... }
```

■**Note** If there are any positional parameters required by the constructor, they must be placed before any named parameters.

Restricting the Usage of an Attribute

You've seen that you can apply attributes to classes. But attributes *themselves* are classes, and there is one important predefined attribute that you will often want to apply to your custom attributes. It is the AttributeUsage attribute. You can use it to restrict the usage of an attribute to a specific set of target types.

For example, if you want your custom attribute MyAttribute to be applied only to methods, you could use the following form of AttributeUsage.

```
                          Only to methods
                               ↓
                  _____

[ AttributeUsage( AttributeTarget.Method ) ]
public sealed class MyAttributeAttribute : System.Attribute
{ ...
```

AttributeUsage has three important public properties, which are listed in Table 21-3. The table shows the names of the properties and their meanings, as well as the default values of the last two properties.

Table 21-3. *Public Properties of AttributeUsage*

Name	Meaning	Default
ValidOn	Stores a list of the types of targets to which the attribute can be applied. The first parameter of the constructor must be an enum value of type AttributeTarget.	
Inherited	A Boolean value that specifies whether the attribute can be inherited by derived classes of the decorated type.	true
AllowMultiple	A Boolean value that specifies whether the target can have multiple instances of the attribute applied to it.	false

The Constructor for AttributeUsage

The constructor for AttributeUsage takes a single, positional parameter that specifies which target types are allowed for the attribute. It uses this parameter to set the ValidOn property. The acceptable target types are members of the AttributeTarget enumeration. The complete set of the members of the AttributeTarget enumeration is shown in Table 21-4.

You can combine the usage types by using the bitwise OR operator. For example, the attribute declared in the following code can be applied only to methods and constructors.

```
                                    Targets
                                       ↓
 [ AttributeUsage( AttributeTarget.Method | AttributeTarget.Constructor ) ]
 public sealed class MyAttributeAttribute : System.Attribute
 { ...
```

Table 21-4. *Members of Enum AttributeTarget*

All	Assembly	Class	Constructor
Delegate	Enum	Event	Field
GenericParameter	Interface	Method	Module
Parameter	Property	ReturnValue	Struct

When you apply AttributeUsage to an attribute declaration, the constructor will have at least the one required parameter, which contains the target types to be stored in ValidOn. You can also optionally set the Inherited and AllowMultiple properties by using named parameters. If you do not set them, they will have their default values, as shown in Table 21-3.

As an example, the next code block specifies the following about MyAttribute:

- MyAttribute must be applied only to classes.

- MyAttribute is not inherited by classes derived from classes to which it is applied.

- There cannot be multiple instances of MyAttribute applied to the same target.

```
 [ AttributeUsage( AttributeTarget.Class,        // Required, positional
                   Inherited = false,            // Optional, named
                   AllowMultiple = false ) ]     // Optional, named
 public sealed class MyAttributeAttribute : System.Attribute
 { ...
```

Using Suggested Practices for Custom Attributes

When writing custom attributes, there are certain practices that are strongly suggested. They include the following:

- The attribute class should represent some state of the target construct.

- If the attribute *requires* certain fields, include a constructor with positional parameters to collect that data, and let optional fields be initialized with named parameters, as needed.

- Don't implement public methods or other function members other than properties.

- For additional security, declare the attribute class as sealed.

- Use the AttributeUsage attribute on your attribute declaration to explicitly specify the set of attribute targets.

The following code illustrates these guidelines.

```
[AttributeUsage( AttributeTargets.Class )]
public sealed class  MyAttributeAttribute : System.Attribute
{
   private string _Description;
   private string _VersionNumber;
   private string _ReviewerID;

   public string Description
      { get { return _Description; } set { _Description = value; } }

   public string VersionNumber
      { get { return _VersionNumber; } set { _VersionNumber = value; } }

   public string ReviewerID
      { get { return _ReviewerID; } set { _ReviewerID = value; } }

   public MyAttributeAttribute(string desc, string ver)
   {
      Description = desc;
      VersionNumber = ver;
   }
}
```

Accessing an Attribute

Now that you know how to create custom attributes, you need to know how to access the metadata they contain. Suppose, for example, that you want to find out whether a particular attribute is applied to a particular class, or you want a list of the attributes that are applied to a class. The .NET class library defines a class called Type, which has several methods that you can use to access this information.

To use these methods, you can start by creating an instance of the class you want to query and calling the instance's GetType method, which returns an object of type Type. Every class has the GetType method, because GetType is a member of type object, which is the base from which every class is derived.

Using the IsDefined Method

You can use the IsDefined method of the Type object to determine whether a particular attribute is applied to a particular class. When this method is called, it returns a bool value that tells whether an attribute is defined on a particular program construct.

For example, the following code declares an attributed class called MyClass, and also acts as its own attribute consumer, by accessing an attribute declared and applied in the program itself. At the top of the code are declarations of the attribute MyAttribute and the class MyClass, to which it is applied. The code does the following:

- First, Main creates an object of the class. It then retrieves a reference to the Type object by using the GetType method, which it inherited from its base class, object.

- With the reference to the Type object, it can call the IsDefined method to find out whether attribute MyAttribute is applied to this class.
    - The first parameter takes a Type object of the *attribute* you are checking for.
    - The second parameter is of type bool and specifies whether to search the inheritance tree of MyClass to find the attribute.

```
[AttributeUsage(AttributeTargets.Class)]
public sealed class MyAttributeAttribute : System.Attribute
{ ... }

[MyAttribute("Check it out", "2.4")]
class MyClass {  }

class Program {
    static void Main() {
        MyClass mc = new MyClass(); // Create an instance of the class.
        Type t = mc.GetType();   // Get the Type object from the instance.
        bool ItIsDefined =       // Check the Type for the attribute.
            t.IsDefined(typeof(MyAttributeAttribute), false);

        Console.WriteLine("MyAttribute is applied to type {0}", t.Name);
    }
}
```

Using the GetCustomAttributes Method

The GetCustomAttributes method returns an array of the attributes applied to a construct.

- The actual object returned is an array of objects, which you must then cast to the correct attribute type.

- The Boolean parameter specifies whether to search the inheritance tree to find the attribute.

```
object[] AttArr = t.GetCustomAttributes(false);
```

- When the GetCustomAttributes method is called, an instance of each attribute associated with the target is created.

The following code uses the same attribute and class declarations as the previous example. But in this case, it doesn't just determine whether an attribute is applied to the class. Instead, it retrieves an array of the attributes applied to the class and cycles through them, printing out their member values.

```
static void Main( )
{
   MyClass mc = new MyClass();

   Type t = mc.GetType();
   object[] AttArr = t.GetCustomAttributes(false);
   foreach (Attribute a in AttArr)
   {
      MyAttributeAttribute attr = a as MyAttributeAttribute;
      if (null != attr)
      {
         Console.WriteLine("Description     : {0}", attr.Description);
         Console.WriteLine("Version Number : {0}", attr.VersionNumber);
         Console.WriteLine("Reviewer ID    : {0}", attr.ReviewerID);
      }
   }
}
```

Using Reserved Attributes

There are several attributes reserved by .NET that are designed to be processed by the compiler. You've already seen AttributeUsage, but there are two others you should know about—the Obsolete and Conditional attributes.

The Obsolete Attribute

You saw the Obsolete attribute in the first example in this chapter. It allows you to mark a program construct as obsolete and to display a helpful warning message when the code is compiled.

There is another overload of the constructor for Obsolete that takes a second parameter, of type bool. This parameter specifies whether use of the target should be flagged as an error or as a warning. The following code specifies that it should be flagged as an error.

```
                            Flag as an error.
                                  ↓
[ Obsolete("Use method SuperPrintOut", true) ]  // Apply attribute to method.
static void PrintOut(string str)
{ ...
```

The Conditional Attribute

The Conditional attribute allows you to either include or exclude all the invocations of a particular method. To use the Conditional attribute, apply it to the method declaration, along with a compilation symbol as a parameter.

- If the compilation symbol is defined, the compiler will include the code for all the invocations of the method, the way it would for any normal method.

- If the compilation symbol is *not* defined, the compiler will *omit* all the method invocations, throughout the code.

The CIL code for the method itself is always included in the assembly. It is just the invocations that are included or omitted.

For example, in the following code, the Conditional attribute is applied to the declaration of a method called TraceMessage. The attribute has a single parameter, which is the string DoTrace. When the compiler is compiling the code, it will check whether there is a compilation symbol named DoTrace defined.

- If DoTrace is defined, the compiler will include all the calls to method TraceMessage, as usual.

- If there is no DoTrace compilation symbol defined, it will not output code for any of the calls to TraceMessage.

```
                    Compilation symbol
                           ↓
[Conditional( "DoTrace" )]
static void TraceMessage(string str)
{
    Console.WriteLine(str);
}
```

Example of Conditional Attribute

The following code shows a full example using of the Conditional attribute.

- Method Main contains two calls to method TraceMessage.

- The declaration for method TraceMessage is adorned with the Conditional attribute, which has the compilation symbol DoTrace as its parameter. So if DoTrace is defined, the compiler will include the code for all the calls to TraceMessage.

- Since the first line of code defines a compilation symbol named DoTrace, the compiler will include the code for both calls to TraceMessage.

```
#define DoTrace
using System;
using System.Diagnostics;

namespace AttributesConditional
{
    class Program
    {
        [Conditional( "DoTrace" )]
        static void TraceMessage(string str)
        {
            Console.WriteLine(str);
        }

        static void Main(string[] args)
        {
            TraceMessage("Start of Main");
            Console.WriteLine("Doing work in Main.");
            TraceMessage("End of Main");
        }
    }
}
```

This code produces the following output.

```
Start of Main
Doing work in Main.
End of Main
```

If you comment out the first line, so that DoTrace is not defined, the compiler will not insert the code for the two calls to TraceMessage. This time, when you run the program it produces the following output:

```
Doing work in Main.
```

■ ■ ■

CHAPTER 22

Preprocessor Directives

What Are Preprocessor Directives?

General Rules

The #define and #undef Directives

Conditional Compilation

Diagnostic Directives

Line Number Directives

Region Directives

The #pragma warning Directive

What Are Preprocessor Directives?

The source code specifies the definition of a program. The *preprocessor directives* instruct the compiler how to treat the source code. For example, under certain conditions, you might want the compiler to ignore portions of the code, and under other conditions, you might want that code compiled. The preprocessor directives give you those options and several others.

In C and C++ there is an actual preprocessor phase, in which the preprocessor goes through the source code and prepares an output stream of text that will be processed by the subsequent compilation phase. In C# there is no actual preprocessor. The "preprocessor" directives are handled by the compiler. The term, however, remains.

General Rules

Some of the most important syntactic rules for preprocessor directives are the following:

- Preprocessor directives must be on lines separate from C# code.

- Unlike C# statements, preprocessor directives are not terminated with a semicolon.

- Every line containing a preprocessor directive must start with the # character.
  - There can be space between the # sign and the directive.
  - There can be space before the #.

- End-of-line comments are allowed.

- Delimited comments are *not* allowed in a preprocessor directive line.

Here are some examples illustrating the rules.

```
                   No semicolon
                        ↓
#define PremiumVersion           // OK

  Space before
  ↓
    #define BudgetVersion          // OK
    #   define MediumVersion       // OK
    ↑
    Space between           Delimited comments are not allowed.
                            ―――――――――――――――――――
                                    ↓
    #define PremiumVersion   /* all bells & whistles */

                            End-of-line comments are fine.
                            ―――――――――――――――――――
                                    ↓
    #define BudgetVersion    // Stripped-down version
```

The preprocessor directives are listed in Table 22-1.

Table 22-1. *Preprocessor Directives*

Directive	Summary of Meaning
#define *identifier*	Defines a compilation symbol.
#undef *identifier*	Undefines a compilation symbol.
#if *expression*	If the expression is true, compiles the following section.
#elif *expression*	If the expression is true, compiles the following section.
#else	If the previous #if or #elif expression is false, compiles the following section.
#endif	Marks the end of an #if construct.
#region *name*	Marks the beginning of a region of code. Has no compilation effect.
#endregion *name*	Marks the end of a region of code. Has no compilation effect.
#warning *message*	Displays a compile-time warning message.
#error *message*	Displays a compile-time error message.
#line *indicator*	Changes the line numbers displayed in compiler messages.
#pragma *text*	Specifies information about the program context.

The #define and #undef Directives

A *compilation symbol* is an identifier that has only two possible states. It is either *defined* or *undefined*. A compilation symbol has the following characteristics:

- Can be any identifier except `true` or `false`. This includes C# keywords, and identifiers declared in your C# code—all of which are fine.

- Has no value. Unlike C and C++, it does not represent a string.

As shown in Table 22-1:

- The #define directive declares a compilation symbol.

- The #undef directive undefines a compilation symbol.

```
#define PremiumVersion
#define EconomyVersion
   ...
#undef PremiumVersion
```

The #define and #undef directives can be used only at the top of a source file, before any C# code is listed. After the C# code has started, the #define and #undef directives can no longer be used.

```
using System;                    // First line of C# code
#define PremiumVersion           // Error

namespace Eagle
{
   #define PremiumVersion        // Error
   ...
```

The scope of a compilation symbol is limited to a single source file. Redefining a symbol that is already defined is perfectly fine—as long as it's before any C# code, of course.

```
#define AValue
#define BValue

#define AValue                   // Redefinition is fine.
```

Conditional Compilation

Conditional compilation allows you to mark a section of source code to be either compiled or skipped, depending on whether a particular compilation symbol is defined.

There are four directives for specifying conditional compilation:

- #if

- #else

- #elif

- #endif

A *condition* is a simple expression that returns either true or false.

- A condition can consist of a single compilation symbol, or an expression of symbols and operators, as summarized in Table 22-2. Sub-expressions can be grouped with parentheses.

- The literals true and false can also be used in conditional expressions.

Table 22-2. *Conditions Used in the #if and #elif Directives*

Compilation symbol	Identifier, defined (or not) using the #define directive.	True: If the symbol has been defined using a #define directive. False: Otherwise.
Expression	Constructed using symbols and the operators: !, ==, !=, &&, ||	True: If the expression evaluates to true. False: Otherwise.

The following are examples of conditional compilation conditions.

```
        Expression
           ↓
      _____
#if !DemoVersion
  ...
#endif                 Expression
                          ↓
                   _____
#if (LeftHanded && OemVersion) || FullVersion
  ...
#endif

#if true    // The following code segment will always be compiled.
  ...
#endif
```

The Conditional Compilation Constructs

The #if and #endif directives are the matching demarcations of a conditional compilation construct. Whenever there is an #if directive, there must also be a matching #endif.

The #if and #if...#else constructs are illustrated in Figure 22-1.

- If the condition in the #if construct evaluates to true, the code section following it is compiled. Otherwise, it is skipped.

- In the #if...#else construct, if the condition evaluates to true, *CodeSection1* is compiled. Otherwise, *CodeSection2* is compiled.

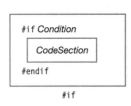

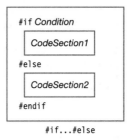

Figure 22-1. *The #if and #else constructs*

For example, the following code illustrates a simple #if...#else construct. If the symbol RightHanded is defined, the code between the #if and the #else will be compiled. Otherwise, the code between the #else and the #endif will be compiled.

```
...
#if RightHanded
    // Code implementing right-handed functionality
    ...
#else
    // Code implementing left-handed functionality
    ...
#endif
```

The #if...#elif, and #if...#elif...#else constructs are illustrated in Figure 22-2.

- In the #if...#elif construct, if *Cond1* evaluates to true, *CodeSection1* is compiled, and compilation continues after the #endif.

  - Otherwise, if *Cond2* evaluates to true, *CodeSection2* is compiled, and compilation continues after the #endif.

  - This continues until either a condition evaluates to true, or all the conditions have returned false. If that is the case, none of the code sections in the construct are compiled, and compilation continues after the #endif.

- The #if...#elif...#else construct works the same way, except that if no condition is true, then the code section after the #else is then compiled, and compilation continues after the #endif.

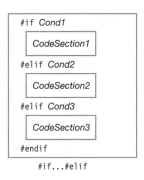

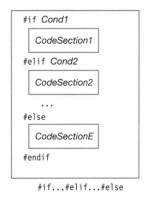

Figure 22-2. *The #elif construct*

The following code demonstrates the #if...#elif...#else construct. The string containing the description of the version of the program is set to various values, depending on which compilation symbol is defined.

```
#define DemoVersionWithoutTimeLimit
   ...
   const int intExpireLength = 30;
   string strVersionDesc = null;
   int    intExpireCount = 0;

#if   DemoVersionWithTimeLimit
   intExpireCount = intExpireLength;
   strVersionDesc = "This version of Supergame Plus will expire in 30 days";

#elif DemoVersionWithoutTimeLimit
   strVersionDesc = "Demo Version of Supergame Plus";

#elif OEMVersion
   strVersionDesc = " Supergame Plus, distributed under license";

#else
   strVersionDesc = "The original Supergame Plus!!";

#endif

   Console.WriteLine( strVersionDesc );
      ...
```

Diagnostic Directives

Diagnostic directives produce programmer-defined compile-time warning and error messages.

The following is the syntax of the diagnostic directives. The messages are strings, but notice that unlike normal C# strings, they do not have to be in quotes.

```
#warning Message

#error Message
```

When the compiler reaches a diagnostic directive, it writes out the associated message. The diagnostic directive messages are listed by the compiler along with any compiler-generated warning and error messages.

For example, the following code shows an #error directive and a #warning directive.

- The #error directive is inside an #if construct, so that it will be generated only if the conditions on the #if directive are met.

- The #warning directive is a reminder to the programmer to come back and clean up a section of code.

```
#define RightHanded
#define LeftHanded

#if RightHanded && LeftHanded
#error Can't build for both RightHanded and LeftHanded
#endif

#warning Remember to come back and clean up this code!
```

Line Number Directives

Line number directives can do several things, including the following:

- Change the apparent line numbers reported by the compiler's warning and error messages.

- Change the apparent filename of the source file being compiled.

- Hide a sequence of lines from the interactive debugger.

The syntax for the #line directives is the following.

```
#line integer           // Sets line number of next line to value of integer
#line "filename"        // Sets the apparent filename
#line default           // Restores real line number and filename

#line hidden            // Hides the following code from stepping debugger
#line                   // Stops hiding from debugger
```

The #line directive with an integer parameter causes the compiler to consider that value to be the line number of the following line of code. Numbering of the subsequent lines continues, based on that line number.

- To change the apparent filename, use the filename, inside double quotes, as the parameter. The double quotes are required.

- To return to true line numbering, and the true filename, use default as the parameter.

- To hide a segment of code from the step-through-code feature of the interactive debugger, use hidden as the parameter. To stop hiding, use the directive with no parameter. This feature has, so far, mostly been used in ASP.NET, for hiding compiler-generated code.

The following code shows examples of the line number directives.

```
#line 226
      x = y + z; // Now considered by the compiler to be line 226.
      ...

#line 330 "SourceFile.cs" // Changes the reported line number and filename.
      var1 = var2 + var3;
      ...

#line default             // Restores true line numbers and filename
```

Region Directives

The region directive allows you to mark, and optionally name, a section of code. The #region directive

- Is placed on the line above the section of code you want to mark

- Can have an optional string of text following it on the line, which serves as its name

- Must be terminated by an #endregion directive, farther down in the code

Although region directives are ignored by the compiler, they can be used by source code tools. Visual Studio, for example, allows you to easily hide or display regions.

As an example, the following code has a region called Constructors, which encloses the two constructors of a class MyClass. In Visual Studio, you could collapse this region to a single line when you didn't want to see it in the code, and then expand it again when you needed to work on it or add another constructor.

```
#region Constructors
   MyClass()
   { ... }

   MyClass(string s)
   { ... }
#endregion
```

Regions can be nested, as shown in Figure 22-3.

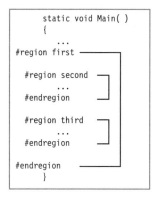

Figure 22-3. *Nested regions*

The #pragma warning Directive

The #pragma warning directive allows you to turn off warning messages and to turn them back on.

- To turn off warning messages, use the disable form with a comma-separated list of warning numbers you want to turn off.

- To turn warning messages back on, use the restore form with a list of the warning numbers you want to turn back on.

For example, the following code turns off two warning messages: 618 and 414. Farther down in the code, it turns on messages for 618 but leaves the messages for 414 turned off.

```
                        Warning messages to turn off
                                   ↓
#pragma warning disable 618, 414
    ...   Messages for the listed warnings are off in this section of code.
#pragma warning restore 618
```

If you use either form without a warning number list, the command then applies to all warnings.

For example, the following code turns off, and then restores, all warning messages.

```
#pragma warning disable
        ...   All warning messages are turned off in this section of code.

#pragma warning restore
        ...   All warning messages are turned back on in this section of code.
```

CHAPTER 23

Other Topics

Miscellaneous Topics
Strings
Parsing Strings to Data Values
Nullable Types
Method Main
Documentation Comments
Nested Types

Miscellaneous Topics

In this chapter, you will look at a number of other topics that are important in using C#, but that don't fit neatly into one of the other chapters. These include string handling, nullable types, the `Main` method, documentation comments, and nested types.

Strings

Zeros and ones are fine for internal computation, but for human readable input and output, we need strings of characters. The BCL provides a number of classes that make string handling easy.

The C# predefined type `string` represents the .NET class `System.String`. The most important things to know about `strings` are the following:

- `strings` are arrays of Unicode characters.

- `strings` are immutable—they cannot be changed.

The `string` type has many useful string manipulation members. These allow you to determine the length of a string, concatenate strings, change the case of a string, and many other useful tasks. Some of the most useful members are listed in Table 23-1.

Table 23-1. *Useful Members of the string Type*

Member	Type	Meaning
Length	Property	Returns the length of the string
Concat	Static method	Returns a string that is the concatenation of its argument strings
Contains	Method	Returns a `bool` value indicating whether the argument is a substring of the object string
Format	Static method	Returns a formatted string
Insert	Method	Inserts a string at a specific point in the object string
Remove	Method	Removes a set of characters from the object string
Replace	Method	Replaces a character or string in the object string
SubString	Method	Retrieves a substring from the object string
ToUpper	Method	Returns a copy of the object string where the alphabetic characters are all uppercase
ToLower	Method	Returns a copy of the object string where the alphabetic characters are all lowercase

The names of many of the methods in Table 23-1 sound as if they are changing the string object. Actually, they are not changing the strings but returning new copies. For a `string`, any "change" allocates a new immutable string.

For example, the following code declares and initializes a string called s. The first WriteLine statement calls the ToUpper method on s, which returns a copy of the string that is in all uppercase. The last line prints out the value of s, showing that it is unchanged.

```
string s = "Hi there.";

Console.WriteLine("{0}", s.ToUpper());       // Print uppercase copy.
Console.WriteLine("{0}", s);                 // String is unchanged.
```

This code produces the following output:

```
HI THERE.
Hi there.
```

Using Class StringBuilder

The StringBuilder class produces strings that can be changed.

- The StringBuilder class is a member of the BCL, in namespace System.Text.

- A StringBuilder object is a *mutable* array of Unicode characters.

For example, the following code declares and initializes a string of type StringBuilder and prints its value. The fourth line changes the actual object by replacing part of the string. Now, when you print the value of the string, you can see that, unlike an object of type string, the StringBuilder object has actually been changed.

```
using System.Text;

StringBuilder sb = new StringBuilder("Hi there.");
Console.WriteLine("{0}", sb);              // Print string.
sb.Replace("Hi", "Hello");                 // Replace a substring.
Console.WriteLine("{0}", sb);              // Print changed string.
```

This code produces the following output:

```
Hi there.
Hello there.
```

When a StringBuilder object is created, the class allocates a buffer longer than the actual current string length. As long as the changes made to the string can fit in the buffer, no new memory is allocated. If changes to the string require more space than is available in the buffer, a new, larger buffer is allocated, and the string is copied to it. Like the original buffer, this new buffer also has extra space.

Formatting Numeric Strings

Throughout the text, I have used the WriteLine method to display values. Each time, I used the simple substitution marker consisting of curly braces surrounding an integer. Many times, however, you will want to present the output of a text string in a format more appropriate than just a plain number. For example, you might want to display a value as currency, or as a fixed-point value with a certain number of decimal places. You can do this by using format strings.

For example, the following code consists of two statements that print out the value 500. The first line prints out the number without any additional formatting. In the second line, the format string specifies that the number should be formatted as currency.

```
Console.WriteLine("The value: {0}."  , 500);        // Print out number.
Console.WriteLine("The value: {0:C}.", 500);        // Format as currency.
                               ⊤
                   Format as currency.
```

This code produces the following output.

```
The value: 500.
The value: $500.00.
```

The difference between the two statements is that the format item includes additional information in the form of a format specifier. The syntax for a format specifier consists of three fields inside the set of curly braces: the index, the alignment specifier, and the format specifier. The syntax is shown in Figure 23-1.

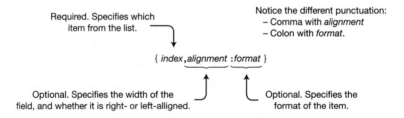

Figure 23-1. *Syntax for a format item*

The first thing in the format item is the index. As you well know by now, the index specifies which item from the list, following the format string, should be formatted. The index is required, and numbering of the list items starts at 0.

The Alignment Specifier

The alignment specifier represents the *minimum width* of the field in terms of characters. The alignment specifier has the following characteristics:

- It is optional and separated from the index with a comma.

- It consists of a positive or negative integer.
  - The integer represents the minimum number of characters to use for the field.
  - The sign represents either right or left alignment. Positive specifies right alignment; negative specifies left alignment.

```
                   Index -- use 0th item in the list.
                              ↓
       Console.WriteLine("{0, 10}", 500);
                            ↑
            Alignment specifier -- right-align in a field of 10 characters.
```

For example, the following code shows two format items, formatting the value of int variable MyInt. In the first case, the value of MyInt is displayed as a right-aligned string of ten characters. In the second case, it is left aligned. The format items are between two vertical bars, just to show in the output their limits on each side.

```
int MyInt = 500;
Console.WriteLine("|{0, 10}|", MyInt);          // Aligned right
Console.WriteLine("|{0,-10}|", MyInt);          // Aligned left
```

This code produces the following output; there are ten characters between the vertical bars:

```
|       500|
|500       |
```

The actual representation of the value might take more or fewer characters than specified in the alignment specifier:

- If the representation takes fewer characters than is specified in the alignment specifier, the remaining characters are padded with spaces.

- If the representation takes more characters than specified, the alignment specifier is ignored, and the representation uses as many characters as is needed.

The Format Component

The format component specifies the form that the numeric representation should take. For example, should it be represented as currency, in decimal format, in hexadecimal format, or in fixed point notation?

The format component has two parts, as shown in Figure 23-2:

- The *format specifier* is a single alphabetic character, from a set of nine built-in character formats. The character can be uppercase or lowercase. The case is significant for some specifiers, but insignificant for others.

- The *precision specifier* is optional, and consists of one or two digits. Its actual meaning depends on the format specifier.

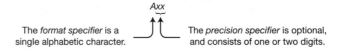

The *format specifier* is a single alphabetic character. The *precision specifier* is optional, and consists of one or two digits.

Figure 23-2. *Standard format specifier string*

The following code shows an example of the syntax of the format string component.

```
              Index -- use 0th item in the list.
                      ↓
Console.WriteLine("{0:F4}", 12.345678);
                      ↑
        Format component -- fixed-point, four decimal places.
```

Some examples of different format strings are shown in the following code.

```
double MyDouble = 12.345678;
Console.WriteLine("{0,-10:G} -- General",                       MyDouble);
Console.WriteLine("{0,-10} -- Default, same as General",        MyDouble);
Console.WriteLine("{0,-10:F4} -- Fixed Point, 4 dec places",    MyDouble);
Console.WriteLine("{0,-10:C} -- Currency",                      MyDouble);
Console.WriteLine("{0,-10:E3} -- Sci. Notation, 3 dec places",  MyDouble);
Console.WriteLine("{0,-10:x} -- Hexadecimal integer",           1194719 );
```

This code produces the following output:

```
12.345678  -- General
12.345678  -- Default, same as General
12.3457    -- Fixed Point, 4 dec places
$12.35     -- Currency
1.235E+001 -- Sci. Notation, 3 dec places
123adf     -- Hexadecimal integer
```

Standard Numeric Format Specifiers

The Windows Control Panel applet, Regional and Language Options, can affect the resulting formats of some of the specifiers. For example, the currency symbol of the country or region specified will be used by the currency format specifier.

Table 23-2 summarizes the nine standard numeric format specifiers. The first column lists the name of the specifier followed by the specifier characters. If the specifier characters have different output depending on their case, they are marked *case sensitive*.

Table 23-2. *Standard Numeric Format Specifiers*

Name and Characters	Meaning
Currency C, c	Formats the value as a currency, using a currency symbol. Precision specifier: The number of decimal places. Sample: `Console.WriteLine("{0 :C}", 12.5);` Output: $12.50
Decimal D, d	A string of decimal digits, with a negative sign, if appropriate. Can be used only with integral types. Precision specifier: The minimum number of digits to use in the output string. If the number has fewer digits, it will be padded with 0s on the left. Sample: `Console.WriteLine("{0 :D4}", 12);` Output: 0012
Scientific E, e Case sensitive	Scientific notation with a mantissa and an exponent. The exponent is preceded by the letter *E*. The *E* will be the same case as the specifier. Precision specifier: The number of decimal places. Sample: `Console.WriteLine("{0 :e4}", 12.3456789);` Output: 1.2346e+001
Fixed-point F, f	A string of decimal digits with a decimal point. Can also include a negative sign, if appropriate. Precision specifier: The number of decimal places. Sample: `Console.WriteLine("{0 :F4}", 12.3456789);` Output: 12.3457
General G, g	A compact fixed-point representation or a scientific notation representation, depending on the value. This is the default, if no specifier is listed. Precision specifier: Depends on the value. Sample: `Console.WriteLine("{0 :G4}", 12.3456789);` Output: 12.35
Number N, n	Similar to fixed-point representation, but includes separators between each group of three digits, starting at the decimal point and going left. Precision specifier: The number of decimal places. Sample: `Console.WriteLine("{0 :N2}", 12345678.54321);` Output: 12,345,678.54

Continued

Table 23-2. *Continued*

Name and Characters	Meaning
Percent P, p	A string that represents percent. The number is multiplied by 100. Precision specifier: The number of decimal places. Sample: `Console.WriteLine("{0 :P2}", 0.1221897);` Output: `12.22 %`
Round-trip R, r	The output string is chosen so that if the string is converted back to a numeric value using a `Parse` method, the result will be the original value. Precision specifier: Ignored. Sample: `Console.WriteLine("{0 :R}", 1234.21897);` Output: `1234.21897`
Hexadecimal X, x Case sensitive	A string of hexadecimal digits. The hex digits A–F will match the case of the specifier. Precision specifier: The minimum number of digits to use in the output string. If the number has fewer digits, it will be padded with 0s on the left. Sample: `Console.WriteLine("{0 :x}", 180026);` Output: `2bf3a`

Parsing Strings to Data Values

Strings are arrays of Unicode characters. For example, string "25.873" is six characters long and is *not* a number. Although it looks like a number, you cannot perform arithmetic functions on it. "Adding" two strings produces a concatenation of them.

- *Parsing* allows you to take a string that represents a value and convert it into an actual numeric value.

- All the predefined, simple types have a static method called `Parse`, which takes a string value representing the type and converts it into an actual value of the type.

The following statement shows an example of the syntax of using a `Parse` method. Notice that `Parse` is static, so you need to invoke it by using the name of the target type.

```
double d1 = double.Parse("25.873");
              ↑              ↑
          Target type   String to be converted
```

The following code shows an example of parsing two strings to values of type `double` and then adding them.

```
static void Main()
{
   string s1 = "25.873";
   string s2 = "36.240";

   double d1 = double.Parse(s1);
   double d2 = double.Parse(s2);

   double total = d1 + d2;
   Console.WriteLine("Total:  {0}", total);
}
```

This code produces the following output:

```
Total:  62.113
```

If the string cannot be parsed, the system raises an exception. There is another static method, `TryParse`, which returns `true` if the string was successfully parsed, and `false` otherwise. It does not raise an exception if the parse fails.

■ **Note** A common confusion about `Parse` is that, since it operates on a string, it is often thought of as a member of the `string` class. It is not. `Parse` is not a single method at all, but a number of methods implemented by the *target* types.

Nullable Types

There are situations, particularly when working with databases, where you want to indicate that a variable does not currently hold a valid value. For reference types, you can do this easily, by setting the variable to null. When you define a variable of a value type, however, its memory is allocated, whether or not its contents have any valid meaning.

What you would like in this situation is to have a Boolean indicator associated with the variable, so that when the value is valid, the indicator is true, and when the value is not valid, the indicator is false.

Nullable types, new in C# 2.0, allow you to create a value type variable that can be marked as valid or invalid so that you can make sure a variable is valid before using it. Regular value types are called *non-nullable types*.

Creating a Nullable Type

A nullable type is always based on another type, called the *underlying type*, which has already been declared.

- You can create a nullable type from any value type, including the predefined, simple types.

- You cannot create a nullable type from a reference type or another nullable type.

- You do not explicitly declare a nullable type in your code. Instead, you declare a *variable of a nullable type*. The compiler implicitly creates the nullable type for you, using generics, as I'll describe later.

To create a variable of a nullable type, simply add a question mark to the end of the name of the underlying type, in the variable declaration. Unfortunately, this syntax makes it appear that you have a lot of questions about your code.

For example, the following code declares a variable of the nullable int type. Notice that the suffix is attached to the *type* name—not the variable name.

```
       Suffix
         ↓
int? MyNInt = 28;
       ↑
The name of the nullable type includes the suffix.
```

With this declaration statement, the compiler takes care of both producing the nullable type and the variable of that type. Figure 23-3 shows the structure of this nullable type. It contains the following:

- An instance of the underlying type

- Several important read-only properties:
    - Property HasValue is of type bool and indicates whether the value is valid.
    - Property Value is the same type as the underlying type and returns the value of the variable—if the variable is valid.

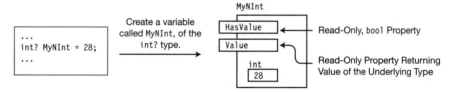

Figure 23-3. *A nullable type is the result of enclosing the underlying type in a struct, with two read-only properties.*

You can use the two read-only properties explicitly as follows.

```
int? MyInt1 = 15;
        Explicitly use the property.
              ↓
if ( MyInt1.HasValue )
    Console.WriteLine("{0}", MyInt1.Value);
                                    ↑
                    Explicitly use the property.
```

A better method, however, is to use the shortcut forms, as shown in the following code.

- To check whether a nullable type has a value, you can compare it to null.

- Like any variable, to retrieve its value, you can just use its name.

```
        Compare to null.
              ↓
if (MyInt1 != null)
    Console.WriteLine("{0}", MyInt1);
                              ↑
                    Use variable name.
```

Both sets of code produce the following output:

15

Reading a variable of a nullable type returns its value. You must, however, make sure that the variable is not null. Attempting to read the value of a null variable produces an exception. You can easily convert between a nullable type and its corresponding non-nullable type.

- There is an *implicit* conversion between a non-nullable type and its nullable version. That is, no cast is needed.

- There is an *explicit* conversion between a nullable type and its non-nullable version.

For example, the following lines show conversion in both directions. In the first line, a literal of type int is implicitly converted to a value of type int? and is used to initialize the variable of the nullable type. In the second line, the variable is explicitly converted to its non-nullable version.

```
int? MyInt1 = 15;                 // Implicitly convert int to int?
int RegInt = (int) MyInt1;        // Explicitly convert int? to int
```

Assigning to a Nullable Type

There are three kinds of values you can assign to a variable of a nullable type:

- A value of the underlying type
- A value of the same nullable type
- The value null

The following code shows an example of each of the three types of assignment.

```
int? MyI1, MyI2, MyI3;

MyI1 = 28;                              // Value of underlying type
MyI2 = MyI1;                            // Value of nullable type
MyI3 = null;                            // Null

Console.WriteLine("MyI1: {0}, MyI2: {1}", MyI1, MyI2);
Console.WriteLine("MyI3 {0} null", MyI3 == null ? "is" : "is not");
```

This code produces the following output:

```
MyI1: 28, MyI2: 28
MyI3 is null
```

Using Operators and the Null Coalescing Operator

The standard arithmetic and comparison operators have been updated to handle nullable types. There is also a new operator called the *null coalescing operator*, which allows you to return a value to an expression, in case a nullable type variable is null.

The null coalescing operator consists of two contiguous question marks and has two operands:

- The first operand is a variable of a nullable type.

- The second is a non-nullable value of the same underlying type.

- If, at run time, the first operand evaluates as null, the second operand is returned as the result of the operation.

```
                              Null coalescing operator
int? MyI4 = null;                      ↓
Console.WriteLine("MyI4: {0}", MyI4 ?? -1);


MyI4 = 10;
Console.WriteLine("MyI4: {0}", MyI4 ?? -1);
```

This code produces the following output:

```
MyI4: -1
MyI4: 10
```

The equality comparison operators, == and !=, have an interesting characteristic you need to be aware of. If you compare two values of the same nullable type, and both are null, the equality comparison operators consider them equal. For example, in the following code the two nullable ints are set to null. The equality comparison operator will declare them equal.

```
int? I1 = null, I2 = null;           // Both are null.
if (I1 == I2)                        // Operator returns true.
   Console.WriteLine("Equal");
```

Using Nullable User-Defined Types

So far, you have seen nullable forms of the predefined, simple types. You can also create nullable forms of user-defined value types. These bring up additional issues that don't come up when using the simple types.

The main issue is access to the members of the encapsulated underlying type. A nullable type doesn't directly expose any of the members of the underlying type. For example, take a look at the following code and its representation in Figure 23-4. The code declares a struct called MyStruct, with two public fields.

- Since the fields of the struct are public, they can easily be accessed in any instance of the struct, as shown on the left of the figure.

- The nullable version of the struct, however, exposes the underlying type only through the Value property, and does not *directly* expose any of its members. Although the members are public to the struct, they are not public to the nullable type, as shown on the right of the figure.

```
struct MyStruct                                  // Declare a struct.
{
    public int x;                                // Field
    public int y;                                // Field
    public MyStruct(int xVal, int yVal)          // Constructor
    { x = xVal; y = yVal; }
}

class Program {
    static void Main()
    {
        MyStruct? MSNull = new MyStruct(5, 10);
        ...
                 Create a temporary instance to initialize the variable.
```

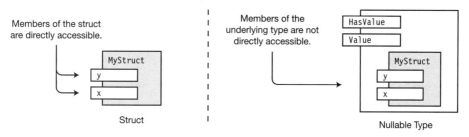

Figure 23-4. *The accessibility of the members of a struct is different from that of the nullable type.*

For example, the following code uses the previously declared struct, and creates variables of both the struct and the corresponding nullable type. In the third and fourth lines of code, the values of the struct's variables are read directly. In the fifth and sixth lines, they must be read from the value returned by the nullable's `Value` property.

```
MyStruct  MSStruct = new MyStruct(6, 11);      // Variable of struct
MyStruct? MSNull   = new MyStruct(5, 10);      // Variable of nullable type
                                    Struct access
                                         ↓

Console.WriteLine("MSStruct.x: {0}", MSStruct.x);
Console.WriteLine("MSStruct.y: {0}", MSStruct.y);

Console.WriteLine("MSNull.x: {0}",   MSNull.Value.x);
Console.WriteLine("MSNull.y: {0}",   MSNull.Value.y);
                                         ↑
                                Nullable type access
```

Nullable<T>

Nullable types are implemented by using a .NET type called `System.Nullable<T>`, which uses the C# generics feature.

The question mark syntax of C# nullable types is just shortcut syntax for creating a variable of type `Nullable<T>`, where T is the underlying type. `Nullable<T>` takes the underlying type and embeds it in a structure, and provides the structure with the properties, methods, and constructors of the nullable type.

You can use either the generics syntax of `Nullable<T>` or the C# shortcut syntax. The shortcut syntax is easier to write and to understand, and is less prone to errors.

The following code uses the `Nullable<T>` syntax with struct `MyStruct`, declared in the preceding example, to create a variable called `MSNull` of type `Nullable<MyStruct>`.

```
Nullable<MyStruct> MSNull = new Nullable<MyStruct>();
```

The following code uses the question mark syntax but is semantically equivalent to the `Nullable<T>` syntax.

```
MyStruct? MSNull = new MyStruct();
```

Method Main

Every C# program must have one entry point—a method that must be called Main.

In the sample code throughout this text, I have used a version of Main that takes no parameters and returns no value. There are, however, four forms of Main that are acceptable as the entry point to a program. These forms are the following:

- static void Main()   {…}

- static void Main(string[] args) {…}

- static int Main()   {…}

- static int Main(string[] args) {…}

The first two forms don't return a value to the execution environment when the program terminates. The second two forms return an int value. A return value, if one is used, is generally used to report success or failure of the program, where 0 is generally used to indicate success.

The second and fourth forms allow you to pass actual parameters, also called *arguments*, from the command line, into the program, when it starts. There can be zero or more of these command-line arguments, separated by spaces or tabs. Each argument is interpreted by the program as a string, but you do not need to enclose them in quotation marks on the command line.

For example, the following program called CommandLineArgs accepts command-line arguments and prints out each argument supplied.

```
class Program
{
   static void Main(string[] args)
   {
      foreach (string s in args)
         Console.WriteLine(s);
   }
}
```

The following command line executes program CommandLineArgs with five arguments.

```
CommandLineArgs Jon Peter Beth Julia Tammi
        ↑             ↑
   Executable       Arguments
     name
```

This code produces the following output:

```
Jon
Peter
Beth
Julia
Tammi
```

Other important things to know about Main are the following:

- Main must always be declared static.

- Main can be declared in either a class or a struct.

A program can contain only one declaration of the four acceptable entry point forms of Main. You can, however, legally declare other methods named Main, as long as they don't have any of the four forms listed previously—but doing this is inviting confusion.

Accessibility of Main

Main can be declared public or private:

- If Main is declared private, other assemblies cannot access it, and only the execution environment can start the program.

- If Main is declared public, other assemblies can call it and thereby start the program.

The execution environment, however, *always* has access to Main, regardless of its declared access level, or the declared access level of the class or struct in which it is declared.

By default, when Visual Studio creates a project, it creates a program outline where Main is implicitly private. You can always add the public modifier if you need to.

Documentation Comments

The documentation comments feature allows you to include documentation of your program in the form of XML elements. Visual Studio even assists you in inserting the elements, and will read them from your source file and copy them to a separate XML file for you. This section does not cover the topic of XML but presents the overall process of using documentation comments.

Figure 23-5 gives an overview of using XML comments. This includes the following steps:

- You can use Visual Studio to produce the source file with the embedded XML. Visual Studio's IntelliSense feature can automatically insert most of the important XML elements.

- Visual Studio reads the XML from the source code file and copies the XML code to a new file.

- Another program, called a document generator, can take the XML file and produce various types of documentation files from it.

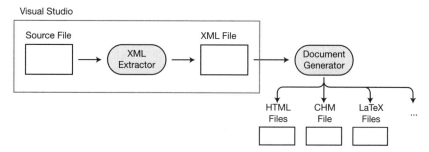

Figure 23-5. *The XML comments process*

Earlier versions of Visual Studio .NET contained a document generator that produced elementary documentation files. It was removed in Visual Studio 2005, and it's unknown whether a version will be added back to a future version of Visual Studio. There are, however, a number of free and third-party document generators that do an excellent job. They are easy to find on the Internet.

Inserting Documentation Comments

Documentation comments start with three consecutive forward slashes:

- The first two slashes indicate to the compiler that this is an end-of-line comment and should be ignored in the parsing of the program.

- The third slash indicates that it is a documentation comment.

For example, in the following code, the first four lines show documentation comments about the class declaration. They use the `<summary>` XML tag. Above the declaration of the field are three lines documenting the field—again using the `<summary>` tag.

```
/// <summary>              ← Open XML tag for the class.
/// This is class MyClass, which does the following wonderful things, using
/// the following algorithm. ... Besides those, it does these additional
/// wonderful things.
/// </summary>             ← Close XML tag.
class MyClass                                   // Class declaration
{
    /// <summary>          ← Open XML tag for the field.
    /// Field1 is used to hold the value of ...
    /// </summary>         ← Close XML tag.
    public int Field1 = 10;                     // Field declaration
    ...
```

Each XML element is inserted automatically by the Visual Studio IntelliSense feature when you type three slashes above the declaration of a language feature, such as a class or a class member.

For example, the following code shows two slashes above the declaration of class `MyClass`.

```
//
class MyClass
{ ...
```

As soon as you add the third slash, IntelliSense immediately expands the comment to the following code, without your having to do anything. You can then type anything you want on the documentation comment lines between the tags.

```
/// <summary>       ← Automatically inserted
///                 ← Automatically inserted
/// </summary>      ← Automatically inserted
class MyClass
{ ...
```

Example of Using Documentation Comments

The following code shows the beginning of a class declaration, containing documentation comments.

```
/// <summary>
/// This is class MyClass, which does the following wonderful things, using
/// the following algorithm. ... Besides those, it does these additional
/// wonderful things.
/// </summary>
class MyClass
{
   /// <summary>
   /// Field1 is used to hold the value of ...
   /// </summary>
   public int Field1 = 10;

   /// <summary>
   /// MyMethod is just a test method to show how the XML comments work.
   /// It does no actual processing.
   /// </summary>
   /// <param name="In1"></param>
   /// <param name="str1"></param>
   /// <returns></returns>
   public int MyMethod(int In1, string str1)
   {
      return 0;
   }
}
```

When this simple code is output to an XML file and run through a document generator, it can produce beautiful and potentially very useful documentation of the code. Figure 23-6 shows just a small sample of the output from this code by one of the readily available document generators. This extensive documentation was produced with almost no work.

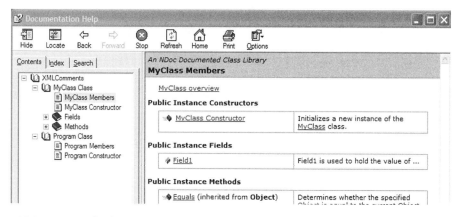

Figure 23-6. *Output of a document generator*

Using Other XML Tags

In the preceding examples, you saw several XML tags that were supplied by Visual Studio. These included summary, param, and returns. There are also a number of other tags that C# recognizes. Some of the most important are listed in Table 23-3.

Table 23-3. *Documentation Code XML Tags*

Tag	Meaning
`<code>`	Format the enclosing lines, in a font that looks like code.
`<example>`	Mark the enclosing lines as an example.
`<param>`	Mark a parameter for a method or constructor, and allow a description.
`<remarks>`	Describe a type declaration.
`<returns>`	Describe a return value.
`<seealso>`	Create a *See Also* entry in the output document.
`<summary>`	Describe a type or a type member.
`<value>`	Describe a property.

Nested Types

Types are usually declared directly inside a namespace. You can, however, also declare types inside a class or struct declaration.

- Types declared inside another type declaration are called *nested types*. Like all type declarations, nested types are templates for an instance of the type.

- A nested type is declared like a member of the *enclosing type*.
  - A nested type can be any type.
  - An enclosing type can be either a class or a struct.

For example, the following code shows class MyClass, with a nested class called MyCounter.

```
class MyClass                    // Enclosing class
{
   class MyCounter               // Nested class
   {
      ...
   }
   ...
}
```

Declaring a type as a nested type often makes sense if it is only meant to be used as a helper for the enclosing type.

Don't be confused by the term *nested*. Nested refers to the location of the *declaration*—not the location of any *instances*. Although a nested type's declaration is inside the enclosing type's declaration, objects of the nested type are not necessarily enclosed in objects of the enclosing type. Objects of the nested type—if any are created at all—are located wherever they would have been located had they not been declared inside another type.

For example, Figure 23-7 shows objects of types MyClass and MyCounter, as outlined in the preceding code. The figure additionally shows a field called Counter, in class MyClass, that is a reference to an object of the nested class, which is located elsewhere in the heap.

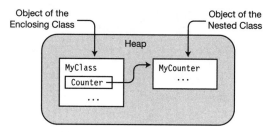

Figure 23-7. *Nesting refers to the location of the declaration, not the location of the object.*

Example of a Nested Class

The following code fleshes out classes MyClass and MyCounter into a full program. MyCounter implements an integer counter that starts at 0 and can be incremented using the ++ operator. When the constructor for MyClass is called, it creates an instance of the nested class and assigns the reference to the field. Figure 23-8 illustrates the structure of the objects in the code.

```csharp
class MyClass
{
   class MyCounter                                      // Nested class
   {
      private int _Count = 0;
      public int Count                                  // Read-only property
      {
         get { return _Count; }
      }

      public static MyCounter operator++( MyCounter current )
      {
         current._Count++;
         return current;
      }
   }

   private MyCounter counter;                           // Field of nested class

   public MyClass() { counter = new MyCounter(); }    // Constructor

   public int Incr()     { return (counter++).Count; } // Increment method
   public int GetValue() { return counter.Count; }     // Get counter value.
}

class Program
{
   static void Main( )
   {
      MyClass mc = new MyClass();                       // Create object.

      mc.Incr(); mc.Incr(); mc.Incr();                  // Increment it.
      mc.Incr(); mc.Incr(); mc.Incr();                  // Increment it.

      Console.WriteLine("Total: {0}", mc.GetValue());   // Print its value.
   }
}
```

This code produces the following output:

```
Total:   6
```

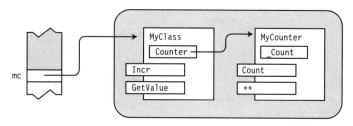

Figure 23-8. *Objects of a nested class and its enclosing class*

Visibility and Nested Types

In Chapter 7, you learned that classes, and types in general, can have an access level of either public or internal. Nested types, however, are different, in that they have *member accessibility* rather than *type accessibility*. Therefore, the following are true:

- A nested type declared inside a class can have any of the five class member accessibility levels: public, protected, private, internal, or protected internal.

- A nested type declared inside a struct can have one of the three struct member accessibility levels: public, internal, or private.

In both cases, the default access level of a nested type is private, which means it cannot be seen outside the enclosing type.

The relationship between the members of the enclosing class and the nested class is a little less straightforward and is illustrated in Figure 23-9. The nested type has complete access to the members of the enclosing type, regardless of their declared accessibility, including members that are private and protected.

The relationship, however, is not symmetrical. Although the members of the enclosing type can always see the nested type declaration and create variables and instances of it, they do not have complete access to its members. Instead, their access is limited to the declared access of the nested class members—just as if the nested type were a separate type. That is, they can access the public and internal members, but cannot access the private or protected members of the nested type.

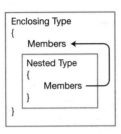

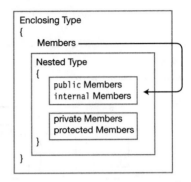

Members of the nested type have complete access permission to members of the enclosing type.

Members of the enclosing type have access permission only to `public` and `internal` members of the nested type.

Figure 23-9. *Accessibility between nested type members and enclosing type members*

You can summarize this relationship as follows:

- The members of a nested type always have full access-rights to members of the enclosing type.

- The members of an enclosing type
  - Always have access to the nested type itself
  - Only have the *declared access-rights* to *members* of the nested type

The visibility of nested types can also affect the inheritance of base members. If the enclosing class is a derived class, a nested type can hide a base class member with the same name. Use the new modifier with the declaration of the nested class to make the hiding explicit.

A this reference within a nested type refers to the *object of the nested type*—not the object of the enclosing type. If an object of the nested type needs access to the enclosing type, it must have a reference to it. You can have the enclosing object supply its this reference as a parameter to the nested type's constructor, as shown in the following code.

```
class SomeClass                           // Enclosing class
{
    int Field1 = 15;                      // Field of enclosing class
    int Field2 = 20;                      // Field of enclosing class
    MyNested mn = null;                   // Reference to nested class

    public void PrintMyMembers()
    {
        mn.PrintOuterMembers();           // Call method in nested class.
    }

    public SomeClass()                    // Constructor
    {
        mn = new MyNested(this);          // Create instance of nested class.
    }                    ↑
            Pass in the reference to the enclosing class.

    class MyNested                        // Nested class declaration
    {
        SomeClass sc = null;              // Reference to enclosing class
        public MyNested(SomeClass SC)     // Construct or nested class
        {
            sc = SC;                      // Store reference to enclosing class.
        }

        public void PrintOuterMembers()
        {
            Console.WriteLine("Field1: {0}", sc.Field1);   // Enclosing field.
            Console.WriteLine("Field2: {0}", sc.Field2);   // Enclosing field.
        }
    }                                     // End of nested class
}

class Program
{
    static void Main( )
    {
        SomeClass MySC = new SomeClass();
        MySC.PrintMyMembers();
    }
}
```

This code produces the following output:

```
Field1: 15
Field2: 20
```

Index

Symbols

#define directive 505, 506

#elif directive 505, 507, 508, 510

#else directive 505, 507, 508, 510

#endif directive 505, 507, 508, 510

#endregion directive 505, 513

#error directive 505, 511

#if directive 505, 507, 508, 510

#line directive 505, 512

#pragma directive 505, 514

#region directive 505

#undef directive 505, 506

#warning directive 505, 511

.NET. *See* NET

@ character 18

A

abstract classes 166–167

abstract members 165

abstract modifier 165–166

access modifiers 53

   accessing members from inside the class 56

   accessing members from outside the class 57

   on accessors 135

   private and public access 53–55

   using access modifiers on 135

accessibility and nested types 539–541

accessors for events 369

acronyms 13

actual parameters 73

addition operator 182

ADO.NET and database manipulation 6

after state 476

All value

   AttributeTarget enumeration 495

AllowMultiple property

   AttributeUsage attribute 494, 495

AND operator

   unpacking bit flags 300

anonymous method event handlers 363

anonymous methods

   delegates 346

   scope of variables and parameters 351

      extension of captured variables lifetime 352

      outer variables 351

   syntax 348

      parameters 349

      params parameters 350

      return type 348

   using 347

ArgumentNullException class 280

arithmetic operators 182

   See also unary arithmetic operators

   using with nullable types 528

Array class

   Clone method 329, 330

   GetEnumerator method 456

   members 327–328

   properties 310

   Sort method 373, 378

array parameters 88

arrays 308

   accessing array elements 313

   as objects 310

   automatic initialization 314

arrays *(continued)*

Clone method 329, 330

comparing array types 331

comparing rectangular and jagged arrays 321

convariance 326

definitions 308

example 316

explicit initialization of one-dimensional arrays 314, 315

foreach statement 322

iteration variables 323

jagged arrays 325

multidimensional arrays 324

rectangular arrays 324

inherited members 327–328

initializing 314

jagged arrays 317–320, 325

points to consider 308

processing with foreach statement 456

shortcut syntax 316

syntax points for initializing rectangular arrays 315

types of arrays 309

as operator 426

using with interfaces 393

ASP.NET

building web-based applications 6

assemblies

configuration files 262

delayed signing 263–264

description 7

identity 255

inheritance between assemblies 157–158

mscorlib library 243–244

private deployment 259

referencing other assemblies 240–241

shared assemblies and GAC 260–261

strongly named assemblies 257–258

structure 253–254

assembly names and identity 255

assembly-level attributes 487

assigning delegates 338

assignment operators 194–195

See also compound assignment operators

associativity 181

Attribute class

attribute classes derived from 489

attributes

See also custom attributes

accessing metadata 496–499

applying 485

Conditional attribute 499–501

declaration statements 96

global attributes 487

introduction 482

multiple attributes 486

Obsolute attribute 499

predefined attributes 488

preview 483

reserved attributes 499

stages 484

targets 486–487

AttributeTarget enumeration 495

AttributeUsage attribute 488

AllowMultiple property 495

constructor 495

Inherited property 495

properties 494

specifying targets 496

ValidOn property 495

■**B**

base class 140–142

accessing hidden members of 145

hiding members of 143–144

using references to 146–147

virtual and override methods 148–152

Base Class Library. *See* BCL

base keyword 145, 154

BCL (Base Class Library) 3
  namespaces 247
before state 476
binary operators and associativity 181
BinarySearch method
  Array class 327
bit flags 300–301
  example 303–304
  Flags attribute 301–302
bitwise AND operator 190–192
bitwise logical operators 190–192
bitwise NOT operator 190–192
bitwise OR operator 190–192
bitwise shift operators 192–193
blocks 21
bool type 33–34
boxing 402, 416
  boxing conversions 418
  creating a copy 417
break statements 66, 212, 227
  ending switch statements 215
  requirements in switch statements 219
byte type 34

■C

C# programming
  as imperative language 482
  as set of type declarations 30
  classes example 45–46, 58–59
  comments 26–27
  documentation comments 27–28
  generics 430
  keywords 19
  Main() method 20
  naming conventions 19
  simple example 16–18
  statements 21
  text output 22
    format string 23

  multiple markers and values 25
  substituting values 24
  Write() 22
  WriteLine() 23
  whitespace 20
Camel casing 19
case keyword 219
cast character and explicit conversions 201
cast expressions 400
catch clause
  catch clauses section 272
  example of searching down call stack 278
  examples of specific catch clauses 271
  forms 270
  throwing exceptions without exception
    object 282–283
  try statement 267–268
char type 33–34
  as character literal 177
character literals 177
checked operators 404–405
checked statements 237, 405
CIL (Common Intermediate Language)
  compiling to 7–8
  contained in assemblies 253
  structure of assemblies 253
class access modifiers 156
class inheritance 140
  accessing inherited members 141
  base access 145
  class access modifiers 156
  constructor execution 153–154
  constructor initializers 154–155
  hiding members of base class 143–144
  inheritance between assemblies 157–158
  Object class 142
  using references to base class 146–147
  virtual and override methods 148–152
class-base specification 140

Find it faster at http://superindex.apress.com

classes
    access modifiers 53–57
    accessibility of constructors 122
    allocating memory for data 50–51
    as active data structure 44
    constants 104–106
    copying from class variable 288
    creating variables and instances of class 50
    declaring 17, 46
    declaring a generic class 433
    fields 47–48
    finalizers 123–124
    generics 432
    indexers 127–134
    instance class members 98
    instance constructors 118
        constructors with parameters 119
        default constructors 120
    instance members 52
    members 96–97
    methods 49
    programming example 45–46, 58–59
    properties 107–117
    readonly modifier 125
    static class member types 103–104
    static constructors 121–122
    static fields 99–101
    static function members 102
    this keyword 126
Clear method
    Array class 327
CLI (Common Language Infrastructure)
    CLS 12
    CTS 12
    introduction 11
Clone method
    Array class 327, 329, 330
CLR (Common Language Runtime)
    compiling to native code and execution 8–9

    introduction 10
    managing program execution at run time 3
CLS (Common Language Specification) 12
CLSCompliant attribute 488
<code> tag 536
COM and .NET 5
combining delegates 339
comments 26–27
Common Intermediate Language. See CIL
Common Language Infrastructure. See CLI
Common Language Runtime. See CLR
Common Language Specification. See CLS
Common Type System. See CTS
CompareTo method
    IComparable interface 372–375
comparison operator 185
comparison operators and nullable types 528
compiler role in producing metadata 482
compound assignment operators 195
Concat method
    String class 516
Conditional attribute 499
    example 500–501
    TraceMessage method 500–501
conditional compilation 507
    constructs 508–510
conditional execution statements 212
conditional logical operators 188–189
conditional operator 113, 196–197
    associativity 181
configuration files, assemblies 262
Console class 243
    printing message to screen 17
    using alias directives 252
    Write() method 22
    WriteLine() method 23
console window 22
const keyword 104
    compare to readonly modifier 125

constants 104–105
  compared to statics 105–106
  local constants 106
constraints
  types and order 442
  where clause 441
constructed types, creating 433–434
constructor execution 153–154
  class access modifiers 156
  initializers 154–155
constructors
  accessibility of 122
  and structs 289–291
  compared to finalizers 124
  positional and named parameters 492–493
  specifying attribute constructors 490–491
  using attribute constructors 490–491
consumers of attributes 482
Contains method
  String class 516
continue statements 66, 212, 228
convariance 326
conversions 398
  boxing 416–418
  explicit conversions 400–401
  implicit conversions 399, 402–409
  reference conversions 410–416
  types of conversions 402
  unboxing conversions 418–419
  user-defined conversions 420–424
CTS (Common Type System) 12
culture information and identity of
    assemblies 255
Current property
  enumerator class implements 468
  IEnumerator interface 458, 460, 461, 466
  IEnumerator <T> interface 469
custom attributes 489
  accessing metadata 496–499

constructors 490–493
  declaring 489
  restricting usage of attributes 494–495
  suggested practices 496
custom delegates 365–367

■D

data members 32, 44
databases, manipulating with ADO.NET 6
decimal type 33, 34
declaration statements 210
declarative programming 482
decrement operator 186, 187
deep comparison 185
delayed signing 263–264
DelaySignAttribute class 263
delegate keyword 335, 348
Delegate value
  AttributeTarget enumeration 495
delegates 334
  adding methods 340
  anonymous methods 346–347
    scope of variables and parameters
      351–352
    syntax 348–350
  assigning delegates 338
  combining delegates 339
  compared to events 354
  custom delegates 365–367
  declaring delegate types 335–337
  deleting methods 341
  events as encapsulated delegates 355
  example 343–344
  generics 447–448
  invocation list 334
  invoking delegates with reference
      parameters 345–346
  invoking delegates with return values 344
  invoking methods 342

Find it faster at http://superindex.apress.com

delegates *(continued)*

name of type required when declaring events 358

private delegates of events 355

type declarations as part of event code 356

delimited comments 26–28

derived class 140

diagnostic directives 511

dimension length of arrays 308

dimensions of arrays 308

declaring one-dimensional and rectangular arrays 311

directions 251

using alias directive 252–253

using namespace directive 251

Dispose method

guidelines 124

IDisposable interface 232, 233, 469

DivideByZeroException class

example 278

example using specific catch clause 271

division operator 182

DLLImport attribute 488

do statements 66, 212, 221–222

can use break statement 227

using continue statements 228

documentation comments 26–28, 533

example 535

inserting 534

XML tags 536

dot-syntax notation 57

double literal 173

double type 33–34

■E

elements of arrays 308

embedded statements 210

empty statements 211

enumerables

GetEnumerator method 456

producing 477

producing with an iterator 478

enumerations 296

bit flags 300–304

further information 304

implicit member membering 299

setting explicit values for members 298

setting underlying type 298

underlying types and values 297

enumerator class

implementing IEnumerator interfaces 468

implementing IEnumerator <T> interface 468

enumerators

creating with iterators 474

example using IEnumerable and IEnumerator 464–465

generic enumeration interfaces 468

IEnumerable interface 463–464

IEnumerator interface 458–463

non-interface enumerator 466–467

producing 477

producing with iterators 479–480

types of 457

using foreach statement 456

equality operator 184–185

event handlers

declaration 356

declaring events 358

description 354

removing 362

event registration 356

EventArgs class

passing data by extending 364

EventHandler delegate type

System namespace 364

using EventArgs class 364

EventHandler generic delegate 365

events

accessors 369

adding anonymous method event handlers 363

as encapsulated delegates 355

as member 358

compared to delegates 354

custom delegates 365–367

declaring 356–357

declaring event handlers 358

EventArgs class 364

MyTimerClass code 367–368

name of delegate type required 358

overview of code components 356

passing data by extending EventArgs class 364

private delegates 355

raising an event 359

removing event handlers 362

standard usage 364

subscribing to an event 360–361

<example> tag 536

Exception class 269

exception handlers 267

example of searching down call stack 277–278

finding handlers for exceptions 274

general algorithm 276

exceptions

COM compared to .NET 5

example of searching down call stack 277–278

exception classes 269

finding handlers for 274

finding handlers for in code without try statement 275

general algorithm for handling 276

introduction 266

throwing 280–281

throwing without exception object 282–283

try statement 267–268

expanded form

parameter arrays 85–87

explicit conversions 199–200, 400–403

and cast character 201

between nullable type and non-nullable version 526

casting 400–401

constraints in user-defined conversions 420

overflow checking context 404–405

explicit interface member implementations 388–391

explicit keyword 420

explicit numeric conversions 406

decimal to double or float 409

decimal to integral 407

double or float to decimal 408

double to float 408

float or double to integral 407

integral to integral 406

explicit reference conversions 413

valid conversions 414–415

expressions 172

associativity 181

evaluating 172

order of evaluation 180

parenthesized expressions 181

precedence 180

side effects 211

statements 211

extern modifier 168

external methods 168–169

■**F**

field initializers and structs 292

fields 47–48

finalizers 123

and structs 291

calling 124

compared to constructors 124

Find it faster at http://superindex.apress.com

finally block
    example of searching down call stack 278
    flow of control 273
    try statement 267
firing an event 354
Flags attribute 300–302
float literal 173
float type 33, 34
flow of control and local variables 66
flow-of-control statements 212
for statements 66, 212, 223–224
    can use break statement 227
    multiple expressions in initializer and
        iterator 226
    scope of variables in 225
    using continue statements 228
foreach statements 66, 212, 237, 373
    accessing elements in arrays 322
    can use break statement 227
    iteration variable 323
    jagged arrays 325
    multidimensional arrays 324
    processing arrays 456
    rectangular arrays 324
    using continue statements 228
    using with enumerators 456
    using with IEnumerator interface 460
    using with non-generic interface code 466
formal parameters 72
Format method
    String class 516
format specifiers 520–522
friendly name and identity of assemblies 255
function members 32, 44

■G

GAC (global assembly cache)
    installing assemblies into 260
    shared assemblies 260
    side-by-side execution 261

gacutil.exe utility 260
GC (Garbage Collector) 4
    disposing of old delegate objects 338
    garbage collection process 37
generic enumeration interfaces 468
GenericParameter value
    AttributeTarget enumeration 495
generics 428
    classes 432
    comparing generic and non-generic
        stack 439
    constraints on type parameters 440
        types and order 442
        where clause 441
    creating a constructed type 433–434
    creating variables and instances 435–436
    declaring classes 433
    delegates 447–448
    in C# 430
    interfaces 444
        example 445
        implementations must be unique 446
    methods 449
        declaring 449
        example 452–453
        invoking 450–451
    stack example 428–429
        continued 431
        using generics 437–438
    structs 443
get accessor 108–109
    indexers 131
GetCustomAttributes method
    Type class 498–499
GetEnumerator method
    enumerable types 456, 466
    IEnumerable interface 463, 468
    IEnumerable <T> interface 468, 472

GetLength method
  Array class 327
GetType method
  Object class 497
GetUpperBound method
  Array class 327
global assembly cache. *See* GAC
global attributes 487
goto statements 66, 212, 231
  modifying flow of switch statements 216
  requirements in switch statements 219
  using inside switch statements 231

H

headers for methods 62
heap 37
HelpLink property
  Exception class 269
hex simple escape sequence 177
HRESULT data type 5

I

IComparable interface
  CompareTo method 372
  example 373–376
IDisposable interface
  Dispose method 233, 469
  IEnumerator T interface derives from 469
  implementing with using statement 234–236
  resources implement 232
IEnumerable interface
  drawbacks to using 466
  example of using with IEnumerator 464–465
  IEnumerable T interface derives from 472
  implementing enumerators 457
  not deriving enumerable class from 466
  using 463
IEnumerable <T> interface 468
  GetEnumerator method 468

implementing enumerators 457
  introduction 472
IEnumerator interface
  declaring 461–463
  drawbacks to using 466
  example of using with IEnumerable 464–465
  IEnumerator T interface derives from 469
  implementing enumerators 457
  implementing with enumerator class 468
  not deriving enumerator class from 466
  using 458–461
IEnumerator <T> interface 468
  Current method 469
  enumerator class implements 468
  implementing enumerators 457
  introduction 469–473
if . . . else statements 66, 212, 214
if statements 66, 70, 212–214
IL. *See* CIL
imperative language, C# as 482
implicit conversions 199–200, 399
  between non-nullable type and nullable version 526
  constraints in user-defined conversions 420
implicit keyword 420
implicit numeric conversions 403
implicit reference conversions 411–412
increment operator 186–187
indexers 127–128
  advanced 131
  and properties 128
  declaring 129
  Employees example 132
  further example 133
  get accessor 131
  overloading 134
  set accessor 130
IndexOf method
  Array class 327

Find it faster at http://superindex.apress.com

IndexOutOfRangeException class
example 270, 278
inheritance
See also class inheritance
accessing inherited members 141
base access 145
between assemblies 157, 158
class access modifiers 156
classes 140
constructor execution 153–154
constructor initializers 154–155
hiding members of base class 143–144
Object class 142
using references to base class 146–147
virtual and override methods 148–152
Inherited property
AttributeUsage attribute 494–495
InnerException property
Exception class 269
input parameters 74
Insert method
String class 516
instance class members 98
instance constructors 118
and structs 289–290
constructors with parameters 119
default constructors 120
instance fields compared to local variables 64
instance members 52
instantiation 31–32
int type 34
integer literals 174–175
interfaces 372
as reference type 380–381
declaring 376–377
example of different classes implementing
an interface 394–395
example with simple interface 379
explicit interface member
implementations 388–391

generics 444
example 445
implementations must be unique 446
IComparable interface example 373–376
implementing 378
implementing interfaces with duplicate
members 383–384
implementing multiple interfaces 382
implementing with structs 293
inherited members as implementation
386–387
inheriting interfaces 392
references to multiple interfaces 384–385
using as operator 393
internal member accessibility 162
interoperability 5
InvalidCastException class 413–414, 425
unboxing conversions 419
invocation list 334
invoking an event 354
invoking delegates 342
with reference parameters 345–346
with return values 344
is operator 425
IsDefined method
Type class 497
iterators
blocks 475
further information 476
introduction 474
producing enumerables 478
producing enumerators 479, 480
statements 66
variables and foreach statements 323
IUnknown interface
COM objects must implement 5

■J
jagged arrays 309, 317
comparing array types 331

comparing rectangular and jagged
  arrays 321
declaring 318
foreach statement 325
instantiation 319
shortcut instantiation 318
sub-arrays in 320
JIT (Just-In-Time) 8
converting CIL into native code 253
jump statements 66, 212, 227
Just-In-Time. *See* JIT

■K
keywords 19

■L
labeled statements 210, 229
goto statement transfers control to 231
labels 229
restrictions 230
labels 229
left shift operators 192
left-associative operators 181
length of array 308
Length property
Array class 310, 327
String class 516
line number directives 512
literals 173
character literals 177
integer literals 174–175
real literals 176
string literals 178–179
local constants 104, 106
local variables
declaring 64
flow of control 66
inside nested blocks 65
Logical AND operator 188, 189
Logical NOT operator 188, 189

logical operators. *See* bitwise logical
  operators
Logical OR operator 188, 189
long type 34
looping statements 212

■M
Main method 20, 531, 532
accessibility 532
managed code 8
manifest and structure of assemblies 253
member accessibility 159
internal member accessibility 162
nested types 539
private member accessibility 161
protected internal member accessibility 163
protected member accessibility 162
regions accessing a member 160
summary of modifiers 164
member constants 104
members 96
instance class members 98
order of member modifiers 96–97
types of 32
memory 36
heap 37
stack 36
Message property
Exception class 269
metadata
accessing by consumers 482
storing of 482
methods 49
adding to delegates 340
anonymous methods 346–352
code execution in method body 63
declaring 17
declaring generic methods 449
deleting from delegates 341
example of generic method 452–453

Find it faster at http://superindex.apress.com

methods *(continued)*

generics 449

invoking 67

invoking generic methods 450–451

local variables 64

flow of control 66

inside nested blocks 65

overloading 93

parameter arrays 84

expanded form 85–87

method invocation 85

parameters 72

actual parameters 73

arrays as actual parameters 88

formal parameters 72

input parameters 74

output parameters 81–83

reference parameters 78–80

types 88

value parameters 75–77

recursion 91–92

return statement and void methods 70–71

return values 68–69

stack frames 89–90

structure 62–63

modifiers

and structs 292

declaration statements 96

MoveNext method

IEnumerator interface 458, 459, 461, 466, 476

mscorlib library 243, 244

MSIL. *See* CIL

multidimensional arrays

foreach statement 324

types of 309

multiple attributes 486

multiple-variable declarations 42

multiplication operator 182

MyTimerClass code 367–368

■N

named parameters 492–493

namespaces 245–246

C# programming 30

further information 248–249

names 247

nesting 250

naming conventions 19

keywords 19

properties 112

nested classes, enumerators as 459

nested types 537

example 538–539

visibility 539–541

.NET

acronyms 13

compiling to CIL 7

compiling to native code and execution 8–9

components of .NET Framework 3

introduction 3

pre-.NET 2

.NET Framework

CLI 11–12

CLR 10

components of 3

programming environment

BCL 6

COM 5

GC 4

interoperability 5

object-oriented 4

simplified deployment 6

type safety 6

new operator

calling constructor 289

creating instance of class 119

creating object-creation expression 50

declaring delegate objects 336–337

hiding members of base class 144

instantiating one-dimensional and rectangular arrays 312

overriding ValueType class 292

non-generic interfaces

compared to generic interfaces 468

non-interface enumerator 466–467

non-nullable types 524

NonSerialized attribute 488

NotSupportedException exception

System namespace 476

null coalescing operator 528

Nullable T type

implementing nullable types 530

nullable types 524

assigning values 527

creating 524–526

Nullable T type 530

user-defined nullable types 529–530

using operators 528

NullReferenceException class

using catch clause for class derived from 272

numeric conversions

explicit numeric conversions 406–409

implicit numeric conversions 403

overflow checking context 404–405

numeric strings

alignment specifier 519

format component 520

formatting 518

standard numeric format specifiers 521–522

numeric types 33

O

Object class 33–34

GetType method 497

inheriting from 142

object-creation expression

new operator 50

object-oriented development environment 4

Obsolete attribute 488, 499

one-dimensional arrays 309, 311

comparing array types 331

declaring 311

explicit initialization 314–315

instantiating 312

operands, constructs that can operate as 172

operator associativity 181

operator overloading 202

example 203–205

restrictions 203

operator precedence 180

operators 172

OR operator

setting bit flags 300

output parameters 81–83, 88

overflow checking context 404–405

OverflowException class 404–408

overloading indexers 134

overloading methods 93

override keyword 166

override methods 148–149

declaring print with new 152

declaring print with override 150–151

overriding 150

P

P/Invoke 5

<param> tag 536

parameter arrays 84

expanded form 85–87

method invocation 85

Parameter value

AttributeTarget enumeration 495

parameters 72

actual parameters 73

arrays as actual parameters 88

Find it faster at http://superindex.apress.com

parameters *(continued)*

formal parameters 72

input parameters 74

output parameters 81–83

reference parameters 78–80

types 88

value parameters 75–77

params keyword 350

parenthesized expressions 181

Parse method

predefined simple types 523

parsing strings to data values 523

partial classes 136–137

partial signing 263–264

Pascal casing 19

platform invoke. *See* P/Invoke

platforms and .NET 3

popping item on the stack 36

positional parameters 492–493

post-decrement operator 186–187

post-increment operator 186–187

precision specifiers 520

pre-decrement operator 186–187

predefined attributes 488

predefined types 33

non-simple types 34

simple types 34

pre-increment operator 186–187

preprocessor directives

#define and #undef directives 506

#pragma directive 514

conditional compilation 507

constructs 508–510

diagnostic directives 511

general rules 504–505

introduction 504

line number directives 512

region directives 513

primary module, structure of assemblies 254

private access modifier 53–55

private assemblies 259

private constructors 122

private member accessibility 161

programming

See also C# programming

C# programs as set of type declarations 30

classes example 45–46, 58–59

goals for next-generation programming 2

Windows in the late 90s 2

properties 107

and indexers 128

associated fields 111–112

declarations and accessors 108

example 109

example of properties and databases 116

performing other calculations 113

read-only and write-only 114–115

static properties 117

using 110

protected internal member accessibility 163

protected member accessibility 162

public access modifier 54, 97, 420

depicting 54–55

public key and identity of assemblies 255

publishers 354

pushing item on the stack 36

■R

raising an event 359

description 354

overview of event code components 356

rank of arrays 308

Rank property

Array class 310, 327

rank specifiers 311

readonly modifier 125

read-only properties 114–115

real literals 176

rectangular arrays 309

comparing array types 331

comparing rectangular and jagged arrays 321

declaring 311

example of creating, initializing, and using 316

explicit initialization 315

foreach statement 324

instantiating 312

syntax points for initializing 315

recursion 91–92

reference conversions 410–411

explicit reference conversions 413–415

implicit reference conversions 411–412

reference counting 5

reference parameters 78–80, 88

invoking delegates with 345–346

reference type arrays 310

reference types 38

classes 50

interfaces as 380–381

storing members 38–39

region directives 513

registry 5

regular string literals 178

relational operator 184–185

remainder operator 183–184

<remarks> tag 536

Remove method

String class 516

Replace method

String class 516

Reset method

IEnumerator interface 458, 461, 466

not supported in compiler-generated enumerators 476

resources

disposing of with using statement 232

multiple resources and nesting 235

packaging use of with using statement 233

structure of assemblies 253

return keyword 68

return statements 66, 70, 71, 212, 237

modifying flow of switch statements 216

return values 68, 69

<returns> tag 536

Reverse method

Array class 327

right shift operators 192

right-associative operators 181

running state 476

S

sbyte type 34

sealed classes 168

sealed modifier 168

secondary modules and structure of assemblies 254

security and .NET 3

<seealso> tag 536

selection statements 66

Serializable attribute 488

set accessor 108

indexers 130

shallow comparison 185

shared assemblies 260

installing into GAC 260

side-by-side execution in GAC 261

shift operators 192–193

short type 34

side-by-side execution 6, 261

sign extensions 399

simple escape sequence 177

simple name and identity of assemblies 255

single inheritance 142

single-line comment 16, 28

Sort method

Array class 327, 373, 378

Find it faster at http://superindex.apress.com

Source property
    Exception class 269
stack 36
    comparing generic and non-generic
        stacks 439
stack frames 89–90
StackTrace property
    Exception class 269
standards and .NET 3
state machine 476
statements 21, 210–211
static access modifier 97, 420
    declaring a static field 99
static class member types 103–104
static constructors 121
    and structs 291
    example 122
static fields 99
    accessing from outside the class 100
    example 100–101
    lifetimes 101
static function members 102
static keyword 121
    declaring events 357
static members 52
static properties 117
String class
    members 516
    System namespace 516
string literals 178–179
string type 33–34
StringBuilder class
    using 517
strings 516–517
    formatting numeric strings 518–522
    parsing strings to data values 523
    StringBuilder class 517
strongly named assemblies 257
    creating 258

structs
    as return values and parameters 293
    as value types 287
    assigning to 288
    constructors 289–291
    field initializers 292
    finalizers 289–291
    generics 443
    inheritance 292
    introduction 286
    methods 63
subscribing to an event 360–361
subscriptions 354
substitution markers 24
SubString method
    String class 516
subtraction operator 182
<summary> tag 534, 536
suspended state 476
switch statements 66, 212, 215–216
    advanced 218
    can use break statement 227
    example 217
    switch labels 219
    using goto statement inside 231
System namespace
    Array class 310
    Attribute class 489
    Console class 17, 22
    EventArgs class 364
    EventHandler delegate type 364
    EventHandler generic delegate 365
    Exception class 269
    IDisposable interface 232
    importing 17
    NotSupportedException exception 476
    String class 516
    Type class 205
    using 17

ValueType class 292, 402

System.Collections namespace

  IEnumerator interface 461

System.Collections.Generic namespace

  iterators require 476

System.Text namespace

  StringBuilder class 517

∎T

targets of attributes 482, 486, 487

TextReader class

  example with using statement 234

TextWriter class

  example with using statement 234

this keyword 126, 154

throw statements 212, 237

ToLowermethod

  String class 516

tools and the .NET Framework 3

ToUpper method

  String class 516

TraceMessage method

  Conditional attribute 500, 501

try statements 237, 267

  appropriate catch clauses for exceptions 269

  catch clauses section 272

  examples using specific catch clauses 271

  finally block 273

  finding handler for exception 274

  forms of catch clauses 270

  handling the exception 268

TryParse method

  parsing strings to data values 523

type arguments 434

Type class

  accessing metadata 497

  GetCustomAttributes method 498, 499

  IsDefined method 497

  returned by typeof operator 205

type libraries 5

type metadata and structure of assemblies 253

type names, Pascal casing 19

type parameters 434

  constraints 440

    types and order 442

    where clause 441

  declaring a generic delegate 447

type safety 6

typeof operator 205, 206, 207

types

  as templates 31

  C# programs as set of 30

  C# programs as set of type declarations 30

  categorizing types 39

  creating constructed types 433–434

  instantiating 31–32

  members 32

  predefined types 33–34

  storing members of reference types 38–39

  user-defined types 35

  value types and reference types 38

∎U

uint type 34

ulong type 34

unary arithmetic operators 198

unbounded type parameters 440

unboxing conversions 418–419

unchecked operator 404–405

unchecked statements 237, 405

Unicode simple escape sequence 177

unmanaged code 8

unsigned conversions 399

uppercase naming conventions 19

user-defined conversions 420

  constraints 420

  evaluating 423

  example 421–422

  example of multi-step user-defined
    conversion 423–424

Find it faster at http://superindex.apress.com

user-defined nullable types 529–530

user-defined type conversions 199–201

   explicit conversion and cast character 201

user-defined types 35

ushort type 34

using alias directive 252–253

using namespace directive 251

using statement 17

using statements 232

   another form of 236

   example 234

   multiple resources and nesting 235

   packaging use of resource with using statement 233

∎V

ValidOn property

   AttributeUsage attribute 494–495

value parameters 75–77, 88

<value> tag 536

value type array 310

value types 38

   structs 287

ValueType class

   overriding with new modifier 292

   System namespace 402

variables

   automatic initialization 41

   declarations 40

   declaring local variables 64

   declaring nullable types 524

   initializers 41

   introduction 40

   multiple-variable declarations 42

   scope of in for loop 225

   using values of 42

verbatim string literals 178

version number and identity of assemblies 255

virtual members compared to abstract members 165

virtual methods 148–152

visibility and nested types 539–541

Visual Studio and documentation comments 533

void methods 70–71

∎W

web-based applications

   building with ASP.NET classes 6

WebMethod attribute 488

where clause and constraints 441–442

while statements 66, 212, 220

   can use break statement 227

   using continue statements 228

whitespace 20

Windows and programming in the late 90s 2

Windows Forms classes

   building Windows GUI applications 6

Windows GUI applications

   building with Windows Forms classes 6

Write() method

   Console class 22

WriteLine method

   alternatives for displaying values 518

   Console class 23

   using alias directives 252

WriteLine statements 69, 71, 228, 251

   accessing elements in arrays with foreach statement 322

   example 270

   reference conversions 410

write-only properties 114

∎X

xcopy deployment 259

XML comments 553

∎Y

yield statements 237, 474–475

You Need the Companion eBook

Your purchase of this book entitles you to buy the companion PDF-version eBook for only $10. Take the weightless companion with you anywhere.

We believe this Apress title will prove so indispensable that you'll want to carry it with you everywhere, which is why we are offering the companion eBook (in PDF format) for $10 to customers who purchase this book now. Convenient and fully searchable, the PDF version of any content-rich, page-heavy Apress book makes a valuable addition to your programming library. You can easily find and copy code—or perform examples by quickly toggling between instructions and the application. Even simultaneously tackling a donut, diet soda, and complex code becomes simplified with hands-free eBooks!

Once you purchase your book, getting the $10 companion eBook is simple:

❶ Visit **www.apress.com/promo/tendollars/**.

❷ Complete a basic registration form to receive a randomly generated question about this title.

❸ Answer the question correctly in 60 seconds, and you will receive a promotional code to redeem for the $10.00 eBook.

2560 Ninth Street • Suite 219 • Berkeley, CA 94710

eBookshop

All Apress eBooks subject to copyright protection. No part may be reproduced or transmitted in any form or by any means, electronic or mechanical, including photocopying, recording, or by any information storage or retrieval system, without the prior written permission of the copyright owner and the publisher. The purchaser may print the work in full or in part for their own noncommercial use. The purchaser may place the eBook title on any of their personal computers for their own personal reading and reference.

Offer valid through 06/18/07.

FIND IT FAST
with the Apress *SuperIndex*™

Quickly Find Out What the Experts Know

Leading by innovation, Apress now offers you its *SuperIndex*™, a turbocharged companion to the fine index in this book. The Apress *SuperIndex*™ is a keyword and phrase-enabled search tool that lets you search through the entire Apress library. Powered by dtSearch™, it delivers results instantly.

Instead of paging through a book or a PDF, you can electronically access the topic of your choice from a vast array of Apress titles. The Apress *SuperIndex*™ is the perfect tool to find critical snippets of code or an obscure reference. The Apress *SuperIndex*™ enables all users to harness essential information and data from the best minds in technology.

No registration is required, and the Apress *SuperIndex*™ is free to use.

❶ Thorough and comprehensive searches of over 300 titles

❷ No registration required

❸ Instantaneous results

❹ A single destination to find what you need

❺ Engineered for speed and accuracy

❻ Will spare your time, application, and anxiety level

Search now: *http://superindex.apress.com*

forums.apress.com
FOR PROFESSIONALS BY PROFESSIONALS™

JOIN THE APRESS FORUMS AND BE PART OF OUR COMMUNITY. You'll find discussions that cover topics of interest to IT professionals, programmers, and enthusiasts just like you. If you post a query to one of our forums, you can expect that some of the best minds in the business—especially Apress authors, who all write with *The Expert's Voice*™—will chime in to help you. Why not aim to become one of our most valuable participants (MVPs) and win cool stuff? Here's a sampling of what you'll find:

DATABASES
Data drives everything.

Share information, exchange ideas, and discuss any database programming or administration issues.

INTERNET TECHNOLOGIES AND NETWORKING
Try living without plumbing (and eventually IPv6).

Talk about networking topics including protocols, design, administration, wireless, wired, storage, backup, certifications, trends, and new technologies.

JAVA
We've come a long way from the old Oak tree.

Hang out and discuss Java in whatever flavor you choose: J2SE, J2EE, J2ME, Jakarta, and so on.

MAC OS X
All about the Zen of OS X.

OS X is both the present and the future for Mac apps. Make suggestions, offer up ideas, or boast about your new hardware.

OPEN SOURCE
Source code is good; understanding (open) source is better.

Discuss open source technologies and related topics such as PHP, MySQL, Linux, Perl, Apache, Python, and more.

PROGRAMMING/BUSINESS
Unfortunately, it is.

Talk about the Apress line of books that cover software methodology, best practices, and how programmers interact with the "suits."

WEB DEVELOPMENT/DESIGN
Ugly doesn't cut it anymore, and CGI is absurd.

Help is in sight for your site. Find design solutions for your projects and get ideas for building an interactive Web site.

SECURITY
Lots of bad guys out there—the good guys need help.

Discuss computer and network security issues here. Just don't let anyone else know the answers!

TECHNOLOGY IN ACTION
Cool things. Fun things.

It's after hours. It's time to play. Whether you're into LEGO® MINDSTORMS™ or turning an old PC into a DVR, this is where technology turns into fun.

WINDOWS
No defenestration here.

Ask questions about all aspects of Windows programming, get help on Microsoft technologies covered in Apress books, or provide feedback on any Apress Windows book.

HOW TO PARTICIPATE:

Go to the Apress Forums site at **http://forums.apress.com/**.

Click the New User link.

JOIN THE APRESS COMMUNITY

READ THE NEW AND IMPROVED ABLOG!

Offering regular posts from Apress authors, technical reviewers, editors, and employees, Ablog offers an assortment of expert advice, industry talk, insider gossip, and tips, tricks, and hacks to keep you one step ahead of the competition.

What Ablog Can Offer You:

- Tips to keep your Linux shop running smoothly

- The value of Vista—Is it worth the wait?

- Taking the leap of faith with new technologies, including Ajax and Ruby on Rails

- IPv4 v. IPv6—Is the transition right for you?

http://ablog.apress.com/

Ablog